20
104
117

JANE WELSH CARLYLE

Jane Welsh Carlyle

from a painting by Gambardella in 1843.

JANE WELSH CARLYLE:
LETTERS TO HER FAMILY, 1839-1863

EDITED BY LEONARD HUXLEY, LL.D.

WITH PORTRAITS

GARDEN CITY NEW YORK
DOUBLEDAY, PAGE & COMPANY
1924

FIRST EDITION	.	.	.	.	*April*, 1924
SECOND EDITION	.	.	.	.	*June*, 1924

PRINTED IN GREAT BRITAIN BY
WILLIAM CLOWES AND SONS, LIMITED, LONDON AND BECCLES.

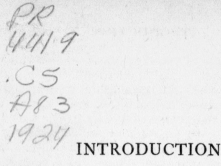
INTRODUCTION

" As to talent, epistolary and other, these letters, I perceive, equal and surpass whatever of best I know to exist, in that kind."

So wrote Carlyle himself in the sad days after his wife's death when he collected and annotated the letters subsequently published by Froude, and readers of those three volumes and the *New Letters* will hardly disagree with this criticism, nor fail to share the feelings which found utterance after the day spent in reading and rearranging the letters of 1857—" such a day's reading as I perhaps never had in my life before. What a piercing radiancy of meaning to me in those dear records, hastily thrown off, full of misery, yet of bright eternal love ; all as if on wings of lightning, tingling through one's very heart of hearts ! . . . Her sufferings seem little short of those in a hospital fever-ward, as she painfully drags herself about ; and yet constantly there is such an electric shower of all-illuminating brilliancy, penetration, recognition, wise discernment, just enthusiasm, humour, grace, patience, courage, love, and in fine of spontaneous nobleness of mind and intellect, as I know not where to parallel !

" . . . But it is difficult to make these letters fairly legible ; except myself there is nobody at all that can completely read them as they now are. They abound in allusions, very full of meaning in this circle, but perfectly dark and void in all others. *Coterie-sprache*, as the Germans call it, ' family circle dialect,' occurs every line or two ; nobody ever so rich in that kind as she ; ready to pick up every diamond-spark, out of the common floor-dust, and keep it brightly available ; so that hardly, I think, in any house, was there more of *coterie-sprache*, shining innocently, with a perpetual expressiveness and twinkle generally of quiz and real humour about it, than in ours. She mainly was the creatress of all this ; unmatchable for quickness (and trueness) in regard to it, and in her letters it is continually recurring ; shedding such a lambency of ' own fireside ' over everything, if you are in the secret " (p. 251).

The letters published in the Froude volumes just forty years ago (1883) number 333, besides some eight and twenty short extracts. Rather more than half were written to her husband, the remainder to various friends and relations. These letters were all that were discoverable by Carlyle himself and Maggie Welsh. In the *New Letters and Memorials of Jane Welsh Carlyle*, 268 were printed by Mr. Alexander Carlyle ; to-day, by an unexpected chance, some 220 more have come to light, all addressed to near relations who figure in the published correspondence. Two are to Mrs. Carlyle's maternal uncle, John Welsh of Liverpool, whose personality is described by Carlyle in his Reminiscences (vol. ii. pp. 142–5), winding up with the " significant " sentence, " No wonder my darling liked this uncle, nor had I the least difficulty in liking him." The rest are to her cousins Helen and Jeannie Welsh, Uncle John's daughters ; her juniors, the one by twelve, the other by eighteen years, but dearest to her of all her kindred, and growing, Jeannie especially, into the spiritual intimacy of true sisters.

Helen, the elder, only survived her father two years, dying of a lingering illness in December, 1855. Jeannie—younger sister in a string of boys, and with the pet name, Babbie, that sticks in such cases, though other sisters should follow—after a long engagement protracted by want of means, married Andrew Chrystal in 1853, and went to live in Glasgow. After Jeannie's marriage, the letters to her grow few and far between. New ties drew her out of the old orbit ; the exclusive intimacy came to a sheer end. No need to hint that Mrs. Carlyle was simply jealous of the husband and child who came between them. A letter of 1849 to Jeannie herself, shows that they both had learned how a child could cut across early friendships. She was woman of the world enough to know how natural it was that Jeannie, absorbed in other interests, should have less of confidence to offer, less of response to give ; and for herself, Mrs. Carlyle, where once she had pitched her friendship so high, was not one to endure its feebler continuance on a plane of incomplete sympathies. Her gift of " divination " saw too clearly into Babbie's heart and her own. Better to have done with the correspondence while it was still warm and heart-felt than let it grow cold and unmeaning.

But Babbie carefully preserved the letters to her sister and to herself, though without, perhaps, realising their intrinsic literary value independently of the freedom and the old heart to heart intimacy which kept for the years of memory the

savour of a friendship so deeply woven into the lives of both.
So they descended to " Babbie's " only daughter as purely
family letters, to be hoarded away the more studiously because
of the family's dislike to the singular and too often unedifying
controversies which sprang up after J. A. Froude had given the
world his strangely perverse account of the domestic incompatibilities between the Carlyles.

Thus the letters have remained undisturbed in their resting
place till Miss Chrystal was persuaded by a friend, to whom
they were shown, that she was keeping for herself what was
meant for mankind.

The correspondence with Helen Welsh had begun while
Mrs. Carlyle's mother was still living ; the more intimate
correspondence with Jeannie started in full flood after the
months of close companionship which followed Mrs. Welsh's
death in February, 1842. For Mrs. Carlyle, hurrying
north at word of her mother's sudden illness, met her cousins
at Liverpool, only to be prostrated by the news that the " first
stroke " had been the final one. When at length she recovered,
Jeannie returned with her to Chelsea and stayed on from March
to October, first with Mrs. Carlyle alone, Carlyle having gone
to settle affairs at Templand, then with both, finally taking
charge of the house while the Carlyles went for a change to
the Bullers' at Troston in Suffolk. Jeannie's quiet charm and
practical sympathy, the tie of kindred blood and love for the
same persons and the same memories, the shared experience of
daily life at Cheyne Row, drew the elder and the younger woman
very closely together. Jeannie speedily becomes " my dear
little sister " ; Mrs. Carlyle writes to her every few days with
entire freedom as indeed to a sister who knows her surroundings,
her household atmosphere, her visitors, her protégés, and whose
living sympathies are constantly with her.

Jeannie knew at first hand the nervous oppression which
consumed Carlyle while a big book was on hand ; his picturesque
flow of language at all times, his doubly picturesque explosions
when the little frets of every day chafed his spirit as it wrestled
for full and exact utterance ; the distracting noises of cocks,
dogs, and pianos ; the incursions of bores ; the mislaying of
papers ; the slightest disturbance of accustomed routine by a
new or careless servant ; the sleepless nights provoked by
the least noise in the house after bedtime ; the " blue devils "
of dyspepsia and the jaundiced angels of castor oil and blue pill.

Mrs. Carlyle could write to her of these things as the familiar troubles of the " wife of a man of Genius," which Jeannie too had seen in the long months she had spent at Chelsea, and could therefore realise at their precise worth, sometimes as merely humorous absurdities in a great man, sometimes overstepping the bounds of the merely humorous and temporarily ruffling the even tenour of daily life. What might seem to be sorry complainings if addressed to one who did not know the real nature of this sort of thing, the broad exaggerations seasoned by a humorous smile or a hearty laugh, count to a large extent as picturesquely coloured details in the matter-of-fact background—elements of the atmosphere in which a letter was written—when chronicled to Jeannie, who knew just how much and how little they meant essentially, however trying for the time being, and when they are marked " private " or " to be burned," this, we are told, means that they are not to be read out to the rest of the family at Maryland Street.

From these letters the reader gains a lively impression of Mrs. Carlyle not only as a centre of social attraction for clever men and women, but as a tender and sympathetic soul under her outward brilliancy, to whom the sad and suffering turned with a certainty of sympathy and help, so long as her keen mind did not detect humbug or vanity.

In her journal for April, 1845, she records that when they first came to London Carlyle had ironically advised her to put an advertisement in the window, " House of refuge for stray dogs and cats." " Now," she continues, " it strikes me I might put in the window more appropriately, ' General audit office for all the miseries of the universe.' Why does every miserable man and woman of my acquaintance come to me with his and her woes, as if I had no woes of my own, nothing in the world to do but to console others ? " These letters show, in some respects even more fully than the letters already published, how truly this was a characteristic of her. She had an open heart for the stray child, the erring woman, the bereaved friend. The noblest of the French and Italian exiles gathered round her as to a responsive spirit ; she could calm and guide even those whose sanity was leaving them ; her treatment of the unhappy Plattnauer and her rescue of him from an asylum form the theme of several letters overflowing with unstudied pathos as well as practical sense.

With her " Shuh-ping-sing faculty of divination," like the fairy in the tale that was a household word, she picks out the inward as well as the outward characteristics of her friends and acquaintances. With careless art they are made to live as we read ; we know the lofty simplicity of Mazzini and Cavaignac ; the ironic charm of Erasmus Darwin ; the blundering step of good John Carlyle, " with best intentions always unfortunate." She has the gift of making us feel as she feels about her friends and her visitors, attractive or unattractive ; the Prussian ambassador, the Mrs. Lyon Hunter from America, the guest who complains of his cold greeting as compared to the warm handshake accorded to Darwin ; the gallant behaviour of the debonair old Jeffrey which shocked more conventional guests ; the conceited cousin from Edinburgh, and the unattractive but wealthy bride who had married Jeannie's cousin ; the " irresistible " ways of young Charles Buller winning his way back to favour.

Lady Harriet Baring ? Yes, there is a good deal about Lady Harriet, afterwards Lady Ashburton, but by no means what the purveyors of romance would have us believe. In the autumn of 1844 (she first met Lady Harriet in May, 1843), she is ironically amused over her fascination and her efforts to add Mazzini as well as Carlyle to her train. " I begin to have a real admiration for that woman—her fascination of Carlyle proves her to be the most masterly coquette of modern times." Carlyle has been " straining his nerves quite preposterously to please " her. Early in July, 1845, Mrs. Carlyle " proceeds with her first season of fashionable life," four days of " fine wits " and four sleepless nights at Addiscombe. Lady Harriet appears to have taken to her. Being unexpectedly in town for two days at the end of September and " too ill to go out," she sends her carriage for Mrs. Carlyle—" More than gracious, incomprehensible upon *my* honour "—and insists " that I had promised to give her my whole winter at Alverstoke ! " Very forthcoming on the part of a great lady with a reputation for haughtiness—" and yet," Mrs. Carlyle adds, mindful, perhaps, of Mrs. Buller's warning that they would never hit it off, " I have an unconquerable persuasion that she does not and never can like me ! "

In November they have been bidden to Bay House ; she is still doubtful, though prospects are better, since she is not in the " horribly excitable state " she was in when she went to Addiscombe. But the visit reveals Lady Harriet's strength and sincerity. " In fact she is a *grand* woman every inch of her —and *not* ' a coquette ' the least in the world—if all the men go out of their sober senses beside her how can she help that ? "

In January, 1846, Lady Harriet follows up with " very nice letters " inviting Mrs. Carlyle to come with her to Rome the following winter, " and *she* always *means* every least syllable she says."

Under date of March 10, 1846, she speaks of a forthcoming visit of a month to Addiscombe, mainly *tête-à-tête* with Lady Harriet. " If all proceeds according to programme it will be a pleasant month. She is ' a bit of fascination ' (as the countryman said of ' *Tagg*lioni ') a very *large bit.* I profess never to this hour to have arrived at a complete understanding of her, but *that* I fancy is just a part of her fascination—the insoluble psychological puzzle which she is and bids fair to remain for me ! "

And in June there is a similar tribute to the sincerity in act, the reserve in words, of this " the woman of largest intellect I have ever seen."

In the following spring, when Lady Harriet has returned to town, she " seems disposed to keep up our country intimacy." Though it is her way that " she never *says* to anyone that she likes them," still " she proves by all her behaviour that she is rather fond of me—the mere fact of her having *kissed* me at parting and meeting again proves more affection for me than twenty reams of protestations from a Geraldine would do—for her Ladyship is *sincere* to death, and would think much less of boxing the ears of a person indifferent to her than of kissing her ! For my part I *love* her now as much as I *admired* her in the beginning. She is the only woman of *genius* I have found amongst all our pretenders to it."

It is from the middle of 1846 that Sir James Crichton-Browne dates the onset of Mrs. Carlyle's nervous derangement, and after the happy letter of June in that year that of October alludes to her " false position " in the Barings' house, though no one but Carlyle himself knows or can divine her difficulties. But these " difficulties," apart from her being something of a fish out of water in frivolous society, if glanced at, are not overtly discussed, though " it is a good job done " when she is home again that autumn. And as to the " false position," it must be remembered that the phrase is one of the Carlyle catchwords, and is applied to quite different circumstances elsewhere, *e.g.* to Miss Jewsbury's visit (p. 90) and the visit of the Grand Duke of Saxe-Weimar (p. 301), and the relation to the Anthony Sterlings (p. 175).

The most open allusions here to the affair are in the letter of 20.1.47, with the thought not only of her arrival ill at Alverstoke, but of " how things would go on *in another department* " (though in the next letter she refers all her anxieties to the fears of being laid up and of the frivolous social round) ; in 5.2.47 where she notes that it looks as if Lady Harriet with her " little contradictions " of Carlyle were " systematically playing my cards for me," and in 15.10.51, where she tells of an imagined slight from the great lady.

Nevertheless there continues much on the other side of the account. Though it is a relief to escape the Alverstoke visit in February, 1848, other visits seem to be pleasurable and new friends are made there. If she ironically declares Lady Harriet's whims to be " as imperative as the ten commandments," yet she confesses to the irresistible cleverness which " even plies *me* round her little finger whenever she sees I am taking a reactionary turn " (20.1.47), and tells of thoughtful consideration and gifts gracefully made.

How did the resentment, the jealousy which undoubtedly existed, arise after three years' cordial intercourse ? She writes on January 18, 1843, that Carlyle is indifferent to *all* women " *as women* " ; and on May 28, 1843, tells her cousin, apropos of her servant's remark that Carlyle " seems to take no pleasure *in new females* "—

" Yes ! there is one *new female* in whom he takes a vast of pleasure, Lady Harriet Baring. I have always omitted to tell you how marvellously that liaison has gone on. Geraldine seemed horribly *jealous* about it—nay almost ' *scandalized* '—while she was here. For my part I am singularly inaccessible to jealousy, and am pleased rather that he has found *one* agreeable house to which he likes to go and goes regularly. . . ."

Here shows the first spring of the romantic Miss Jewsbury's melodramatic tale which Froude swallowed with such avidity. Mrs. Carlyle herself is but happily amused at this " pleasing titillation of the philosophic spirit " by " the intellectual Circe," whom she speedily found to be " a very lovable spoilt child of Fortune."

Mrs. Buller, who introduced them to one another, foresaw the possibility of a clash between them ; nevertheless, Mrs. Carlyle confesses in September 1845 that—

" I dare say, in spite of Mrs. Buller's predictions, we shall get on very well together ; although I can see that the Lady has a genius for *ruling*, whilst I have a genius for—*not being ruled !* " (N.L. i. 177.)

We may well surmise the origin of the trouble to have been the almost inevitable rivalry for intellectual leadership between two brilliant women, each accustomed to queen it in her own sphere. Mrs. Carlyle was the superior intellectually ; but the scales were weighted for Lady Harriet in her own house by her position as hostess, her social prestige, her unquestioned throne among her friends, the still youthful charm and beauty of the " spoilt child of Fortune." Hers was the first word as well as the last.

The secondary effect of morphia, we are told, is to engender baseless suspicions against those who are nearest and dearest. This now came into play with Mrs. Carlyle. If she had lost the primacy in this new circle, could continuance of the friendship mean that she had also been deposed from the first place in her husband's regard ? In her normal state she laughed at the mere idea. She can make fun about the sort of wife Carlyle ought to have married, a good-humoured creature with plenty of solid fat (No. 119) instead of a woman as full of nerves as himself. But baseless imaginings offer nothing for reason to lay hold of. No assurances of Carlyle's could touch it, so long as the poison remained in her system. He, and he alone, she tells us, knew of her " false position " there, if these words really refer to her imagined grievance ; but he knew also of the admiration and affection which had subsisted between her and Lady Harriet for the past three years, and realised to the full that the real cause of the change lay in his wife's health. Ten years of this " mental dyspepsia " lay before her, with constant contemplation of madness or death, from the time when it first found sad utterance in her birthday letter of 1846 :

" At least to quiet myself I will try to believe. Oh ! why cannot I believe once for all ? that with all my faults and follies I am still dearer to you than any other earthly creature."

He knew, and in this knowledge lies the pathos of such utterances of his as this :

" Adieu, dearest, for that is, and if madness prevail not, may for ever be your authentic title."

The present letters display no trace of the morbid intensity of feeling which appears in Mrs. Carlyle's Journal for 1855-6, which after her recovery and the return of love and confidence she recognised as being delusive.

She sees the futility of much of the social round ; the irony of great people being slaves to the whims of their servants ;

she is glad, often, to escape to her little home where she can be just herself instead of hiding her real feelings under a gay mask ; glad sometimes to be kept from one of these grand visits by a bad cold.

All the same, it may be repeated, she goes frequently to Bath House in town and to the country houses, sometimes when Carlyle was away, sometimes even on a *tête-à-tête* visit to Lady Harriet. She recognises the grace with which the Lady makes her a valuable present, uncomfortable though it is to be unable to requite it with anything of equal value. For a long time, certainly, the balance must have been on the side of her own pleasure, with friends to talk with and celebrities to meet, though she did not feel the additional attraction that was felt by Carlyle. He found with the Ashburtons not only a second appreciative and attentive circle, both social and literary, but the company of leading men in politics and affairs through whom he might get his strenuous ideas of reform into practical currency, might himself even be called upon to share in the work.

Indeed, most of his books were written, Mr. Larkin suggests, with other than a merely literary purpose ; his desire was to make history rather than to write it. His chief—and last—chance of giving such active aid came in the acquaintance with Sir Robert Peel, in whom he saw a statesman with sympathy for his fundamental ideas and with power, if he would, to carry something into effect. That Peel's sudden death was a cruel and crushing blow to his hopes is shown by the letter of July 4, 1850.

Thus there is nothing sinister or hateworthy in Mrs. Carlyle's slowly and deliberately formed judgment on Lady Harriet in the first years of their acquaintance, before the sad years when imagination was partially clouded over by prolonged insomnia and the hurtful pursuit of sleep by the aid of drugs. These letters, like others that have been published, afford glimpses of those wearing times that followed sleepless nights and useless draughts of henbane, or morphia, from the spring of 1846 onwards. They lead us also to a very full view of another character whose assiduities, tempered at length to a reasonable pitch, helped to bring comfort to Mrs. Carlyle at this hour of unhappiness. She too had long suffered from the black darkness of nervous depression, and knew how to sympathise, to distract and to heal. This was Miss Geraldine Jewsbury, the novelist, who thenceforward remained a friendly and devoted member of Mrs. Carlyle's inner circle, yet with one or two periods of misunderstanding, notably when in the late 'forties, Mrs. Paulet's irresponsible tongue—she never could keep counsel—made mischief between them. But though Mrs. Carlyle found comfort and support in her vivacious society and passionate personal devotion, and described her later as " my chief friend " (to Mrs. Russell, July 8, 1856), she knew her for an unstable, impulsive creature who possessed a " besetting weakness by nature, aggravated by her trade of novelist, the desire of feeling and producing violent emotions " (N.L. ii. 126) ; who made scenes of " tiger-jealousy " in the early days over a supposed preference for another woman, or of oppressive endearments over her sick-bed a dozen years later, and whose very talent made her at length, in Mrs. Carlyle's words to a friend, " the most gossiping and romancing of all our mutual acquaintance " (L.M. ii. 396 *seq.*; N.L. ii. 217). Even in 1858 a temporary estrangement ensued between them, " partly because her head has been pack-full of nonsense, and partly because I made no secret of that opinion " (N.L. ii. 172). The frank letters to Jeannie, who also had come to know Geraldine Jewsbury since 1842, and her Liverpool friend Mrs. Paulet, give a full and connected account of her early vagaries and emotional excursions in the evocation of Passion, many revelations of which have appeared in the *New Letters and Memorials*, giving good ground for the Carlyles' opinion of her unreliability on matters of unadorned fact. The papers in the possession of Froude made him fully aware of this opinion. It may have been proper to avoid mention of it during Miss Jewsbury's life ; it was not legitimate to doctor the facts. Carlyle's note on the mythical nature of her reminiscences of Mrs. Carlyle is emphatic, together with his command that these reminiscences should be shown to no one but the lady for whom they were put together. Yet Froude not only disregarded this prohibition and published the reminiscences, but used the details which had been pronounced mythical as well as other unsupported romancings of this imaginative weaver of plots as the fabric of his tragical theory of Carlyle's life and of his relations with Mrs. Carlyle. His curious idiosyncrasies as a biographer have been pitilessly analysed by several hands ; a very complete and accessible summary of the case appears in the Introduction to the *New Letters and Memorials of Jane Welsh Carlyle*, to which readers may be conveniently referred.

In making this selection, many letters or portions of letters have been omitted which deal with illness, with episodes fully told elsewhere, and with minor domestic details, but a characteristic passage has been retained, which shows her keeping on a deaf servant to her own great inconvenience, not only because she hated change, but from concern lest this disability should prevent the girl from finding another place.

Only one of these letters is fully dated. Mrs. Carlyle's habit was to date by the day of the week, and no more. The dates, given in brackets, have been in many cases recovered from the postmarks on the envelopes, where preserved, though occasionally it is clear that letters had been put back into wrong envelopes. In other cases internal evidence and examination of the Carlyle material already published give the necessary clue. A final test in every instance was the calendar giving the day of the week for every month in each year. Thus a fairly accurate chronological order has been secured.

In the matter of punctuation, Mrs. Carlyle, writing at breakneck speed, mainly relied upon a hurried dash to represent any form of stop, and her rare use of a semicolon is very frequently at variance with established usage. Convenience demands that these marks should often be replaced by the conventional signs. On the other hand, the constant underlinings which denote stress on the word if spoken, have been retained. They help to give the written words their conversational quality. The spelling, too, and that not merely of proper names, is sometimes fitful. Even the new gold pen with a platinum tip, warranted to spell automatically, was known to betray its owner's faith. But though these casual lapses may be indications of a nervous temperament as well as a hurried hand, there is no need to preserve them.

In the frequent references to the previously published letters L.M. stands for Froude's *Letters and Memorials of Jane Welsh Carlyle*, and N.L. for *New Letters and Memorials of Jane Welsh Carlyle*, by Alexander Carlyle, with an Introduction by Sir James Crichton-Browne, F.R.S.

A copious index, including references to Mrs. Carlyle's turns of speech and " coterie-sprache," will also prove helpful to the reader who wishes to gather up impressions or recapture passing allusions.

NOTE TO SECOND EDITION

AMONG the corrections I have been able to make at short notice, thanks largely to the kindness and unique knowledge of Mr. Alexander Carlyle, the more important are the re-dating of Letters 113 and 120, and the further evidence as to the date at which Mrs. Carlyle became acquainted with Lady Ashburton.

L. H.

23 *May*, 1924.

CONTENTS

xvii

B

CONTENTS

CONTENTS

LIST OF ILLUSTRATIONS

FAMILY LETTERS OF
JANE WELSH CARLYLE

1. *To Helen Welsh*

Penny Post impending—Return from Templand direct—Servant Helen and the household gods—Pepoli marriage.

At the beginning of July, 1839, Mr. and Mrs. Carlyle had gone to Scotsbrig by way of Liverpool. From the middle of August she had made Templand her headquarters, while Carlyle, after taking her there, returned to Scotsbrig.

The other " Helen " mentioned in this letter is the Carlyles' servant, Helen Mitchell, famous for her apt sayings and unconscious humour, who in spite of many " breezes " and threats of parting, stayed for about eleven years, first leaving to join her brother in Dublin, and after a couple of years returning for a time. Like the other servants at Cheyne Row, she was personally devoted to Mrs. Carlyle, but varied her devotion with petulant outbursts. No doubt this lack of self-control was connected with her tendency to strong drink, of which Mrs. Carlyle cured her for a while ; but though three or four relapses were repented of and condoned, drink was her final undoing. (See p. 323, and L.M. i. 121.)

The Fergus family lived at Kirkcaldy, where Carlyle kept school, 1816–18, and became the fast friend of Edward Irving. Elizabeth, who had just married an Italian refugee, Count Pepoli, a man much her junior, appears frequently in the Letters as a constant friend and neighbour in Chelsea.

Darwin is Erasmus Alvey, elder brother of Charles the famous naturalist, a man of great charm and a faithful friend of the Carlyles, but burdened by ill-health.

Thomas Spedding of Mirehouse on Bassenthwaite Lake, was, like his brother James the editor of Bacon, an old-standing friend of Carlyle, as well as of Tennyson and his circle.

I

" Old Sterling " and his family played a considerable part in the Letters of the 40's. He was the father of Carlyle's friend John Sterling, and was nicknamed sometimes the Whirlwind, from his character, sometimes the Thunderer, a nickname extended to the *Times*, because, as chief leader-writer on that paper, he had begun one of his leaders with the words, " We have already thundered forth this opinion."

5, Cheyne Row.
Sunday (22nd Sept., 1839).

MY DEAR COUSIN,

After the first of January, when the penny-post bill comes into action, I shall surely send " Sibilline leaves " all over the world, and you shall get your share of them. But in the meanwhile (our members being all serving their country in the moors a-shooting of innocent grouse) it is a questionable kindness to take fourteen pence out of your purse for any good I can do you by writing. For the consolation of my own conscience, however, I must articulate my thanks for your irish-collar—must give some explanation of our crow's-flight southward—must assure you that my cousinly feelings towards you have by no means been steeped out of me by my wet sojourn in Scotland, but have been preserved quite snug in a warm corner of my heart to bloom luxuriantly, I trust to the end of time—that is to say—of *my* time. There was in the Liverpool letters, which came while I was at Templand, indications of a beautiful delusion in the cousinly mind on the subject of my " *improvement* "—tho' in what, if not in the virtue of patience, I was at a loss to conceive. For my looking-glass assured me that I was growing thinner and yellower every day —and headaches, rheumatism, ennui and desperation were my portion every day and all. How could it be otherwise—it rained without ceasing, my occupation was gone, and there was no human speech to be got out of Mundells Macveahs and the like—but only inhuman clatter. I cannot conceive how my mother manages to exist in that place, yet she appears to find it quite satisfactory, nay to think it a sort of fairyland where everybody *must* thrive, unless thro' own perversity, and wilful resistance to its " improving " influences.

When the time came for returning Southward all heart

for other visiting was entirely cut out of me. I longed for my own No. 5 Cheyne Row with the passion of a lover ; where I might at least declare myself unwell, if I felt so, without offence to mortal, and where my hands should find something to do more or less profitable. Nevertheless we were all in readiness to start for the lake country, as in duty bound, having promised Mr. Spedding to that effect for the last two years— but just then, a death occurred in his family which put our visit to him aside for the present—and the other two visits, my husband and I taking sweet counsel together opined might be *shirked* without much harm done—so we made our excuses like a couple of liver-hearted travellers, as it must be admitted we are, and tempted by my Brother-in-law John's experience who had just come down by the Preston Railroad we renounced Liverpool also, and putting ourselves into a coach at Carlyle Carlisle (is that it ?), found ourselves in London twenty hours after. At twelve on Tuesday we started from Scotsbrig in our gig—at half after one on Wednesday we were in London. This was losing no time. Our little maid had arrived according to orders the night before, and opened the door to us with a half glad " half Magdeline " aspect. There was nothing a-missing—but a pair of scissors had been put in. Darwin, who had my sheets and silver spoons in keeping, was out of town, which caused a serious destitution at first. But we have got all back now except the sugar tongs and my work box, and are restored to tolerable order. Helen goes on well hitherto, and I only pray that she may not bethink her some fine day that her " *resolution deserves a dram.*" Miss Fergus had become " La contessa Pepoli " two days before our arrival, and is now domesticated with her angelic Conte within a quarter of an hour's walk of me. They both look well content ; if the romance of the thing could but hold out ! She will be an acquisition to *me*, and I hope her bold step (not to say rash) may be justified by a better future than onlookers predict for her. Old Sterling, who had been to see her, said to me to-day " Heavenly Father ! what a wreck she is ! She is fifty by Jove ! " But love has no arithmetic. Cavaignac says " Voilà un homme condamné à rendre sa femme heureuse ! J'espère

qu'il se donnera cette justification ! " I hope so too. Mr.
Darwin says " *Ah!* " —and perhaps that is the best that can
be said of the matter. London is very dead at this season—
but one gets the more good of the people that *are* in it. It is
also contrary to custom very rainy. What are you all doing in
your City ? How is my uncle ? Is the worsted work all done ?
Surely you will write and instruct me of your doings and sufferings. . . . Carlyle joins me in kind love to you all. Is my uncle
going to Templand ? * My mother never ceases to expect him.

Ever, dear Helen,

Your affectionate cousin,

JANE CARLYLE.

I see nothing in the world to hinder your taking a forenoon
drive here. Is there anything ?

2. *To Helen Welsh*

Delay in answering a letter—Harriet Martineau—Stay at Newby—
Better view of Cheyne Row.

Newby Cottage is on the Solway coast, close to Annan.
The Carlyles had spent a month there from July 26, 1841,
then went to visit Mrs. Welsh at Templand, driving in their
own gig. Thereafter Carlyle went to Annandale, hoping
afterwards to visit the Speddings in the Lakes. Mrs. Carlyle,
who " had not the strength of a robin-redbreast in her," was
unequal to the visit. They did, however, visit Harriet
Martineau at Tynemouth on the way home. The favourite
catchword " realised ideals " is the title of the second chapter
in Carlyle's " French Revolution."

Monday (11th Oct., 1841).

Who could have foretold, dearest Helen, in marking the
fine glow of cousinly enthusiasm with which I perused your
Newby letter, that I should only for the first time acknowledge
it in the month of October ! Alas, sweet one, there are depths
of inconsistency in human nature which human nature's self
stands astounded before, when it is at the pains to fathom
them ! For my part, I own at once, I am born to fallibility
as the sparks fly upwards ! " But then," as a certain old

* Not the village of that name in Annandale, but the farm just outside
Thornhill in Nithsdale. It had belonged to Mrs. Welsh's father, and after
her daughter married Carlyle, she left Haddington and lived at Templand
till her death in February, 1842.

MRS. WELSH.
From a miniature in the possession of Miss Chrystal.

woman of Haddington told some charity-ladies who were reproaching her with her shortcomings, " but then, dear *hinnies, I repent a great deal !* " I assure you I have *repented* late and early of the damnatory fact above mentioned—and it has required all the illusions I could make to myself, of its being *superfluous* to write from Templand, whence others were sending bulletins world without end,—of its being *impossible* to write from Tynemouth, where Harriet Martineau exhausted in talk my every particle of intellect, imagination, and common sense,—of its being next to mad to think of writing from here, while everything about me is in a transition state—old things giving place to new—a house blooming forth in new carpets and our " rather humble way " getting itself improved into a certain modest *respectability*—it has required, I can tell you, all these flattering unctions to my soul to enable it to sustain its load of self-reproach in thinking of my shameful silence towards *you*, kindest of cousins and bonny white-skinned Missy !

Happily when I do write I have no ill news to tell you. Since my return to London I have been gradually recovering from the nervous excitement occasioned by the winds and waves and " *industrious* fleas " and other unimaginable horrors of my husband's " realised ideal " " a cottage by the sea-shore ! " It went hard with me at Newby—another month of it and I must have lost my wits or taken to drinking—or died of ennui and flea-bites—but my escape was effected just in time to spare the world the cruel shock of such untimely loss of one of its brightest ornaments. And surely my husband will never tempt Providence in so daring a manner again ! Since we have been here, the scales one would say, have fallen from his eyes, and he has awaked to some sense of the quiet and comfort of No. 5 Cheyne Row in comparison with all the other places he has tried and found wanting—" it must be confessed his bedroom here *is* the very freest from noise he ever slept in " —and several other things have been to be " confessed," which hitherto he has most sceptically denied. And so we are not to *flit* as he threatened me with next Lady-day—at least I infer so not only from these verbal concessions, but from the still more conclusive fact, that he is investing a small amount of capital in new carpets for the stairs and library, which were an imprudent outlay if he had still thought of leaving in six months—and imprudence in spending is a thing which no man —or woman—can lay to his charge. You cannot imagine what an amelioration of my earthly lot it were to be delivered, tho' only for *one* year, from his hitherto unceasing speculations about " *flying* presently," he knows not whither ; but to some " remote region," or " solitary shore of the sea," or even " solitary island in the sea "—where, the beauty of it is, in six months' time he would be ready to cut his throat. With some people the difficulty of realising their desires is small, compared with the difficulty of ascertaining for themselves what their real desires are. And my husband belongs to this perplexing and perplexed section of humanity. . . .

3. *To Jeannie at 5 Cheyne Row*

Restfulness of Troston and its people.

Between the Bullers and the Carlyles there was a close tie. While Carlyle was tutor to their two elder sons, Mr. and Mrs. Buller, " ex-Indians of distinction " and culture, instantly appreciated his great gifts under his " rustic outside or melancholy dyspeptic ways," treated him with the highest consideration, and were no less quick in discerning Mrs. Carlyle's talents and charm. The eldest son, Charles, M.P., was a young man of great wit and charm, the idol of society ; the high promise of his career was cut short by his early death in 1847. Arthur obtained a law appointment in Ceylon ; Reginald, the youngest, " an airy, pen-drawing, skipping, clever enough little creature " in the tutor days, took Orders, and obtaining a comfortable country living at Troston, " placidly vegetated thenceforth." Despite his laziness and muddling habits, writes Mrs. Carlyle (L.M. i. 171), he " deserves really the only epithet that remained to him—seeing that there was already ' the clever Buller ' and ' the handsome Buller '—viz. ' the good Buller.' "

In March, after Mrs. Welsh's death, Babbie returned to Chelsea with Mrs. Carlyle. She stayed there till mid-October, taking charge of the house in August and September with Helen the maid to help her, " bad leg " and all, while Mrs. Carlyle, and soon Carlyle also, went to the Bullers at Troston.

Jeannie was studying German, and *Don Carlos* is Schiller's

play, which she was reading. Creek is G. L. Craik the elder, from 1849 Professor of English Literature at Queen's College, Belfast, whose assiduous friendship sometimes proved tedious and is made fun of by Mrs. Carlyle. " Universal Knowledge Craik," Carlyle dubs him, as a leading writer for the Society for the Diffusion of Useful Knowledge, and the title of one of his books, " The Pursuit of Knowledge under Difficulties," became a catchword in Cheyne Row.

" Borne through with an honourable throughbearing " was " the helpless phrase of a certain conceited extempore preacher " in his " thanksgiving of a sacramental occasion."

Mr. Ogilvie was a weak-minded patient for some time under the care of John Carlyle.

Theresa, who appears to have grown up rather a handful, was a young girl the elder Bullers had taken under their care ; her mother, living in the south of France, " a most amiable and unfortunate woman, Mrs. Buller says. But Mrs. Buller reads George Sand, like me."

Troston.
Sunday (14th Aug., 1842).

My " Blessed Babbie,"

Another long letter—so far I find you perfect ! Go on in this laudable course and not only will it soothe *my* pains of absence, but tend much to the good of your own soul. " The devil," they say, " is always at the elbow of an idle man "—still more of an idle woman—and to think of the devil at Babbie's elbow ! and I not there to exorcise him ! My dear, it would give me serious apprehensions.

But with the daily letter to *me*—and *Don Carlos*—and *Helen's wants*—and such *Himmel-sendungs* (look in your German dictionary) as the immortal Creek, I have no fear but you will be " borne thro' with an honourable thro'-bearing."

For myself I expect to return to you " improved physically at least " (to use Mazzini's words). The first day things looked very black about me, and twenty times, like John's Mr. Ogilvie, " I wished to God that I had stayed in London ! " but I have been better every day since. The place is all that a visitor could wish it—green as emeralds—with plenty of fine old trees—and just that amount of picturesqueness which is compatible with comfort and " *elegancy*." Some people would object to the little churchyard so near—but in these bright days I find *it* rather comforting to look at than otherwise. It is a relief after the horrible London cemeteries to see a quiet spot like this where the wicked *really* cease from troubling and the weary are at rest. Every time I step *out of the window*, I go over to the little churchyard, and draw in a sort of breath of quietude from it, and think to myself, " Just so will the churchyard of Crawford * be looking in this blessed sunshine."

For the people, they are what I have always known them for, the politest, best-bred people alive. They make you feel in their house, exactly as if you were in your own, which is the perfection of hospitality. I get up about eight—when I hear the man knock at Mr. Reginald's door; dress with a deliberation !—my hair has not got as much combing nor my neck as much washing for I know not how long—not that I am more caring about the *effect* I produce, but that it is a pleasure to dress slowly in such a large bright room, looking out on such charming " *natur !* " I descend to the breakfast room about nine—where the letters await me beside my plate—and then Mr. Buller prepares the coffee, and we breakfast according to the " simplest expression " of that meal—toast and butter just as at home. After breakfast out at the window—in again at the door—and upstairs to my own room—where I have both a beautiful sofa and an easy chair—white all covered over with coloured birds. In the centre of my carpet are two white swans kissing each other among reeds ! round them a hexagonal field covered with pagodas and Indian trees—and round that a border of green and rose-coloured dragons tied together by the tails ! and separated into pairs by a square of hieroglyphics. You never saw such a strange carpet in your life ! I am sure there is witchcraft in [it], which I shall not rest till I have found out. My bed is of bamboo—shaped like a tent—the curtains, as also the window curtains and toilet, white india muslin—embroidered—and lined with straw colour—the whole thing has an exotic character which produces an effect on my imagination little as I care for *fine* furniture merely fine. There is a mirror over the chimneypiece which shows me myself in the bamboo bed ! I wish it showed me something lovelier.

* Mrs. Welsh's burial place.

Mrs. Buller does not come down till about two—so all the fore-noon I may write or read, or think, or run out and in, according to my own sweet will—hitherto what I have *done* is not capable of being embodied in words.

There is no lunch—happily—but dinner at three—no fuss about it, but everybody getting up so soon as enough has been eaten—then to the *sofas* for half an hour—then out for a two or three hours' drive. At eight we *all* make an excellent tea—last night I came in mind of poor Alick's " Aunt Jeannie, me's a terrible eater ! " Before going to bed I play a game at chess with Mr. Buller, and last night to my own astonishment and still more to *his* I beat him ! Mrs. Buller retires at *ten*— and after that I may read if I like in my own room.

Such, Babbie, is my life—very *harmless* at all events—and farewell. I do not mean to write two such long letters every day, for I am here not to write but to run about—and meditate. Bless thee, my Babbie. Give my kind regards to Helen and take care she does not hurt her leg.

Your affectionate
[Signature omitted].

Please to enclose me a dozen or two of stamps.

4. *To Jeannie Welsh at Cheyne Row*

Babbie's excellent letters—Confidence in her—Recovers power to play chess—Wasps—Mr. Dobbie and memories of Templand.

Troston.
(18th August, 1842).

BABBIE OF MY AFFECTIONS,

Thanks to thee for thy nice long clever letters ; which supply for me the place of John Sterling's powerful telescope—a Babbie that really shines in *narration !* Every-thing, from Sterling's champagne down to Helen's sore leg, is set before me with a most praiseworthy distinctness, and " not without " (as Carlyle would say) " a certain sly sarcasm, peculiar to the family." Continue to keep me up with the current state of my household—it is the least you can do in return for the generous confidence I repose in you ! I do not mean in the matter of *allowing you* to run up and down stairs, tiring your life out, and to take on yourself the charge of a sore leg—but I mean in having left you alone with my husband, without having first possessed myself of that seductive dressing-gown ! He writes to me the other day, " little Jeannie comes down in the morning in a kind of shawl *dressing-gown, almost with the air of a little wife* to make coffee to me ! " Oh yes, I know very well how *like a little wife* she looks ! and if there were a spark of jealousy in my disposition I would have taken out my seat in the next Bury coach, immediately after reading that sentence ! and returned in all haste to put a check to such dangerous illusions. . . .

Our life is the most quiet and regular heart could desire—the drive and the game at chess are the *excitements* of the day, the last indeed is becoming rather *too* exciting. It is long since I laid aside my chess-playing honours—and that anybody has been welcome to beat me. I was sure that I could never play well again because I had lost all interest in the game, and could not conceive myself recovering the interest—but one night soon after I came, Mr. Buller having beaten me with his usual facility, said in the most provokingly slighting tone : " I *do* wish you could improve a little ! " And at this all my past triumphs stood up before me, and somehow I felt myself injured—he should see I was determined that I *could* play if I liked—and so I *beat* him the next game and the next—and he has had sore thrashing of his brains for any game he has won from me since. His astonishment is very amusing, but such laborious play is not a good preparation for sleep. Among our excitements I should not have omitted to mention *the wasps !* We have no flies here, but in their stead multitudinous wasps that take all the liberties of flies, congregate on the spoonful of apple tart one is putting into one's mouth, drown in the cream jug and the wine decanter, and keep up a continual attack on the public tranquillity—at this moment while I write they are buzzing all about me and lighting on my hands as if I were made of sugar.

I was so sorry to have missed old Mr. Dobbie,* but I *must*

* Emeritus Rev. Dobbie, father of Mrs. Russell of Thornhill, and so connected with Templand and memories of Mrs. Carlyle's mother.

see him before he goes. I hope you were both very kind to him—and that you will tell me when he returns. I feel somehow as if he were come from the place to which she is gone, instead of only from the place she has left. Alas, alas, he— nobody can bring me any news from her more, but only the Angel of Death—in that must be all my hope henceforward— hope full of terror too—for how unfit I am to die—but, dear Babbie, I was not meaning to sadden you with any talk of this sort. God be with you, dear—and believe me,

Always your affectionate,

JANE C.

Tell Carlyle I have on his collar and cuffs to-day—and cannot sufficiently admire myself in them. I do wish Helen were better—poor little Cinderella that you are.

5. *To Jeannie Welsh at Cheyne Row*

Carlyle's walking tour plans—Visit to the Cartwrights—Virtue lies in the stomach.

Troston.

Monday (29*th Aug.*, 1842).

MY DEAR BABBIE BUNTON,

Last night it was the thunder !—but, as John says, " there is no use at all rebelling against Providence," so we make no Jeremiahad about having been kept awake by *that*— it might have thundered anywhere as well as at Troston. It looks now to my weather-wisdom, as if the fair weather were broken, and we were to have a spell of wet days, which will be sorely against the white hat-and-knapsack-mode of travelling. Pray say what you can to repress his youthful enthusiasm, and to point his decision towards the Cornwallis, or the Phenomenon.* These walking-over-all-England schemes are excellent in idea—an innocent stimulant to the imagination, but they are not meant to be executed—at least by the like of him—" A long, sprawling, ill-put-together thing from the very beginning "—as his mother said of him—and with a nervous

---

* Two coaches running, the former to Bury, the latter to Ixworth, only two miles off Troston.

C

system that renders him peculiarly unfit for being " thrown out, *sang froid*, to charity." . . .

Except Nature and the persons of this household I have seen nothing and nobody since our tea-visit to the Squire's—than which nothing could be a completer failure—still I am glad that we went, for it gave me the idea of a new sort of man, and new sort of menage—a very detestable sort to be sure—but still as God permits Mr. Cartwright and his *Priory* to exist in the same world with me I should not disdain the knowledge thereof. I never saw a man that looked more like the pig pushing towards Cork while made to believe itself taken to Kilkenny—a stubborn contradictory brute—rapturising over Sir Robert and the income tax—finding all the distress of the country to be occasioned by the *cheapness* of victuals ! ! and ready to *knock down* any one—male or female—that dared to be of a different opinion. His wife, a most elaborate piece of formality with a very questionable fixture-smile, did what she could to keep the peace—and succeeded but indifferently—and gave us the worst tea and the most meagre supply of butter and bread I remember to have seen in this world.

On the whole, the sight of that Place with its magnificent avenues of cedars and vaulted *crypt*, and " gloomy bits of colour," and worst tea, worst talk, worst taste, to be found in Christendom, was enough to make the humblest peasant contented with his lot.—N.B. Mr. Cartwright's eyes are almost close together in his face.

. . . I am truly thankful that Helen's leg is restored to a state of efficiency. Give her my congratulations, and kind regards. I hope she will take double and triple care of you when you are left alone—unfortunate Babbie, what is to become of you ? But it will not be for long. Mind above all things that you take your victuals properly—one is so apt to neglect that department of things when one is alone—and if virtue lies, as most people seem to believe, in the stomach, the consequence would be a demoralised babbie at my return. . . .

Bless you my good child.

Ever your affectionate
JANE CARLYLE.

6. *To Jeannie Welsh at Cheyne Row*

A fireless house.

Troston.
Thursday (1st Sept., 1842).

DEAREST BABBIE,

I write you just one word of blessing in your loneliness—and if it were not for the thought of your loneliness I could not muster faculty enough to-day to send you even that much.

It is raining—and searchingly cold—and I have not slept—and am otherwise unwell—and there is no fire in the whole house except in the kitchen—where it is not very pleasant to warm oneself in the midst of four or five servants, nevertheless I have been to the kitchen fire once this morning and must go again soon—or die. Why *would* Carlyle put off and off until the weather broke entirely ; but for his coming I should have been back to-day and had the prospect of a good fire, at least to-morrow. And why do not people above all in country houses put on fires at the shortest notice ? I meant to have gone with Mr. Buller to meet Carlyle at Bury ; but unless it fairs it were a wrong measure, quite knocked up as I feel myself.

I shall go in quest of Regy for the present and see whether I cannot put it into *his* head—as John puts things into Mr. Ogilvie's—to have a fire in his study—since Mrs. Buller does not like it in the drawing-room—it makes it, she says, " so insufferably close." Pardon me to-day, Babbie—for I am really sadly out of sorts—worse than I have been any day since I left you.

God keep you well and not *quite* unhappy till we come.

Your affectionate,
COUSIN JANE CARLYLE.

7. *To Jeannie Welsh at Cheyne Row*

A chill; and a warm carriage—Carlyle arrives—Meeting with Dr. Donaldson of Haddington—Regy and his affections— Mrs. Buller described.

The *New Cratylus* (1839) was a treatise on Greek philology by the eminent scholar, Dr. John William Donaldson, D.D., from 1841 to 1855 headmaster of King Edward's School, at Bury St. Edmunds. He, like Mrs. Carlyle, was a native of Haddington, where his grandfather had been Town Clerk.

Troston.
(*2nd Sept.*, 1842.)

To-day also my excellent Babbykin, I cannot put you off with a mere scrap—for I am not what Mazzini calls " responsible." The cold I imbibed into my system yesterday, followed by another sleepless, entirely wretched night, has given me as bad a headache as I can well carry—out of my bed. But you will be glad to learn that Carlyle got an inside place and was picked up at Bury in a state of perfect dryness and considerable vigour. The rain abating somewhat—and having in vain tried upon Regy a cap and woollen shawl—those infallible symptoms of a fire-needing human being—I resolved to have the carriage closed and go with Mr. Buller to meet my husband, thinking that the motion with the help of a *warm bottle* in the carriage might put a little heat into me—would not be so bad at least as sitting shivering at home. I had met the *New Cratylus* riding in Livermere park the night before —odd !—two persons issued out of the same Haddington to meet, each taking exercise in Livermere Park ! I had saluted him with unwonted urbanity—the creature looked so immensely delighted at the encounter ; and informed him of what was expected from the *Cornwallis* the following day—" upon which hint he acted " and was on the ground under an umbrella at our arrival ; so my husband was most abundantly welcomed to Bury. Cratylus *would* have us dine with him—or return to dine with him—is coming on Saturday to urge that thing— *vainly*, I should hope—but do you know all the while who I mean by that Greek appellative which I am not perhaps even spelling aright ? I mean the horrid Donaldson—who " with his foot " (*not*) " on his native heath " but on *his acquired Bury*, is much less horrid, however, than you saw him at Chelsea. Carlyle is in high heart this morning—was fortunate enough to have fallen on a quiet night, for his first—slept very fairly—breakfasted more than fairly—and is now off on foot to Thetford, a town some seven miles off—his contentment with the place verges on the ecstatic. Regy has asked him twice over why he did not bring " Miss Jeannie." Poor Regy ! he is developing into something not so bad—if he would but, as his mother suggests, " *starve himself*," he might indulge dreaming of Miss Jeannie—without absolute distraction. He says he will give me some honey-comb when I go away—and will send me some *walnuts* when they are ripe—and that he will have asparagus ready for me *when I come again next year*—and that I had better take Mr. Loft's house which is to let and stay here altogether—and he told his mother privately that if Mrs. Davis (the housekeeper) went away he was meaning to ask *me* to send him one in her place ! ! Poor Regy, I question if he ever before lavished as many marks of affection on any woman except his own mother.

Mrs. Buller is kind to me beyond expression—not as people are kind to their visitors generally, but as if I were the daughter of the house. She speaks to me so *out of her heart* as women of the world rarely speak at all—and hardly ever to a person so much younger than themselves. When I came home yesterday I found her with a large fire in the drawing-room, altho' it hurts her breathing. She had heard of my warm bottle—and scolded me for my " *scrupulosity and too little* selfishness," which was very amiable, she said, but kept me very uncomfortable in this world. It is all she knows about it I often think I am just the *most selfish* person in existence.

With all my faults,

Your affectionate cousin anyhow,

J. WELSH.

Kind regards to Helen. Tell her to look to the moths and the carpets.

8. *To Jeannie Welsh at Cheyne Row*

Writes to James Baillie—Successive interruptions—The daily paper
 is sent on—Carlyle upsetting—His trip to Cromwell's country—
 Indecision about return—" Feasting."

James Baillie, Mrs. Carlyle's once-rich cousin, now broken
down but unabashed, was in old days " the reigning Dandy of
London "—" the leader of the Hunt in the country." In
1845 he was reported to be " getting up in the world again by
speculating in Railway Shares." (N.L. i. 182, and Letter 84.)

Mr. and Lady Agnes Byng—" one of the Pagets ' whom
we all know ' "—were " the grandees of the district." (L.M.
i. 168.)

Anthony, the soldier, afterwards K.C.B., was Thunderer
Sterling's eldest son.

Troston.
Thursday (7th Sept., 1842)

DEAREST BABBIE,

It was not headache that prevented my writing to
you yesterday, and still less was it oblivion—it was a combination
of petty contretemps which cheated you out of your letter. I
sat down to write immediately after breakfast, but when the
pen was in my hand, the first words it traced, from some
mysterious and sudden movement, were not " *dearest Babbie* "—
but " *dear cousin* "—and I found myself, without the smallest
forethought, writing first to James Baillie. In that there was
no harm ; as he asked me for neither help nor commiseration,
nor for anything I could not give him, it was but common
humanity to fling him the civil word he *did* ask for—in answer
to his question how I did. But having told him with cold
brevity where I was and how I was, something inspired me,
instead of remaining his obedient, humble servant, to personate
Minerva for the time being, and to write him four mortal
pages of passionate remonstrance against the folly—not to say
infamy—of his past and present course of life ! My little
sermon was so very impressive, that it made *myself* cry when
I read it over—but I am afraid it would have no such salutary
result for him. " At all events," said Carlyle, " it could

do him no ill." That don-Quixote-like speculation accomplished, I started again, " dearest Babbie "—when Carlyle
knocked at my door. Would I go with him to the village to
" help him to buy a box of matches and a pennyworth of
pipes " ? So modest a petition could not be refused by
anybody with Christian bowels—so to the village we went and
made the small purchases.

Again I sat down to write—to " dearest Babbie " were
added another pair of words, when the manservant proclaimed
outside my door that " lunch was on the table," and Regy
insinuated the same fact the same moment, outside my window.
Carlyle has overset all our household arrangements here as he
oversets all household arrangements wherever he goes. Here
were we eating lunch, and dining at six ! that we might go to
Bury before dinner to enquire about coaches to St. Ives, &c.
Lunch eaten with more or less appetite, I was hurrying upstairs
to proceed with my letter having still half an hour before the
time at which the carriage was ordered, when Mr. Buller
called after me : " You will not object to calling on Lady
Agnes on the way ? "—Lady Agnes ! and I in my wearing
gown !—absolutely *fringed* round the skirt with *rags* as no
woman unless lost to all sense of shame would like to present
herself to a be-satined and be-diamonded Lady Agnes. I had
to run and strip and re-clothe myself with the speed of a house
on fire—and had just time left to make up the newspaper.
Nay, after all I went—as I only discovered this morning—with
two stockings of different sorts ! And thus had the poor
solitary Babbichen no letter written to her that day—only
many kind and somewhat remorseful thoughts wafted to her
over space !

This morning the Great Traveller breakfasted alone with
me at eight o'clock, and immediately after set off on a horse
which Mrs. Buller, who is like *the beautiful lady* of fairy tales
had, as it were, " stamped out of the ground," for him ! He
felt, he said, " like a man setting out on some great commercial
speculation by which he hoped to make his fortune ; yet full
of apprehensions and an invincible repugnance ! ! " It is not
battle fields that he is hunting out, after all !   At Huntingdon

Oliver Cromwell was born—at St. Ives he had a farm—and at Ely he was elected Member of Parliament. I tell you this that you may not, as Mrs. Buller and I have been doing, perplex people's historical reminiscences by talking of Mr. Carlyle's being gone to visit certain battle fields of Oliver Cromwell's in Suffolk—where no shadow of a battle ever " transpired " ! His luggage consisted of a razor and two shirt collars :—he calculates on being back by possibly on Thursday—more probably not till Friday—when certainly he *ought* to be here, having invited " the new Cratylus " to dinner *at six* ! No great treat for the rest of us ! " And when are we to go back to London ? " I asked, with a sympathetic sigh, " to my Babbie." " On Saturday, if you like ! " That I am afraid will never be *listened to*—seeing that he has done nothing here as yet except throw all our still regularity into hubbub wild. Besides, Charles will be come before his return and he must in common decency stay at least one day for him. But the beginning of next week I do hope to get back—altho' I foresee great pressing on the part of all here, and great *indecision on his part*, which will throw all the *odium* of an unpersuadable resolution on *me*.

Mrs. Sterling writes that she is perfectly well and is " feasting on the produce of Anthony's garden." I wish her wellness may last long ! The wasps have been the chief *feasters* with us. Did I ever tell you the Annandale woman's exclamation on hearing an account of the luxurious living at some squire's house in the neighbourhood ? " Wae's to them wi' their *bags* ! " I declare it is entirely beastly in people to go from home *to* " feast." If I were so " left to myself " (as the pious Scotch phrase is) that I should do such a thing, at least I should think shame to tell it ! Speaking of garden produce, Regy " wishes you were here to make bags for *his* grapes "—positively I think I must bring you here some time to take a look at the creature. You might do such a world of good in the village ! ! as parson's wife—and it would be a nice rustication for *me* every summer ! Meanwhile tell Helen to keep up her heart, that I do not seriously mean to stay for ever. And now adieu, my bambina—love me as I do you.

Remember me to Mazzini and Darwin if you see them and if they seem to have forgotten me.

Your
J. W. C.

9.   *To Jeannie Welsh at Cheyne Row*

A long sleep—Expected recital of Carlyle's travels—Charles Buller coming.

Carlyle soon after his return from Ghent in August, 1842, wrote a lively account of his journey. Passages are quoted from it in Froude's *Life ;* the full journal was printed in the *Cornhill Magazine* for October and November, 1922.

Troston.
(7th Sept., 1842.)

What have I to tell you since yesterday ? Absolutely nothing, dear Babe, except that this morning I had a long, very interesting letter from yourself ! Yes, I may add that I slept last night from twelve till six *without awaking*, a fact at which I felt almost *frightened !* No word of Carlyle. I suppose he will not have opportunity of writing—and so we shall have a fine *deluge* of spoken autobiography when he comes ! surpassing even the voyage to Ghent !

We are rather *excited* here to-day from the anticipated arrival of Mr. Charles. Mr. Buller is just going off to fetch him, but none of us can accompany him for a drive ; " Charles brings such a quantity of luggage and a valet over and above." . . .

10.   *To Jeannie Welsh at Cheyne Row*

Charles Buller's selfish conduct, but subsequent charm.

Troston.
Thursday (8th Sept., 1842).

. . . I do not remember when I have been more angry at a thing I had so little business with as yesterday, when Mr. Buller returned from Bury cold, wearied, sad-looking and with no Charles ! Had it been the *first* disappointment

he had given them, I should have concluded at once that
he had missed the coach, and been as sorry for him as
for his parents—but he has been doing nothing but disappointing them ever since I came here. He was to have come
when Parliament rose, and he went instead to " Lady
Harriet's "—as if he had not flirted with *her* the whole
season thro' ! Then he went to Havre " to be near the
sea " ! What on earth could be the benefit of *the sea* to a
political town-wit and *diner-out* like Mr. C. Buller ? Then he
would surely come at last ! but no—not yet—off to the Lady
Harriet's again—then he finally fixed Tuesday—then some
Thompson or Johnson asked him to dinner and he changed the
day to Wednesday ; and of his Wednesday's appointment *this*
was the result ! All this time his poor father and mother have
tried to pretend indifference, declaring they know him too
well now to *care* when he came, or whether he came at all—
but every day they have been plainly sickening with " hope
deferred "—and yesterday when there had been a sort of
slaying of the fatted calf—when everybody had been at work
all morning to have things in apple-pie order for him—when
his mother had put on her most becoming cap and gown—and
his old father had gone off all smiles to fetch him—and he did
not come after all, I declare I could not help crying for the poor
parents of this *distinguished* son ! and a little too, for the son
himself, in thinking what a store of remorseful remembrances
he was laying up for himself in after years—when he would
not be able to buy back with all his blood one single hour
of those caresses to which he was now preferring the poor
frivolities of *flirtations* and *fine dinners !* Oh mercy, if we could
but, *all of us*, see the present thro' the future ! if we could but
give to it the significance which the future will give to it, when
it has for ever escaped from among our hands ! how differently
would we live with those we love ! But never was there a
truer saying than that " we only recognise our blessings when
we have lost them " ; and if sad experience makes us sensible
of this fatal tendency of our nature, what we do is to bewail the
evil that has *already* resulted from it, rather than to prevent
future evil by striving with all our soul and strength to recognise

whatever blessings we still have ! You may be sure I *exerted* myself to help them away with their dull evening ! From a sudden impulse I put my arm round Mrs. Buller's neck and kissed her. " O," said she, *with tears in her eyes*, " I am not disturbing myself—I am merely sorry that Mr. Buller had the long drive to no purpose ! " " O well," said the poor Father, as we sat down to an unusually lavish dinner, " the fatted calf, you see, Mrs. Carlyle ! but *no* Charles ! " " My dear," said his wife kindly, " I thought you had grown *philosophical* about Charles—as *I am ?* " " O hang it ! " says he, " so I am, but I dislike going to fetch anyone and having to come back without my errand, *suppose it were only a pointer !* " " Well," said she, with one of her lovely smiles, " you *may* be provoked to-day, for you have been cheated of *both a pointer* and *Charles*." He has been ransacking all Suffolk this week back for a dog for Charles to shoot with—and one was to have been sent in the carriage—but had not been procurable. I recommended to him Carlyle's remedy for all ills—a tumbler of hot brandy negus !—which he at last agreed to take, on my declaring I wanted some myself—and instead of one we played *three* games at chess ! Mrs. Buller and Regy went to bed at ten—Mr. Buller and myself at eleven, when the chess was finished. About twelve I was just falling asleep when a horse in the park under my window began to neigh with all its might. " The devil fly away with you," thought I. Then there was a loud rumbling —" more thunder," thought I—then there was a great opening and shutting of doors—and finally something in creaking boots entered the room adjoining mine. " It must be Charles," I said to myself, now broad awake—and so it was. He had been *too late* for the Bury coach—had come by the one to Newmarket and so on in a post chaise.

I was glad at his arrival, tho' it did cost me half my night's sleep. To-day all faces have a look of sunshiny gladness—only Mr. Charles's face I have not yet seen. I had breakfasted with Mr. Buller before he came down—and have kept in my room ever since, tho' it is now one o'clock— in a sort of spirit of reaction against the extravagant homage which he is used to receive from all people, especially women. . . .

11. *To Jeannie Welsh at Cheyne Row*

Being " Charlesed "—Carlyle returns—Plans for going home.

Petrucci, an Italian exile of Mazzini's circle, whose gloom earned him the nickname of Heraclitus, the weeping philosopher.

Friday (9th Sept., 1842).

. . . According to programme I did not go down yesterday till I was summoned to dinner, when I met Charles with a certain armed neutrality. He should see that I, at least, was too wise a woman to be *Charlesed*, that his society-graces and society-talents should not *come over me!* One would say he had divined my humour and prepared himself to wheedle me out of it—I never saw him so agreeable, not to say *amiable*—still by a sublime effort of *grumpiness*, I withstood all his attempts to win from me a cordial smile! Till at last the fated moment came—we were all standing at the hall-door, looking out into a dripping world, when suddenly, as if struck with an inspiration from Heaven, he exclaimed : " I will shoot a hollyhock ! Wait, Mrs. Carlyle, till I fetch my gun, I *must* shoot a hollyhock ! " The gun was fetched—he took his aim with the most sportsmanlike intenseness, and a tall hollyhock dropt its head upon its breast ! Then, flinging down the gun, he pulled a large knife from his pocket, ran up to the shot plant, severed the broken part from the stem and carrying it, dripping wet, between his finger and thumb, presented me with this his curious *game!* Mr. Petrucci himself in the character of Heraclitus must have laughed at this ridiculous scene—and laughing—that is to say, *honestly laughing* with anyone—is for me what *taking salt* with anyone is among savages—all ideas of hostility were dismissed from my mind—and to the disgrace of my originality I am to-day disposed to subscribe to the general opinion that Charles Buller *is* " the most *agreeable* person alive."

Carlyle came in the *evening* drenched with rain but otherwise in good condition. Had seen enough to fill three octavo volumes—accomplished all he intended, and a vast deal more—

and lived that day on *a quart of greengages !* He still stands by *Monday* in spite of Regy's entreaties for " another fortnight." Whether he will hold out against Mrs. Buller's *gracious mockeries* remains to be seen. . . .

12.   *To Jeannie Welsh at Cheyne Row*

Lady Cullum's " Museum "—On adopting a baby.

Sir Thomas Cullum, of Hardwick House near Bury, was distinguished as a botanist, following in the footsteps of his father, to whom Sir J. E. Smith dedicated his " English Flora."

Lady Bunbury, sister of Sir Charles Napier, had married Sir Henry Bunbury, of Barton Hall, Suffolk ; soldier, politician and connoisseur.

Troston.
Monday (12th Sept., 1842).

CARA BABITHA MIA,

I have only time for a good day to you ! and keep up your heart ! for surely to goodness we will come on Thursday ; I have kept saying constantly " Thursday, Thursday," till it seems to be finally received as a settled thing, even by Carlyle.

We are going off again to Lady Cullum's—a long journey comprising *a lunch* and other laborious adjuncts. All her own *curiosities* are not enough for her—she must also see the Author of *Hero worship*, which book she professes to admire infinitely and therefore one would suppose to *understand*—tho' hang me, if I think she has ever got beyond *Mammon* worship, with all her high pretensions ! My heart sinks at the thoughts of having to dawdle for *a second* time thro' all her show-rooms— her " *old* curiosity shop " served up to suit the most aristocratic taste—to hear a second time : " This was an altar of Latona, isn't it a love of a thing ? " " This is *supposed* to be a bronze of Benvenuto Cellini." " That silver paper cutter represents Dante's Angel ! " " These gold boxes were taken from the carriage of Napoleon after the Battle of Waterloo ! Isn't it nice to have them ? " etc., etc. To all which I felt inclined to answer in Helen's favorite phrase of admiration : " How expensive ! " If *I* were mistress of *fifty thousands* a year, I would not make myself into a *show-woman*! but there is no accounting for tastes! What will Miss Hunter do with all *her* money? Give Babbie a marriage portion? With all her love for you I see not that she can restrict her generosity to a velvet gown and diamond ring! I wish you would suggest to her, to found a little female La Trappe, to which people of an earnest turn of mind might retire from time to time, to consider *what they want!*—to attain to some glimmer of an idea as to *that*, would be an immense step gained for the female mind in these days—and an impossible one amidst the deluge of idle babblement, and pressure of the most unlily-of-the-field-like small cares in which the most of us spend our lives—God help us poor women!—especially such of us as have not our daily bread to work for—and small children to bring up, better or worse!

Lady Bunbury was advising me to *adopt* an American baby of fourteen months—advertised in the newspapers as to be had for nothing. I thought that in " the present distressed state of the country " a good many native babies might be had *for nothing!* But a full grown *babbie* were a better speculation—don't you think?

> Bless thee dear Little,*
> Your affectionate cousin,
> JANE W. CARLYLE.

13. *To Jeannie Welsh at Cheyne Row*

Resists being magnetized—Home preparations.

> Troston,
> *Wednesday* (14th Sept., 1842).

. . . Well, I have undergone the process of animal magnetism,† and with the impracticability of the Bass-Rock —which proves merely, according to Charles, not that his animal magnetism is a piece of downright nonsense, but that

---

* See p. 64.

† On September 11 she wrote, " Charles has undertaken to *magnetize* me provided I will give him an hour and not laugh, nor make any noise all the while—so perhaps I have supernatural revelations to report you next time."

I " have an ill-regulated mind." But what use is there
in writing any more, seeing that I will follow my letter
in a few hours ? The coach leaves Bury at half after nine so
that at the same rate of travelling we should reach London at
four. You may order some dinner to be ready at half after
four. *Broth* and boiled mutton if you like—for we shall probably be rather *feverish* and inclined to *slops*.

We are in expectation of Lady Cullum to-day to lunch here.
Charles has escaped to shoot partridges; Carlyle, who is retained
almost per force, looks not indisposed to shoot *himself*—or her.

Yours affectionate,

J. C.

14. *To Jeannie Welsh*

Babbie goes home—Panegyrics by Carlyle and Helen—The envy of
the inarticulate—A picture to be hung.

Monday (17th Oct., 1842).

MY DEAR GOOD CHILD,

To think that yesterday I was looking at you, speaking
to you, holding your bits of hands in mine, and that to-day I
am *writing to you* with two hundred milestones betwixt us !
It is one of those things which one does not realise to oneself
just at once ! Every time the door opens I fancy you should
come in, and you do not come in ! will not come in any more—
for a while !—and the house looks sad and strange—and I do
not know very well what to make of myself this foggy day.

Carlyle's manner of consoling me after you drove away was
characteristic. He fell to pronouncing an exceedingly long and
eloquent eulogy on you—particularizing everything from your
" *fine instinctive sense* " to the " *daintiness* " of your person, and
winding up with a prophetic felicitation to *the man* who should
get you for his wife !

Very gratifying for me to hear under ordinary circumstances
—but just then it sounded rather too much like a funeral
oration !—and I was not sorry when he resumed his reading of
the old Latin book. How I envy people who have the gift of
putting all that they think and feel into words ! Who never

lose their voice, literally or figuratively, whatever becomes of them ! But this power of utterance is a greater blessing to the people themselves than to those about them—witness Helen ! how often one wishes her struck dumb for the next twenty-four hours ! This morning she spent I am sure a whole hour in removing the breakfast things, that she might have repeated *flys at me* with her Job's comfort. " Poor thing ! I wonder what sort of night she had ? I never saw a sweeter Cretur ! " " Isn't it a pity, mem, but Miss Welsh were nearer—*for* it's quite surprising how fond she is about you !—*and* she left half a crown with me to give the Postman—I am sure he'll wonder ! *so* you see she behaved uncommon genteel."

I flew upstairs to be out of the road of her—and when I came back—she emerged out of the china closet saying as she crossed the floor—" Poor thing, the last thing she said to me was to take good care of cousin ! " You can fancy how all this worries me. To-day too we have the worst fog that has been this year—just as if it had kept off till you were out of the road of it. And Carlyle has already *three times* this morning requested I would " take *immediate* steps about getting that picture framed " and finally I had a bad night and my head aches—" and altogether," as the Dumfries Courier says, " the time is out of joint " for me. There is a frightful proposition about the picture that it should be hung over *this* mantel-piece to the sweeping away of all my dear little ornaments ! and to the utter destruction of *my privacy*—for I could never feel alone with that picture over me ! I almost *screamed* at the notion—but fortunately checked myself in time, as a passionate resistance would have clenched the matter. I merely suggested that it could not be seen to advantage—when brought so near one—as it would necessarily be in this small division of a room, so it is to be hoped it will still go upstairs.

I will not write any more just now, for I am not well enough for writing to any other purpose than the momentary gratification of my own feelings of loneliness. In truth, my babbie, I feel *very* lonely without thee—nevertheless, since you were to go, I am thankful you are gone ! just as, had I made up my mind to having an arm or leg cut off, I should be thankful the operation was well over.   No letters this morning but one from Cordelia Marshall [Mrs. Whewell] another of the *in*articulate people of this world—never able to give themselves fair play.

You will write to me a great deal, my dear little sister, till we meet again ?—and you will love me, more in proportion to the goodness of your own trustful heart than my deserving.

Remember me to them all with kindest regards—

Ever your affectionate
JANE W. CARLYLE.

15.   *To Jeannie Welsh*

Babbie writes at once—Dr. Adam Hunter and consumptive tendencies—Loses her way to Sloane Street—Darwin to the rescue —Robertson—Mazzini calls—Carlyle dines with the Macreadys.

Dr. Adam Hunter's cousinship was through Mrs. Carlyle's paternal grandmother, a Miss Hunter.

Robertson, in Carlyle's words, " is the blusterous John Robertson, whom Mill had at that time as Sub-Editor, or Subaltern generally, in the *Westminster Review* ; and who took absurdish airs on that dignity." (N.L. i. 124.)   In one case at least, as we learn, the " fancy " on which Mrs. Carlyle twits him, was not mere coxcombry on his part.   Jeannie had already met Mazzini and knew him as one of her cousin's truest and most high-minded friends.   The " donation " she sends is in support of his Italian school, of which more hereafter.

Miss Horton was a singer and actress who charmed her world as a " delicate Ariel."   A later generation knew her as Mrs. German Reed, a lady of massive proportions.

Dr. Quin was the earliest English homœopath ; popular in London society, and a friend of Dickens, Thackeray and Macready.

(*19th Oct.*, 1842.)

You did well to write, my poor Babbie, even before taking a wink of sleep ! for I should have been greatly disappointed had I not heard from you yesterday.   Tho' nothing had been settled about the *when* at parting—indeed it were difficult to say what *was* settled at parting—I calculated on a letter from you yesterday with as much certainty as on the sun's rising—or *more* certainly, for the sun I think has ceased rising of late days.

D

Your letter, however, made me very *wae* in picturing your physical state ! Had it been me, a violent headache of twelve hours' duration must have been the inevitable and mortifying issue of that amazing fluency of speech and noble disdain of sleep—but you, I think, do not (as Carlyle phrases it) " *go upon* " headaches—so perhaps you have escaped the reaction, at least in that its most torturing shape. Having finished writing to you on Monday, I went about a while, very much in the condition of the " wee woman who lived in a shoe "—not knowing the least in world " What to do." Finally I got up a resolution to set forth in an omnibus and call for Mrs. Buller. I had just got my bonnet and shawl on when Helen brought me up a card bearing the distinguished name of Dr. Hunter. Strange fatality ! on the first day of finding myself without one cousin, had Providence provided me in another ? and *such* another ! or was it the Dr. Hunter whom John had brought us ? I hurried down, not without a certain tremor—and beheld, him of Leeds sure enough ! but so altered ! thin, bent, feeble and in the act of unmuzzling himself from a *respirator*. His first words were characteristic—" Do not be alarmed, my dear Lady ! at least do not alarm yourself *too much !* I am not so ill as I seem ! " But to do the poor fellow justice, he seemed, after having got the first meeting over, considerably more concerned about my appearance than he even *expected me* to be about *his !* It was plain to the meanest capacity that he considered me a pretty way gone in consumption. " Dear ! Dear ! " he said, looking at my face and placing his finger and thumb on the hollows of his own cheeks—" Dear ! Dear ! this is not as it should be ! " and then he gave his head a great many slow prophetic shakes.

He told Carlyle that his own spitting of blood (in quarts !) was all brought on by over-excitement—had nothing to do with consumption—(poor unfortunate !)—" for tho'," he added, with *a courteous bow towards me*, " tho' there is a strong consumptive tendency in *this* family, it all came by old Mr. Welsh's side ! " He has been all this while in the Isle of Wight—is now in a lodging in Brompton for a week or two, and goes afterwards, by Sir James Clark's advice, to Hastings for the winter. The next winter he is to pass in Madeira—but will he live to see it ?

He told Carlyle he was very sorry to see " the way his wife was in "—and that " he must freely say to him, not merely as her cousin, but as *a medical man*, that he ought to take her abroad and use *any means under Heaven in the way of gratifying her wishes* to get her out of it." (No wonder he was a well employed doctor among the women at least, if this be the sort of advice he deals in !) " At lowest he thought I should try coming to *him* at Hastings for a month or two—the climate was fit for *weak lungs*. I would have the benefit of his medical advice, and Mrs. Hunter I would find *a chatty body !* at all events ; he did not say it to alarm me, *but merely in the way of conversation* "—if it was necessary for me to leave England next winter and my husband found it inconvenient to go with me (C. had looked monstrous glum at the speech about gratifying my wishes), need he say that in him, Adam, I would have *a warm friend and attentive protector*. Alas ! would one wish to prolong existence on such terms ! I mean, however, to take the opportunity of getting some reasonable advice from him regarding the pain in my side—since John will absolutely have nothing to do with it. He came in a cab and was to walk home—to Montpelier Place—near the Sterlings. Old Buller came in while he was here and told me Mrs. B. was gone to the Dentist, so there was no use in calling at Chester Place and I turned my benevolence into the channel of Adam, proposing to guide him the shortest way home, and a pretty guide I showed myself—fairly lost my way—to the Sterlings ! ! walked on and on, hoping always we should emerge into the Fulham Road, and finally emerged into Sloane Street ! opposite my shoe-shop ! ! The fact was, the seeing of him—absurd ass tho' he be—had thrown me into a sort of agitation and I hardly knew my right hand from my left —so I recommended him to Providence at that point—and stept myself into an omnibus returning from town—but *whither* it was returning I did not stop to enquire, and after carrying me a hundred yards it set me down in Sloane Square ! ! I felt really altogether ashamed of myself—even the omnibus cad seemed to compassionate my case—for he would not *take* my sixpence ! and providentially, as I was wondering how I should get home on my feet, Darwin drove up and relieved me from all further charge of myself.   That evening who should present himself but—Robertson !   I thought at first he must be come to ask why I accused him of " fancying women in love with him "—but his intentions proved to be entirely amicable.

Yesterday I had to go in two omnibuses to Fitzroy Square about the framing of that picture—on the instantaneous completion of which C. seemed to have hung all his hopes for this world or the next.   I returned at dinner time tired to death, having been again on the Gower Street end of the town *picked up by Darwin* and deposited in a regular Piccadilly omnibus ! " Mr. Mazzini waits "—the disagreeableness of finding even a Mr. Mazzini when one returns from such a worrying expedition, and needs porter and animal food to restore exhausted nature !—and moreover, it was the day of the Macready-dinner, and Carlyle was all demoralized in the awful prospect—lounging about from the mantel-piece to the table—from the table to the chairbacks—(you know his way) touching everything and contradicting everything—and neither taking the good of Mazzini himself nor letting me get the good of him—so I told him flatly to go away, and leave me to eat my dinner in peace and come again in the evening when I should be recovered and alone —which he did for three hours.

I gave him then the little donation,* but I will keep his speeches on the occasion till next time, for this letter is already too long for the time I have to spare.

C. returned at one in the morning—I having sat up for him —rather pleased it seemed with his lark.   Dickens, Longfellow, Dr. Quin and the Butlers at dinner—Mrs. Dickens and other " honourable women not a few "—and men came to make a soirée of it in the evening, and Miss Horton sang them all into bliss !

And now I must go and prepare for another attempt on Mrs. Buller, who writes to me that she will be at home all day.

Bless you, darling,

Your affectionate,
JANE C.

My love and kisses—as a general rule.

* See the following letter.

16. *To Jeannie Welsh*

The current of correspondence—Mazzini and Babbie's donation—
    Visits the Hunters—James Baillie—A pamphlet mislaid—
    Visitors.

Gambardella was an Italian refugee driven from Italy for
his too liberal political opinions, first to America, then to
England, bringing an introduction to Carlyle from Emerson in
October, 1841. He supported himself by painting portraits
and was successful with Mrs. Carlyle and the Welshes, but not
with Carlyle. His abrupt and tempestuous ways offered a
lively target for Mrs. Carlyle's pen.

The Wedgwoods are the Hensleigh Wedgwoods ; he a
grandson of Josiah Wedgwood of Maer and a cousin of the
Darwins ; she a daughter of Sir James Mackintosh.

(21st Oct., 1842.)

I am not sure, dear Babbie, that consistently with my
duties to " *Humanity*," to my numerous friends and admirers,
to my own household (such as it is), and above all to my own
me, little spirit of unrest, which, that it may not fly all into
shivers, needs to cultivate in itself above all things the great
holding-together cement of *stupidity !*—am not sure that consistently with these manifold duties, I can *go on* writing to you
at the present rate. But my imagination (surely a most fertile
one !) representing you to me in these days as a Babbie getting
herself *weaned*, how can I resist thus spiritually holding out to
you (if I may so speak) a finger to suck ! Alas the small
nourishment that is to be drawn from it ! but if the Babbie's
imagination be comforted thereby, is it not well, and may not
the shirts * and all other things lie over, for the accomplishment
of so laudable a purpose ?

First then of *the donation*. Mazzini was telling me that
Gambardella had stopped payment ! Two surprising facts
respecting G. I learnt from him in the same breath—the first
that he (G.) *can* write, the second that he has no money ! " *The
Administrator* " (old Heraclitus) † waited upon him to ask
the amount of his subscription (£1) or leave to erase his name

---

* See next letter.   † Petrucci.

from the list of subscribers. G. told him he would communicate on the subject with Mazzini himself, and this was the purport of his communication made *in writing ;* that he had not £1 to give at present, but would send it when he had ! Has he invested his whole capital in velvet linings ? While M. was bidding a sad adieu to this one pound as well as to Lady Byron's five, I put yours into his hand. Having cautiously unfolded it, he asked, " What *is she ?* " (the sovereign was it, or the writing of which he made a female ?). " Read and you will see." " J. W. Jeannie Welsh " ? (quite unconscious that he was taking the smallest freedom with your name). " It is of her ? " " Of her." " And without suggestion ? " " Entirely without suggestion ! " " Well, it is *good* upon *my* honour ! But I should not have thought—I mean—in a young person—I rather wonder how the thought came to her ! " " I assure you she is quite old enough to have good thoughts." " Jeannie Welsh—well, do I put her by that name on the list of those who have *gifted* our school ? " " That is her name of endearment—*you* had better call her Miss Welsh." " And what is *Babbie ?* Is *Babbie* in Scotch the same as *Jeannie ?* " " My dear, you are getting so abstruse that there is really no answering of your questions." " Never mind ! Jeannie or Babbie as you will ; she is *good*— and our school *stands in debt* to her ! " Well for " our school " if that were *all* the debt it stood in !

. . . The visit to the [forlorn] Hunters both fatigued and sad- dened me so much that I was fit for nothing more that day. Mrs. Hunter I found a sensible, unaffected, very affectionate looking woman—suffering great anxiety of mind and exerting herself to do the best under it. She told me at the door with a very pale face and tears in her eyes that the Drs. gave her almost no hope. Their little girl, about 11 or 12, is a beauty, and a smart, well mannered little thing. She is to remain at her school here during their stay at Hastings, so I must really take some charge of the poor little thing. By the way, there seems to have been a general turning up of *Cousins* for me since you went. The day I went about the picture frame, I saw in Regent Street from my omnibus (and thanked Heaven it was from an omnibus) James Baillie, still in the white trousers and heaven-blue coat, and his *mustard unsold.* It were a curiosity of rascaldom to know how that man lives, and gets his washing done !

Yesterday morning I had your letter, to hearten me after a considerable of a row about a missing pamphlet, which C. had kicked up (in pleasant consequence of the Macready-dinner), "one of those books seen for a moment—laid out of his hand, and then swept away *irrecoverably* into the general chaos of this house."   It was found of course in his own book-press, the first thing I saw on opening it.   But the music of our souls was jarred for the day ! . . .

You perceive that I am writing without paper fit to spell upon.

Here is the Postman already with another letter from you ! a thousand thanks, my darling.   I must not begin to answer it, for even of this sort of paper there is no supply *—and for time ! only consider !

Yours affectionate,

JANE C.

17. *To Jeannie Welsh.*

The domesticities leave time for a letter—Revolution by balloon—Dickens on America.

Saturday (22nd Oct., 1842).

I have mended *two* of the shirts this morning—and *effectually* —having put entire new tails to them !   So now I may do a little in the way of fondling my innocent offspring, without the sternest moralist being entitled to say to me " black is the white of your eye ! "   Besides, I feel as if writing a few lines to *you* were some small expression of thankfulness to Heaven for this particular thorough wet day !   But for the conclusive rain, I could not have got staid in the house to-day—again—the third day—without having had a fight for it—and really chicken-hearted as I am grown, there is nothing I can muster nerve to show fight about—nothing except my *right* to treat " poor Creek considerably worse than a dog ! "   *That*, with God's blessing, I will maintain to my latest breath.

---

* The letter is written on one ordinary sheet of notepaper and three slips of ruled paper—pages cut out of a little notebook.

Mazzini was here yesterday—radiant over an " *aviso interessante* " which he produced from his pocket, setting forth that one Mussi, or some such name, had discovered a power for regulating balloons as perfectly as a steamboat or railway carriage, in confirmation whereof behold certificates from *the Grand Duke of Tuscany* and the heads of *the Academy of Science at Florence*, etc., etc., before whom his model had been displayed ! The practical application you cannot for a moment be at a loss about ! The man, having not a shilling in the world, no means of subsistence but simply this small model-balloon, is willing to sell his secret for the trifling sum of *two thousand* pounds. If Mazzini can find him work in the interim, the man *may be induced not to part with it !*—till some member of *the Association* in Italy may be found to make the purchase. " Then," says Mazzini, " the power of directing balloons *ours ;* all is ours ! " " You mean that you would invade Italy in balloons ?—that *the Association* would descend on the Austrians out of the skies ? " " Exactly ! And I confess to you—you may think it childish—but there is something of romance, something which flatters my imagination in the idea of *starting up a nation* in a manner never before heard tell of ! " " *A la bonne heure*, my Dear ! but if it be decided that we are to begin the war by personating the fallen angels, adieu to *my* share in the expedition."

" Now, why so ? " (with a look of the most grave astonishment). " It was just in reference to *you* that I felt the greatest preference to *this means*—to think that you could go without incurring the physical suffering of a sea-voyage, and all the dangers—what shall I say ?—of being sunk perhaps by a volley of cannon from the shore ! and then there would be something so new and so—what shall I say ?—*suitable* for *you*, in descending as it were out of Heaven to redeem a suffering people ! " All this with eyes flashing hope, faith, and generous self-devotion ! Surely between the highest virtue and the beginning of madness the line of separation is infinitesimally small ! But is it not almost a desecration, a crime ever to *jest* with that man ? He lives, moves and has his being in *truth*, and take him out of that, he is as credulous and ignorant as a two-year-old child. . . .

I am reading Dickens' *Notes on America* which he has sent to Carlyle. At first I found the humour too strained and burlesque—his usual fault—and the plain narrative dull; but it improves as one goes on. He is much to be commended for avoiding utterly that detestable practice with travellers of turning their entertainers' houses and almost their entertainers themselves inside out. In the second volume he gives up dancing on the crown of his head for halfpence (if I may so speak) and becomes quietly entertaining, and entertainingly instructive.

Now farewell, my Babbie, and

love me well and long.

18. *To Jeannie Welsh*

On remembering omissions—Servants : a grave interest—Pensioners :
    her mother's generosity—Miss Gillespie—A local burglary—
    Presents to the family.

Henrietta is one of the Welshes' servants. Mrs. Martin is an old friend whose daughter Sophy afterwards married Babbie's brother Alick. Miss Gillespie, a former pensioner of Mrs. Welsh.

(26th Oct., 1842.)

DEAREST BABBIE,

. . . I could not but smile at the first words of your letter—having been thinking to myself that *all* the things I had meant to say to *you* had been omitted in my last letters. Yesterday it rained from morning till night without ceasing—nobody came—nothing happened—and it is wonderful how the human memory freshens all up in the vapour bath of such a day ! Ever so many things which I needed to ask you and to tell you came out like invisible ink-writing held to the fire—it was as if the pitter-patter of the rain whispered them to me—Lord bless me ! I am so figuratively disposed this morning ! I suppose it comes of having spent all yesterday in reading Jean Paul. But I will try to check the oriental tendency of my imagination and keep to the businesses " before *the House*." . . .

Poor Henrietta ! and poor Mistresses of Henrietta ! God be praised it is not typhus-fever ! It would have been a horrible anxiety for me to have known such a thing in your house !— to say nothing of her own and your more immediate concern with it.

One [of] the questions I had meant and failed to ask was precisely about *her*, and the other—how they went on ? and especially the new cook ?—fellow-feeling makes one take a grave interest in these sublunary cares, which young ladies think beneath the dignity of modern correspondence.   Another of my forgotten questions was : Has Mrs. Martin opportunity of sending things to old Miss Gillespie, and, if not, what is old Miss Gillespie's special address ? Poor old woman, I know next to nothing of her personally, but she has lost a most kind friend, and I would be glad by any little attention in my power to give her a moment's pleasure—often I used to feel vexed at my mother for spending so much of the little she had upon others, and getting so few comforts and pleasure out of it for herself—fool that I was, I made that a reproach to her which was her goodness, her wisdom.   Oh, I am very thankful now that she followed the thought of her own generous heart instead of my mistaken counsels !   What comfort were it for me now to think that she had for so many years of life had a little better food, and better clothes, and more travelling about, and more company at home, compared with the comfort of thinking that she made herself *loved* as a benefactor while she lived, and has made for herself in the hearts of so many an eternal regret ? All that she *enjoyed* is useless to her now—and useless to me in the remembrance—*it* belonged to her life on earth, and her life on earth is finished ; but all that she *gave* belongs to another and higher sphere—its fruits remain for ever and ever.

What were the other things I had to say to you ? They are all escaped again—and I know they amounted to something like half a dozen.   Well ! perhaps I may recover them by to-morrow. . . .

Love to the whole of No. 20.

Your own,
JANE CARLYLE.

19. *To Jeannie Welsh*

Busy on other people's business—Carlyle's impatience, especially
about the " improper " Mrs. R.—The picture framed and hung—
Mazzini and the watches—Call from Mr. Finlay—A rap to the
piano-player—Mazzini's English—The Italian School Anniversary—Solitude best for letter writing.

" Plato " is Plattnauer, of whom later. See Note on
Letter 21.

The Geneva watches belonged to Mazzini, who was trying
to sell them in order to clear off a fellow-exile's debts for which
he had made himself responsible. See Letter 26.

Mrs. R. had cut an unhappy matrimonial knot by flying
to France with her lover.

Mr. Carlyle's visitor is George Finlay, Byron's companion
at Missolonghi, who published his *History of Greece* between
1844 and 1861.

Saturday (probably *29th Oct.*, or *5th Nov.*, 1842).

Oh, sympathetical Babbie, sympathise with me ! If I
had three heads like the hydra, three pairs of hands and ditto
of legs, with three times the largest female patience (setting
aside, of course, such impossible examples as the *Lady Godiva*,
patient Grizzel, etc., etc., mere creations of the masculine brain
got up for its own diabolical purposes !), if I had all this tripled
power to think, and do, and run, and bear, it would all have been
little enough to meet the demands of the last few days ! It has
been *too* bad, " upon *my* honour " ! so much " *receiving* " (as
Plato calls it), so much obligatory writing, so many other-people's-
businesses devolving on poor me—unsought, unlooked for—
as the kittens that came " tumbling from on high " and put out
Mazzini's candle ! If I could tell you all I have had to undertake for " the welfare of others " this week, you would not
know whether, most to wonder at the *part of Providence* which
my friends put on me, or to grieve for my being so little *up
to it !* A correspondence about a housemaid for Mrs.
Wedgwood—a correspondence about a theatrical engagement
for the now *starving* Madame Fochetti !—new correspondence
about the immortal Mariotti-five pounds, a journey after

" inconceivably cheap chintz " to cover the delicate furniture of Mr. Charles Buller—three journeys and as many notes about the Geneva watches—deep consultations about the *getting up* the anniversary of the Italian School—with a running accompaniment of small household worry—such as : " Am I *never* meaning to take any steps about getting home that picture-frame ? " " Strange ! that a man cannot have a morsel of cake baked in his house, having the meal, an oven, and *two women*." And with all this and much more, too long to tell, you are to take along with you that two days ago his wisdom " kicked up a rumpus "—thereby flurrying me out of *two* nights' sleep. This time it was not for my *in*humanity, as in the case of " poor Craik," but for my " George-Sandish excess of humanity," à propos of poor Mrs. R. ! " My *doctrine* on that whole matter, he would have me to know, was *infamous*—and also, my *practice* in making myself the advocate of W——s—it behoved me to reform ! " I should have laughed at a charge so preposterous and which he himself was ready to laugh at five minutes after. But as I had spoken of Mrs. R. merely to amuse *him*, when, tired and cold, I would much rather have eat my dinner in sullen silence, I felt that virtue had *not* been its own reward, and *cried* like a simpleton and so made bad worse. All this, of course, is strictly private. And the result was, as I said, two heart-beating nights.

This morning we breakfasted very late, and then came the picture-frame beautiful—for only three pounds ! A deal of time was spent in dethroning poor Mrs. Sterling and hanging up the new Lady instead. She looks not at all amiss—better there, however, than *here*. When I told Helen Mr. Carlyle proposed to hang her over *this* mantel-piece she set down some plate she held in her hands with a slam, and uttered an " impossible ! " from which there could be no appeal. " Oh, mercy no ! " she added, " *that* can never be ! it *would* be a fell sicht *there !* " The picture business well over I sat down at last to write to my Babbie by this day's post—but hark, the softest possible rip tip, tip ! Enter Mazzini. A day's delay had been gained in paying some bill he owed, so that one more trial might be made to sell the poor watches at £6 each, instead of 5—

but only one day—so I had to start up and set off, first to
Boulter's and then to Collier's the Jeweller at the top of Sloane
Street.   Collier, *I think*, will take them at that money—but
would not say positively till his workmen had examined their
insides.   In short, my dear, I have been " troubled about many
things," and so *you* have been kept waiting.

I remember now two of the things I meant to tell you—one
dates from the day I went that far journey in quest of the picture-
framer—in the evening, as I was lying very tired on the sofa,
C. said quite suddenly :   " He seems a great talker that Mr.
Thingummy."   " Mr. Whatummy ? " says I—never having the
gift of divination.   " That Mr. What-d'you-call-him who was
here to-day ? "   " I know of nobody that was here to-day but
Countess Pepoli."   " Oh, I forgot—you did not see him—it
was that brother of Walter Macgregor's ! "   For the rest he seemed
to be rather disappointed in his " interesting appearance,"
he supposed, because I had led him to expect too much.   He,
Mr. Finlay, told him he was going to write a book upon Greece—
expressed the greatest detestation of London—and the interview
seemed to have gone off, if not rapturously, at least amicably
enough.

The other thing was still less momentous and yet worth
telling *to one's Babbie*—it was a shock that was given to " the
deep, deep sea."   The young Lady had been very incessant
one forenoon—and Carlyle was in a *fix* with his writing.   He
tried to vent his impatience in walking violently to and fro over
my head—at last seized with a movement of fury he took up
the poker, and with the head of it gave two startling blows on
the wall " exactly opposite where he fancied the young Lady
seated."   The music—if music it can be called, ceased in one
moment—and all was quiet as death in No. 6 for the next twelve
hours !

Darwin and Mazzini met here the other day and the three
of us sat with our feet on the fender—the folding doors being
closed—and talked about " things in general," forming the most
confidential little fireside party I have seen for a good while.
Mazzini said that Sismondi had at one time been " nearly
lapidated."   " Nonsense," said I, " you should say *stoned*,

there is no such word as lapidated in that sense." " Let him alone," said Darwin, " he is quite right, *lapidated* is an excellent word." " Do not mind him," said I to M., " he only wants to lead you into making a mistake." " But are you sure ? " asked M. with the greatest simplicity—" in the Bible, for instance, does not *She call it lapidated* in speaking of St. Stephen ? " This femalizing of the Bible so delighted Darwin that he gave a sovereign to the school ! *the* deficit will surely get filled up in time. Nay, he almost promised to attend the anniversary— when all the organ boys are to have *a supper* and the best learners receive medals. Carlyle will not go I fear—but if I am well enough and can front all the black, black eyes that will flash out on me if I present myself along with the Capitano, I will go and put *my* sovereign into " the bason or box, what shall I say ? " that is to be placed at the door. Elizabeth also wants to go—but Pepoli hesitates—from *political* fears. Pepoli, I think, needs only to show his face to make *Austria* entirely at ease respecting his purposes—whether he appear as a patron of the school or no.

Dear child, I write you all this *wash* to-night while I have leisure—and one knows not what to-morrow or next day may bring forth. I have generally leisure in the evenings, but when C. is sitting opposite to me at the same table, besides his objecting to " the squirting of my pen," I feel always as if there was a shadow between me and the person I am addressing— you will understand this feeling better than you once could have done—having got accustomed yourself to a certain seclusion while writing or doing anything with your head ! To-night C. is gone to Darwin's.

. . . My love and kisses to them all. Love me, my child, and be sure that I love you always, always like the dearest little sister.

Ever your,

J. CARLYLE.

20. *To Jeannie Welsh*

Mazzini and the watches—Mrs. Sterling ill—Old Sterling falls asleep while paying a call—The Laings—Irregular hours in the house.

Monday (31st *Oct.* or 7th *Nov.*, 1842).

DEAR,

My letter being of rather ancient date (Saturday night) I add a line that you may know me, up to Monday, still in the land of the living and the loving.

Already (at 12 o'clock) have I been up, poor wretch, to Collier's [the jeweller]—in omnibus—respecting those melancholy watches—delivered after all—found to be " of inferior quality," so that Mazzini has nothing left for it but to sell them to the Frenchman for £15—well if he gets the money from him even at that absurd price ! " Virtue its own reward "—was there ever a greater *bêtise* than that current among articulate speaking men ! *Virtue its own punishment* were a maxim much less liable to exception.

Old Sterling came yesterday giving lamentable accounts of " my poor dear wife." . . .

The old gentleman in the midst of our *tête-à-tête* suddenly dropt silent. I looked round at him after a minute or two, and saw him with his features all pinched together, his mouth a little open—profoundly asleep !—and I thought it one of the most rational and friendly-looking modes of transacting a forenoon visit that I had fallen in with for a good while. He awoke after a quarter of an hour or so, exclaiming " Gracious God, have I been dreaming ? " " You know best," said I. " I only know that you have been asleep." You may figure the apologies ! The Laings, male and female, were also here yesterday—a pretty little thing she is but I think a considerable of a goose. She made the most loving inquiry after *you*. I told her I had set my heart on your marrying her Father-in-law. She laughed immoderately but said you were not to be taken in by his assiduities, for he was a very general lover of young ladies—" he said there is so much more *freshness* about them than older women "—naturally.

Our house is on a sort of climax of irregularity just at present —C. orders the dinner at half after four and keeps it waiting

till six—goes to bed at two—and the breakfast prolongs itself
into midday. It is an evil in its way to a punctually disposed
person like myself. . . .

21. *To Jeannie Welsh.*

A day's occupations—A housekeeper for R. Buller—A note from the
Macreadys—C.'s portrait by Gambardella—Plattnauer comes
to bid farewell—A difficult trio of visitors—Anne Fox's copy
of C.'s portrait—C.'s hair, and cottonwool—Mazzini and the
watches—Sponged on by his compatriots—Cavaignac and his
character—C. forgets to post a letter—Humour and virtue.

Mrs. Strachey, Anglo-Indian by birth and by marriage, was
younger sister of Mrs. Buller ; her father, General Kirkpatrick.
The charming Kitty Kirkpatrick, Carlyle's early admiration,
was a cousin, child of their uncle's romantic marriage with an
Indian Begum.

Rio, "a wandering, rather loud and headlong, but innocent-
hearted, French friend, Neo-Catholic, etc." (T. C. in L.M.
i. 313), and again " a sort of French John Sterling " (N.L. i. 73).

Mrs. Jameson, the indefatigable writer on art, who rejoiced
in an " extraordinary wealth of accomplished friends."

Mrs. Milner Gibson, wife of the M.P. and Cabinet Minister
who was one of the apostles of free trade and free newspapers,
was the daughter of Sir Thomas Cullum mentioned in Letter
No. 12. Her salon in London was frequented by the literary
celebrities of the day and the French and Italian political exiles,
including Mazzini. She was godmother to one of Dickens'
children.

Plato, nickname for Plattnauer, a German of good family
connexions, at that time tutor to the Marquis of Ailesbury's
son (see p. 124). His queer ways culminated in active madness ;
subsequent letters tell how Mrs. Carlyle, who had much influence
over the poor soul, delivered him from a madhouse, and got
into touch with his " hochwohlgeborn " relatives.

William Cunningham reappears as a collector of pictures.

William Weir, first editor of the *Glasgow Argus*, migrated to
London, and finally became editor of the *Daily News*. His
drawback was deafness.

George Darley, poet and mathematician (d. 1846), was at
this time dramatic critic of the *Athenæum*. The Carlyles
liked him, but conversation with him dragged, as he had a bad
stammer.

The " tame Foxes " are the Quaker family of Falmouth.

Godefroi Cavaignac, "the chivalrous and grandly humorous" (T. C. in L.M. i. 248), was the one among the exiles with whom Carlyle ever had any intimacy, the superior, he thought, of his younger brother Eugene, subsequently President of the short-lived French Republic.   Godefroi and Mrs. Carlyle had a deep affection and regard for one another.   Cf. Letter 160.

The author of the sketch of Walter Welsh is probably the Mr. Hick mentioned in Letter 25.   Harriet is Miss Martineau.

Now stop !   Have you eaten your breakfast ? if not, eat it— the letter will not cool by keeping—the tea and toast will !

Sunday (? 13th *Nov.*, 1842).

BELOVED BABBIE,

Take yesterday as a sample of my whole week, and then wonder, if you can, that I was so many days without writing to you !

I rose at half after seven ; early enough in all conscience for a November morning ! It was rough weather, both without and within—one of those mornings in which " the Devil " is requested to " fly away " with things, and does at all events fly away with one's whole comfort ! The breakfast over, I sat down in my dressing gown to repair my only wearing gown —three days before I had put *one* new wristband to it, and now it was full time to finish with the other.   As I *cannot* work in the Miss-Tanner-fashion it was eleven before I had got myself dressed.   Then arrived, by appointment, the Housekeeper for Mr. Reginald Buller, on her way from Glasgow to Troston, to receive my instructions as to the remaining fraction of her journey and to be told by me I know not what—for the last day I saw Mrs. Buller she " did not know the least in the world " what she was saying—one of those days with her in which when she asks for a *comb* she means *her shoes*.   The woman satisfied me entirely, a large, effectual, maternal looking woman, whom I should have chosen out of a thousand to put poor dear Regy into the hands of.   After an hour's speech with her, I sent her off to the Golden Cross to secure her place for Monday, and sat down to inform Reginald she was under way—and would need to be picked up with her boxes at Bury—that done, the

E

house-keeper concern at least would be finished off, and then I would write to my Babbie in peace. But in the midst of my writing enter Helen with a letter post-marked Ixworth. Here you must stop and read the said letter, which I will enclose.

Well !—was not there a pretty mess ? What on earth to do ? let the poor woman go on and plump into the thick of this cabal, or try to stop her till it had settled itself—I absolutely thumped my brow in despair—at last I decided on letting Destiny take its course, but you may fancy how many more pages it required to make all the reasons plain to the capacity of a Regy, besides soothing his agitated mind. And then an equally long letter had to be improvised to Regy's mother—and that again enclosed in a few lines to Mrs. Strachey—Mrs. Buller's new address having escaped my memory—sixteen pages of close writing went among them—and I am sure there was not one superfluous line !

All this scribbling brought me to the post hour and a dinner of stewed beef—and an hour on the sofa afterwards was hardly enough to compose my distracted " *brains* " (as Rio says). After tea I sat down with the gathered up wreck of my faculties to mend the *last* of the shirts—when tap tap—another note from Mrs. Jameson (about the five pounds) the contents of which required to be immediately communicated to Pepoli. That done, again I turned to the shirt—feeling even sewing a blessedness after so much writing—but again the knocker with loud single stroke shook me to the centre of my poor being— and Helen brought me a note to which an answer was to be returned by the Bearer—I tore it up with a quite piteous " Oh merciful Heaven ! " and found it a hurried request from Miss Macready that I would send *Madame Fochetti's* address, or if I did not know it, send the Bearer to where it could be had, as " William " very particularly wished to have it that evening— some *fix* at the Theatre most likely—in which William had kindly bethought himself of my protégée—a note to be written to Mazzini—and another to Miss M. in case of Mazzini's being from home—and Helen to be sent off with the man to show him his way—being a servant of the Theatre (" quite a stranger *in this part of the country* "). I could hardly help saying to myself when I went to bed after all this : " If ever I undertake anything for the good of any human again ! "

To-day (Sunday !) Carlyle is sitting to Gambardella ! In passing to Mrs. Sterling's one day I seduced him into G.'s room to see Harriet and Mrs. Milner Gibson—with both which pictures he was *enthusiastically* pleased and readily yielded to —nay almost anticipated Gambardella's request of another two hours to make the picture for America a little uglier and more cross-looking. I do not understand how G. should be at a loss for *one* sovereign—sitters seem to be pouring in upon him and paying him large prices—young Laing is done, as cleverly as the father. I declined going because it bores me to see C. sit—and also because I half expected Plato, who came, at eleven, in a cab—poor fellow !—he looked sadly wearied—and out of humour with the world—one of the fatalest symptoms of which was the accusations he made of me for being " so *calm*—to look at me and read my letters one would say that I had never a cross moment—a very enviable state of *indifference*, which he admired but was sorry he could not imitate ! " *Before* the church dismissed a rap came to the door, whereupon he said with some emotion : " there is someone coming ; now I have seen you, and must bid you farewell "—and so saying, he took my hand and kissed it rather impressively—kissing one's hand is so much *selon les règles* in *foreign* leave-takings, that I thought nothing of it at the moment, but considering afterwards, how remarkably reserved this particular foreigner has always shown himself in *practical* things (recollect, for instance, the washing of his hands !) it struck me all of a heap that he had taken leave of me for good and all—that he is *meaning* to quit his Ailesburys in Paris and return to England no more if he can help it. Several words he let fall were in accordance with such a hypothesis. If so—I shall be sorry—" This minds me," (as Helen says) of something Helen *said* the other day—speaking of *you* she remarked that " certainly you were *most* insinuating ! and if Mr. Plattnauer (! ! !) or any nice mannerly gentleman like that wanted a real, good, most *virtuous* wife, and a pretty cretur, he might think himself blessed to get you "—decidedly, so he might !—But to return, the someone who came in was Mr. Lucas, as dreadfully happy as usual, and he has worn me out with laughing at I know not what——

Evening.

Oh Babbie, such a day of human speech—I was interrupted by William Cunningham who sat two hours and a half !—sat out Craik, Weir and Darley !—Now consider that party and fancy me, with my uncertain voice, in the midst of it !—Darley who cannot speak—Craik who cannot be spoken to, and Weir who is as deaf as a post ! But the three incompatibilities went before I was tempted to take my dagger to them and left me to resume an ethical discussion with William Cunningham. The motives of human action, the aims of *ditto*, the nature and qualities of *ditto*—finding there was going to be no end to it I told him at last, that the *action* which was always stopping at every step, to ask from whence it came, and whither it was going, and what was its merit or demerit, appeared to me in danger of getting into " a regular fix," at all events of becoming inordinately self-conceited—and that I could sooner forgive a man who did wrong unconsciously than one who lived in a continual pretension to do right.

But all this while I have not thanked you for your dear long letter. " *Ah !* " your little *imagination* moved me almost to tears—and I could have stretched out my arms and caught the visionary Babbie and " kissed " her not once or twice, but twenty times over. I kiss nobody at present—I do not know how I may *look* to Plattnauer, but I certainly *feel* " cross "— and excessively.

I was twice to Knightsbridge during the last week. Mrs. Sterling is really ill—is threatened, the Dr. says, with disease of the heart—and I must go to her often so long as I keep on foot—not because her husband asks it of me with ever ready tears, but in gratitude for all the kind nursing she bestowed on myself when she was less wearisome than now. It is to be said, however—and that is really the most serious looking symptom I see about her, that her disposition is strangely softened and improved from what it was in summer—the continual fret about

everything and nothing has quite subsided. She has become
affectionate and studious about other people's comfort as of
old, and seems to cling to *me* as of old to cheer her solitude.
I am glad that it is thus—for I should have felt myself *bound* to
be good to her, in whatever frame of mind—but the continuance
of the mood she had got into in summer would have made all
kindness from me of no avail to *her*, and very uphill work to
myself. But it is a pity she is so far off in this cold weather.

The basket Harriet spoke of is come, and I wish that I
could send you a sight of it. . . . Another present I have
received last week of a much less satisfactory nature. One of
the nice little *tame Foxes* has copied for me the sketch of my
husband carried away in triumph from Lawrence's by John
Sterling—the intention was beautiful, but the performance
—never, never was anything so hideous in shape of a likeness !
I not only would not hang it up on any wall for the world, but
wish very much that " the devil would fly away with it " out of
the house ! It is carefully secured under glass too ! poor
little well-meaning but mistaken Quakeress, and of course I
had to write her a letter of *thanks !* you may conceive the
difficulty !

Carlyle is going on much as usual—Helen ditto—the cat
only seems *better* than usual—its spirits are almost too much for
me ! Helen says " it is the strangest cat, it is just *dottedly*
fond of her ! really adores her, to say the truth, and yet it will
not suffer her to touch it." In what manner it had expressed
its *adoration*, I could not discover. Mercy, I had as near as
possible forgotten—the potatoes—I can say now quite decidedly
No, do not send any—the man's are so much improved that it
were ingratitude both towards him and Providence to seek
further.

C.'s hair is creeping slowly over the tops of his ears, but that
is all the way it has got. Meanwhile the *cotton* is still used for
one ear—in which, however, it never stays long, but is generally
to be seen (not without astonishment by the uninitiated)
sticking, a small white pellet, at the end of some stray hair—
for all the world like a snowberry ! The Frenchman did not
give the fifteen pounds for the watches—would give no *money*

—only *hopes* of money—which were not available for paying a bill—and then, as I had always foretold, *he* got fourteen pounds to pay in addition, at the very same moment for that thriftless Scipione Petrucci—of course there was nothing for it but the old resource, borrowing on exorbitant interest from the money-lenders ! He said to me with a bitter smile : " I am fortunate, you see !—I have always *credit*." Surely he has been so imposed on by one and another of them of late that he will become a *little* wiser.

Now if I have left what I am about to tell you to the very end, it is not by any means that I reckon it the least event of the week. I had a letter the other day from Cavaignac and he will come before the winter end, if all go right. With all men " appearances are deceitful," *sometimes*—but with Cavaignac they are almost *invariably* so !—and having found this on long knowledge of him, I never now judge him by appearances ; accordingly his silence all these months, which in any other so related to me, I should have accounted ungracious, not to say unfeeling—in him I accepted merely as one of his *eccentricities* from which no sure indication was to be discovered of his actual feelings towards me ; which ought not therefore to be allowed to influence *my* feelings towards him. And this time as always he has justified my great *faith*. After alluding quite slightly to vexations he has had and illness he has had, he says with that manly frankness which so delights me in him : " n'avoir pas senti un besoin de vous écrire un mot de sympathie et d'amicale consolation qui l'importât sur tout ce qui me tenait— c'était à ne pas se reconnaitre soi-même "—so long as the *soi-même* continues friend to me I am mighty indifferent about the rest. Oh, Babbie dear ! I do think that the men in con- stituting themselves our judges are very unjust to us ! One thing for example : how often we hear them say ! that women value the *small change* of friendship quite above the solid gold— or to speak in plain English, that we prefer those who " *set in* chairs " for us and pay us all sorts of small attentions, to those who, in neglecting them, have nevertheless our interests really at heart ! Silly women do so, and do many other silly things. And I should like to know, is the conduct of silly *men* always

CAVAIGNAC.

From a photograph by Gwyn Collier.

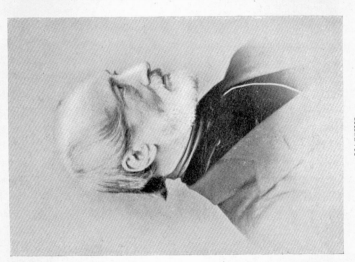

MAZZINI.

From a photograph by Elliott & Fry.

perfect ?—But a woman of sense—I judge by myself (!) can dispense with the " *small change* " without a sigh, where she knows that a true affection is felt for her—only where she has no ground to believe in such an affection, if she pocket the small change with " *a certain* " thankfulness, is not *that* her goodness rather than her folly ?

Monday morning.

You received my last letter a day later than you ought to have done.   Carlyle took it with two others of mine to the post office—put in some letters of his own out of a separate pocket and brought back my three an hour and half after post time— " It was no fault of his " however !—" he had no recollection of ever having charged himself with them." . . .

I return Walter's image—which is indeed a rare work of art ! the man who did it must have genius—at all events *virtue* —as according to Carlyle all *genuine* humour has its foundation in virtue—nay *is* virtue's self.   Love to them all—

Your affectionate

J. C.

22. *To Jeannie Welsh*

Early rising and Babbie's letters—Carlyle looks askance at the Italians.

(15*th Nov.*, 1842.)

MY EMPHATIC AND *insinuating* BABBIE,

Be good then !—or rather—*continue* good ! and I will not Miss-Babbie you any more.   I know your difficulties, my poor child, and it is just *because* I know them, that I regard the first step of giving way to them as a thing to be counteracted by all means, gentle and ungentle. . . .

I want your letters for myself—they are very cheering to me in my solitary forenoons, especially *when we have risen early* and my enviable *calm* has had itself ruffled.   I find that I can get thro' the rest of the day more contentedly and good-temperedly with the kind words of Babbie in my ears—

and so—I wish naturally to have them always in my ears—at least some audible echo of them.

It seems to me I have a great many things to tell you, but must keep them till my head is clearer, for as I said it is aching to-day still, and prudence recommends that I should allow it all possible repose—but I could not let alone giving you my blessing for two such nice long letters. Thank heaven it could not be the Italian *Anniversary* that has made me ill—or I should be hearing of it on the deafest side of my head—I did not go to the Anniversary—tho' the Pepolis offered to take me with them in their fly and I had almost got the length of *wishing* to go—C. had looked so thundery on the whole business —as if the education of organ boys were something nearly amounting to felony—and has in fact taken up of late such a spirit of persecution (for I can call it nothing less) against everything connected in the remotest degree with " young Italy " that I foresaw an amount of ill-humour on account of my lending my countenance (that is to say, *his* wife's countenance) to " a nest of young conspirators " which would be too dear a price, I thought, to pay for any satisfaction I might have or give by going—so I staid at home and was *rewarded* for my conjugal docility by having Craik ! Mrs. Jameson and Elizabeth were highly pleased—but I will tell you all about it when I am abler. . . .

Bless you, darling—pray for me.

Your own J. C.

23. *To Jeannie Welsh*

Mazzini's School Anniversary—Gambardella's portraits of C. and Mrs. C.—His letter from Mrs. Reid—Gambardella and Mrs. C.'s age—Young Laing's MS.—The old Dairywoman and her husband —Fasting—The musical neighbour.

" Upon *my* honour "—one of Mazzini's idioms.

Dr. Rossetti was Professor of Italian at King's College, and father of Christina and Dante Gabriel Rossetti.

John Forster, best remembered as the friend and biographer of Dickens, was in his day one of the foremost figures in literature and criticism. He was affectionately known to the Carlyles as " Fuz "

Wednesday (16th Nov., 1842).

Darling—the four ill-written pages I sent you yesterday, evinced a more determined concern for your *happiness*, than twenty well-written would have done under more favourable circumstances !   For yesterday was a bad day with me, " upon *my* honour," and the *second* bad day too which made it the worse to bear up against.   Now I am " *pretty well* " again and hasten to make hay while the sun shines, that is to write while the rain rains—With dry weather one may foresee there will come a flight of visitors to make up for time lost—to *them*—I have set a sempstress to work—*in the kitchen*—finding that the needlework of this house was threatening to engulf me bodily. I have written a trio of other-people's-business-notes, and now I am all for my Babbie !

First of *the Anniversary :* " the moral satisfaction was complete, the *financial* rather disappointing."   Thirteen pounds was the sum collected including the immortal five—from which deduct the expenses and there would remain, I am afraid zero—or perhaps even *a deficit*—the *supper* of itself must have gone with a half—*forty-five* gallons of beer, *fifty* pounds of macaroni, and roast beef of unascertained quantity ! to be sure there were two hundred and fifty sat down to what the *Dumfries Courier* would call " the festive board," and the fine times of miraculous loaves and fishes are long gone by ; tho' God knows if ever there was a time when men had more need of them ! think of the boiled dead dog !—The supper transacted itself in a tavern hard-by, at the close of the business—leaving the schoolroom to more poetical purposes—to distribution of prizes—speeches of " the *founder* " (anglicé the Committee) and " what shall I say, strange things upon my honour " ! You may be sure that old Petrucci would not let slip so fine an occasion of gratifying his melodramatic propensities and accordingly a series of *scenas* were most unexpectedly introduced which the audience must have been charmed to find themselves " *assisting* at "—*for nothing*—I mean *gratis*.   Of the first, poor unsuspecting, horror-struck Mazzini was made at once the hero and the victim !   When all had spoken who were to speak, he came forward—very shame-faced, as you may fancy, and " unveiling himself as the original founder " (in defiance to Baldanoni who had said he *dared* not) he made a most moving address to the school as *learners* and as *patriots*. When he had finished amidst shouting like to bring down the ceiling there stepped forth from the pupils' benches the *least* boy— some twelve years old—who advanced blushing, and laid a bouquet at his feet ! then putting his little hand in his breast, he pulled out a little paper, and proceeded to read a little sonnet to his (Mazzini's) honour and glory !—Just fancy this ! and consider the sort of man ! and admire him that he did not turn round and brain old Petrucci on the spot—from whose goose-head of course this *coup de théâtre* must have emanated ! Nor was that all the trials his modesty had to undergo—an Italian girl next advanced from the pupils' benches (there are nine female pupils—some English, the wives of Italian opera- tives—and some Italian) a very beautiful girl too,—came forward in an accès of enthusiasm genuine—for this part of the exhibition was *spontaneous*—and humbly besought him to give her one flower of his bouquet ! ! and an English woman, who would not be behind the foreigner, called God to witness that he was the *Prophet* of her time ! ! The moral satisfaction might well be " *complete*," *more* than complete one would say !—Nor had Petrucci forgotten himself—when the company were about to disperse one of the pupils again stepped forth, and declared that it would make their enjoyment perfect if Mr. Petrucci would favour them with an *improvisation*. " Oh, *impossible, impossible !* "—with all sorts of coyish grimacing—at length he allowed himself to be so far prevailed upon that " he would read them a composed poem of his own—" which he thereupon drew *all ready* from his pocket—and calling to him " *the* Dr. *Rossetti* " the two old fools proceeded to deliver in horrible recitative a dramatised poem written for the occasion ! What the " well-wishing English " thought of all this, I cannot pretend to say—a good deal of inward laughter must I should think have transacted itself—fortunately there were few English present—of women only Elizabeth and Mrs. Jameson, the one, half Italian by marriage, and the other, two-thirds so by nature.

Did I tell you the fate of Gambardella's picture of Carlyle ?
I think not.   At C.'s desire I stept in to see it one day in passing
to the Sterlings'—Spiridion (his other name is quite too long for
writing) almost without opening his lips set it up before me.
He had put in a small triangular light just at the joining of the
nose and brow which gave it the appearance of *smelling something*
to which *assafoetida* was a joke, and another very broad,
circular one in the middle of the under lip—which I cannot
describe unless you can fancy such an unheard of thing as a
lip *ignited* by a lucifer-match !—I looked at it for a moment
with all the gravity I could muster, and then looked at the
painter.   Our eyes met, and *both* exploded with laughter !
" The fact is," said G., " that poor man can *not* sit ! and will
never get himself painted in this world—unless from *memory*
by someone who has studied his face " (in this last observation
I believe there was a deal of sound sense).   " But we must
not tell him so," he continued, " it would vex him, and the
poor man has done the best he could !   just let it pass for *my*
want of talent, and I will do him a picture of *you* to make up
to him for his lost time ! "   And then he made me sit down and
read two letters from Mrs. Reid which I had heard of already
from Carlyle and which had " excited him very much."   No
wonder !   The first was a honeyed production enough, setting
forth the inducements of Tynemouth—and beseeching him
to come and paint her a picture of her " dear and admirable
friend Miss Martineau, who was just now looking unusually
well."   She, Mrs. Reid, would cheerfully bear his expenses, a
steamer would bring him in two days, etc.—The second
letter was on receiving his charge twenty pounds for the
picture (not at all too much) and 6 pounds for expenses—three
pounds less—observe—than what it actually costs to go and
come by railway.   A more coolly impertinent, ungenerous,
unladylike epistle than this of the " amiable Mrs. Reid " I
never in my life read—it might well excite him.   She re-
proached him with having neglected her directions about the
steamboat and thus added *several* pounds to her expense
" without one word of motive or apology."   If he must go by
railroad, at least he might have gone by the second class

train ! ! !—She feared such want of consideration would hinder
his success among English people, " for whom nothing was
more offensive than a *want of delicacy* in money matters ! "—I
absolutely blushed for the woman in reading her vile letter,
and felt heartily sorry for the poor fellow.   Such language to a
man who had dined at her table—a gentleman by birth and
breeding—shame on the old haddock !   I always considered
her a humbug with her virtue-doing and penny-ladyisms *—
and I was not deceived.   He was very confidential—spoke of
my letter to him about the five pounds in the warmest terms
of gratitude—and also of his regrets that after C.'s " capricious "
behaviour to him he could not visit at the house.   " There
were just two perfect women for him in the world, Mrs. Follen
in America and I in England.   I was not so old as Mrs. Follen
(good God how old *is* Mrs. Follen ?) but *that* made no difference
in the *disinterestedness* of his friendship for me—" whenever I
needed him he was ready to spill his blood for me, or go to the
world's end for me "—but to visit at the house under such
circumstances could be no good either to him or me—" he had
said so to Dr. Bute," and a great deal more he appeared to have
said to Dr. Bute which he might as well have kept to himself—
moreover he told me as coolly as if I had been *a hundred years
old*—that he spent *all* his evenings with Dr. Bute—he *must* go
somewhere, for his nature was social—he *could* not go to me—and
so he went to Dr. Bute—for unless he had *virtuous* society he
would take up with vicious—would turn blackguard—and
ruin himself *every way*.   Heaven have mercy—" that *minds
me !* " † only think Babbie of young Laing having written a
Drama and actually sent it in to Macready !   Do not mention
this for *perhaps* it is a secret—when he confided the fact to
Carlyle and requested his intervention with Macready, C. said
(nay wrote it to Macready himself) that he " received a sort of
shock—as if his maid servant had informed him that she had
fallen with child ! ! "   If poor Laing had seen that sealed note

---

* " In Scotland the ' Penny Ladies ' (extraneously so-called) were
busy, ' benevolent ' persons ; subscribers of a penny a week for educating,
etc., not with much success." (T. C. in L.M. i. 349 n.)
† A saying of Helen Mitchell's.

of *recommendation* which he unsuspectingly forwarded along with his MS. !

Mrs. Wright the large Dairywoman at the corner died the other morning, and her husband has been a great object of interest to the neighbourhood especially to Helen ever since—it was a sort of Mahomet and Kadijah affair—the woman a prosperous widow advanced in years took him, a poor lad to keep not her camels but her cows—and finding him a good lad married him. She has died at seventy-two—and he—still a young man is inconsolable ! " He cannot be persuaded," says Helen, " to taste either meat or drink." " How long is it," said I, " when did she die ? " " This morning at nine o'clock " —it was then eleven !—the poor fellow *may* have loved his old wife, however, very sincerely, and be sincerely to be pitied—altho's the *fast* was nothing to speak of. A propos of fasts—C. was reading out of one of his big books last night the only fast worth mentioning I ever heard out of them (the old chronicles I mean). A certain Sir John Compton displayed his vocation to holiness at so early an age " that when he was yet an infant on his mother's breast he fasted two days in the week—on Wednesdays and Fridays he did wholly abstain to suck ! ! " *there's* a kid !

Thursday.

. . . Oh that horrible squalling girl ! in these wet days she is worse than ever ! every morning that I get leave to sleep a little longer than usual she rattles me up with her accursed scales vocal and instrumental ! the idea of any creature out of Bedlam falling to work to practise at eight o'clock in the month of November !

There is C. tramping in his boots overhead so I must seal and be ready—bless you darling—dispense my love *liberally* yet according to desert.

Ever your affectionate,

JANE W. C.

I send Helen a caricature of Forster and Dickens to put among her autographs—I need not say who did it.

24. *To Jeannie Welsh*

Domestic distractions—Rival MSS. : a novel and *Past and Present*
—Death of Mrs. Milner Gibson's child—The old dairywoman's
husband again.

Lady Morgan, the Irish novelist, lived in London for the
last twenty years of her life, making the most of her position
in society. Miss Jewsbury, coming to London in 1854, helped
her in writing out her Memoirs.

Mrs. Paulet, an early friend of Miss Jewsbury, and later
much attached to the Carlyles, was "a strange, indolently
ingenious, artistic, &c., creature," wife of a " good, cleverish "
Genoese merchant (T. C. in L.M. i. 288), who lived at
Seaforth House, three miles or so down the river from Liverpool, once occupied by W. E. Gladstone's parents.

Wednesday (late Nov., 1842).

MY DARLING BABBIE,

Before committing myself to the general stream of
things, I must beg your attention to a brief exposition of my
difficulties in the one matter of writing.

For the last week or two we have breakfasted later than
usual, C. seldom coming down before half past nine—*tant
mieux*, so far as that goes—by the time the table has been cleared
for writing and oneself emerged out of dressing-gown into
fit-to-be-seen-in gown eleven has probably struck. Say that
I then fall to writing—first comes Helen : " What about the
dinner, Mum ? " " *Chops !* " that at least is quickly settled,
but then perhaps comes Carlyle to say : " Jane, these cloth-
boots of mine are in eminent need of some repair," or " Jane,
these cloth trowsers of mine must have a new hem at the
bottom," or " Jane, something or other " alike inconvenient
at that particular moment—or perhaps Elizabeth Pepoli comes
(she comes very often at present) " to catch me before I go out "
—or perhaps the Postman brings some note or letter that makes
it imperative for me to turn my writing into another channel
than the premeditated one of Babbie. There is hardly a day
that one or other of these *perhapses* does not come to pass

—then, if *all* the forenoon were at my own disposal, as it used to be, Babbie might still get her letter—but at *one* o'clock—I am *forced* to go out every day, unless it rains— which at present it seems resolute not to do.   Now that this odious walking forms part of my *medical* treatment there is no evading of it without getting myself into worse trouble.   If, after coming in, there be a leisure half hour or so before dinner I am too much fagged to turn it to any earthly account—and in the evening I have neither privacy nor strength for writing—I am always wearied and *sick* in the evenings—the effect I suppose of the walking and the blue pills.   The beautiful part of it is that this sort of thing may go on for ever so long— John tells me that " If I can trace any perceptible improvement in myself after having continued the pills for a *month*, it will be as soon as I have any business to look for it."   Well, patience— and do you dear help me to be patient by writing always as if I made you the most liberal returns.

I received yesterday by railway a bundle of manuscript from Geraldine and Mrs. Paulet—of which I am to give my opinion—partly from a sort of *vague apprehension*, partly for another reason I have not yet untied the parcel—this other reason is, that Carlyle has also a considerable bundle of MS., *not* about Cromwell at all ! but about that old Abbot of St. Edmonds Bury ! ! which he " rather wishes me to read and give him my views about "—and until I have *studied* that, which will be no light matter, I must abstain, for *decency's sake* from showing any curiosity about the other literary produc- tion in which I have only a *friend's* interest.   My Dear, tho' we are not trained here as in China, to " the three-thousand punctualities "—we are always needing to look to our doings that we may not stumble over some nicety or other. . . .

Did I ever tell you that Mrs. Milner Gibson lost her *only* child about two months ago, a little girl of eight years old ? After so long she was not likely to have more children—and with her immense fortune I thought she must feel herself the most desolate woman on earth.   I felt a more real compassion for her than I ever felt for an unknown person before.   Well— see how one wastes one's " *fine feelings* " *!*   Elizabeth went to a

brilliant soirée at Lady Morgan's the other evening, and there
sat Mrs. M. Gibson, and Elizabeth " really saw no change in
her ! " How *do* people get such griefs tumbled out of their
minds in that way ? Why ! a cat will turn sick and go about
pining for as long after its kittens have been drowned ! Another
fact of an opposite sort I must tell you, for the rehabilitation
of poor human nature. I mentioned to you the death of the
old dairy-woman and that her young husband was sore afflicted
by it ? I saw him yesterday leaning against the lamp-post
at his door—and if it had not been at *his* door I should not have
recognised him—from a stout, middle-aged man, he was
become pale and emaciated, and as old-looking as the old wife—
a very picture of woe—and the wife was turned of seventy—
perhaps Pepoli loves Elizabeth after all !—but no—it is not *in*
Pepoli to love anyone as that Milkman-Mahomet must have
loved his Kadijah.

. . . Now I must go and tramp thro' the ocean of mud—
and with such a side ! I do trust it will be some better " *in a
month* " for at present it is worse than ever.

Helen's letter has come since I began writing, give her my
thanks and three kisses for it—a kiss for every sheet—Oh dear,
how I wish we were all together.

Bless you, my Babbie, love to all the rest.

                                        Your own cousin,
                                           J. W. C.

25. *To Jeannie Welsh*

Experiments in paper—Gambardella to Liverpool—Uncle's portrait
essential—Orthodox piety—Dining out.

Anne Welsh is one of Mrs. Carlyle's three aunts, her father's
younger sisters, who lived in Edinburgh. They constantly
tried to " convert " her to their beliefs, the old Presbyterian
orthodoxies which Carlyle and his wife had long outgrown.

The question of writing paper was one that frequently
troubled Mrs. Carlyle. Her letters are often hastily scribbled
down on half sheets of note-paper, economically saved, no
doubt, from other people's letters, or, as is here recorded, on

little, ruled pages torn out of one of the tradesmen's account books.

MY DARLING, *Monday night (21st Nov., 1842).*

To account for certain phenomena in the paper department that must have filled you with astonishment, I may as well mention while it is in my head, that we are making a course of paper-experiments at present, buying it in very small quantities from this and the other stationer, to see if by God's grace we cannot discover one man who sells " genuine unadulterated " paper of rags—not " an abominable compound of plaster-of-Paris " !—oh, that accursed Reform Bill !—Meanwhile every now and then I find myself without even plaster-of-Paris note-paper to wear the points of my pens upon and am reduced to tearing sheets out of—the Butcher's book !

I should have had a hot pressed gilt edged sheet for the present writing—to communicate such news as will cause you to dance for joy. Only think Babbie—by the time this reaches you Gambardella will be in the same town with you—ready to paint my uncle at a moment's warning ! Now does there not seem to be the finger of Providence in this sudden resolution of his to start for Liverpool ?—just when I was pondering how I could put the thing into his head—so as to *persuade him to go voluntarily*—as John does with Mr. Ogilvie. I send the note that has just reached me from him—whereby you will perceive once for all that he can not only write, but *spell*—better or worse —well enough for all practical purposes. I need not bid you give the poor fellow a warm welcome ; you will remember our sails, etc., and do *that* of your own accord—nor do I feel his going to see you will embarrass you *anyhow*—for I am sure my uncle will be greatly amused with him, and see the good that shines thro' his manifold folly. Now Babbie if you do not make something out of this best of all possible opportunities for getting my uncle painted, I shall make it a reproach to you as long as I live. A man should not let his modesty (however praiseworthy *modesty* may be in the *abstract*) thwart the wishes of a whole virtuous family, and me at the head of them !—

F

urge this on him my uncle—emphatically—there is no surer way of succeeding with him than appealing to his sense of justice.

I shall give G. an introduction to Geraldine and Mrs. Paulet —I know no one else in Liverpool that is not more your acquaintance than mine—the Sketchleys ?—shall I introduce him to Miss Pen ? Better not !—he would kick too recklessly thro' their cobwebs. Perhaps you will introduce him to Walter as an admirer of his Aspiration *in shift* and to Mr. Hick as a fellow Artist ! * By the way do send me the said Mr. Hick. The man who drew that sketch can be " no fool "—and besides as he is shortly to be connected with the family, I may as well commence my relations with him betimes.

. . . Give my most affectionate regards to Mrs. Martin and Sophy—poor little Sophy ! she used to make *her* caps I remember ; and she always spoke of Mrs. Martin with such kindness ! Do not let them forget *me*—I would not be forgotten by anyone she loved.

I had a letter from Anne Welsh to-day—enclosing a block-head of a tract entitled " *Knowledge of Sin* " and a printed hymn about " *the fullness of Jesus* "—these things do not make me angry—only horribly sad—to feel oneself and those one is bound to by natural affection separated so widely, widely even in the same world of the living—is scarcely less melancholy than being parted from them by death. A letter from Mrs. George Welsh, which crossed one from me about her son on the road, is much more comfortable. She seems a good sensible woman that—a remarkable instance of *nothing* made into *something*, and a very self-subsistent, creditable *something* by the *educating* process of misfortune. . . .

I have only been once out for a week—to call for Mrs. Allan Cunningham—the weather has been heartily bad and myself *ditto*. The Booths came this forenoon—and engaged C. to dine on Sunday. I refused—make a point of *always* refusing Dinings out are desperately fatiguing ; and as an Annandale farmer said of Carlyle's *Sartor*, " what's 't ouse on 't ? " I am better at home writing to my Babbie or even looking into th

* See page 43.

fire tho' ever so drearily !—right, even-down, unconstrained sadness is better than *company-gaiety* got up at a frightful expenditure of the little nervous energy one has remaining.

Ever your affectionate

J. C.

26. *To Jeannie Welsh*

Miss Jewsbury and Gambardella—Passion—Asserted likeness of Babbie to Mrs. C.—Picture of Uncle John—Furniture for the house—Sketch of C. smoking—Potatoes.

(8th Dec., 1842.)

DEAREST BABBIE,

. . . I had a long letter from Geraldine the other night—in which she treats the question of Gambardella as if I had sent him to her on purpose that she should fall in love with him, and either marry him, or make with him what she calls " a *modified arrangement*." " If she lived long beside him she could grow to *love him very sisterly* but *not otherwise*," " he is too *overproof*—wants *body*—is in fact *too good* and that sort of people she cannot love with passion." What is all this ? who wanted her to love him " *with passion* " ? Not I, sure enough. The less *passion* in the world the more *virtue* and *good-digestion !* I would have nobody *cultivate* passion " for its own reward " for *that* is even a degree more unsatisfactory than virtues. It is bad enough to love *with passion* when one cannot help oneself—but to set about it, malice prepense, as a piece of the natural business of life, whenever a man presents himself—and without the slightest inspection of the proba- bilities of being bored in return—that does seem to me an exuberance of " *the social feeling* " which ought to be kept down by *cold pudding* or anything however disagreeable that is found to answer the purpose—all this *entre nous*. Geraldine is a fine spirit in spite of all her vagaries—and she is mighty fond of you now as well as of me. " *Jeannie*," she says, " is really a charming creature and has taken root here very nicely "—and " the other sister " comes in for a share of her praise—by the way will you tell *the other sister* to write to me ; I want to hear from her own self *her* impressions of this " *Feast of pikes*."

—Except for the continual recurrence of the monosyllable
" *we* " ! in your letters I am very much left in the dark respecting " the graceful Miss Welsh " as Gambardella called her
in his letter to me.   Geraldine says of you further (and I doubt
not but that was meant for the crowning praise) that " you
have got *a trick* of *my* countenance, and even some of my
attitudes."   Now as to " the trick of my countenance " keep it
and welcome !—for I have always been given to understand
that my *countenance* was " remarkably expressive "—and so I
suppose that if you imitate it in its imitable points—not indis-
criminately, like Kate Gilchrist—turning up the whites of
your eyes *par exemple* in the monstrous idea that " it looked so
pooty ! " there will be no harm done to your own little cherub-
face from this remodelling in the likeness of mine—but for
my *attitudes !*—humph !—you had better hold by *your own*,
Babbie, at least until a less prejudiced judge than Geraldine has
told us that any attitude or attitudes of mine would not mar
your natural grace.   When I was so young that people could
take liberties, that is to say, would speak the truth to me—I was
told often enough that I walked " as if I were in tight breeches."
My first dancing master used to lift me up by the two hands
exclaiming in desperate accents " heavy ! heavy ! " My
last dancing master, a highly figurative as well as exaggerative
sort of man, used to ask me " if I fancied I had Arthur's Seat
on my back ? " Our miller's wife, a prophetic woman in
her way, declared " one had but to look at me to see that I was
a stickit callant "—in short, never never since I came into this
world has it entered into the head of any mortal I believe before
Geraldine that " my *attitudes* " could be worth picking up—
but such are the illusions that come of loving " *with passion.*"

  I am so glad about the picture ! actually I shall have it
then in my menagerie ! and yet last night I cried myself sick
about that very picture—every thing like happiness is so
spoiled for me now—it came into my head how often *she* had
wished to have one—how delighted she would have been with
this—what a joyful new year gift it would have been for her—and
the thought there is *only me* to give it to now—only me to rejoice
over it, went to my heart like a knife—and I could not help

bursting out acrying even with Carlyle sitting there—but when I told him what had been all day in my head he said it was " quite natural " and did not *lecture* me as he sometimes does which shuts up all my sorrow in my own heart for weeks after.

He works very hard—all the forenoons till three or four o'clock—and often in the evenings also. He has got an immense bookcase erected in the upstairs room. Elizabeth's carpenter took the vile old black press at the surprising allowance of £4 (the original cost was only £4 10s.) and for three pounds more has made him a really handsome mahogany bookcase covering the whole end of the room. I wish he would order a little sofa for *me* when he is about it—for I do not see how I am to exist up there thro' the winter if I am always to be *upright*—however I have spoken twice for it without result, and will not, as Helen's phrase is, " so far demean myself " by speaking again. I told you the lamp was discontinued ? well I washed it with my own hands, which were none the better for the potash—and in washing it had occasion to take it in bits—and could not put it together again—well every day now I am asked when is that lamp to be ready for action—because the candles it seems " smell as bad as the oil." I can readily believe it.

You are quite welcome to keep the little smoking Carlyle till all have seen it—I must not forget to tell you that there is no cause for a single regret about the potatoes—we boil them now with the skins on and find them *all* eatable and *some* of them excellent—I think they need very long and slow boiling—our nan's are *prettier* to look at but have not such a " genuine real unadulterated " potato-taste—Having more than I saw the prospect of eating I sent one of the barrels to Elizabeth—she sent back word that she must return it " being amply supplied from the same quarter "—the deuce you are thought I !—but it turned out she fancied mine a present from Kirkaldy—as they had spoken to her of sending me some—" it had better not be sent back however " said Carlyle " desire her to send it on to Craik poor fellow—who never gets good potatoes ! ! "—My potatoes, my own uncle's potatoes to—Craik ! ! I answered

not a word but my whole face burned with righteous indignation
—I must stop.

Your own
JEANNIE BIG.

[N.B. Babbie is Jeannie little.]

27. *To Jeannie Welsh*

Xmas gifts and memories—The cushions' magic for sleep—Little
Miss Hunter—Gambardella—Geraldine's MS.—Darwin's gift of
a shawl.

(*25th Dec.*, 1842.)

MY DEAR KIND BABBIE,

I fancy you almost understand by instinct, without
being told, how it was with me yesterday; that I did not
notify the safe arrival of those affectionate presents by return
of post. I had made up the little packet for Maggie the night
before—while Carlyle was dining at the Helps's—and the little
packet for my uncle immediately after breakfast—and I had
written to poor Harriet * of whom I have been rather neglectful
lately—all before the Postman came—for he was later than
usual—did not come till half after twelve—no wonder; if
many people had taken the same advantage of the post that
you had done! And then, when I saw those parcels—so like
what used to be and yet not what used to be—and read your
letter so kind, and yet not from her—I could not help a long fit
of crying—which *you* will not think an ungrateful return for
your wish to make me feel myself still loved and cared for—it is
only a very narrow hearted person that could fancy grief for
what one has *lost* incompatible with gladness over what one has.
Before I had recovered myself, Carlyle came in upon me,
and urged as usual that I should " get out into the open air "—
oh that weary " open air " which is to do all for me and does
so little!—Mazzini met me at the door, and came back with
me; and so the post-hour had come before I was let alone.

The cushions are perfect beauties, and both have been
already slept upon! indeed I began to think that Geraldine
had taught you some of her magic †—which had enabled you to
make of Carlyle's one a sleeping talisman!—After dinner
he fell to examining it anew, and asking anew if I could not

---

* Martineau.   † Of going to sleep anywhere.

" *open it up* so as to let his head in " for " it would really make
a very comfortable cap "—on my advising him to apply it
rather to its proper use ; he said " well ! how does one do with
it ? So ? "—placing it at the back of his head against the
green chair—and in one moment he was fast asleep ! and slept
without moving a muscle for two hours !—I was almost
relieved when Helen's entrance with the tea-tray broke his
supernatural looking repose. I myself had in the meanwhile
been sleeping by snatches on mine—but never profoundly
enough to get rid of the apprehension that my hair might be
dirtying it ! Carlyle seemed really pleased with his present
and letter—repeated several times over with an air of com-
placency " poor little Jeannie ! " and I daresay at that moment
you wore the shawl-dressing gown to his Imagination ! *
The beautiful little bag and handkerchief might have been an
offering to Titania the Fairy Queen ! I never saw anything
more dainty ! Kiss Helen for them, with a heartiness ! You
are very good to me my dear *little* cousins—and that is all I
can say ; for I have not little Miss Adam Hunter's knack at
making speeches. Oh that preposterous child ! I cannot
get her out of my head—" Mrs. Carlyle, I am enjoying myself so
much ! and feel so much obliged by your goodness in inviting
me ! " " Oh Mr. Carlyle you do speak so like my papa, it is
quite a pleasure to listen to you ! " Once he was cross-
questioning her about something she called " her *Mangnall's
questions* " and turning to me with a look knowing enough for
fifty she said " *Ah !* I perceive Mr. Carlyle is a dreadful
quiz !—now aren't you sir a great quiz ? " And remember this
creature is not struck *ten* yet !

Certainly, Jeannie, Gambardella is getting mad with
success, like his favourite Masanello and like him will need to
be shot before long !—just see such a note as I have had from
him ! along with a book of the most distracted poems that
even this age has yet produced—and this note † you are to

---

* See Letter 4.
† Asking Mrs. Carlyle to write a short review of it in the *Athenæum*, or
get " Someone who to oblige a friend of yours (me) will notice it. I know
that you are equal to Geraldine if not greater in the *questionable* power of
making your friends do whatever you fancy."

bear in mind must have been sent *open* to the author of the poems—for it came to me open inside the book which was addressed in another hand—" I must *wait patiently !* " and all in the imperative mood ! patiently ! Yes I shall wait with a patience never surpassed !—except so far as my uncle's picture depends on his coming. He is a good fellow in the main—but he ought to learn the difference between a man and a woman— I mean in addressing them.

I have read the Seaforth novel and, as was to have been anticipated, with a feeling little short of *terror !* So much power of genius rushing so recklessly into unknown space ! Geraldine, in particular, shows herself here a far more profound and daring speculator than even I had fancied her. I do not believe there is a woman alive at the present day, not even George Sand herself, that could have written some of the best passages in this book—or would have had the courage if she had had the ability to write them—but they must not publish it, " decency forbids " ! (as they write at the street corners). I do not mean decency in the vulgar sense of the word—even in *that* sense they are not always *decent !* but then their *indecency* looks so purely *scientific* and so *essential* for the full development of the story that one cannot, at least I cannot get up a feeling of outraged modesty about it—nay I should feel as if *I* were the indecent person should I find anything to blush at in what *they* seem to have written just *for fact's sake* without a consciousness of wrong—but there is an indecency or want of reserve (let us call it) in the spiritual department—an exposure of their whole minds naked as before the fall—without so much as a fig-leaf of conformity remaining—which no respectable public could stand—which even the freest spirits among us would call " coming it too strong " ! I wish a clear day would dawn for me that I might give them a full and faithful deliverance upon it—for it is a difficult task they have put on me to criticise such an extraordinary jumble of sense and nonsense, insight beyond the stars, and blindness before their own nose ! One thing I feel no doubt about that this Geraldine will either " make a spoon or spoil a horn "—she is far too clever to do nothing in her day and generation.

Darwin heard Mazzini telling me the other day I should
" really wear a shawl in the house "—a *fixed* idea he has got!
Darwin seemed quite indifferent whether I wore a shawl or
even a shift, but the next time he came he brought me an
immense gauze-looking shawl of white lambswool!—So like
him, was it not?

28.   *To Jeannie Welsh*

Xmas gifts—John Carlyle sends a parcel without paying carriage—
   Tennyson comes to dinner—John admires Helen Welsh more than
   Babbie—His prescriptions.

(*28th Dec.*, 1842.)

DEAREST,

If all went the right road you would receive a parcel
this morning which you would not be able to make either head
or tail of. Not a line of explanation along with it!—and
carriage to pay for other people's things!—but surely your
imagination would exculpate *me* from being at the bottom of
such a piece of blockheadism—altho' my handwriting *was*
mixed up with it! When John dined here on Sunday he
declared his intention of sending you a copy of Schiller—and
politely suggested that if I had " any little thing to go it might be
sent along with the books." I thought it would be a good
opportunity of returning the Seaforth manuscript—and added
the packet for Sophy—taking it for granted that he would
pay the carriage, otherwise his *offer* was a sheer *bêtise*. Last
night he was here again to dine with—Alfred Tennyson
(Ah Babby what you have lost) and having a scientific curiosity
to get to the bottom of that matter of rail-way carriage—also to
form some notion of what I was *indebted* to him I asked:
" What did you pay for that parcel? "   " *Pay* for it! how do
you mean? "—" The carriage to Liverpool? What was it? "
" I never dreamt of paying the carriage! What puts it into
your head I should have paid the carriage? "   " Why nothing
—only that it would never have entered into *my* head *not* to
pay it. Then did you tell Jeannie how I came to send her
my parcel? "   " No—I had not *a moment's leisure* to-day to
write any *note* along with it! "   In fact that man does things

like nobody else, even his kind actions are stript of all gracious-
ness by the stolid way he sets about them.   As to the books do
not *flatter yourself* they are a love-token—he does not *love* you
the least bit—loves no woman—never did, and never will—
not tho' Trojan Helen should return from the shades to tempt
him—" Accursed vegetable that he is ! " as old Sterling said
of him one day—" not a man at all but a walking Cabbage ! ! "
Indeed if he were going to dream of setting about trying to
persuade himself to consider whether by possibility he could
bring himself to get up a feeling of love for one of the family—
I rather think it would be for " Miss Welsh "—not you.
Whenever I speak in your praise he interrupts me always
with—" but Miss Welsh don't you think Miss Welsh is an
interesting sort of person ? "   " Not a doubt of it, Sir ! " . . .

> Your own
>
> J. C.

29. *To Jeannie Welsh*

New Year reflections—John Carlyle's books are only a loan—The
Butcher's book provides writing paper—Happiness and life
—Active benevolence : its pleasures and disappointments—The
begging woman and her son—Gambardella's picture of Jeannie
—Little Miss Hunter—Her innate gaiety precludes dullness
—Seven barrels of potatoes—The lamp—Cromwellian oppression
—Result of being an only child—Stupidity a sign of affection
—Cavaignac—A visit to Seaforth—Geraldine's effusiveness—
Writing paper.

He " is but a man after all "—" The Corporate Weavers at
Dumfries elected a deacon, or chief of weavers, who was
excessively flattered by the honour.   In the course of the
installation dinner, at some high point of the hep-hep-hurrahing,
he exclaimed, with sweet pain, ' Oh, gentlemen, remember I
am but a man ! ' "   (T. C. in L. M. i. 116.)

Sunday night (1st Jan., 1843).

MY DEAREST BABBIE,
        Here we are then in the beginning of a new year !
May we do as much of good in it and as little of harm as
possible ! for this much we may pray with an assured conscience
—for all the rest, it is in God's hands, where we had best leave
it ! We know not what more to ask—what it were good for

us to have for the asking, whether to live or to die—to be well
or to be sick—to be at ease in Zion, or to be troubled about
many things. All these are transitory conditions, and their
joy or their sorrow is transitory—but no joy, no sorrow, no
anything I suppose is given to us in vain—and the *ultimate
issues* lie far beyond our poor human vision stretching away away
into eternity. So for my part I ask of heaven only what I have
said—that I may live my life wisely thro' this new year—not
foolishly—not wickedly, and I advise you, Babbie of my
affections, to ask neither more nor less than this same.

John dined here to-day—as usual—and now Carlyle is
convoying him home—and I am here alone, and shall sleep the
better for having written you, if not a letter, at least the beginning
of a letter.

First as to the *books*, for *business* should always take prece-
dence of other topics. The books, my dear, are after all a
loan ! ! " Why do you ask ? What could make you suppose
I should have meant them as anything else ? " Aye, what
indeed ? The fatal romance of my character could alone have
made me suppose such a thing ! And yet there are traditions
in the world of men who have laid crowns and kingdoms at
the feet of a beautiful woman, never to . . .

Friday (6th *Jan.*, 1843).

There *is* some paper in the house to-day, but I absolutely
dare not go in for it, so let us be thankful for the unfailing tho'
rather prosaical resource of the Butcher's book ! * My
Darling Babbie, the " moral satisfaction " I have in you is
great ! almost my only " *unmitigated* satisfaction " (as Sir R. Peel
would say) in the present existing state of my affairs ! " *The
trail of the serpent* " is over all else that pretends to give me
comfort or pleasure ! My Aunt Anne writes to me—as if it
were great *news*—that " happiness is not to be found in this
world ! it was not God's purpose with us in sending us into it ! "
Good gracious ! Have not I known that much for upwards
of a quarter of a century and put it into a formula too for my

* This letter is written on seven half-sheets.

own behoof, before *she*—wise woman, as she now thinks herself—had discovered that " God's purpose in sending us into
it " was *not* to run after " the *fashion*," a seeking of happiness
in the very lowest walk where it could be imagined findable.
It is not *happiness* which I ask of Heaven, however much I
might *like* to have it (in conjunction, I believe, with all my
fellow-mortals, even the most philosophical, if they would
but speak without cant), *that* I agree to the impossibleness of,
and should be a fool if I did not leave it out of my prayers—but
what I *do* ask of Heaven, and with ever-increasing earnestness,
and ever-increasing protest against the " lions in the way,"
is *calm*—let me be sad as death if God wills it so—but let me
be left in peace with my sadness ! *that*, it seems to me, one
has a right to demand of one's fellow-creatures, especially
of those who profess to have our well-being at heart, and
the unnecessary griefs which *they* cause us look to me not so
much of God's sending as of the Devil's ! Oh, but I am
wrong in taking this view of the matter ! these everyday
highly superfluous worries and tribulations are a part of
our allotted trials, as well as the inevitable irremediable
bereavements and afflictions—granted they *are* a part—but a
part to be struggled against—protested against—only *submitted* to because one cannot help oneself. Why otherwise
should God have planted in our hearts a sense of *justice* and of
self-preservation ? Meanwhile I have swallowed a seidlitz
powder which as yet has had no beneficial results. A vision
of a tea-cupful of soup crossed my mind—but Helen was
ironing and I would not trouble her to make it for me. Helen,
however, seeing me look ill, of her own accord *broiled* and
brought up (with a little air of self-complacency which it would
have been a thousand pities to dash) a morsel of mutton !
as opposite a thing to the tendencies of my " interior " at the
moment, as could have been hit upon by the wit of cook !
However, like a simpleton I ate it to please her and now I am
wishing " the devil had flown away with it." I am not *well*,
certainly, but so long as I *keep on my legs*, and have nothing
that needs to be *taken care of*, I should be thankful. I have
no cough, only a perpetual dull headache of now a fortnight's

standing, very bad in the mornings and evenings and less so during the middle of the day.   It seems to make no difference in it what I do or abstain from doing—it would be worse for me if it hindered me from writing.   Fontenelle, I think it was, who observed in speaking of Hell that " he *flattered himself* one would get used to it "—it rather makes against this theory of the force of custom, that I still make such an outcry about headache, for certainly I have had opportunity enough to " get used to it."   For the rest the weather has been more adapted for Ducks or the Witches of Macbeth than for a delicate female like me.   I went out a little yesterday, however, between two showers and made excellent use of my time.   I was not absent an hour and half in all and in that brief space I executed a scold on Mr. Boulter—shopped to the amount of sixpence— made three new acquaintances and did three good actions ! I should have returned then with a comfortable sensation of *virtue* you will say.   Alas, no, I returned cold and wearied, and forlorn—on the whole the pleasures of *benevolence*, between ourselves, are not a whit less visionary than other sublunary pleasures—at least I find them so.   There *is* a moment of moral satisfaction in putting a starved old woman into a warm flannel petticoat, but one reflects the next instant—" of course she will pawn it "—and so on of everything else of the sort one attempts in the way of charity.   That you may not be forming too magnificent an idea of my " good actions " of yesterday I must tell you that they *cost* me *in all* only half a crown, and wet feet.

Some nights ago Carlyle, in one of his dark walks along the King's Road, observed a " remarkably decent, even *dignified*- looking woman " sitting on some steps with a baby in her arms —" if he saw her again he would give her a penny "—he did see her again the following night and gave her not only a penny, but three halfpence.   The next night also she was " still there with the same *sad calm* look."   He addressed her and found her pretty deaf—she professed to be a soldier's widow—that night he " had not a penny " so he told her to come down to me and I would give her some old clothes.   I am sure he thinks I can invent old clothes—for it was only a

few days before I had given all the duds I had to the widow of
that pale-faced street-sweeper in the King's Road—now
relieved from street-sweeping for ever more. The woman
arrived the next morning at ten o'clock, strongly perfumed with
gin !—a decent-looking woman, nevertheless—and if a poor
wretch have no fire, no warm breakfast, and for three farthings
can get gin enough to both warm and strengthen her, who shall
say that her taking it is a fatal sign of her—not I !—So in spite
of the *questionable* smell, I entered on a searching examination
of her claims to my assistance. She told me she was the
daughter of a hotel-keeper in Dublin, had eloped from a
boarding-school with her soldier-husband at fourteen—had
never since been taken the smallest notice of by her relatives
—her Parents had died—her husband had died, and here she
was a beggar—with three children—a boy of twelve who had
been taken into the Chelsea *Institution* for soldiers' orphans—a
girl of six and the baby at her breast. She " never went to
see her son—for fear of disgracing him among his companions
—he did not know what was become of her—but she lived here
for the sake of knowing herself near him." All very touching
if true. " She could *sew* perfectly well, could do any work she
was put to—but none was to be had." I *did invent* some
clothes for her—among the rest a most *massive* petticoat out of
the old floor-cloth ! !—gave her a shilling and promised to
inquire about her at the address she gave me. And accordingly, yesterday I set forth on that errand, when it occurred
to me that the truth of her story was to be got better from her
son (if she had one) at the Institution than at her lodgings where
they tell lies for one another. I addressed myself to the book-
keeper who discovered in his ledger the name—John Wood—
and took the trouble to bring the boy for me into his private
room—a dear little fellow, full of spirit and intelligence, but
the terrified expression of whose face at being brought in to
me gave one a mournful idea of his young experience of his
fellow-creatures. He looked as if he thought I *must* be come
to tell him his mother was hanged. His answers to all my
inquiries were clear as spring-water—he had seen his mother
three weeks ago ! she lived in Union Street ! his father died

six years ago ! there was no baby ! (a borrowed baby !) his
Mother's Mother was alive ! he had an uncle in Smithfield !—
in short on a basis of truth I had been amused with a whole
super-structure of lies—and the woman was just an inveterate
never-do-well. I patted his head, gave him a shilling for his
fright—and inwardly resolved to take some further charge of
the son since nothing could be done for the mother—and there,
you see, how imprudent it is to enter on a long story !—with
limited time and limited paper—such histories are only for
being *chattered* by the fireside. So I spare you my other
good actions hoping that I may do some more another day.
No—the *last* is soon told and you may like to hear it—it was
calling on little Miss Adam Hunter at her boarding-school
which, after having been vainly inquired about, at Knightsbridge
and Kensington, turns out to be five minutes' walk from my
own door ! exactly over against Newman, the dyer's ! That
little Miss Adam is a cousin nobody need be ashamed of—a
remarkably pretty, graceful, intelligent child with a strange
dash of *the old Adam* in it—a sort of old-fashionedness—not
displeasing in a child, however, but on the contrary rather
" *insinuating*." When she came into the room to me, instead of
leaving *me* to *do* the cousinly to her, she tripped up holding
out both hands and exclaiming with a tone half of " *reception* "
half of childish gladness—" Oh, thank you, thank you,
Mrs. Carlyle, for coming to see me ! " The Mistress came by
and by and rather checked her *expansiveness*—we were getting
on finely ! I must write to the Father to send his orders to
the Mistress that she is to be allowed to visit me when I ask
her—the cross-looking spinster seemed quite disinclined to
much intimacy—the old fool ! as if the child would not learn
far more from me than from her ! But perhaps that was the
very reason.

I hope *the picture* will be speedily set agoing before
Gambardella gets his head turned and raises his prices to a
hundred guineas ! Give him my kind remembrances when he
comes again and tell him to remember that he is but a *man*
after all !—I am glad the family of Welsh is likely to atone to
him for the ingratitude of the family of Carlyle. As for my

uncle and Johnnie, I am sure they will be charmed with him, the sober Mr. Alick I am not so sure about. I am obliged to him for his sympathy over my *dullness*—tho' superfluous—if six years of Craigenputtock could not *break me into* a dull life I must have a fund of *gaiety* in my character little short of super-human ; so that in either case, dull or not dull, I am not to be pitied on that score. The *dullness* truly is the least of it !

No fear of our leaving the potatoes on the quay—but *seven* barrels ! it is difficult for me to imagine barrels so diminutive that seven of them should not be something alarming. In looking at the paper there came over my mind the long-forgotten dread-inspiring yet delectable reminiscence of *Morgina* (was that her name ?) and *the Forty Thieves !* Your consideration about the manner of delivering oneself from the empty barrels was worthy of you ! By the by, I have to thank you also for a very nice japanned kitchen lamp and a tidy little tin saucepan ! If you disclaim having made me any such present, I bid you not be too sure—I had them in exchange for the snuffers ! Oh, *the* lamp !—it is still in action—has never failed to do *its* part for a single minute !—but it is ordered to be " flung out of his way " so soon as the present stock of oil is burnt out—" it makes an atmosphere that no mortal can breathe in "—as I am a living woman I have never been able to detect the impurity !—but no matter about that, it must go. Much else will have to go before Cromwell is finished—perhaps the animate as well as the inanimate.

Dearest Babbie ! I sometimes wish I had you here just to assure me by your contented looks that everything in and about this establishment is not actually but only *Cromwellianly* fallen into a state of *detestableness* disgraceful to hear tell of— and then again I thank Heaven that you are not here—" Night must it be ere Friedland's star can burn "—and so is it for me tho' no Friedland !—*support*, tho' most soothing at the moment, only weakens me in the long run when I have much to bear. When I feel myself quite, quite *alone* and with only *myself* to rely upon—then I am true to myself !—at least have been hitherto — but the petting and consideration I have of late been used to once more, has revived the *leaning* tendency of earlier days—and I feel dreary and helpless as in the *first unlearning* to be a much-made of Only Child.   In a few weeks it is to be hoped " the winter of our discontent " being fairly set in, I shall have wrapped myself in my fur-mantle of imperturbability, and be living on my own individual resources—such as they are !—Happily one does not live for ever—nor even very long !

Saturday (7th Jan., 1843).

I am afraid, my Babbie, that your contentment with this long letter will be greater *before* you have read it than *after*. So many closely written pages containing what ? fretful egoism and the story of a beggar-woman !   Ach, *du lieber Gott !*   But perhaps you may think with Cavaignac that being stupid with you is a sign of particular affection.   One evening that I was talking to him rather " *wittily* " (as I thought) he said to me *brusquely*—" Spare me your *cleverness, Madame*.   Je ne le veux pas—*moi !* it is not *my pleasure* to rank among those for whom you have to *make minced meat* of yourself ! ! "   regal words, truly !   as all his words were !—if that man be not an absolute monarch yet before he die, Nature will have missed her intention with him !

I left my letter unsealed last night to see what reportable thing to-day's post might bring forth—that I should hear again from yourself I was not presuming to hope—thank you all the more !   Foolish " Gam " !   why don't he come and dine at once and put you all *out of pain*—Dear !   I would be the last person in the world to dissuade you from any good work, but could not you delay your visit to Everton till *the picture* is fairly achieved, and till you have had the visit of Geraldine and Mrs. P. [Paulet] ?   I know they will *do* the impossible to get you off to Seaforth, and I do think you would find Seaforth " very exciting," especially with Geraldine there to *weep on your hands* and show you how *a woman of genius* demeans herself !—having some notion of setting up for the part yourself, you cannot begin to study it too soon !—Helen, too, I want to go.

G

Carlyle finds your paper plaster of Paris also !—he is meaning to order a quantity " such as it is " from the shop in the Strand. . . .

Your own heart's-sister,

J. C.

30. *To Jeannie Welsh*

A rushing-about day—Geraldine's MS. not for Maryland Street— Fragment : on reasons for marrying Carlyle—Walter Welsh and Carlyle's form of praise—Visit from Mrs. Sigourney and her friends—Old Sterling and John S.'s illness—Carlyle is writing not Cromwell, but Abbot Samson.

The first sheet of the following was by way of postscript to what had been written the night before.   In the original letter Mrs. Carlyle, it seems, casting back her memory eighteen years, had described the feelings that led to her engagement to Carlyle, apropos, it may be, of Babbie's engagement to Andrew Chrystal. Of this only a fragment remains.   Did she counsel Babbie not to marry without the touch of romantic passion to which she denies any part in her own decision, or was she to be satisfied at the outset with what had been decisive for herself—the plain impossibility of living without the man who had come to fill so large a part in her own existence ?   Did she confide to Babbie what seems clear from her early correspondence, that as time went by, her feelings did grow warmer ?

For " decency," see p. 66.

Monday (9th Jan., 1843).

DEAREST,

I have opened my letter to announce the arrival of yours—for mine was written last night while *they* were drinking their brandy-punch up stairs and *sealed* last night that Helen might not edify herself with the contents in the morning— according to her usual fashion—I have no time however to write a new letter. This has been one of my rushing about days, *cleaning* the lamp, etc., etc. (for we are returned to the poor lamp at *his* particular desire), and now—" Babbie I want you to do my hair " ! these words will give you the liveliest image of my state ! But instead of that soothing operation I must off to

Sloane Street to buy new stuff for blinds—for *his* room is to undergo a thorough cleaning to-morrow—" The troubles that afflict the just in number many be." . . . Geraldine was right not to let her MS. be read at Maryland Street—the religious ideas set forth in it would have seemed very shocking to those who had never heard anything said about religion except in the orthodox tone—This *entre nous*.

(*Fragment, on a torn sheet.*)

just because, in virtue of his being *the least unlikable* man in the place, I let him dance attendance on my young person, till I came to *need* him—all the same as my slippers to go to a ball in, or my bonnet to go out to walk. When I finally agreed to marry him, I cried excessively and felt excessively shocked—but if I had then said *no* he would have left me—and how could I dispense with what was equivalent to my slippers or bonnet? Oh, if I might write my own biography from beginning to end—without reservation or false colouring—it would be an invaluable document for my countrywomen in more than one particular, but " *decency forbids !* "

. . . . .

Walter was here the night before last—talked of being off this morning—Do you know I find him far more intelligent and agreeable away from all you young ones—He staid that night till near *twelve*, and I was not sleepy ! *You* may infer from that how miraculously well he must have managed ! And Carlyle too thinks him, " *not* at all a bad fellow ! *Not* at all without sense "—which means in his dialect—what Pepoli in *his* would call " *un angelo di bonta*—and PIENO PIENO d'ingegno."

I send Helen an autograph of the American Poetess Mrs. Sigourney—which does infinite credit to her total want of penetration !—the evening of which she makes such grateful mention—would have been remembered by anyone else with feelings of quite another sort—even *I* who do not give much way to remorse, have often had qualms of conscience in thinking about it. Her coming and still more her bringing along with her two geerpoles of the name of " Johnson or Tomson," a male and a female (as little Miss Adam would say—did I tell you of her asking me in the presence of Mazzini whether *Gorgon* whom she styled " *one of the graces*," for my better understanding, " was a male or a female ? ") her coming with this tag-ragery quite spoiled a pleasant party that happened to be here—the Wedgwoods, Darwin, Mrs. Rich * and Julia Smith— We had all set in to be talkative and confidential—when this figure of an over-the-water-Poetess—beplastered with rouge and pomatum—bare-necked at an age which had left *certainty* far behind—with long ringlets that never grew where they hung—smelling marvellously of camphor or hartshorn and oil —all glistening in black satin as if she were an apothecary's *puff* for black *sticking-plaster*—and staring her eyes out, to give them animation—stalked in and by the very barber-block-ish look of her reduced us all to silence—which effect was heightened by the pair who followed at her heels—the *male* in an embroidered satin vest—the *female* also in satin with—fancy it in *that* room—and in *that* company !—with *a gold tiara on her head !* These two never spoke a word but sat with their eyes fixed on Carlyle as if they had paid their shillings at the door—Mrs. Sigourney also made large eyes at him—and *she* took the liberty of poking at him now and then to make the lion roar, but he was not in the vein—and would not roar finely that night for all she could do. The rest of us meanwhile, feeling ourselves aggrieved at being regarded with no more curiosity or politeness than as many domestic cats in comparison of the Lion, repayed them in their own coin—*I never addressed one word to them !* this is a literal fact—of " her who helped to make that evening so pleasant to remembrance." Faith it is not true that " we reap not where we have not sown "—my harvests are far oftenest of that highly improbable sort.

I will send old Sterling's last note as another instance of this infraction of the laws *of nature* in my favour. John had again broken a blood-vessel—in lifting tables to save the servants trouble ! madman that he is !—it was a hanging in the wind with him for two days—and the communication of his state had to be made to his father thro' us—for fear of doing mischief to his mother who you know has a disease of the heart

* Daughter of Sir James Mackintosh.

hat requires the utmost quiet. When the old fool came down here, after receiving Carlyle's note, I was prepared to be very sorry for him—but at the very outset he set all my sympathies against him by his theatrical fuss clapping his hand on his *stomach* and declaring " no ! this *heart* must not break *yet !* I cannot afford to sink under my griefs !—I have five *orphans* depending on me." So little of humanity did I show him—that I answered merely " bless me !—you had better see the end of it—they are not *orphans* yet ! " And when he sent his servant for news the next morning I wrote—" Since the accounts are favourable you had better give up your distracted project of setting out to Falmouth. Do keep yourself *quiet if you can*—it were the greatest kindness you can show to those you are interested in "—or *this* he writes to me all these little ecstatic pages !

Dear I will tell you a secret but see that you keep it to yourself—Carlyle is no more writing about *Oliver Cromwell* than you and I are ! I have known this for a good while—you will wonder that I should not have known it all along—the fact is his papers were a good time more resembling hieroglyphics than finished manuscript. I could not be at the trouble of making them out—then when I came to find, on days when I chanced to look, pages about *the present fashion of men's coats*—about the rage for novelties—puffing everything or anything except " *Cromwell Oliver* "—I had no misgivings—I know he has such a way of tacking on extraneous discussions to his subject—but when I found at last a long biography of that *Abbot Samson !* then indeed—I asked what on earth *has* all this to do with Cromwell—and learned that Cromwell was not begun—that probably half a dozen other volumes will be published before that. Nevertheless for I know not what reason he lets everybody go on questioning him of his Cromwell and answers so as to leave them in the persuasion he is very busy with that and nothing else. Absolutely I will not begin another sheet.

Yours,

J. C.

31. *To Jeannie Welsh*

"Cause and effect"—Novels from the London Library in Darwin's
name—Lady Harriet's appeal to C.'s charity : the cause of
Mazzini's hearing a lecture on the Corn Laws—Geraldine's MS.
criticised—Her invitation to Cheyne Row at Carlyle's suggestion
—Gambardella's portrait of Carlyle has a gallows-expression.

James Greenacre was a notorious murderer, executed in
1837, whose *modus operandi* largely anticipated that of Crippen
in recent days. "Betsy" is Mrs. Paulet.

(*18th Jan.*, 1843.)

My best Babbie,
                I would have written to you yesterday forenoon
if it had not rained last Monday. The connection of cause and
effect here will not be very apparent to you—what the rain
of Monday had to do with the writing of yesterday—but so it
was—as certainly, as that my husband's having received a
seductive letter from the *Lady Harriet* a few days since will be
cause of Mazzini's hearing a corn-law lecture in the Strand
to-night ! "Ah" things are very curiously linked together
in this little world—the Chinchinnopoli chains of invisible
workmanship are not half so intricate as some of the connecting
chains between the simplest causes and the simplest effects—and
I cannot fancy a readier way of losing one's wits than just sitting
down to consider how *this* comes out of *that !* or a readier way
of settling one's pride on the great question of man's *free-agency !*
If you would know how the rain of Monday produced the
silence of yesterday, I should be sorry to balk your scientific
curiosity—so attend and you shall hear. On Monday at one
o'clock there being every appearance of a clear, dry day I set
out in an omnibus to buy tea and coffee at *Fortnum & Mason's*
meaning thereafter to pay a *charitable* visit to poor Darwin
who was (and is) confined to the house with cold, but no sooner
had I issued from the omnibus according to programme, than
contrary to all human expectation, it began to rain on me—so
I made for the nearest refuge that offered itself, viz. the
London Library—being in the Library what could I do but
choose myself some books ? Everything I asked for was as
usual "out"—so *as usual* it ended in bringing away French

novels—a book of Sand's which I had not before seen and two of
—Paul de Kock ! Having still however some sense of *decency*
remaining I coolly entered my name in the ledger for these books
Erasmus Darwin ! to the wonderment of the book-keeper
doubtless, who must have thought me an odd sort of *Erasmus* !
(this by the way). Well having the books in the house, it was
natural that I should read them—yesterday after breakfast I
took up *Frère Jacques*—meaning to read in it only till the table
was cleared for writing—but it proved so amusing that hang
me if I could lay it down till dinner time when I had quite
finished it. So you see if it had not rained on Monday I should
have gone to Darwin's—if I had gone to Darwin's I should
have had no time to go to the Library, if I had not gone to the
Library I should not have fetched away *Frère Jacques*, and but
for the fascinations of *Frère Jacques* I should have written to
you. So now you see how the two things hang together the
same as Lady Harriet Baring's love-making to my husband and
Mazzini's hearing Mr. Fox on the Corn-law ! " But how is
that again ? " Oh you cannot guess—Well—I will tell you that
also—for it is good for your morality that you should be made
to reflect on this subject of cause and effect—one can never be
too much alive to the consideration that one's every slightest
action does not end when it has acted itself, but propagates
itself on and on, in one shape or other, through all time and
away into eternity. Lady Harriet writes to my husband that
she is ill—that she dines at four o'clock and is allowed to go
nowhere in the evenings—to do nothing, but speak—and that
" there is nobody—(she may really say almost nobody in the
world) she likes so well to speak with as him "—Pray mark the
fine truth-giving effect of the modifying parenthesis !—" So
he sees what a work of *charity* and *piety* is cut out for him " !
When a handsome, clever, and reputedly *most haughty* woman
appeals to the *charity* and *piety* of a simple man like Carlyle you
may be sure she will not appeal in vain. So he writes to her
engaging to visit her on Thursday evening—and *forgets* to
tell *me* he has done so. Then comes a ticket of admission for
one gentleman and one lady to Mr. Fox's lecture for the same
Thursday evening—and he asks me would I like to go ? The

Devil puts it in my head to answer unexpectedly " Yes."   In
fact, I have been long wanting to hear this Fox lecture—for I
understand him to be a first rate speaker—and observing that
his place was this time on the straight line of the omnibuses I
thought I could never have so good a chance—" Very well,"
says he rather perplexedly—" but *I* cannot go with you—I
promised to go to Lady Harriet to-morrow evening—Can you get
any other man ? "—Mazzini is the never failing man in every case
of need but I would not propose him—for young Italy has been
horribly out of favour this long while—seeing that I remained
silent he himself however proposed him.   As *he* was going *his*
road he felt the fairness of allowing *me* to go mine—so now you
see that chain of consequences also—so far as it yet extends—

But I myself have written a letter the consequences of which
I feel more interested in than in any conceivable consequences
that can follow out of the Lady Harriet's.   After reading the
Seaforth manuscript I wrote to Geraldine some of my notions
about it, and she answered me in a whole *pamphlet* of witty,
devil-may-care objections to my objections—" C'est assez "
I said to myself, " if she *will* run about the streets naked it is
not I who am her keeper."   However " she had sent on my
protest to Betsy " and accordingly in a few days came a letter
from " Betsy " also—extremely clever—and what was more
to the purpose perfectly *rational*—assuring me that I had merely
" said in other words what *she* had been telling Geraldine all
along."   Since my letters were sent from one to another I saw
no need of writing to both—and Mrs. Paulet being clearly the
most reasonable of the two I addressed my next to her, and
certainly did not conceal the displeasure which Geraldine's
levity had occasioned me.   Now things said *at* one are more
annoying than what is said *to* one—and so poor Geraldine
" moped," and has had " sore eyes "—and seems to have been
sincerely vexed—and finally writes me the best-natured, most
penitent little letter in the world.   As nobody knows better
than I do the difficulty of confessing oneself *gravely* in the wrong,
there is nobody more touched by such confession from another.
So I could not help reading a part of her last letter to Carlyle
and declaring that she was after all a good little soul—Carlyle

seemed never to have doubted it and winded up his praise of her
with " You should ask her to come up here for a little while ;
it might be of great use to her " !—a proposition of such a *novel*
character on *his* part quite took me by surprise, and I sat staring
at him without making any answer. " Why," says he, " you
seem *doubtful* about it—she is very easy to do with is she not ?
and you like her company ? " " Oh," said I at last " as to the
doing with I have no misgivings about *that* but——" " But
what ? " " Why I am afraid that having her beside me from
morning till night would be dreadfully wearing ! " " You
had Jeannie beside you from morning to night—what would
be the difference ? " " Jeannie ! Jeannie was not always in a
state of emotion ! dropping hot tears on my hands, and watching
me and fussing me as Geraldine does ! " " Oh as you like !
only I think it would be a kindness to *the poor lonely girl*—
and that her company might be useful to yourself when you
have so little of mine." I lay awake half that night endeavouring
to resolve whether I should ask her or no—but there was so
much to be said for and against ! a little of her would be very
enlivening—but a continuance of her does really fatigue me—
and then to say the truth—tho' I am not jealous of my husband
(pray read all this unto yourself and burn the letter) tho' I have
not only his habit of preference for me over all other women
(and *habits* are much stronger in him than *passions*) but also
his indifference to *all* women *as women* to secure me against
jealousy—still young women who have in them, as Geraldine
has, with all her good and great qualities, a born *spirit of
intrigue* are perilous sort of inmates for a married pair to invite
—they may make mischief in other ways, than by *seducing the
husband's affections*. Then again ; it might as he said really
be of use to her in several ways—and should I let my purely
selfish misgivings hinder her of the possible good—professing
as I do both to herself and other people to have a friendship
for her ? Another argument *for*, the invitation arose out of my
consciousness that I am letting myself grow too indolent—
perhaps I should be the better of being roused out of my
habitual still life and forced to exercise my faculties again in
human speech—especially of the intellectual sort, which

Geraldine takes delight in.   Still the thought of those ecstatics she goes on with introduced an immense questionability into the project—so that it was with a hesitating mind I wrote to her finally inviting her *in a sort of a way* to come " *for two or three weeks* "—and it is with an unsettled mind that I await her answer—not knowing whether I wish it to be a *yes* or a *no*—and foreseeing that if she come, there will be consequences from her coming either good or evil.   I took precious good care not to tell her that the invitation originated with Carlyle—that fact would have been sufficiently flattering for her to have founded a whole prospective Romance on it ! —and really the sober sadness of this life weighs too heavily on me that I should have much patience with the romances of other people !—I wish I might talk with you for a couple of hours about this and other matters—one's mind does sometimes make such a foolish uncertain figure on paper !

But enough for the present. . . . . I was charmed at your discovering that gallows-expression in Carlyle's picture *—I have all along been calling it *Greenacre-Carlyle*.

Your letter came in the midst of this.   Bless you—Kisses to all.   Write me instantly that you have news of Walter.

Your affectionate,

JANE CARLYLE.

32. *To Jeannie Welsh*

The excitability arising from constant stillness—Conversation with Robertson—Episode of the vinaigrette—Harriet Martineau has her letters destroyed—Correspondence—Geraldine coming : a dubious satisfaction.

Robertson's interest in the laws of pawnbroking led to a ridiculous episode, told in Letter 68.

Spring-Rice is Stephen, son of Lord Monteagle and deputy chairman of the Board of Customs, who accompanied Carlyle on his trip to Ghent (p. 19).   His sister married Sir Henry Taylor (p. 369).

MY DARLING,   *Thursday* (*26th Jan.*, 1843).

I believe I should do wisely to make " a sacred *week* " of it—to wholly abstain for eight days, from writing to man,

* By Gambardella.

woman or child ! Seeing that in the week past I have nearly
written myself into *delirium tremens.!* at least, (to stick by *the fact*)
I have written myself clean off my *sleep !* and *that* is a grave
consequence in my particular case—the exception being so
apt to become the general rule. This is one of the *disadvantages*
of that " *constant stillness*," which you protest against ; the less
one is excited the less can one bear excitation. I have observed
this in myself, in Carlyle, in all people that I have had
opportunity of seeing into. Long continued stillness in
purifying the blood, seems to have the effect of *thinning the skin*,
so that the merest flea-bite pierces into one, and inflames,
and irritates, as thick-skinned people cannot have the smallest
idea of ! A curious instance of this occurred to both C. and
myself a few days ago. *He* went to dine and *stay all night*—
not with *Mrs. Laing*—but with young Spring Rice, at Lewisham
—it was no party—quite a domestic transaction, and attended
with no bodily fatigue. He returned with rheumatism in his
back, nameless qualms " in his interior "—there has been the
devil to pay ever since—and nothing less than a blue pill and
dose of castor-oil have been needed, to counteract the quiet
visit ! Then, for my part in the illustration ; it happened that
Robertson came the evening that C. was at Lewisham—and
sat two or three hours—so that I was under the necessity of
talking a little—C. not being there to take the trouble off me.
Well, this mere talking—and to Robertson—for whom *anything*
is good enough—threw me into such a flurry, that I went to bed
as excited as a young lady after her first Ball—and never closed
my eyes till four in the morning ! Did you ever hear of such
a thin-skinned pair ! Nor was this all the consequence to
me of Robertson's visit that evening. He had come to request
that I would put down in writing for him " my little history
of the vinaigrette "—to be published along with other docu-
mentary evidence he is collecting against the present order of
pawnshops—I promised quite readily, without considering the
quantity of writing it would take—but it *made* me consider
it when I found myself filling sheet after sheet—yet if I told
the story at all I must do it in *my own* way—not in the dry way
of a police-report. So there was *one* good spell of writing for

me !—then just at the same moment Harriet Martineau took
it into her head to involve me in writing *her two long letters*
" in quick succession " of the *reasoning* sort ; the sort of all
other which are most apt to murder *sleep*. Poor Harriet seems
to me to be got into a dreadful state of " *self-consciousness* "
of late—to be fancying always that the world has nothing more
important to do than to occupy itself with her, and *her*
" *principles* of action " !—that affair of *the pension* having
subsided—and full time that it should !—she has got up a new
excitement for herself—fully as absurd it strikes me, as
Gambardella's " letting his hairs grow." She is demanding
thro'out the whole circle of her correspondence which is almost
as wide as the world—that there should be a general thorough
conflagration of her letters—in fear of their publication at her
death—and this she calls—not what it really is, a diseased anxiety
about her future *biography* but " *her protest against the laxity
of society in the matter of letters.*" " She feels it her *duty*
(varnish !) to set this example," etc., etc.—I felt it *my* duty
(without varnish) to tell her that I considered the whole uproar
" *unworthy* of her "—to tell her a great many very sensible
things, which have been entirely thrown away—" she perceives
that I think her a little *mad*—morally," but the only inference
she has drawn from that is that *I* must be a little mad—morally
—and so she goes on exciting this letter-conflagration as if it
were " the burning-up of all the sins of the world." I have
done the *practical* in the matter—keeping only an autograph
for Helen—but for the rest, have told her that I must be allowed
to retain my own *opinion*.

Besides the " *history* " and these *controversial letters*, my
acquaintance here have all *conspired* one would say, to write me
notes at one time, requiring immediate answers—more or less
long ! Even Anna Maria * of Falmouth writes " wilt *thou*
have the goodness to inform me, etc., etc." They are all
settled with, now however—having cost me a good deal in
valerian †—and I write to my Babbie not from duty but
affection. . . .

Yes, of course—Geraldine comes !—A perfectly ecstatic

* Fox.   † *I.e.* a medicament for her heart.

acceptance by return of post made me almost angry with myself that I could not share her transports ! could only look into the thing with a *dubious* satisfaction. I hope it will turn out well for *her* at all events—such *faith* deserves fulfilment—the *when* is not settled—there were *shifts* to be provided ! ! She seems herself to have some idea of my misgivings—for she assures me that I " will find her much quieter to *live* with than to see just for a day "—and that as she has two other invitations she will not be altogether " *on my arms*," as I once said to her ! God grant [it] for " my arms " are of the weakest !

God bless you my own good child—my love to Helen—and please remember me to your beautiful-eyed cousin.

Ever thine,
JANE CARLYLE.

33. *To Jeannie Welsh*

Uncle John's illness at the anniversary of Mrs. Welsh's death.

(18th Feb., 1843.)

MY DEAREST JEANNIE,

I hardly know what I am going to write—only I feel a need to write something by return of post. Your news of this morning has quite confused me—I feel only one thing quite distinctly that you are the best wisest little soul that ever was made. Oh yes, let none of us ever more have concealments ! You were right to tell me the whole truth—but how few in your circumstances could have told it in such a wise considerate way !—told anyhow, it could not fail to make me very anxious, and, somehow just in this particular month when my heart is quite full of last February it could not fail to make me very sad—but I am better pleased to be ever so anxious and sad than to be kept in the dark. Oh if all people had had your sense—what bitter regrets would have been spared me for my life long !

My child you are an example to me—for all so much older and more experienced I am—your quiet affectionate good-sense rays itself into my mind even at this distance, thro' all the tumultuous nonsense that is fussing round about me and through all the natural temptations I have to get nervously excited myself. I say with you in calmness and faith " let us hope the best." Yet it is hard for me to have to wait till Monday for further intelligence. Oh that I were beside you—to see how things go on with my own eyes. If my uncle does not get better *soon*—and if you feel that my company would be of the slightest use or comfort to you say so without hesitation. I am quite aware that every one of you makes a better *nurse* than I do— that in fact I am a very helpless being—but I feel myself so much your elder sister that it seems unnatural for me not to be beside you all, to take my turn in reading to him and all that, and to share your anxieties on the spot. You understand? I would not officiously set off in the Geraldine fashion—to " do " what will be perfectly well done without me, or may be perfectly well left *undone*—or to parade *my* anxieties among anxieties which must be naturally still greater than mine—but if my going to you could in any conceivable way make you more comfortable—you have only to bid me. I will not say any more for indeed I am very confused.

Only that I pray God to make this danger pass swiftly away —and to have you all in his keeping.

Your own,

JANE CARLYLE.

34. *To Jeannie Welsh*

Geraldine an unsatisfactory visitor.

(*24th Feb.*, 1843.)

. . . it were also a good thing if Geraldine would lay it to heart that I asked her for just two or three weeks—it will be three weeks on Monday since she came—three most uncomfortable weeks—and when she received a note yesterday from a Mrs. Green in St. John's Wood reminding her of her promise to spend some time there and saying that she had actually accepted an invitation for her to a ball on the 3rd of March she asked *me* what she was to do ? " of course you should go " I said " a ball is not to be lighted on every day." "And stay all night?" said she—"but then the long visit?—when is that to be executed?"—"I wonder," said I, "that you should go at all on a *long* visit to a person you dislike so excessively"—for she had been *abusing* this woman the whole morning. "Oh my dear," said she, "I shall only be too happy to stay on here—till you *desire* me to go"—a pleasant footing to have her stay set upon! My astonishment is that she is not as thoroughly enraged at me as I am weary of her—for I have a hundred times been quite unable to conceal my provocation. Of Carlyle she sees very little for ever since she came he has sat upstairs in the evenings as well as in the forenoons—and of other people she has seen very few—and all of these decline talking to her. One would say she had the poorest life of it here that can be figured—all the mornings she scribbles letters on her knees—and all the evenings she lies on the sofa and sleeps! I speak little with her—for her speech is so extremely insincere that I feel in our dialogues always as if we were acting in a play—and as we are not to get either money or praise for it and not being myself an amateur of play-acting I prefer considerably good honest *silence*. Intellect! Carlyle made a grand mistake when he held this Geraldine up to me as something superlative—she is sharp as a meat-axe—but as narrow—there is no *breadth* of character in her and no basis of truth—in fact she is what Dunlop * described the Dumfries woman's hen—"nothing but just a fluff of feathers." She is off to-day to wheedle Mrs. Sterling. She is also wheedling John Carlyle at a great rate pretending all the while to have the greatest dislike to him. Every Sunday and on no other day— she makes a *grande toilette*—*comes down in the forenoon* with *a bare neck*—and a black satin gown—or coloured silk!—all wasted I assure you. I wish to-morrow were come that I might have another letter.

Your own,
J. C.

* "An eccentric old minister in Dumfries, buying a live fowl, weighed t in his hand, and used this expression. M. C." (Note in vol. lxxxviii,). 306 of "Letters to Thomas Carlyle, 1826–1836," by C. E. Norton.)

35. *To Jeannie Welsh*

John Carlyle : a tiff and an amende—Geraldine disliked by visitors —On swearing everlasting friendships—Illness of Darwin, Forster, and Mrs. Sterling.

(*2nd March*, 1843.)

DEAREST,
　　. . . John Carlyle—suddenly taken with I know not what movement of superhuman generosity—sent lately to Carlyle a *Tweed !* if you know what sort of a garment that is— and to *me* some oranges—figs—French plums and a Yorkshire Ham from Fortnum & Masons—which ham is the very best I ever ate. I believe it was a sort of *amende honorable* for certain purblind, impertinent criticisms which he had been making to C. on his book, the which, by the way, he has *never read* and so was in no very competent state to pronounce an opinion of it— but he was sure that Carlyle " formed a wrong judgment of the Aristocracy—he had not had the same opportunities which he (John) had had of observing their dispositions and pro- ceedings ! ! ! " To which Carlyle who had been fretted too long with his *blether* answered " No ! perhaps not Sir, I was never attached to any Nobleman or noble woman—in capacity of flunkey or in any menial capacity whatever ! ! "

　　The result of this quarrel was the above mentioned *Tweed* and eatables. Geraldine I dare say secretly persuades herself— that *her* Sunday's bare neck—and *grande toilette* was the moving spring of his generous proceeding—but that is incredible truly ! Oh no—Geraldine does no execution on either man woman or child here. No living soul takes to her—several, Mazzini, Elizabeth, Darwin testify a sort of *sacred horror* of her—and the curious part of it is that every new-comer after surveying her with questioning eyes, begins immediately to ask me a hundred questions about *you !* Even Carlyle has come to the conclusion that, " that girl is an incurable fool—and that it is *a mercy for her she is so ill-looking ! !* " *There* was a remark " *indicative of several things !* " I really wish she would go away now for she places me entirely in " a false position." Besides so long as she remains I am not likely ever to have C.'s company except at meals. From all which several practical inferences may be drawn—1st. Beware of "swearing everlasting friendship" on "a sudden thought"—(a thing I might have known at this time of day without any new experiences)—2nd. Put no faith in the intellect which is *purely theoretical ;* when you ask it for bread it will give you a stone—3rd. Choose your friends by their qualities to *excite* love and esteem—not by the love and esteem which they profess to *feel*—or may even in reality feel for *you*—4th. Follow your first impulses—not the impulses which you have cockered up in yourself by dint of special pleadings. That is to say—if you be a reasonable woman— if you be not a reasonable woman all will be folly, the first impulses as well as the last—your best course in that case were to tie your hands together, and deliver yourself over to some wise person, begging him or her, to take the responsibility of living off your shoulders—to *order* you in the way you should go.

Has Helen got a cook ? Poor Darwin is still very suffering— he came one day a week ago bringing with him three beautiful hyacinths in pots—a white, a blue, and a pink. The smell of them makes me sad somehow.

Forster has also been ill, and is ill—all that prodigious " Brummigam enthusiasm " and foaming vitality bottled up in a sick arm chair—very deplorable to see ! for I actually went to see him. One is so sorry for a man *ill* with only a tiger to look after him—tho' *his* is the pink of Tigers !—Poor Mrs. Sterling is confined to bed at present. Indeed everybody seems ill or miserable. Bless thee my sweet wee Babbie—I would give a crown piece for a kiss of you at this instant.

J. C.

When is that monster of a Gambardella to come home with my picture ?

It is too bad to make you write every day still *—but so pleasant !

* To give news of Uncle John.

36. *To Jeannie Welsh*

Geraldine Jewsbury's officiousness—Letter and parcel from Babbie—
  Chinese Exhibition—Geraldine and Garnier—The piano next
  door subdued—Geraldine induced to depart.

Garnier—" big German refugee, dusty, smoky, scarred with
duel-cuts ; had picked up considerable knowledge in his
wanderings, was of intelligent, valiant, manful character ;
wildly independent, with tendency to go mad or half-mad—as
he did by-and-by." (T. C. in L.M., i. 33 and more fully,
p. 247, where we learn of his introduction to the Carlyles by
J. S. Mill in 1834, of the help given him by Carlyle and other
English friends, and of his death in his native Baden during
the risings of 1848.) Mrs. Carlyle's influence that " soothed
the troubled soul of him " is told in L.M. i. 243, in her letter
of August 21, 1843.

(*9th March*, 1843.)

Dearest,
            I was very disappointed yesterday forenoon, when
no letter arrived from you—and over and above, a little out of
humour—but my humour was quickly restored to its natural
calm, by what was meant to aggravate it—the fussy officiousness
and superfluous enthusiasm with which Geraldine struck into
the concern, wondering how it ever should happen that " any
one whose letters I was at the pains to wish for should not feel
it worth the pains to write," etc., etc., produced a speedy
reaction in your favour, just as the wife who was getting herself
beaten by her husband—fell foul of the stranger who interfered
in her behalf—demanding " what it was to *him* if her husband
chose to beat his own wife ? "—After dinner came the parcel—
truly a beautiful and most luxurious wrappage ! but in spite of
my admiration of it, I did not willingly leave off shaking it,
and shaking the books, in hopes that a letter would fall out—
" Perhaps," I said, " the letter will be coming by to-night's
post "—and at that same *moment* Helen, who had come in
without my noticing her, my attention being absorbed in the
shawl, put the letter into my hand—*then* finally my contentment
was complete ! When I had finished reading it I put on the

shawl, drew the delicious little hood over my head—and
stretched myself on the sofa to be supremely comfortable.   I
had been in the forenoon to the Chinese exhibition—which
like all *exhibitions* had tired me dreadfully—I was soon asleep
—Carlyle was stretched on the green chair and two others—
he had yesterday finished his book ! *—he also slept profoundly
—as he had good right to do.   Geraldine makes herself a
bed with the *priedieu*-chair and a sofa cushion and the hearth
rug—*every day* after dinner—and sleeps like a person under the
influence of liquor—or drugs—a singular phasis of a young
lady.   Yesterday evening she was stretched out and sound as
usual !—Into this enchanted looking room walked Garnier—
considerably distracted.   Singling out me to catechise he
asked " Why do you *tender* yourself in this way ? or are you
really not well ? "   Geraldine who had got on her end, and
always bursts out of sleep into volubility—poured forth a
torrent of words about " the poor creature having been to that
confounded Chinese exhibition, etc., etc."—but she was cut
short by Garnier's uplifting his two hands, and saying to me
with an affectation of dismay—" Oh my goodness ! how fast
that lady does talk ! it is quite impossible for me to follow her !
Mrs. Carlyle is she a relation of yours ? "   She pretended to
be vastly amused—and vastly amused with the quizzing which
he carried on the whole evening—but I believe she had her own
private misgivings about it !   After tea Carlyle and Garnier
went down to smoke and in the interim a gentleman sent in his
card—Helen whispered it was the gentleman of next door—
and that you may understand all the awfulness of this announce-
ment for me, I must tell you that Carlyle had yesterday put
into effect his long matured purpose of trying the fair musician
with a letter !   I was out at the time and did not see it—but
he gave me to understand that it was of the most chivalrous
description professing his conviction that " a young beautiful
female soul working in the most beautiful element that of *music*
would not willingly give annoyance to any fellow worker ! ! "
etc., etc.—What he required of her practically to do—or rather
to not do, was to refrain from playing all days of the year till

* *Past and Present.*

after two o'clock ! ! !　A modest request to a young lady whose
whole existence seems to be in practising ! *—I feared " the
gentleman next door " must be come to make a *shine*.　But the
first glance at him as he entered, hat in hand, reassured me.
He looked at me most benignly from head to foot—sat down
on the chair I motioned him to and then observed, " We have
had a delightful day Mam ! "—I myself led the conversation
to the piano—saying that I understood my husband had been
invading his house to-day with a most unheard-of remonstrance
—but the amiable gentleman would not let me finish—he
bewailed the annoyance his daugh*ters* must have given us—
bewailed our patience in having suffered so long without
protest—would do unheard of things to spare us in future—the
piano should be drawn into the middle of the floor—the *top*
should never be opened—there should be no playing in forenoons unless when the mistress came on Wednesdays—and if
she could possibly change the hour it should be done—in short
there never was such a complaisant gentleman as " the gentleman of next door " since this world began !—When Carlyle
came he seemed ready to fall on his knees before him to implore
his forgiveness for having daughters who played on the piano—
I assure you we were quite melted by his super-human politeness and he seemed to find himself quite melted by our grateful
sense of it—and he stayed talking—till supper-time !—and
then there was such a shaking of hands—and repetition of
civil speeches on both sides.　Nobody knows what he can do
till he tries !　The putting down of a piano under such circumstances would have seemed desperate even to me !—To-day
the *faintest* sound of it was heard as if for trial for about a
minute—it was hardly audible—Heaven knows how they have
deadened the sound.　So pray my dear have a fly at your
chimney can !—that is an unsupportable thing *and ought not
to be* tolerated for twenty-four hours.

Geraldine goes on Saturday thank heaven—I did not
absolutely give her notice—but I took precious good care to
avoid uttering a word that could be a second time misconstrued
into an invitation to stay longer.　On Monday she said, " I

* See Letter 23.

must write to that horrid Mrs. Green—to say when I am to pay
her the long visit—she wanted me before to-morrow evening
for a music party." The " *horrid* Mrs. Green " you should
know is a pretty, gentle—rather silly—but very innocent and
good-natured looking young woman who has shown her first
and last a deal of kindness—and who when she came here the
other day was caressed and flattered all over by Geraldine—just
as she caresses and flatters *me !* before my face too—but *that*
I *think* was an oversight she afterwards bethought herself of—
certainly it was a sad oversight, for the credit of her *sincerity*
considering the atrocious things she had said to me of the poor
young woman. I was reading when she began to speak of her
visit to her—I turned over a leaf and made no answer—she
scribbled a few lines—then looked up to me pen in hand—
and asked—" Well ! when ?—will you tell me *when* you would
have me go ? "—I answered dryly—" Surely it is for *you* to
decide the *when* not for me "—and continued my reading.
She wrote a note naming Saturday then handed it to me to
read—I glanced it over, and giving it back said merely—" it
seems all quite right ! "—This I think was the next thing to
" giving notice ! "—but indeed I am sick to death of her—and
I have not her gift of showing kindness where I feel only
annoyance and disgust.

Your own,

J. C.

A passionate kiss to my uncle for the shawl and dozens
for abstract affection. Love to all the rest—Mary's note
was too short to entitle her to any special thanks. The devil
fly away—or rather fly home with Gambardella—home first
and then away after beyond the realm of chaos and of night
if he like.

37. *To Jeannie Welsh*

Relief after the sentimental guest's departure—Books for Uncle
John's reading—*Past and Present :* a great book—A gift to the
lady of the piano—Dr. John prescribes a whiff of tobacco.

" Thanks God " and " What shall I say ? "—phrases of
Mazzini's.

Pattenisms—the mode of certain Pattens, friends of Miss
Jewsbury.

Sunday (12*th March*, 1843)

My Babbie,

" Thanks God," the house is quiet again ! oh so
quiet ! so quiet !—How worthy of being remarked is that
apparent platitude of a remark that " all happiness is comparative "—the mere *negation of worry* is indeed as much
happiness for some of us, as for others would be a rich succession or the realization of " love's young dream."   She went
yesterday, according to programme—on *her* side, of *course*
the parting was a dreadful business !—floods of tears—even
a sort of mild hysterics—on our side it was transacted with dry
eyes, with a composure of soul impassive even for the claims
of sympathy.   In fact, it must have been from seeing such
women as Geraldine in tears that old Burton came to his
conclusion that " the spectacle of a woman weeping was no more
moving than that of a goose going barefoot."   Some few times
in her life I will believe she has *wept*—really wept from heart-
fulness—unconsciously—not " according to programme "—
But all the tears that I have seen her shed have been of the
programme-sort—with no more *real* sorrow in them than there
is in drops of rain or in the *drops of steam* that gather on the lid
of a tea-kettle !—they are the same sort of half-constitutional,
half-voluntary thing, these tears of hers, as the little nervous
cough on the strength of which some women set up for being
interestingly consumptive !—and which they carry about them
all their lives without being either better or worse for it !

" Dear me ! how hard-hearted Cousin is this morning ! "

No my angel-babbie—I am not harder-hearted this morning
than any other morning—*thy* soft true tears—the tears of no
true woman—would suggest to *me* on this or any other morning

" a goose going barefoot." But I am, very naturally, in a state of reaction against the *cant* of sensibility, which has led me such a devil of a life for five weeks back.—It is come to an end now however—she is gone and my good wishes go with her and abide with her, so long as she keeps far away ! But never let us try to live under the same roof again ! this time the trial has passed over without bloodshed, or any very flagrant outrage— but it might not be so always !—That we have not already quarrelled outright, I will say in her praise is to be attributed to her *good nature* or *self-possession* (I know not which) rather than to any virtue of mine. My behaviour to her as my guest —and on my own invitation—has been very far from perfect —from the first day I have been for her cold, cross, ironical, disobliging—and this evil disposition on my part, instead of getting itself disarmed by her *unfaltering* flatteries and caresses has rather been aggravated thereby—flatteries and caresses so out of season and so ill responded to appearing to me in truth a what shall I say ?—*bassesse*—*toadyism*—or else a hypocrisy— in either case a thing alike incompatible with an *honest friend-ship*, which would have found itself *enraged*, and with good right, by such repulsive behaviour—Carlyle seems not a whit less relieved than myself—altho' he had so little of her.—He said to me last night with a beautiful *naiveté* " Oh my dear what a blessing it is to be able to sit here in peace without having that dreadful young woman *gazing* at me ! " To be sure she did *gaze* at him—and try all sorts of *seductions* on him, with a hope that seemed to " spring eternal in her human breast ! "—but the poor man proved absolutely *unseducible*. Even when she took the strong measure of stretching herself on the hearth rug at his feet and sleeping there—in the manner of Ruth—all that came of it was a remark to me afterwards " that he looked at her face when she was lying sleeping on the rug and could not help thinking how like she was to an old snap-wife ! " But more than enough of her and her *Pattenisms*—I only wish that I had seen into her in the beginning as I see into her now— that I might not have committed the memorable folly of taking her for my confidential friend !—

And would not one say to read all this much ado about

her that I had not an uncle in the world to think about and write about ? and nevertheless he is not out of my head for an hour together. He and all the babbies are really as much before my eyes as the portraits hanging on the wall are.

The weather has not been weather for mending *rapidly* and besides rapid recoveries are not always the surest so I suppose we should content ourselves with the progress he makes—still I should so like to hear of his being out again— if it were only for a drive in a carriage—men shut up in a drawing room put me in mind of the wild animals in the zoological gardens !

Have you ever tried for Bamford's book ? *—or the *Neighbours* ? * You will soon have a new one of our own †—in four or five weeks—the printing is going on rapidly—I consider it a *great* book—calculated to waken up the Soul of England if it have any longer a living soul in it—and " *thanks God* " he has got thro' it with less bodily harm than was to have been anticipated. He intends sending a copy to the young lady of No. 6—as an acknowledgment of the extraordinary courtesy of that household. I do not think they have played an hour in the day since the remonstrance was sent in—sometimes I could find in my heart to send round a request that they would play—the silence becomes so oppressive to me in fancying what it must be costing them—

Monday.

The foregoing was written yesterday by way of taking Time by the forelock. I was interrupted by The Editor of the *Tablet* and an *Artist* whom he called Herbert—Robertson came just as we finished dinner, and an hour or two later Mr. Spedding. After Robertson came in I rose to go up stairs.

* See L.M. i. 187, 188.
These books she had already recommended to Helen Welsh for her Uncle's reading : the former is *Passages from the Life of a Radical*, by Samuel Bamford, a silk-weaver of Middleton. " He was one of those who got into trouble during the Peterloo time ; and the details of what he then saw and suffered are given with a simplicity, an intelligence, and absence of everything like party violence, which it does one good to fall in with, especially in these inflated times." *The Neighbours* was a domestic novel, translated from the Swedish by Mary Howitt ; but Mrs. Carlyle " is not sure that it has not a little too much affinity with water-gruel."
† *Past and Present.*

John followed me, saying he wished to talk with me a few minutes. We went into the Library where there was a good fire—I wondering what he was about to say—judge of my amazement when he fell to asking me more questions about my side and all my *et ceteras* than he had done from first to last putting all together since I first complained to him !—The more I told him my side was much better than it used to be, the more he showed himself *inquisitive*—almost anxious about it ! ! and the result of the consultation was his inviting me—should rather say *prescribing* for me that I should take part of—his cigar ! !—" there were certain states of the stomach in which a little *mild* tobacco-smoke was extremely good for one ! —I had better take a little more !—I had not had enough yet to do me any good." I protested that more of it would make me sick—" Oh no !—I would find it *highly* useful for me—*provided I did not send it thro' my nose*, which was very dangerous —very dangerous indeed " ! Can he be going out of his wits ? Such attentions to me would almost make me think so—

He spoke of Geraldine as " a very *unfortunate* young woman "—" Did I know how she had been brought up ? it would be curious to know how she has arrived at her present absurd figure !—Perhaps the best she could now do were to go into the Catholic Church, it might be the means of keeping her out of worse mischief—— "

. . . Bless you my child—

Your own
J. CARLYLE.

38. *To Jeannie Welsh*

Neglect which was no neglect—Love present and absent—Portrait of Uncle John.

(*End of March*, 1843.)

" It is abominable of cousin to be writing to Gambardella, writing to Geraldine, and all the while neglecting little me ! " Hush my child !—there is not common sense even in what you there say ! I have *not* been neglecting thee ; but on the contrary, forwarding thy bits of interests with all my might. Listen ! I have only been *up to* a very small quantity of writing this last week—my headache has altered its figure from the *dull* sort to the *throbbing* which latter is always aggravated by writing —unable then to write to all of you as I wished, how would I serve *your* individual interests more practically, than just in directing my letters so as to fan the flame of brotherly-love which is kindling all hearts in Liverpool and promising to bring back a Parisian " *Feast of Pikes* " into that commercial city. Yes depend upon it ! both Geraldine and Gambardella would be ready to enfold not only one another but you ! Helen—my uncle (!) everybody in a more strict embrace after having had my letters, and alas my Babbie ! it is a truth which even the sentimental souls must candidly admit—that *present* affection exercises a more sensible influence on one's *daily life* than that which is *not* present, tho' in itself far more vital—*the inward exceptional life* may derive its chief strength and heavenliest moments from affection thousands of miles away—even removed perhaps to another world—but it is the *love of those about us* that makes " the breakfast go off cheerfully " and promotes good digestion and enables one to live long—*on the earth.* Ergo—I would increase affection for you as much as possible in the *there* living and moving—Geraldines and Gambardella's and Mrs. Paulets—and I see no surer way of doing so than to keep them in good humour with *myself.* What an amount of head- aches and heartaches it does take to drive the *conceit* out of one !

So the picture is done and successful—my good *patient* uncle, give him twenty kisses for his compliance—but Babbie— you say you wish that I could see it, and you wish that I could see it !—am I *not* to see it then and that speedily ?—is not the picture for *me* ?—it certainly was meant so in the beginning—you asked my uncle to send me his double and he answered " why not one of myself ? " but now that it is satisfactorily done, you little avaricious gipsy, perhaps you think to appropriate it ! as if I could have so far belied my nature as to take up the question merely as one of public good, and not of my own individual interest—impossible ! common honesty common sense direct that the picture should be hung up in this house rather than yours—I am willing to regard it as a family possession, only ! *I must have the keeping of it*—you understand ?

JOHN WELSH.
From a portrait by Gambardella in the possession of Miss Chrystal.

39. *To Jeannie Welsh*

A "subdued temper"—The story of Gambardella's portrait of
Mrs. Carlyle—His portrait of her Uncle.

(End of March, 1843.)

MY HEARTS-BABBIE,

Never apologise to *me* for being " *cross* "—I should
not like you half so well if you were always the same sweet
placid Babbie " without shadow of change "—I should not feel
sympathetic with you, if you had either an *imperturbable temper*
or what is called " a *subdued temper* "—as Darwin says " defend
me from a *subdued temper* " !—and the *imperturbable* is nearly
as bad !   Your last note I assure you was very much after my
own heart—and I would have sent you a little word of encouragement by return of post—only that I had something else to do
for you, which I considered would be of more permanent
use—What ?— "

> " Ah that is the mystery
>   Of this wonderful history
> And you wish that you could tell ! "

But it were cruel to keep you puzzling your bits of brains !
Well then—know that on Saturday I sat from twelve till four
to—Gambardella—for my picture !—to be given to *you !*—
and again yesterday from eleven till four—and you all the
while expecting him in Maryland Street on his way to London ! !
On Friday morning he scampered up to this door on a
grey horse—and took the house as it were by storm—I found
him fatter—more hairy—and more in love with himself than
ever—but the same good hearted fellow as ever. He spoke
of you all in grateful and approving terms—but it is my Uncle
who is his *passion* in the family—" He was a *grand* man "—" a
noble man—*especially when excited* "—" Oh there was nothing
in Liverpool he liked so well as to see *Welsh* excited." He
talked a vast quantity of nonsense, not without flashes of good
sense—and ended by telling me that I *must* come to him
immediately to sit—" without any words about it "—he had
" promised the picture to *Jeanie,* and if he did not do it before

he began the other *wo-k* he would never probably find leisure to do it at all "—Of course I was quite ready to sacrifice my *humility* or as you consider it my *vanity*—when " Jeanie " was to be the gainer—so I appointed to go to him the following day— I was very unwell however the morning he came—but as he complimented me on my looks, I thought it needless to call myself ill—and besides I hoped to be better by the time I should need to go to him.   Thackeray and FitzGerald were to dine with us that day (Friday)—I baked a mutton pie and a raspberry tart in a state of great suffering—got thro' the dinner —hoped to get thro' the tea, and then promised myself to go to bed—but just before the men came up stairs, my affairs reached a consummation—I fainted—and had to be carried to bed— and lay for three hours alternating between fainting and retching—Helen blubbering over me—and the men, increased by the arrival of Spedding and Robertson, raging and laughing in the adjoining room.   Oh I assure you I have not passed such an evening for a good while.   The following morning I felt too broken to get up to breakfast and was still in bed at ten o'clock, when down came G. again—Helen told him I had been ill and was not up—" *Well* then "—says he—" you tell her not to be later than *twelve* and to be sure to bring the black veil I have seen on her head " !—" Lord preserve me " says Helen " you can never be expecting the mistress to sit for her picture to-day !   *The thing's an impossibility !* "   " Did *she* bid you say that ? " says he—" No," says Helen, " but anybody may see by her that she is not fit for anything of the kind ! "   " Oh never you mind," says G. " you tell her what I say "—and off he went like a passing whirlwind !   Nobody knows what he can do till he tries thought I—and so I rose and dressed myself and actually went and sat four hours !   And yesterday again five hours !—and I am not dead—only near it.   I hope the result will be satisfactory for you.   One is not a good judge of one's own likeness and no one else has yet seen this of mine— I incline to suppose it is extremely resembling but not very well conceived—the features are every one of them exactly what I see in my looking-glass—but the expression he has given them I never saw there—it *may* be that my " habitual look " is as he says it is, this which he has painted me with—the look of a rather *improper female* DOING a sort of St. Anthony's ecstasy ! and *doing* it not well—but you will see it in good time and perhaps it will strike you differently.   However it strike you—you will be pleased with the great pains which he has bestowed on it.   If it had been to have yielded him fifty guineas he could not have taken more.

But all this while I have said nothing of my uncle's picture— my own more immediate concern.   In the first moment I was disposed to quarrel with the eyes—he held it too near me—and I was not used to the want of the spectacles—still I thought it a good likeness on the whole, and was fully as content with it as I had expected to be—but after a while, rising to warm my feet at the fire, my eyes fell on it unexpectedly where he had placed it behind a screen, which let in the light on it only from above—and absolutely I gave a little scream—and ran forward to kiss my own identical little uncle.   Oh it is perfect in that light—the dearest little life-like kissable thing !   If Gambardella had not been by ; I must have cried over it when I recognised how good a picture it was—you can understand why.   Oh, I am so much obliged to him—give him a whole smotherment of kisses for me (my uncle I mean).   I have not got it home yet—it was framed—beautifully framed—but he must send the frame he said for a few days as a pattern to make the others by—for he meant to frame my picture for Jeanie himself— " as a present."   This is equal to " Authors giving *bound* copies of their works ! "

. . . I have still an inquiry to make in Carlyle's name of Alick—Will he (Alick) be so good as discover to a nicety the last day on which it would be quite safe—without the smallest chance of being belated for a packet or parcel to be in Liverpool to go to America—Carlyle thinks it is the fourth of April on which a vessel will sail but is not quite sure.   Also will he mention the name of the steamer—and give a guess if he can at what would be the probable charge for carriage from Liverpool to Boston of a packet weighing some three or four pounds— the last query is the least important to have answered with precision.   Moreover could you tell me all this if possible by

return of post—as I shall have no peace till he knows about
it—

I have a great deal more to say—and do not end—only
interrupt my writing—Bless you loveliest

Your own

J. C.

40. *To Jeannie Welsh*

Servants, a most important item in female existence—Gambardella's
quest—His portrait of Mrs. Carlyle a mark of his devotion to
Babbie—Mrs. Carlyle goes to a party and feels like a ghost—
Plattnauer again and Geraldine's letter—Lord Jeffrey shocks
William Cunningham.

(*27th March,* 1843.)

My goodness Child ! why *do* you make bits of apologies
to me for writing about the servants—as if " *the servants* "
were not a most important—a most fearful item in our female
existence ! Do you forget how I was always while you were
here, finding fault with Helen and the rest, that they would not
tell us about the servants ?—whether they were doing well or
ill ? I think, talk, and write about my own servant as much as
Geraldine does about her lovers—and make myself sure that
everybody that cares for me will sympathize with me in the
matter—that everybody who asks me with a real interest " how
are you ? "—would ask also if it were passed into a fashion of
speech " are you comfortably *suited* ? " With respect to these
damsels of yours ; I have to remark for the thousandth time
what a mercy it is for us, that we never discover all the misconduct of the " vile creatures " till they are gone or going !—
I shall be really anxious to learn your hopes from the new-
comers, or your fears. . . .

Darwin came the day before yesterday, apparently to ask
me " if I had found Gambardella a mistress yet "—for it was
his first question *—He carried me with him to Michael Place
to see the picture which he pronounced a master-piece—" the
only picture of G.'s he had seen that gave him any idea that he

---

* The artist's unfortunate advertisement and its consequences are
described in the next letter.

could ever become a good artist "—" from which," says
Carlyle, " it is plain that Darwin knows nothing at all about
you " ! !—G. told Robertson who asked, that his charge for
such a picture would be forty guineas ! and Darwin thought
it not at all dear !—" He must be very much in love with
Miss Welsh " says Darwin " to bestow so much work on her
gratis "—" He must be very much in love with *the subject* "
says Carlyle, " that is all ! "—I suppose Miss Welsh and *the
subject* have *the love* between them.

I went to *a party* at the Chadwicks' on Wednesday evening—
and the misery of it I cannot express to you—Carlyle has been
for a long while showing himself excessively discontented at
having to go everywhere alone—I really think he was getting
afraid that people would suspect him like Mr. Liston * of
having made his wife into an anatomical preparation—some
month ago I undertook at his particular desire to go to a party
at the Procters' (Barry Cornwalls) but when the night came I
sent him as usual with my apology—and as I was really plainly,
to outward eyes even, extremely unwell, he did not force me.
On Wednesday then—I determined to go—to sacrifice myself
for one time and then be done with it for months to come—as
I can now say to him under the next score of invitations " I
went to the Chadwicks'—I have publicly testified that I am
alive—what more would you have ? "

If you had seen me getting under way you would not
have known whether to laugh or cry over me—I rather fancy
you would have preferred the *latter* thing.　I went off at half
after eight to dress myself, as pale and trembling as if I had
been preparing for the scaffold—my hands would not put in
the pins—and then I had forgotten how to *dress for a party !*
—my head ? first of all—to go with it in its usual state of bare
simplicity—would pass for *affectation*—the black scarf came
most naturally to hand—but no—the spiteful people would say
" Mrs. Carlyle being desperate of enacting the *girlish* any longer
with advantage, is now for *doing* the *nun-like* "—I bethought
me of the wreath of *your* old black bonnet (the bonnet by the
way Helen had sorted up for herself with coloured ribbon and

* Liston was a marvellously skilful operating surgeon.

it has been her Sunday's bonnet ever since)—*that* I twiste
round my small knob of hair—with what effect those who foun
themselves *behind* me only know—then my silk dress, which ha
not been on since I was in Suffolk ! your chemisette—in i
pristine *unwashed* purity !—and Helen's beautiful little pocke
handkerchief finished my decoration.   When I heard my nam
bawled from servant to servant I was really within a trifle c
fainting—and instead of getting slipped quietly into a chair, t
recover myself, I was presently surrounded with acquaintanc
all expressing the most importunate *surprise* over me —
" *You* actually come," says one, " I declare it almost frighter
one like seeing a ghost ! "   " How *is* this," says another, " ar
you *well* now ? "   " But good heavens," says Mrs. Booth, " wi
you explain it to me ? *how is it* that I see you out ? " &c. &c.-
till I was tempted to start up like a wild deer, and rush dow
stairs, and out of the house again, and home to my safe bed
Oh dear dear when I *did* get home to bed I cried like a chil
that had been *lost* for so many hours !   And this was what peop
call *pleasure !* a pleasure to be purchased with *eight and si*
pence for a fly !—And next day I was so ill—no wonder—for
really suffered that night—horrible things.

To make not only the impression but to have the sensa
tions of a ghost—while one is yet alive, is a state of contradictio
which those only who have felt it can appreciate the horror of-
I shall not do such violence to myself in a hurry again—indee
with such continued ill health as I have I do not see that I nee
any got up excuses for avoiding *general society*. If nobod
else can see that I am *too ill* for going about to soirées and la
dinners and all that *I* at least see it, and feel it and know it-
and *that* should suffice to justify me in staying at home, an
saving my small stock of strength for more essential purpos
than visiting.

Meanwhile I have got back my Sunday morning's *congreg*
tion—Plattnauer presented himself unexpectedly the la
Sunday and had the door opened to him by Carlyle (Hele
being gone to church)—He looked much better—and *strange*
glad to see me again. He asked most cordially after " *her*
nodding towards your picture and expressed unmitigate

disgust over Geraldine's letter to him *—" One *half line* from myself would have been better than all that *strange stuff—which of course required no answer.*"   He never saw Cavaignac ! ! ! *C. twice left a card for him*—But he dined sometimes with George Sand and found her " really very charming—for a French woman."

. . . William Cunningham comes here very often—he came in yesterday and found Lord Jeffrey (who was also just arrived) kissing me *à plusieurs reprises* and calling me " my darling "—mercifully however with the grave presence of Mr. Empson † to justify or at least palliate the procedure—William nevertheless looked perplexed.   Love to them all.

Your own

J. C.

41.   *To Jeannie Welsh*

Mrs.   Carlyle's   portrait   finished—Gambardella's   unfortunate advertisement and its consequences.

(4th *April*, 1843.)

Great news for thee, " insinuating " Babbie !— . . .

. . . your picture is finished—I sat again on Friday from ten till two ! and he worked at it by himself all the rest of that day ! so in point of *finishing* you may fancy it has had all manner of justice done to it—indeed I think Mrs. Milner Gibson looks coarse beside me !   As for the *likeness ;* you are to know for your comfort that he has now worked the *estasi* pretty well out of it—and it looks *simple* enough—Carlyle thinks too simple " *for anything* " ! (as you say in Lancashire)—The eyes, he says, " want expression " the mouth " wants character "—but for one person that finds it less *inspired-looking* than the original there will be twenty finding it excessively flattered. Gambardella's own criticism on it when finished was (with a look of ineffable self-complacency), " It looks too young !   I must put in some wrinkles ! "—The frames are not yet ready— and besides he seems to wish that I should keep it here for a few days that the visitors may see it—a harmless vanity in which

---

* Cp. Letter, 17th April.   † Jeffrey's son-in-law.

I

it were but fair to indulge him. So be patient—it is not even dry yet.

My last day's sitting was enlivened by the most extraordinary of all *excitements* he has yet found out for himself—I do not speak of the " *wittels* " he produced for me—about a hundred-weight of rusks in a great paper-bag—a whole hoop of figs—Guinness's Porter, Scotch Ale—Indian Ale—Cyder and something else with an incomprehensible Italian name !—This gigantic lunch was laughable enough but not to be recorded as in the sphere of the absolutely extraordinary. However that you may have a clear understanding of what I am about to tell you, we must begin further back.

At my second sitting he was telling me of sundry new household arrangements which he contemplated. He had engaged the two upper rooms in addition to those he had—partly that he might [have] a place to show visitors into besides his studio and partly because the gentleman and his wife who at present occupied them are so—dreadfully *ugly* that he cannot endure to meet them on the stairs ! Then he was going " to have a gu-l all to himself ; the lodging-house gu-ls being vile creatures who left fingermarks on everything "—and this gu-l should wash his brushes, mend his linen, make fancy-dresses for his pictures, according to his own directions, out of " very rich *stoffs* " which he intended to buy—and most important of all should " have beautiful fo-ms " and sit to him for model whenever he needed one. In fact he had already sent an advertisement for such a person to the *Times* newspaper !

Poor Mrs. Sterling's two hundred and eighty nursery-governesses rushed thro' my mind—and I thought ; God help you ! you know not what you are bringing on yourself. But as the thing was *done* I saw no use in frightening him about the consequences beforehand—they would disclose themselves only too soon—I asked merely how his advertisement was worded—

" Wanted a very genteel girl to do *very genteel work*—not under fifteen nor exceeding eighteen years of age—wages from twenty to thirty pounds per annum " ! ! !

Could there be two ideas as to what sort of functionary this advertisement had in view ?—I groaned in spirit for the poor blockhead who, without having the smallest ill meaning (I am very sure) was thus exposing himself to the most atrocious imputations !

I called on Thursday forenoon to ask when I was to be needed again—the door was opened by himself—as mad looking as a March-hare—his eyes were gleaming like live coals—his " hairs " in a state of wildness—his whole figure expressing the most comical excitement blended with perspiring perplexity.

Tho' heretofore so respectful of my *years ;* he on this day flung his arm round my person—as if I had been the reed of a drowning man, and almost *carried* me up stairs ! I sat down and asked " Well ! what on earth is it ? "—but he turned his head to a side as if listening, then darted down stairs again to the door—then back—then down again—and so on for half a dozen times before he could find two spare minutes to tell me his story. At length I got it out of him, but with immeasurable parenthesis of opening the street door. That morning at eight gu-ls began to troop into the street from all points of the compass—congregated in groups of threes and fives—till the clock struck nine—and then there was a general rush of *fifty* to demand admission !—and fresh ones were continuing to pour in—as I saw—— " The people of the house were furious "—no wonder !—" Mr. Blore had sent him up a most impertinent note "—" neither mistress nor maids would go to the door any more and so he had to open himself "—and then if I could only have seen " the detestable ugliness " of all that had come !—" vile wretches calling themselves *eighteen* who were *thirty*, if they were a day ! "—To make a long tale short he had from three to four hundred applicants that day and not *one* of " beautiful forms "—or even passable forms among them !—he had also six and thirty letters from the country ! not containing a single inquiry as to the nature of the " very genteel work "—but all passionately eager to have the place, whatever it was, for some daughter, or sister, or friend ! Does not this give one a horrible glance into life—as it is at present— even worse it seems to me than the *boiling of the dead dog !* *That* at least involved no immorality !—On the following day

which was that of my last sitting, they were still coming—but
not in such numbers—and the people of the house having been
heaven knows how restored to good humour Mrs. Blore was
opening the door to them herself—and by his desire showing
them all in succession up to the painting room—" that I might
just see what ugly wretches they were!"—But Fortune
favoured me—for among the *twenty* who were thus shown up,
I found *three* very pretty—the rest certainly were hideous!
One of the three himself even was pleased with—but tho' she
looked to *me* as improper as improper could be; she expressed
some hesitation about *sitting as a model*—she would consider
of it and let him know in a couple of days—the fact was she
preferred transacting with him without witnesses, I believe—
for she came back the same afternoon and declared herself
ready to come. But when he (much to her astonishment
doubtless) proposed to *see her parents* on the subject before
coming to a final engagement she answered that they were *both*
ill in bed and could not be spoken with—which he thought
" sounded ill for her *respectability* " and so he would have no
more to do with her! The last of the three pretty ones was a
very sad spectacle, indeed she was a gentle innocent looking
girl—not more than sixteen—brought in like a sheep to the
slaughter by a wicked-faced devil—as to whose *business* in life
there could not be two opinions—Gambardella hardly looked
at the girl—but told the woman in a grave imperative manner
that he was already suited—and the pair went off to seek a
less scrupulous customer—leaving me very much shocked upon
my honour!—I was at his house again yesterday—went with
Carlyle to see the picture in its finished state—and stayed
awhile behind him, helping the *Unfortunate* to concoct a new
advertisement! more *precise*, and not so liable to misinterpreta-
tion as the first. In addition to the female help he is minded
now to have a—tiger! Lady Morgan having laughed at him
for having the door opened by a maid with a *baby* in
her arms!! It is impossible to make him conduct himself
like a reasonable being—and so he must flounder along like a
very unreasonable one. The only comfort is that sort of
headlong unbalanced character has a wonderful knack of

lighting always like a cat on its feet. There I must stop abruptly —Mazzini has been here and as it pours down rain I had best send the letters with him.

You *might* have written to-day if you had liked—for your last was short.

Your own
JANE WELSH.

42. *To Jeannie Welsh*

Sympathy with Babbie and her character—John Carlyle leaves the Ogilvies ; settles at No. 5—Geraldine ; inconsistent—Her letter to Plattnauer—Walter.

The Walter here mentioned is Walter Macgregor, a cousin of Babbie's. See p. 122.

See p. 122.

Monday (early April, 1843).

MY BELOVED BABBIE,

There is a tone of *weariness* in your last letter—weariness with " things in general "—which has something more than *cold* at the bottom of it. But *whatever* be at the bottom of it ; I long to have you in my arms, to cover the babbie's face of you with kisses !—I feel so sympathetic with you *thus !* not that you were not loveable for me in your *placidity*—that " *beautiful equability of temper* " that " *disposition to be pleased with everything* " which gained you such approbation from Carlyle and the rest was not thrown away upon *me*, only. For your *normal state* (as Mazzini would call it) such equability, such disposition to be pleased is good—the very best, and in an utilitarian point of view even, it was almost indispensable for living well alongside of *me*, whose *normal state* is unfortunately very different—but if you had never exceptional moments, hours, days, of longing after an unrealizable ideal—of protesting against the mean, worrying actual—I could never have felt thoroughly sympathetic with you—there must always have remained a Bluebeard's Chamber in my heart of which I durst not have given you the key—you would have remained my *Babbie*—literally. You could not have become what you are, my *friend*—my *sister*—the one being alive that I can turn

to in *every* mood with assurance that neither her kindness nor
her sympathy will fail me. I have been thinking this morning
that I have written very little from *me* to *you*, this long while
back—and that with all my writing you are not kept up as you
ought to be with the current of my *personal concerns*. The fact
is, ever since my Uncle has been confined to the house my letters
have been more for *him* than for *you*—I have written more with
a view to making him laugh than to relieving my own mind of
what I had a *besoin* to say. Hence long stories of Gambardella
etc.—while much more important things have remained untold.
Just to think for instance, that I should not yet have told you
of the breaking up of John's engagement with Mr. Ogilvie
altho' it took place a fortnight ago, and will exercise a rather
malign influence on my individual comfort for a pretty while to
come, I am thinking !—Mr. Ogilvie went off to Cheltenham
some weeks ago, with his *maternal* uncles—(there are two sorts
of them *maternal* and *paternal*—the former considering their
nephew an exceedingly wise man—the latter those who
appointed John to *keep* him)—Well the maternal uncles wrote
from Cheltenham that they considered Mr. Ogilvie needed
nothing now, " except to learn to *think* and *act* for himself "
(a pretty considerable of a need one would say) and that the
companionship of a man of his own years—not a physician—
would perhaps help him better to that end. Of course John at
once acceded to the suggestion considering that " on the whole
perhaps they were in the right." Mr. Ogilvie sent him thereupon, his half year's salary with a quarter's over and above
as " an expression of his sincere gratitude and affection "—
and so the thing smoothly terminated. John left their house
in Chester Terrace some days ago—and went into the country
for a *week* with Bunsen the Prussian Ambassador—but finding
Bunsen's house " *too full* " he arrived here last evening—with
bag and baggage when Helen was in the midst of a *washing* and
myself in the midst of a headache—and now the question presses
itself on me with some emphasis " what will he do or attempt
to do next ? Above all how long will he stay *here* ?—running
up and down stairs—fretting me with distracted queries and
remarks—making the house—what he has on so many former

occasions made it—a scene of *worry* world without end !—
When one has renounced all the gaieties of life one does hold
rather grimly by one's *quiet*—and where John is you know
whether there can be any quiet.　That he will ever muster
energy to take up house for himself—altho he is now as able
to keep a house as we are—I have not the smallest hope—he
finds it always much easier and less expensive to live as *our*
visitor—and what suits himself he is in the habit of thinking
must perfectly suit other people—so that this time, as on former
occasions, I see no deliverance from him, except in Providence
sending unsought the offer of some new tempting *situation*—
unless indeed Carlyle gets provoked into telling him flatly that
he cannot keep him here—now that he is well enough off to
keep himself elsewhere—and it would be long before Carlyle's
brotherly nature could get itself provoked to that point—while
for *me* in the meanwhile—the *Sister-in-law*—nothing of course
remains but to submit, and even with a good grace. . . .

Geraldine was here yesterday.　She wrote from Essex the
beginning of last week, that she was " dreadfully anxious about
me."　I would not tell her about myself—but " thanks God "
she would now be able to see with her own eyes how I was—as
she was coming to town on the morrow and would be with me
the first leisure moment after her arrival—Well ! she *did* arrive
on the Wednesday and her leisure moment turned up for her
only yesterday a week after ! ! and even then, she went round
by Mrs. Hall, so as to arrive here after two o'clock when she
knew that if well enough I should be *out !*—unfortunately I
was *not* well enough and so she found me in !　And then the
excuses !—she had been " mad to get to me—absolutely mad "
but without making " the most horrible grievance " she could
not absent herself for an hour till that day ; there were such
endless schemes for her amusement !—(she is with the X's
at present)—What would she have said to *you* had you let
difficulty or even impossibility keep you away so long.　I was
heartily obliged to her for having staid away—but such
flagrant inconsistency between her words and her deeds dis-
gusted me to a degree that I did not even try to conceal.　As
for Carlyle he went out to walk without coming into the room ! !

Her staying with these X's after the way in which the *man* has shown his utter contempt for her, insulted her—even by her own showing—is in itself a horror !—even now " he will not be a moment alone with her " !   But to keep a footing in the house she is laying the hair of her head under the feet of his wife and daughter—his wife ! whom she told me when here two years ago " was absolutely *loathsome !* a creature that made your blood run cold to think of any being bound to her for life "—an excellent woman all the while—as I told her even *then*.

She goes back to Manchester on Monday—whence *I* will never thro' all eternity be the means of bringing her again— she is " a vile creature "—and that is the short and long of it.

I thought I had told you of the letter to Plattnauer at the time—It was one day soon after she came that after having fussed me in all sorts of ways she said suddenly—" Now what *can* I do for you ? tell me something to do for you ! "   I was thinking of Plattnauer at the moment she spoke—how long it was that his letter from Paris had lain unanswered and I said in *perfect jest* of course—" really I can give you nothing to do unless you will write a letter to Mr. Plattnauer "—" Well " said she jumping up " tell me where to get a sheet of paper." " Goodness Geraldine " said I " you are not going to do it ? " " Why not ? "

" Because you do not know the man—and how is it possible you can write to him ? "—" My dear there is no such word as *impossible* where your convenience is concerned "—

Seeing she was in earnest I determined on letting her proceed just to see how she would get thro it—And she wrote not only a letter but a very long letter—most *free and easy*—and I let it go—to amuse the poor youth—and had better have thrown it in the fire as it did *not* amuse him at all but made him vexed at *me*.

My darling I am not half done—but I must stop for my head is getting bad again.

I do wish the weather would grow milder for my uncle's sake and yours and mine—If *I* cannot sympathize in your feelings of cold who can ?   According to Geraldine it would seem that " fellow-feeling makes us wondrous *un*kind "—which is quite a new reading of the proverb. I am glad that Walter *even speaks* of coming. Shall I try to keep him out of mischief by engaging him in a *platonic* affair with *me* ?—A woman of a *certain age*—*married* and above all *three hundred miles off* is the *safest* of all possible *divinities* for an excitable youth like him. Bless you dearest—love to them all

Your own
J. C.

Give Alick the enclosed from Carlyle.

43. *To Jeannie Welsh*

A returned letter—Miss Jewsbury undamped by cold water—Old Sterling courts a rebuff from Gambardella—An advance sheet of *Past and Present*—Mr. Martin.

Wednesday (April, 1843).

MY DARLING,

. . . Here is the letter *—come back to me—having like the Dove of the ark found no rest for the sole of its foot ! to think of the botheration I have caused to so many poor post-men thro' this bêtise of an address ! our own post-man had been tried with it, he told me, from its bearing the Chelsea post-mark. But for James Baillie's letter inside they would not even have known where to *return* it—for it had no signature —nor date !—what I feared was they might perhaps have sent it to James whose letter *has* a date ! !—I have read it over with some curiosity—and should rather like to know if " *the officer appointed by Her Majesty's Postmaster-General for opening letters* " *read* this one as well as *opened* it ! and if he be a man that one is likely ever to meet in society !

. . . Your gladness over the picture is very pleasing to me— an ample remuneration for any " *trouble* " I had with it—I must go and see it again finished, for there was still a good deal to do to it. But I must tell you it has cost me more than *trouble*— it has cost me—the adoration of—old Sterling ! Yes Babbie— that picture has made a breach between us which can never surely be healed in this world ! " Deevil may care " !— Sterling called here during my last sitting, and was stupidly

---

* A letter to Jeannie dated March 20, not printed here.

enough told by Carlyle where I was gone and how occupied—
of course he came puffing off to Michael Place—and demanded
admission. G. had given orders to his maid that " nobody
whatsoever " was to be let in to him that day—that he was
" not at home "—and that point settled he had turned the key
of his door on me. Well Sterling insisted—persuaded the
woman to take up his name—G. indignant at having his *fiat*
protested against, roared out " No ! I repeat to you stupid woman
as you are—I am not at home." Sterling thereupon ought
certainly to have gone away—but the thing which he *ought*
to do is seldom that which he does—very curious to see the
picture doubtless—for *he* has long been wanting a picture of me
the old fool—he again sent up the poor maid to say it was Mrs.
Carlyle whom he wished to see for a few minutes. " Are you
mad ? " cried Gambardella now perfectly furious—" go back
you vile woman, and repeat that I am not at home "—this
order was given with an authoritative wave of his hand to *me*—
on my compliance with which, I felt that the fate of *your*
picture depended, so I kept my seat and left the thing to take
its course. Tho' every word he said must have been heard at
the street door and far beyond it—Sterling nevertheless, as
wilful as himself, persevered—actually proceeded to ascend
the stairs—*without a search-warrant*—to look for a woman whose
pleasure it was, clearly enough, not to be found ! This was too
bad—for it was a liberty he would not have dared to take in
the house of a private Gentleman—it was showing Gambardella
that he regarded his study *merely* as a *shop*. I cannot then be
very angry with G. for what followed—his behaviour was
savage—*brutal* if you will—but he was in a state of justifiable
excitement. He stood with the door in his hand looking like
a concentration of a hundred lions—facing Sterling, whom I
heard but did not *see*, on the stair.

" I wish to see Mrs. Carlyle," said S. in a tone of forced
politeness. " *I* am engaged Sir," said G. fiercely—" I am
painting—I desired my servant to tell you I was not at home."
" Sir," repeated Sterling warming into wrath—" it is Mrs.
Carlyle that I wish to see ! " " Sir," repeated Gambardella
in a voice of thunder, " I tell you I am painting—I am engaged

—*I have a sitter*"—and with that he—slammed the door in the man's face ! ! The pause that followed was awful !— G. snatched up his brushes and began to paint—but his hand shook like the leaf of the lime—he rung his bell—told his maid she was " a vile creature "—then tried it again—but his hand still shook, so he laid aside his brushes, took a pinch of snuff and burst into a perfect earthquake of laughter. Sterling has not been heard of since—in fact I do not see how he *can* come here again—for tho' it was not personally *I* who so insulted him, he must know that I was witnessing the insult and letting it take its course. But his own conduct was far from perfect. Gambardella bade me tell you that he could not have called for you on his way thro' Liverpool without putting off his journey a day and he had two *wagers* depending on being in London on the Thursday—on the one day he stayed he began and finished a picture—which left him not a moment to go anywhere.

I send you a sheet of C.'s book but my uncle will not be able to make either head or tail of it I fear in that disjoined state—And now dear I had better stop before I become entirely illegible. . . .

Distribute kisses as usual and little Benjamin's share to yourself—my Babbie.

J. C.

44. *To Jeannie Welsh*

Death of old Mrs. Sterling—Geraldine's promise not performance—
Criticism on the portrait of Mrs. C.

Tuesday evening (18*th April*, 1843).

MY DARLING,

There is a sort of hurry scurry in my moral as well as material atmosphere just now which makes it prudent for me to take advantage of any quiet hour that turns up—so I write to-night, tho' the letter cannot go off till to-morrow. . . .

You have seen in the newspaper what has happened at Knightsbridge ? Perhaps not—Mrs. Sterling died last Sunday morning *—not unexpectedly—her end had been foreseen for

---

* April 16. The news about his mother reached John Sterling at Falmouth on the 18th, the day of his wife's death. The D.N.B., misled by an epigrammatic phrase in Carlyle's *Life of Sterling*, assigns both deaths to the 18th.

many weeks. The poor old fool of a man is in such a state as
you can figure. Anthony mercifully arrived on Thursday
last—John is still detained at Falmouth by the confinement of
his wife who is critically situated at these times. I had not been
seeing her for a good while back—no one was allowed to see
her except her husband and Alicia Campbell who has been her
most unwearying affectionate nurse—the last look I got of her
was from the open door of her room where she was asleep
in an easy chair—with her mouth wide open—I wish they had
not made me look at her *so*—it was a sad almost horrible look
to have itself fixed for ever in my mind as *the last*. I came home
with a bad headache which lasted all thro' the night and next
day I was too ill for rising out of bed, which is eternally to be
regretted—for on that day—just that one day on which I *could
not* go she expressed a wish " to shake hands with me "—
adding " to-morrow I shall not be able "—but they did not tell
me the latter words till after, or I would have gone at night when
I *was* able to get up—but Anthony came down here at night
and from the way he spoke I flattered myself that she would
be able to see me and know me next morning. And when I
went next morning—she was quite unconscious—alternating
between stupor and delirium. I was in her room but came away
again without looking at her. She was talking wildly—and
seeing her in such a state had no consolation in it. To add to my
regrets they told me that she had said that morning during a
little interval of consciousness : " there now ! I said that I would
see Mrs. Carlyle yesterday and you see she has not come ! "—
So like her ! the pettish affectionateness of her nature still
strong in death ! Anthony who seems for his mother's sake
to have suddenly taken to behaving towards me as if I were
their sister, promised that if she recovered her consciousness
before death he would instantly come himself with a cab for
me—but she never recovered her consciousness. I went up
on the evening of the day she died—and saw Anthony and
Alicia—but not the old man—Anthony and William Cunningham
walked home with me, trying to talk on indifferent subjects
what unnecessary restraints people lay themselves under in this
world for [the] sake of something that they account manhood !—

as if manhood could consist in talking about the favour-change
in the weather and the effect of St. Luke's steeple against the
blue sky when their hearts were full of the dead.   Truly we live
all our days in a vain show.   I went next morning to see the
old man for I was sure he would be better for getting a good
cry with me—which he had ; with his head on my shoulder
poor old fellow—but at such a moment he was welcome to make
any use of me that he pleased.   Anthony speaks of leaving the
army, and bringing his wife to live there—and really I do not
see what else can be made of his Father.   *He* is as unfit to keep
up a house about him as a child of five years old.

To-day I had Jeffrey again and several others besides—and
among them my purposed letter to you again fell to the ground.
So you see between the solemn and the frivolous I have had my
hands full—Geraldine made her farewell visit on Sunday,
along with her Miss Patten—she had written that " *grievance
or no grievance*, she *would* and *must* come for two hours *alone* on
Sunday immediately after breakfast." She came at *two*
o'clock—I said—" I had ceased to expect you." " Oh yes,"
said she, " I meant—but *could* not get sooner "—With my heart
at Knightsbridge I was in no humour to make even an attempt
at patience with her—" Really," said I " it is a consolation to
my self-complacency to see you in *action*—when you tell me
there is ' no such thing as *impossibility*—no such word as
distance where *I* am concerned,' I look at myself, not only
recognising *impossibilities* at every turn, but even giving way
before very slender *difficulties*—and think what a cold-blooded,
ineffectual character must *I* then be in comparison !—but when
it comes to the test of *doing*—I find that the difference between
us has been merely in *dialect of speech* not in *matter of fact* ! "
For the first time in her life she had not a word to answer—but
sat looking not unlike a fool.   What think you ?   Walter made
the very same observation that Carlyle, John and Mazzini made
on her—each for himself—that " it was a *mercy* for her she was
so ill-looking " ! Do not however in speaking of her ever
quote me to her disadvantage—not to do her any mischief
in her own circle, even at the cost of being supposed a bad
judge of women, is the last duty that imposes itself on one who

committed the imprudence of constituting myself her friend
before knowing anything about her.   Her friend I have ceased
to be for ever and a day but from the consequences of having
been it in the beginning I cannot wholly emancipate myself—
Heaven grant that the consequences may be only *boring*—not
" *fatal* "—But our *imprudences* often enough cost us dearer than
our *crimes*. . . .

Your picture is here—and will go back I hope with Walter—
but Gambardella has not yet got the frames—I am afraid that
some day he will *shoot* the frame-maker or " send an arrow
right thro' him."   Everybody likes the picture except Carlyle
and Elizabeth.   *She* says " it is a *young* lady that never knew
a day's sorrow or a day's ill-health "—My kindest love to all—

Your own

J. C.

45.   *To Jeannie Welsh*

Old Sterling's wails for sympathy—The Babby picture.

Tuesday (25*th April*, 1843).

MY DEAREST,
        I was hurried off yesterday at the early hour of
twelve o'clock before I had got well begun.   In fact I begin
to be sick of the extraordinary occupation that has been
appointed me for these last ten days, viz. : dry-nursing my
great, big, obstreperous infant of an old Sterling !   Actually
I have not had five minutes' speech with Mazzini for the last
week !   At first I went to him from the impulse of my own
compassion—then I ceased to go, really thinking that at least
until the funeral was over they would be better without visitors.
On Tuesday forenoon I was desirous of having a mouthful of
quiet talk with Elizabeth whom I had not got a sight of for many
days.   I had not been seated more than ten minutes when we
were startled by the sound of Carlyle's voice in the lobby
enquiring for me—I thought the house must have taken fire,
such an occurrence as C.'s coming to seek me anywhere was so
unprecedented—" My Dear," says he opening the drawing-
room door " here has old Sterling been to seek you *roaring*

greeting ! and I have had to bring him after you ! You
must go away in the carriage with him somewhere and keep him
quiet ! " I departed with a sigh on my difficult mission—and
we drove all thro' *the streets !* crying the whole way (that is to
say *he crying*) and I bottled up beside him in his very small
carriage—looking I am sure the very picture of what Harriet
Martineau defined Queen Victoria to be " a young woman
in prodigiously difficult circumstances " ! On Wednesday
Mazzini had just come in and we had just placed our two pairs
of feet on the fender when the little carriage drove up again
and in *rushed* the old man exclaiming " Oh my friend—my dear
dear friend comfort me ! soothe me ! " I was on the point
of lifting up the poker to kill him—when he disarmed my wrath
by adding—" I have a *new* disaster ! John's wife has been
carried off by inflammation ! " You know *I* never felt any
affection for Mrs. John but the news of her death under such
circumstances was truly shocking—and I became quite sick—
" Oh come with me " says he—" come and let us walk a few
turns in the pure air of Battersea Bridge ! ! "—" I am *unable*
to walk at this moment " says I—" Then I won't go—I
must not separate myself from you ! We will drive since you
cannot walk—only for the love of God let me stay by
your side ! ! " Mazzini was *standing* all the while—*staring*
as you can fancy—the sound of his voice was not heard any
more ! So off we set again—*thro' the streets !* Thursday
ditto—Friday ditto—Saturday ditto. On Sunday he came with
Mrs. Anthony who had arrived—but mercifully I was already
gone with Walter to the Pepolis'. And yesterday he came
again while I was writing to you. But I begin to see he is merely
prolonging his wailing in the view of exploiting my compassion
and getting better treatment from me than he has been used
to. His real sorrow is already pretty well cured ! ! already !
Yes it will be just as his son Anthony told me. " You will
see that in a few weeks he will be back to his Carlton Club
and all his old haunts and the past will be for him as if it had
never been." I thought Anthony cruel to say so but he knew
his Father better than even I did. In the depth of his despair
he proposed to me to go away with him to the Isle of Wight

or some secluded place for a few weeks—and I in my simplicity
actually did not positively refuse and Carlyle in his simplicity
said "yes it would be well done." But my last drive with
him has given me other thoughts. . . .*

You have seen Walter ! and heard from him perhaps that
all the Laings were in raptures over your Babby-picture on
Sunday—taking it for a youthful likeness of Carlyle ! in his
"indivisible suit of yellow serge"—made mention of in
Teufelsdröckh !—By the way your old Lover inquired after
you in the very first breath—and the young Mamma (now)
had heard you were to be married to Gambardella. . . .

Your own
J. CARLYLE.

46. *To Jeannie Welsh*

Robertson and the Authors' Association—A tiff with Carlyle—Walter
Macgregor's engagement—Geraldine less extravagant.

Walter Macgregor, the Welshes' cousin, in love with a
Quaker lady, was now in London. Mrs. Carlyle had not yet
tried her gift of "divination" on his "palpitations and
Quaker-mania"—only her "commonplace faculty of observation"—but never found a calmer young gentleman.

George Rennie, a nephew of the great engineer Rennie (a
Haddingtonshire family), was an early lover of Mrs. Carlyle's,
to whom she was engaged for a short time. He is described
by Carlyle in the *Reminiscences* (ii. 92) as "a clever, decisive,
ambitious, but quite *unmelodious* young fellow, whom we knew
afterwards here as sculptor, as M.P. for a while, finally as retired
Governor of the Falkland Islands . . . a man of sternly sound
common sense (so called), of strict veracity, who much con-
temned imbecility, falsity, or nonsense wherever met with
had swallowed manfully his many disappointments."

(3rd May, 1843.

MY DARLING,
          I was hindered from writing to you yesterday by
headache, the day before by Robertson—who has been hanging
about us of late like a physical malady—time after time he has
come here—*always out of season* (which is his peculiar faculty
to bore Carlyle into taking active part in something which he

* The trip and its discomforts are fully described in L.M.

calls *Association of British Authors*. If C. be either out or
" engaged " when he comes he doggedly sits down to wait for
him—three or four hours it may be—an hour or two makes no
difference to him !   And so on Monday he came in at twelve
and sat till three—in spite of all that I could prudently suggest
about the risk he ran of wearing out Carlyle's patience by urging
him too pertinaciously—I knew in fact that C.'s patience had
already reached its *Ultima* Thule and that at one word more on
the hated subject he would certainly explode on the unfortunate
Blockhead.   Accordingly when C. came down at three and
was passing out *determined* not to see him, Robertson intercepted
him in the Lobby and thrust a paper on him like a bailiff
serving a writ.   Had you seen C.'s look ! ! " *Oh Heavens* " !
and then how he fell to brushing his hat saying the while—
" Sir ! I have told you already I will have nothing more to do
with that business "—" Why ? " says the other ; " Because
nobody but a madman can expect any good out of it under the
present circumstances ! "   How far a conversation commencing
in such terms would go, you can imagine without being told—
suffice it to say : Robertson went off in a *red* fury and left
Carlyle in a *green* one.   It is to be hoped however we have
seen the last of him *now*.

Walter ? Why ! to be sure ! Another case of *wasted
commiseration* it would seem ! for *palpitations* arising from a
prosperous passion are neither very distressing for the time
being, nor likely to terminate fatally.   Poor fellow ! I trust in
heaven that this " emanation from the Moon " (as the Chinese
call a beautiful woman) is one who will do him good—not
harm.   If she be an ambitious woman (that is to say ambitious
on the small scale) he will be not unlikely to follow in the path
of George Rennie—and end in a restless acrid egoism.   She
will have much in her power at the present turning point of his
life to make him or to mar him—God grant she may use her
power like a sensible woman and a true one !—His letter to me
was excellent—I will answer it soon. . . .

God bless you my Babbie—and all that belong to you.

Ever your own

J. C.

K

47. *To Jeannie Welsh*

Plattnauer and his little pupil—Carlyle's large plans for Cheyne Row—Dines too late at C. Buller's—Quarrel with old Sterling.

Plattnauer was now acting as tutor to the son of the 1st Marquis of Ailesbury by his second wife. The boy was nine years old at this time.

(*9th May*, 1843.)

My Sweetest

. . . To yourself, I have hardly any time remaining to write. Plattnauer having been cheated out of his Sunday visit by a sudden whim of the Marchioness's that he should go *with her* to church—made himself amends by putting his baby-Lord in a street cab this wet morning and bringing him here *for exercise!* The dearest, prettiest *kissablest* little Lord it is that ever I set my eyes on! No wonder he always calls him " *my* boy "—he is worth the appropriating. Now he is gone I must go out on divers business—the most noteworthy an investigation about houses. Since it became wholly indifferent to me, whether we remained in this house or not, Carlyle seems to have been growing in attachment towards it—even the accursed piano which " must be got rid of " does not always drive his imagination forth into new streets or a new county, but only *on to the roof*—or *up to the top of the garden!* One day he is for building a sort of well deafened observatory aloft—and the next he will build a good-sized room at the end of the garden !—

But preparatory to so strong a measure, there would be need of our having the house on some other principle than from six months to six months. It would be best he says to *buy* the house ! ! !—*this* house which he has a thousand times over sworn to be " out of before he was a month older " as if his life depended on being out of it !—Now however he wants to buy it—and then he will build the room in the garden—and throw the Library and *my* bedroom into one reasonable drawing room. He would like he says " to have a soirée now and then " ! ! " once a fortnight or so " !—Is he going mad ? or is it I who

have been mad all this while in fancying that he disliked company—and cared nothing about " appearances " ? If I cannot
get any satisfaction about this house I am to enquire after one
in the same street—it seems we are attached even to the street !—
I am at my wits' end ! my bedroom turned into a drawing room
—soirées once a fortnight with *one maid* servant ? the realization
of these wild dreams is still a great way off—but I confess they
appal me ! And this particular day I am not ill to appal—for
I went to Charles Buller's to dine yesterday—the father and
mother are returned—and instead of dining at six as I had
laid my account with we were kept starving till eight—and eating
then made me sick—and Mrs. Buller insisted on my telling *three*
long stories which I had told to her at Troston—and when I
went to bed I could not sleep and to-day I am " heavy and displeased "—Thank Heaven John is not here to " aggrawate "
me !

So good-bye to you love till a more auspicious moment—a
kiss to my uncle for the envelope—which was anything but a
comforting sight to me—only do not tell *him* that !—

I had a furious quarrel with old Sterling on Sunday gone a
week—I went to dine there with Mrs. Anthony—at her earnest
entreaty—her husband having left her with the old goose alone.
Well the way he took of testifying his gratitude was to fall
foul of my husband's book which *I knew that he had not read*—
and utter the most monstrous impertinences about it. I gave
him of course as *good* or a pretty deal *better* than he brought
and came away—abruptly—telling him that he must learn
good manners before I visited his house or received him into
mine again. He had been in fact *brutally insolent*—as his
nature is when he loses command of himself—two days after he
stopped his carriage a few doors off—came to the door on foot—
rung the *bell*—handed in a letter and walked away miserable in
spite of Helen's officious entreaties that he would " come in
and rest himself." I enclose the letter—to show you what sort
of arrant fools are the Rulers of our Israel !

Ever your own
JANE C.

48. *To Jeannie Welsh*

The mantle of Ninon de l'Enclos—Apparent high spirits—Vittoria
Accorombona—a woman after her own heart—Servant Helen on
widowers—The intellectual Circe—First meeting with Lady
Harriet—Escape from a bevy of Americans—Mazzini makes
himself mincemeat for the universe.

The present letters show that the first meeting with Lady
Harriet Baring took place more than two years before the call
at Bath House, September 28, 1845, which Mr. Alexander
Carlyle thought probably the first meeting. (N.L. i. 184 and
175.) The latter was but the first visit to Bath House (*cf.* p. 254,
below, September 30, 1845). After the introduction effected
by Mrs. Buller in May, 1843, we read of Lady Harriet calling at
Cheyne Row in June, 1845 (p. 246) ; of a visit to Addiscombe
in July, 1845 (p. 248). Moreover in L.M. i. 344, under
date of September 23, 1845, Mrs. Carlyle refers to Craik
having sat out Lady Harriet one day when she called in
Cheyne Row, while T.C. in Reminiscences ii. 192, gives their
first visit to Addiscombe as "about 1843 or so ? " A similar
visit is assigned doubtfully to Easter 1844 in L.M. i. 276.

Private.　　　　　　　　　　　　　　　(*28th May*, 1843.)

MY DARLING,

I have been dissipated all this week—extremely
dissipated *on programme*—not settling myself to anything—
writing to Babbie included !

The fact is a *sublime absurdity* occurred to me the other day,
and threw me into a sort of nervous flurry which I saw more
likelihood to get rid of in everybody's or anybody's company
rather than tell a tale with myself. My goodness ! surely the
mantle of *Ninon de l'Enclos* has fallen upon me ! One might
have thought that in this year of grace I was pretty safe from
having my tranquillity assailed by *the grandes passions* of *young*
gentlemen ! But as the old Countess of Essex said when asked
at eighty by a young jackanapes ; " when does a woman have
done with love ? " " Ask someone older than me ! "

Be all that as it may I have *done* a great deal of company this
week—and talked—oh good heavens, *such* a quantity ! *You*
would have been perfectly *terrified* at my *liveliness* had you been
by—but those, who have had the benefit of it, have seen in it

the simple souls, only a most sudden return to good health and good spirits—on which they cannot sufficiently compliment and congratulate me ! At a dinner party at the Wedgwoods' on Tuesday Miss Darwin, who was there, said to me before I came away—" Mrs. Scott and I have just been remarking to one another that everybody that has sat next *you* thro' the evening has been one after another in incessant fits of laughter ! what a comfort it must be to have the consciousness of being so entertaining ! " An immense comfort to be sure ! especially when one has the additional comfort of having just made a person one likes and wishes well to, extremely miserable (for the time being) in the abstract cause of *virtue*.

Well ! John Sterling has given me a German novel by Tieck—Vittoria Accorombona—which contains a woman he said " exactly after my own heart "—I was curious to see *his* ideal of a woman after *my* heart—and so far as I have gone which is but eighty pages I find he has made a wonderfully good hit ! Poor John ! he has recovered his spirits with a rapidity ! *
" You will see," says Helen while clearing away the breakfast things the other morning, " that Mr. John Sterling will very soon be married again !—but indeed I don't, for *my* part, think there is any *love* in the world nowadays like what used to long ago !—If one hears of it at all it is just *momentary and away* ! *There* was *No. 4* how soon *she* got over the death of *her* lover !— And Mr. Brimlicombe the milkman was married seven months after *his* wife's death !—But I *do* think," she resumed after some interruption of dusting, " that Mr. Carlyle *will be* (admire the tense) a very *desultory widow* ! he is so *easily put about*— and seems to take no pleasure *in new females* ! " Yes ! there is one *new female* in whom he takes a vast of pleasure, Lady Harriet Baring—I have always omitted to tell you how marvellously that liaison has gone on. Geraldine seemed horribly *jealous* about it—nay almost " *scandalized* "—while she was here—for my part I am singularly inaccessible to jealousy, and am pleased rather that he has found *one* agreeable house to which he likes to go and goes regularly—one evening in the week at least—and then *he* visits them at their " farm "

* His wife had died on the 18th of the preceding month,

on Sundays and there are flights of charming little notes always
coming to create a pleasing titillation of the philosophic spirit !—
Mrs. Buller in her graceful quizzical way insisted I should " see
a little into the thing with my own eyes," and promised to give
me notice the first time she knew beforehand of the Intellectual
Circe's coming to her house—and accordingly Mr. Buller came
last Monday to ask me to meet her that evening at tea at seven
o'clock—She is in *delicate health* you may remember and not
up to parties or late hours—I said at once yes—and appointed
him to bring the carriage for me at half after six. He was not
long gone—when it flashed thro' my mind that a whole bevy
of Americans male and female were coming *here* to tea by
invitation at seven—Dr. Howe the man who puts souls into
people blind and deaf and dumb—you would read about him
and his Laura Bridgman in *Dickens' Notes*—his wife—a Mr.
Mann and *his* wife and a Miss *Peabody*—What to do ? I
posted off to Chester Place to explain the necessity of my giving
up the Lady Harriet for that time.   But the Bullers would not
hear of it—" it was my husband not *me* all these Americans
were coming to stare at—I would simply pour out the tea for
them—and if I spilled it or committed any awkwardness they
would go home and *put it in a book* " ! there was truth in these
suggestions and finally it was agreed that Mr. Buller should still
bring the carriage for me, and unless Carlyle made violent
resistance, should snatch me away like Proserpine out of the
American environment !   C. was at first quite furious at the
project—but I got the better of him by saying " Well then there
will be nothing for it but to let Mr. Buller when he comes *stay
here* ! "—the idea of *that*—the deafness and the trumpet was
worse than anything—so he told me " in Heaven's name to do
anything rather than introduce such an element into the
concern."

Happily Mr. B. came first—and off I went in cold blood—
leaving C. to pour out the tea himself and make what excuses
for me he pleased !—I do not remember when I did such a
spirited thing or one which I so little repent of doing—*I* have
no reason to study politeness with the Americans.   But Lady
Harriet !—I liked her on the whole—she is immensely *large*—

might easily have been one of the *ugliest* women living—but
is almost beautiful—simply thro' the intelligence and cordiality
of her expression—I saw nothing of the impertinence and
hauteur which people impute to her—only a certain *brusquerie*
of manner which seemed to me to proceed from exuberant spirits
and absence of all affectation.   She is unquestionably very
clever—just the *wittiest* woman I have seen—but with many
aristocratic prejudices—which I wonder *Carlyle* should have
got over so completely as he seems to have done—in a word
I take her to be a very lovable spoilt child of Fortune—that a
little *whipping*, judiciously administered would have made into
a first rate woman—we staid till eleven—and as there were no
other strangers, I had ample opportunity of estimating the
amount of her seductions.

What *she* thought of *me* I should rather like to know—she
took prodigious looks at me from time to time.   In the *last* note
to Carlyle inviting him to Addiscombe for next Sunday she says
—" I meditate paying my respects to Mrs. Carlyle—so soon as
I am again making visits—she is *a reality* whom you have
hitherto *quite suppressed*."

Mazzini is all in a worry about a concert he is getting up
for the Italian school—indeed he has been of late so over head
and ears in what Richard Milnes would call " beastly little
businesses " that I get next to no good of him—I never saw a
mortal man who so completely made himself into " minced
meat " for the universe ! . . .

Bless you my love—Remember me to all.

Your own
J. C.

49.   *To Jeannie Welsh*

Inferences from silence—Good works—Mazzini ill—A letter from
Cavaignac.

(*9th June*, 1843.)

So young Lady ! you must have been *living fast* since you
have been so slow to write !—As Harriet Martineau says of me
I am " dreadful at drawing inferences " !—You *have* written
at last however—and you will say perhaps it was not your

turn—that I owed you a letter—Bah, Debtor-and-creditor-accounts between you and me are a thing not to be spoken of. Had you been in your " normal state " my silence would only have been an additional reason for your writing to me, you would have felt a besoin to know why I did not write. Well ! I did not write because literally I *could not*—I took unto the doing of good works like Mazzini one day—rushed about from two in the forenoon till near eight at night, without having eaten from eight in the morning—*verifying* a case of extreme misery—preparatory to exerting myself for its alleviation—and the result—" virtue's reward " as usual was a severe attack of rheumatism in the head and shoulders which kept me lying several days on the flat of my back—and which is not entirely removed even now—for I am still obliged to move myself *all of a piece*, and my head feels as if it had been pounded in a mortar. Mazzini too has been and is very ill—an abscess inside his cheek—headache of several days' standing and fever —I am very unquiet about him for in that accursed Tancioni establishment there is no help for a person who is incapacitated from helping himself. He persists too in declining to send for a doctor. But I have written to that Dr. Toynbee who has shown himself so friendly towards him—stating his melancholy predicament—and urging him to lose no time in going to his assistance—Mazzini will be angry at me for this but no matter— if he be the sooner recovered.

In fact it has been all going ill for the last week—the only consolation a letter from Cavaignac—to Carlyle—but containing some precious words for *me*—he is not coming—cannot come —has to go to Africa his brother's health making him " *inquiet de nouveau* " and being besides " *pauvre comme Job* "—but he says " *je voudrais bien vous voir, voir Madame, bonne et noble âme s'il en fût !* "—And Madame is almost as content as if he had come !—And the letter ends with " Adieu, chère dame, je déclare que de vous on peut dire *bien !* toute mortelle que vous soyez, je me suis dit plus d'une fois, depuis que je vous ai quittée : par le ciel, il n'y a pas sur cette terre trois femmes comme celle-là ! Adieu tous deux—Madame une lettre ! "— Now such words from any other man might be mere *words*—

and I should not care rigmaree for them—but from *him !*—
Ah c'est autre chose ! *he* never praises *except as it were on
compulsion*. . . .

50. *To Jeannie Welsh*

Interruptions—A Scottish Bishop—Story of the Mudies.

The Scottish Bishop was nicknamed " Cuttikins " (L.M. i.
209 ; cp. 207, 210, 213) from his gaiters, which formed a part
of his " episcopal uniform, unsuitable to the little bandy-
legged man." " Indisputable man of talent and veracity,
though not of much devoutness, of considerable worldliness
rather, and quietly composed self-conceit—gone now, ridiculously, into the figure of a bandy-legged black beetle, as was
thought by some."
" My poor family " are the Mudies, of whom T. C. gives
an account in L.M. i. 263, the grown-up daughters of
" a Mr. Mudie whom I recollect hearing of about 1818 as a
restless, somewhat reckless, and supreme schoolmaster at
Dundee." For twenty years he had subsisted in London as a
literary adventurer ; broke down and left a family " with
a foolish widow and next to no provision whatever for them.
The case was abundantly piteous, but it was not by encouragement from me, to whom it seemed from the first hopeless, that
my dear one entered into it with such zeal and determination."
In this and subsequent letters (54, 59, 60) Mrs. Carlyle gives a
much fuller account of her endless trouble on their behalf—
and its ultimate failure—than appears in L.M.

(15*th June*, 1843.)

Here is half a sheet of *pretended* foreign paper for you
Dearest—the other half is gone *only yesterday* to Cavaignac—
you may think what a worry I have been in since I have not
answered even *his* pressing demand for a letter sooner !—The
Devil has been in the wind for me these two or three weeks—
every kind of thing that could be imagined in the shape of
business and interruption has come to trouble me at one time.
My *business* is still at the thickest but I may anticipate some
alleviation from the interruptions ; one fertile source of these
embarked in a steam-boat for Scotland last night—not to return

these two years God willing. I think I mentioned to you that
Bishop —— was here—but you could hardly attach all the
sad importance to the fact which it deserved. The man is mad
I think—when I admired him long ago as *the clever man* of the
place he scarcely showed any preference for me—now that I
admire him no longer but on the contrary regard him as what
Mazzini would call a " *self-constituted impostor* "—and have
hardly patience to be reasonably civil to him for old acquaintance's sake ; he seems to have *constituted me* into his *Santa
Maria !*—has been coming during his stay in London at a rate
which it is almost fearful to look back upon—staying each time
three mortal hours at the least—making me all sorts of extraordinary confidences—never seeing Carlyle who *hates* him,
and kept himself determinedly out of his way—and in short
keeping me I will not say *in hot water*—but in a sort of *luke warm
water* even more detestable. Thank heaven he is gone at last—
with his bits of black leggings and shovel-hat—and *shovel-
heart and soul !* In all the arguments we had—and they were
many—it seemed to me that it was *I* always who defended the
religious side of the question, and he the worldly—the devil's
side—and he *dares* to go about in black leggings and call
himself Bishop !—Bah !

Then that *German romance* which I spoke of *—I am
still in the third volume of it—and the *interest* (to use Godwin's
curious phrase) is " rather exquisite "—with all my remarkable
foresight I cannot predict the catastrophe—but certainly
George Sand in her most impassioned moments never *wrote*
anything equal to it—you understand me ?—But the engrossing
business of all—my poor family—Heaven and Earth ! what *am*
I to do with them ?—I will enclose you something that was
printed about the Father at the time of his death—about a year
ago—so that I need not speak of *him* (send me back the paper).
But the family's history has been this—briefly ; for it would
take hours to tell it with all the *details* I know—The widow and
five children, all daughters except one, a boy of fourteen—" a
very bright boy " (the poor mother called him) were left quite

---

* Probably Tieck's *Vittoria Accorombona*. See p. 127, *ante*, and L.M.
i. 192 ; N.L. i. 109, 114.

destitute—a small subscription was raised among those they
were known to which just sufficed to pay *the undertaker's bill*
of £30—and some such like bills. Their rent was still unpaid—
the landlord put an execution in the house—and all their
furniture books etc, were sold for an old song. They removed
into one wretched apartment for which they paid five shillings
a week and subsisted—or rather starved on what they could
earn by sewing " slop-shirts " at a *penny-farthing* a piece—and
stitching fine stays for EIGHTPENCE ! With hardship of one sort
and another the mother fell ill of Typhus fever—she recovered
—but the boy—the one boy—her hope in life—caught it—
lingered six weeks—died !—*another burial to pay for !* and then—
a chandler with whom they had accumulated an account of £5
during this agonizing period seized the mother—and before
her first tears were dried for her only son—threw her into
prison—*for* £5 ! She lay there three weeks—*desperate* it
would seem for she appealed to no one—a stranger—a Russian
—heard tell of her case and set her free—another stranger gave
her £5 more for immediate need—and this was her situation
when I first heard tell of her. She thought that if thirty pounds
were given her she could start a small school—being an educated
woman—a woman that has herself written things for journals—
and that by this together with needlework she and her daughters
might make an independent livelihood—she talked like a
practical well meaning woman—I thought one should get her
a hundred pounds—to give her a fair start—too little would only
be flung away in an impossible attempt—and I seemed in a
fair way of getting it till there arose certain insinuations that she
had been *improvident* in her better times—nay that she had
indulged too much in stimulants—all that by the minutest
investigation I have been able to ascertain to her disadvantage
amounts to no more than what would be quite easily pardoned
in anybody but in *one who is asking help*—in matters of charity
however people's consciences are *extremely* nice ! And so
because in her hard labours of writing to her husband's dicta-
tion from morning till night for fifteen years—and being often
very savagely used by him—and educating at the same time all
her children herself—because thus situated, she *may* have been

tempted to take more drink than was lady-like—the subscription—I am told—must be abandoned—can only at least be carried on among private well wishers—and where are they? except myself and Professor Gillespie of St. Andrews—I know of none that trouble their heads about her. I must move heaven and earth to find situations for the girls—such of them as are fit for situations—and then they if they are good for anything will be able to assist their mother. Geraldine who has continued like the wonderful being she is to write me twice or thrice a week—the longest letters—without ever getting a word of answer—wrote last week to beg that I *would* send one line at least to say if I were ill—so I wrote that I was occupied—with a family in great economical affliction. On this small notice she writes instantly again proposing——

Enter people——

No more then

Your own,
JANE CARLYLE.

51. *To Jeannie Welsh*

Geraldine's help ; is reconciling—Carlyle's two worries.

(21st June, 1843.)

DARLING,

I am afraid you will get no good of me until the Mudie concern is off my hands either as a success or a failure—I have just been writing a long letter to Jeffrey about them till my head is all in a mash—yesterday ditto—to Geraldine!—that unwearied girl has fairly *conquered* me into a hot correspondence with her again after all—by taking up this matter I have so much at heart with an enthusiasm—even surpassing my own! I cannot but feel *grateful* to her at least for what she has done and is in the way of doing—nay *at times* I am almost over-persuaded back into my old illusion that she *has* some sort of strange, passionate—incomprehensible *attraction* towards me that leads her thro' what is even more repugnant to natural feeling than " fire and water "—thro' *the miry puddle* of teazing and *begging*—to do me pleasure. Whatever be her *motive* her *results* are worthy of admiration—and lay me under a considerable debt of toleration towards her.

Then here has been Carlyle fretting himself—and family— that is, me and Helen—to fiddlestrings—having two incompatible worries acting on him at once—the thought of his Brother's departure to America with all the *practical* work *that* brings with it—such as writing of recommendatory letters— gathering of all sorts of information for his guidance, etc., etc.— And on the other hand an *article* for Forster's Review which *must* be finished by Saturday night ; if he would not run the risk of Forster's hanging himself, and so—we have sleepless nights—terrific explosions at breakfast—and all the et ceteras you can figure ! . . .

Your own bedevilled,
JANE CARLYLE.

52. *To Jeannie Welsh*

Youth and happiness—Summer plans—Mazzini would not wait.

(*Before* 30*th June*, 1843.)

MY GOOD DARLING

You must not lose heart—easy to say ! but when it comes to *doing !*—Well—no one knows better than I do the immense difference betwixt saying and doing ; still I am not ashamed to *say* to you you must not lose heart, because I really see good cause why you should not ;—setting aside all *moral* obligation in the matter.

Amid all your present troubles, whatsoever they be, you have a ground of comfort which *I* have not, which so many have not ! *You are young*—very young—with youth on one's side depend on it one has *the odds* on one's side against the sorest trials. One may not feel this at the time—nay, one may find the prospect of a long life to come only aggravation of one's suffering. But in the long life to come lie so many glorious possibilities ! And some fine morning, without knowing precisely how, one awakes to a recognition of these, and can smile over the despairing past as over a bad dream ! I can only guess at what ails you—I may or may not be near the truth—but of this I am certain as I live—that *whatever you*

are suffering *I* have suffered, and under more terrible conditio
than can in your case be possible. And see, after all, I am he
alive, speaking *hope* to my Babbie ! Not very *gay* certain d
—not " *happy* "—who in a world like this, that has any more*rs*
reflection than the Brutes can be what they call *happy* at my
age ?—but I am better than happy in having learned to do
without happiness—and I have this knowledge to communicate
to you, drawn from my own life-experience ; that the heart even
of a woman can stand an infinite deal more breaking without
being broken than one can form the smallest conception of at
five and twenty. There is a beautiful proverb and it is as true
as beautiful that " the darkest hour of the night is nearest the
dawn." So have I found it, and so will you too find it—*Wait*
and hope for the dawn in patient faith. There is no use in
tormenting oneself into got-up good spirits. That is, as it
were, to light a parcel of farthing candles, and call that " the
dawn " ! A sort of beggarly brightness that serves only to
make the darkness visible—to show one how *very* miserable
one is ! But *wait*—Mazzini you remember did not like that
word—nevertheless it is a good word—and one which if *he*
had better appreciated he would not have lain under the reproach
of having been turned back from revolutionary Italy " by a
toll-bar " ! and under many other consequences sad to think
of. Wait—not in sloth indeed—but in inward prayer—with
your face towards the East—till the *true* God-sent brightness
comes—and pours itself afresh over all your world and into the
depths of your soul—you know not how—but no matter *how*
so it be there ! Oh *that* is joy ! such as one knew not of *before*
having suffered ! When one feels oneself again *awake—alive—*
no longer a ghost among the living and the loving—but living
and loving like a newborn creature, in a newborn world ! My
darling, if I had you here I could *make* you believe that all will
be well with you in good time. I could *kiss* the belief into you !
I am sure that I could !—But the things that are in one's heart
to say grow so cold on the paper—Well, the practical inference
from all that is, that we must speedily meet— . . .

Your own

J. C.

53. *To Jeannie Welsh*

On hanging in the wind—Carlyle starting for Wales—Other plans ;
house cleaning—Mudies' affair—Mazzini's abscess.

(*30th June*, 1843.)

. . . I do wish you were *settled* one way or other—I know
no state which it is so difficult to lead a rational never to say a
contented life under as that state of hanging in the wind.   God
knows *I* have had enough of it in my time but even custom never
reconciled me to it the least in the world.   Carlyle has finally
determined on starting for Wales on Monday or Tuesday.
We have just been emptying the portmanteauful of books which
you packed—to replace them with the necessary clothes—so
I suppose he is *really* in earnest this time.   He has no idea
how long he will stay or whether he will come straight back or
go round by—Scotland ! or the moon !—He " hopes that *I*
will go *somewhere* during his absence "—and then the next
minute agrees to the necessity of my staying to take charge of
the house until at least I can find some safe person to put into
it besides Helen—Then half a minute after asks if I am not
going down next week to the Isle of Wight ?—I have an
invitation to go to John Sterling there—and of course a most
pressing invitation to Troston.   But the confounded house—
and the scattering in Liverpool confuse my mind beyond all
power of scheming even.

When *He* is fairly out of the way—and the ceilings whitened
and the carpets beaten and *some* painting done—even if I should
do it out of my own pin-money—then I will *try* to " go
somewhere."

Meanwhile I shall not be lonely—never fear for that.   I
have always visitors enough and to spare—when I am *single*—
and when a domestic earthquake is going on there is no leisure
for *feeling* lonely suppose no one came near me.   I hope to get
the Mudies put into some sort of small line of business in a
week or two—thanks chiefly to the active exertions of Geraldine !
—and then I *must* positively wash my hands of them—for they

take up far more of my time and thought than is at all
able—I believe if I had sat down at once and written a
in three volumes—and given them the proceeds it w
have been easier work for me than the writing of all the *lette*
I have had to write on their account, and all the talking and
walking besides. . . .

Poor Mazzini is again very ill with his cheek—the
swelling has ended in an immense tumour outside—which is
fearful to look at and think of—I went to see him yesterday
the one side of his face looked as sweet and placid as if nothing
ailed the other—but the other ! made me absolutely sick—
with apprehension chiefly—I wish I could bring him here and
nurse him—he is very ill cared for where he is. In fact we are
all of us *you* included in a baddish way—love to my uncle and
the rest— . . . I know I have forgotten a hundred things but
better this than nothing.

Your own
JANE C.

54. *To Jeannie Welsh in Glasgow*

Illness and Babbie's aid—Mazzini ; Dr. Toynbee and the sympathy
of his Association.

Wednesday (*Early July*, 1843)

. . . I must not write you a long letter to-day for I have a
rush of things laying violent claim to my time and faculty,
illustrating for a millionth time the proverb that " it never rains
but it pours "—a few lines, however I *must* send you to bid
you be of good cheer, my dear Babbie—for my displeasure is
only *inverse* affection—and also to tell you that my cold is
quite gone—indeed I am *happy* to have had something sharp
in the way of illness, for I had been going on a great many weeks
with a general feeling of *malaise* which was taking all spirit and
sense out of me, and which I felt could not be got rid of without
a *crisis*. Now I hope to be better than I was before the going to
bed—and do not you fancy that I would be either so forgetful of
my promise or of my own interest as to be either " dying or near
dying " or at all *seriously* ill without telling you, and calling

on you to come and help me though you were at the furthest
end of the kingdom—but I have always an *inner* feeling when
I am *seriously* ill—quite different from that which attends
a passing illness however painful for the time being and I
had none of that *presentiment* on this occasion—I knew that
it was only "*a summing up of many things*" (chiefly moral)
as Mazzini declares his face to be—and that the rest and quiet
of bed would bring me speedily round. Oh dear me, Babbie,
I am very anxious and sorrowful about Mazzini. After many
entreaties he has at last begun to take care—some care of
himself, but God knows whether it be not too late. He went
with Toynbee yesterday to a consultation with Hawkins, the
chief surgeon of St. George's Hospital—who probed the
wound and declared it to be already at *the bone*—and John
Carlyle told me again last Sunday night "that if it reached the
bone nothing could hinder its becoming a cancer"—"Well,"
says Mazzini, "but my dear—*even if it does*—there can still
you know be an operation!" Such comfort! and this he said
to me to-day as calmly as if he had been speaking of a hole in
his coat! He went yesterday and had a tooth drawn by order
of his new surgeon to see if Nature would turn the *matter*
perhaps into that course—and came here to-day all the way from
Queen Square where he now lives! and when I scolded him
for coming, he said "well, but since the tooth was pulled upon
my honour the wound has not discharged anything." I could
not help crying half the time he stayed—he looks so emaciated
and so calm! if his Mother were near or any human being to
nurse him I should not mind so much, but he has nobody but
poor helpless me—helpless because the accursed convention-
alities of this world would make it *disgraceful* to go and nurse
one's dearest friend if he happened to be a young man. A
strange thing took place at *the Association* the other night—so
pathetic and at the same time almost ridiculous. After Mazzini
had made a short speech—pleading his inability to speak more
at one time—a working-man took the chair and moved a
resolution that "Mr. Mazzini should be . . . *laid under
obligation to take care of himself!* his life being not his own but
Italy's property; that *constraint* should be exercised if necessary

L

for his preservation "—the sensible working-man ! And then he proceeded to move the details of his resolution—firstly for instance that if the doctor considered quiet necessary an Italian guard should be in constant attendance at his door to prevent any one passing in to him—etc. etc., and this movement was followed by a deputation of Italian men waiting on Dr. Toynbee to ask what particulars of treatment he wished to have *enforced*. The only comfort is that he *does* now *begin* to feel himself the insanity of neglecting his health to the same extent as formerly—God grant the sense may not have come too late.

I have no spirits to write about anything else after this—besides that I have already written longer than my other botherations left time for—Pray do write a few lines to Mazzini—any kindness always cheers him, poor fellow and the shortest note will be better than none—his address is 4' *Devonshire Street*, *Queen Square*, and for the love of Heaven i you stay longer in Glasgow send me *your* address—don't you see I have to send all my letters round by Liverpool which puts off time—to be sure I might have told you sooner without trusting to your drawing the inference.

Ever yours

J. C.

55. *To Jeannie Welsh*

House-cleaning — Sterling — Plattnauer and Babbie — Mazzini ill-cared for.

This letter is written on four half-sheets of notepaper both grey and white.

(*7th July*, 1843

Oh Babbie ! Would thou wert here to do my hair !—Words cannot paint it Babbie ! *Infernal ?*—that is too mild an epithet by far, for the " hubbub wild and dire dismay ' which I am now actually in the midst of !

[Follows a very full account of the house-cleaning already described in L.M. i. 202, which incidentally proves, as Mr. A

JEANNIE WELSH.
From the portrait by Gambardella in the possession of Miss Chrystal.

Carlyle has pointed out (N.L. i. 110) that Froude has misdated the letter as the 18th instead of the 7th July.]

. . . Most days however, you will be glad to hear, that Sterling brings his carriage and drives me wheresoever I please —I have him in perfect subjection at present. On Wednesday I dined there to meet Charles Barton poor Mrs. John Sterling's brother—he told me that Sterling's phrase of invitation had been " Will you come to me at half after five—that angel dines with me to-day—that Angel of Consolation and Mercy " ! ! !

Last evening I had a quiet walk in Battersea fields with Plattnauer—the only good hour I have passed since Carlyle went away—we talked of " *that sweet girl* " as we often do— that young man improves under my " *angelic ministrations* " —there is an *earnestness* a something of *noble*, of *self-sacrificing* in him now which gives him about the same amount of re- semblance to Cavaignac *spiritually* which I used to find in him *externally*—it is not very *striking*—but still something to be glad of.

Mazzini is still confined to the house with his face but he *professes* to be quite well otherwise—I have not seen him for a week. It always puts me into such a bad humour going there— to see the *mess* in which these wretched Tancionis keep him ; and the silly way in which he submits to be made their *prey* as it were—that I never go except in case of necessity—and last day the sight of his face was a sight to make one dream bad dreams of him for a week after. Had he taken care after the first abatement of the swelling it would have been all well—but he went fussing out day after day on the business of the Italian School and got more cold in it—and then the tumour came outside and burst and had to be lanced—and heaven knows when his face will look as it did—but what cares *he* how it looks ? I wish you would write him a little note of inquiry— he needs all the kind attentions possible from without, his consolations at home are so few !—And now what of *your*self— after all this about *my*self—are the rest gone ? I hope so— for the getting of certain persons fairly off is a devil of a business, as I was fully sensible the last Sunday and Monday morning.

I have no paper—so be thankful for the backs of old notes—love to all that are at home and to Walter—I hope he will soon seek me in my chaos—Bless thee darling of my heart—

Your own
J. C.

56.   *To Jeannie Welsh*

Sympathy ; like that of the Siamese Twins—Painters in the house—A neighbour's precautions against thieves.

(12th July, 1843.)

DEAREST BABBIE,

The sympathy between us continues to be perfect in all respects—both materially and morally—to a degree unprecedented I really believe except in the case of the *Siamese twins !* Unfortunately it is not oftenest sympathy in bliss ! at this moment ?—Oh good Heavens, after all !—The unspeakable is going on in this house !—Every morning at six of the clock a legion of devils rush in under the forms of Carpenters, Painters, whitewashers, and non-descript apprentice-lads who grind, grind, grind, with pumice-stone, and saunter up and down the stairs whistling and singing as if I had hired them to keep me in *music !*—At the first sound of this *Legion* spreading itself over the premises, I spring out of bed—dash down stairs, and " in verra desperation " take a shower-bath !—After which I feel more up to standing the noise—and smell, and hideous discomfort ! I am oil-painting the staircase and passages and the wood of the Library—so you may conceive the smell in this warm weather ! Sterling predicts my *death* in consequence —various persons remonstrate against my staying—above all sleeping—in it—but what can I do ? If I were not here to look after what is a-doing I can see that there would be fifty blunders made—and to leave Helen alone during the night—or to bring any stranger in to keep her company while the house is in such disorder would be equally inexpedient—" death " indeed were to be avoided on any terms and if I saw *that* likely to ensue I would accept a sleeping room in Sterling's house—but by keeping my bedroom door always closed and sleeping with the two windows wide open I do not feel the smell very bad thro' the night—" And *the thieves* Cousin ? two wide-open windows and plenty of ladders lying quite handy in the court underneath them " ?—My dear, when one is painting and papering one's house, one has no time to think of thieves !—It did occur to me last night in lying down, that " heavy bodies " * might drop in thro' the night and be at my pillow before I heard them —but my nerves are pretty strong at present—I took the precaution to lay the Policeman's rattle on the spare pillow—and went to sleep without thinking more about them—a curious contrast to Mr. Lambert next door—father of the young pianists—who sleeps in the back room of the ground floor—" for protection to his house "—he told me—and besides his quick-eared dog has ever in readiness a loaded gun—pistols he says are " worth nothing in such cases." I told him that rather than pass my life in such a state of armed defence, I would adopt Darwin's plan of leaving all the plate &c. every night on the lobby table —I told him also of your screams of delight in seeing " a small cannon " carried into his house last year—and thinking what an unexpected reception the next thieving party was likely to encounter. He laughed himself till the tears ran down but told me " the small cannon " was a small steam engine—he seems to be some sort of military engineer. All this passed between us yesterday morning when in return for an amiable note of regrets about the noise &c. which I had felt it polite to write to him, he came himself to assure me " he had never heard the noise "— and to *offer me* " *his protection* "—(in the virtuous sense of the word of course)—from all he said, he left me with the idea that *he* stood much more in need of *my* protection than I did of *his*.

. . . You tell me *our Walter* was to meet my uncle and the others at *Greenwich ! !* In that case had not I better go too ?— but perhaps you meant Greenock my Dear ? Bless you love —perhaps even in your material *earthquake* you will find more time to write to me than when they were all at home in the usual routine—

Your own
J. C.

* A phrase of Helen's.

57. *To Jeannie Welsh*

Confidential correspondence—The Mudies.

Carlyle, after visiting his friends Redwood and Bishop
Thirlwall in Wales, went on to Liverpool for the last week of
July.   There he was to meet his brother John, and proceed
with him for a further tour in N. Wales.   Thereafter John was
planning to descend upon Cheyne Row, while Carlyle went to
Scotsbrig.

The Father Mathew episode told in L.M. i. 220 is here
omitted.

Sunday forenoon (6th August, 1843).

My own Babbie,

Have you *comprehended* me the least in the world ?
I fear not—I fear that your faith in me, steadfast as it is, must
have received a shock more or less, from this prolonged silence·
If so, now hear " *the solution* " and be sorry for having doubted
a moment.   Babbie I *could* not write to you while my husband
was there, because I could and would and needed to write to
thee more confidentially than to *him* even, and I felt that it
were placing you in an embarrassing predicament to send you
letters which he naturally would wish to see and which you
would not feel at liberty to show him—better—easier and more
prudent to write always straight to himself than to be writing
as it were *for* him *thro'* you or else *for* you to the exclusion of
him.   Not that I have had any mysteries of iniquity to communicate—but all my bits of household troubles—all my
sympathy with *you* in *your* troubles, which with two such
men must have been considerable—all my amusement at their
planlessness—their *lionizing* &c. &c.—all my apprehensions
of having John landed with *me*—all in short of the *intimate little*
things which it came naturally to say to Babbie and to no person
else, all *that* it would have puzzled you to repeat to *them*—and
when I tried to *compose* a letter to you—a letter for the public—
Ach Gott I found it not possible—I have got so into the
way of *splashing* off whatever is on my mind when I write to
you, without forethought or back-thought that I must go on so
if at all, to the end of the chapter—Well ! now the coast is

clear again—and now my Babbie how do you do ? For *me*
I have been but indifferently all last week—Carlyle would
perhaps tell you that I had been to Tunbridge Wells,* and that
feeling out of sorts next day I took an immense dose of shower
bath to enable me to *do* the Kay Shuttleworths. The step
I believe was too energetic—all that cold water drove my cold
not *away* but *in*—and so I have been in a *curious* and rather
wretched state ever since. . . .

. . . I had letters from both Mrs. Paulet and Geraldine
yesterday—full of enchantment over the " angel visit "—and
comprising even John in their *questionable hero-worship :*
" Jeannie looked nice and pretty as she always does "—
Carlyle seems to have been rather charmed with Mrs. Paulet
and not displeased with Geraldine—indeed with all his hatred
of being made a lion of he seems to tolerate those who make
him so marvellously well.

. . . Juliet Mudie goes off to Manchester to-morrow
morning and I have just packed the picture and the frame into
her trunk—to the care of Geraldine who will easily get them
forwarded to you—I do not think they can possibly take any
hurt—wrapped up as they are.

. . . What a quantity of things I still have to tell thee my
Babbie—and see already what a letter—again you perceive I
have had recourse in case of need to the Butcher's book. Write
to me here—if I am in the Isle of Wight the letter will follow
me there—Love to the boys and Walter—

> Your own
> Cousin and Sister and friend.

58. *To Jeannie Welsh*

A bond of sympathy—Needlework—A gift to Darwin—Her portrait
being copied at Manchester.

Thursday (18*th August,* 1843).

My Child,

The sympathy that is between you and me has something of—what shall I say—supernatural in it. Morally and

---

* A one day's visit on July 27, with John Sterling to his aunt, Mrs. Prior.
(M.L. i. 126.)

materially we go on at this distance in the beautifulest fellow-ship of worries—first heart worries that cannot be put on paper—then household-worries from cleanings, &c.—and finally indignant worries with one's maid—during the last week I have been exercising a quantity of philosophy that will never be known or estimated " *here* down," * in merely abstaining from taking a poker and killing Helen for the woe she has brought me.

But to start fair—After I wrote to you last I was really very ill—I did not get over my horrid Ryde expedition so easily as I expected—I had a spell of *headaches* and the most extraordinary aches in my limbs as well making it im-perative on me for one day to keep my bed. Well I had got on foot again, Carlyle had begun to *talk* of coming home—I must wind up my fag ends of radical reform and get in readi-ness for him—and just when I was sitting down to breakfast with a feeling of the necessity of despatch making me rather flighty—says Helen " My !—I was just looking up at the corner of my bed this morning and there ye ken what should I see but two *bogues* (*anglice* bugs !) I hope there's nae mair ! " " Good God " said I " you hope ? It will be a precious affair if you have let bugs into your bed again after the fright you got five years ago ! " And off I ran to investigate with my own eyes—I had *killed* two in the first instant—and on pulling the bed separate I saw—oh heaven and earth plenty of " little *beings* " (as Mazzini would say) moving—I told her so in despair. But now she considered her honour concerned—went and investi-gated after me and returned very angry to tell me " there was not a single *bogue* there—*she* had looked and there was nothing of the sort. . . . "

[Follows the devastating episode told in L.M. i. 240 *seq*. The newly cleaned house was found to be infested with vermin introduced by the carelessness of Helen, who angrily refused to help in the ensuing campaign of destruction.]

So you may figure that when the letters that must be written to the master of the house were written I had little faculty never to speak of time remaining—the idea of his arriving at home after

* Another phrase of Mazzini's.

such a time consumed in brightening the outside of the platter
and finding me in a beastly mess of this sort being an idea that
has chased me all thro' the day and even haunted my dreams.

Surely some time again we shall be at leisure Babby !—It
does not look like it yet— . . .

Your own

JANE C.

The garters ! have never once thanked you for them—Ah—
but they had passed away from me !   Only think, I gave them
to Darwin and said you worked them for him and the poor
man blushed up to the eyes and so will you at hearing of it—
never mind, I put it all to rights; after I told him you had worked
them for me who *cannot* wear that sort and that I could not have
them wasted on anybody *you* did not care for, he declared he
should be delighted to wear them !

.   .   .   .

Just as I was going to seal I bethink me of that eternal
picture—(and I have not a bit of writing paper left)—only
fancy it—when I was thinking that at last you had it safe—for
they were so beautifully packed in wadding—and tied up and
all *sealed*, there comes a note from Geraldine—saying " she had
received from Juliet Mudie a *sealed* parcel for you to her house,
that she knew at once it was my picture—she struggled with her
inclinations for two days—finally she could hold out no longer
but broke the seals and now there *I* was *sitting very like myself*
on the drawing room table ! ! ! "—So much for confession—
the humble request " might she—surely she might get Patten
to make *her* a sketch from it ! "   Considering all the dreadful
trouble she has taken for me about these Mudies I could not
refuse so small a mercy—nor blame her very severely for what
she had done tho' it *was* unjustifiable—So this is why you are
still without it.   Better say nothing to Gambardella of this, he
might chance to take it ill.

59. *To Jeannie Welsh*

Jeannie's letters appreciated—John in the house—His unfortunate
civilities — Carlyle at Dunbar, etc. — Walter Welsh assistant
minister at Auchtertool.

(*About 12th Sept.*, 1843.)

MY BABBIE !

You *are* good, to make apologies to me all the same
when I am your debtor as your creditor ; it is well-judged
moreover ! for *the which* makes in fact no difference in the
impatience with which I look for letters from you and my
disappointment when they do not come. I do not know how
it is ; but I have somehow of late cut the cables of all my
customary habitudes and got far out at sea—drifting before the
wind of circumstance in a rather helpless manner—not that I
am become lazy or indifferent—I was never more full of energy
and *emotion* " *since I kennt the worl* " (as they say in Annandale),
but a Destiny seems to have taken possession of me body and
soul—and orders me this way and that—and thro' *my* head and
hands performs *its* will, without giving me the smallest voice in
any matter. To look at me *in action* you would say that my
whole heart and life was in it—and so it is ; but then there is a
something dominating my heart and life—some mysterious
power which mocks my own volition and forethought. The
results are good so far—useful—contributory to " the greatest
happiness of the greatest number "—" never," says Bishop
Terrot, " have I seen anyone so *improved in amicability* as you
are !—Why you seem to aim at superseding Providence on the
face of the earth ! " Letters come to me commencing with
" *ange tutelaire* " and such like recognitions of my practical
helpfulness—and then my zeal and superhuman success in the
rehabilitation of my house makes me pass for the model of
wives—and all the while Babbie—between ourselves hang me
if I have the slightest natural bias either to the career of *benevolence* or of *notableness* !—Neither do I wish to *act* either of
these *rôles*—I tell you they are *put upon me* by some superior
power and I go thro' with them like a person in the magnetic

state doing the bidding of his magnetiser—with a vague, internal, spell-bound protest which goes for nothing.

But I should like much better to talk to you of all this than to write about it. The only direction in which I seem to have got myself put out lately—in any thing like a voluntary spontaneous way has been, in revolting every day and hour of the last week against the infliction of John ! *—Of course I do not mean that I *openly* quarrel with him—in Carlyle's absence *that* would be a sad impropriety—but I concentrate all my forces into a position of grim impassivity, which any power of teasing and boring except his own would *échouer* against. There is something so irritating at the very outset in having a man fix himself down in your house—palpably for *its* sake not yours —so that his material wants be all supplied—it is no matter by *whom*—nay one would say that he considered the act of administering to *his* wants like virtue its own reward !—for he will sit morning after morning munching away at his break- fast and gazing into vacancy without once addressing me as if I were the Chinese figure that one sees in some of the tea-shop windows ! "The Devil fly away with him " for having come to hand before my husband returned. I should have been glad to have had my new house hanselled by *him*—rather than this other who makes *confusion* wherever he be—and I *should* have liked after so long an absence to have been a day or two with *himself* in peace and reason—but John's peculiar talent, as I have long known, is to be " *toujours hors de propos* " † so there is no help for it. In his attempts at being civil even—" few and far between," this *hors de proposness* discloses itself. Just *one* such attempt has he made since his return—On Thursday last I was feeling particularly knocked up—and just on Thursday and on no other day he *would* have me to go out somewhere with him. " I lived too quietly," he said, " I should go out more and *see things* "—" it would be good for me to go that evening to the Surrey zoological gardens "—I refused at first on the score of

* " Never one of the quietest men in this house." (T. C., L.M. i. 256. She speaks to T. C. of John's " self-conceit," 259.)

† " Like Mademoiselle de l'Espinasse, *son talent est d'être toujours hors de propos*." To T. C. on August 31, in expectation of John's arrival. (L.M. i. 256).

being too weak—but as he continued to press me I yielded at
last merely to show a disposition to receive anything so unwonted as a courtesy from *him !* He told me the place was
" close by Vauxhall " to which we were to go in the steamboat—
it was at least two miles beyond Vauxhall—when I was breaking
down however Providence sent a stray cab to my aid. The
gardens we finally reached and there I " saw things " with a
vengeance ! You may fancy how he would lead one this way
and that, backwards and forwards, to this and the other beast
and bird—and tell me its name and properties over and over and
over again—in an hour I was half dead with it and declared if he
did not let me sit down on a seat that presented itself I should
certainly faint—" Much better come this way—there was
something well worth seeing farther on—one might find a better
seat than that "—so I dragged after him till we came in view
of the *grand wonder* of these gardens, " the Indian City of
Ellora " all *done* into pasteboard, as large as life, and shone on
by the *real* moon ! " And it was nothing now," he told me,
" in comparison with what it would be by and by "—and he
handed me a bill by which it appeared that at half after *eight*
o'clock (observe it was then only half after five) *the Indian City
of Ellora* would be " all lighted up with *fire* "—there would
be *fire* in the caves in the palaces—" *jet d'eaus of fire* (as the bill
had it) from the Lake "—*fire*-dragons—" A sacrifice to the
Spirit of Fire "—" Brilliant Apotheosis of the Fire-God "—
&c., &c.—So much *fire* that my poor head *took fire* at the bare
thought of it !—and when in addition I found it was to be
waited for *three hours ;* a sacred horror crept over my heart
and I felt for the moment that my whole happiness here and
hereafter depended on my getting away from that place
without an instant's delay !—John protested, argued against
" the stupidity of going back without having seen what I had
come for "—God is my witness that I knew no more *what* I
had " come for " than the Babe unborn ! Away I came anyhow
and mercifully was *just in time* for the last steamboat—he had
no scheme for getting me home *the seven miles*, had we stayed !—
there was no cabstand, no omnibuses—and for this tremendous
adventure he had chosen just a day when I was pale as a ghost

and to the outward eye even more than usually *suffering*. Of course I had to go to bed quite ill—having realized a cruel head-ache—and when I was taking off my clothes he knocked at my door and proposed that I should come upstairs and look thro' his telescope at the four moons of Jupiter ! ! "A chance when I should see them to such advantage again ! "—"Oh," I thought, "if *you* were in one of them !—or *quartered* into the four ! "

How much more insupportable is that inveterate egotism which has absolutely lost all sense of other people's feelings than a good downright, spirited vice ! If Helensburgh were not in Scotland I should long so much to fly away to you all ! your letter gives me such a feeling of a place all sunshiny and hearts all sunshiny. Next year—if we live to see it I have a scheme for a *grande réunion* at the Isle of Wight—I even looked after *a house* for my uncle there !—I believe the *place* would be charming under ordinary circumstances—and so accessible !

Carlyle is to be home on Friday I expect. He has been to Haddington (!) and Kirkaldy * and is now off to Thomas Erskine at Dundee !—It was very strange for me getting a letter from him dated Haddington. He went there for the sake of a *battle field of Oliver Cromwell's* at Dunbar—whither he *walked*— (eleven miles and back again) spending two nights with the Donaldsons at Sunny Bank. He was at Thornhill too by my desire—much against his own feeling—he saw old Mary and Margaret and the Russells.† He has seen all that remains for me in Scotland—two graves—I do not know what good it does me that *he* should have been there—at Crawford and at Haddington —but I am pleased to have as it were sent a message to them since I want force to go myself. Oh Babbie I am horribly sad always at the bottom of my heart—my external life is all smoothed over again, and flows on noiselessly enough—but underneath ! Happily the world troubles itself little what we have *deep down*—and the thing to be chiefly guarded against in

* So spelt invariably by Mrs. Carlyle.

† Friendship with Mrs. Russell (formerly Miss Dobbie, see p. 10), wife of Dr. Russell of Thornhill, began in Craigenputtock days. Through her devotion to Mrs. Welsh at Templand, she became Mrs. Carlyle's most intimate and dearly loved friend, by whom she sent yearly gifts of remembrance to her mother's old servants, such as Mary Mills and Margaret Hiddlestone.

suffering is plaguing one's fellow creatures with one's individual griefs.

Carlyle rode over to Walter's and found not only Walter but his Landlady gone—he brought down Mr. Fergus's pony and peeled one of its knees and bruised his own ankles and wrists in the business ! . . .

How very glad I am to hear such good accounts of my uncle—a dozen kisses to him—and love to all the rest—I do not forget that I owe Helen a letter—bless you my child ever

Your affectionate

Jane Carlyle.

60.   To Jeannie Welsh

Reaction after activity—German novels—London deserted—Carlyle returns out-of-sorts—Earthquake on earthquake in the newly decorated house—Babbie's health.

(*2nd Oct.*, 1843.)

D'abord, you are an angelical Babbie, to make me never a reproach for my silence—never a reproach for anything ! I am sufficiently conscious, without being told, of the imperfection of my actual manner of being, but I console myself with the reflection that, if not *inevitable* absolutely, it is at all rates the *very natural* reaction against the outrageous activity and universal benevolence which I have been carrying on for the last two or three months.

My husband has been returned this fortnight back, and since then I have not written to you—have not written to anyone— have not *done* anything except occasionally mend my stockings and read in the dreamy novels by the Gräfin Hahn Hahn (Countess Cock cock ! What a name !) She is a sort of German George Sand *without the genius*—and *en revanche* a good deal more of what we call in Scotland *gumtion*—a clever woman, really—separated from her husband of course, and on the whole very good to read when one is in a state of moral and physical collapse. For the rest nothing can exceed this great City in these weeks, for absence of all earthly objects of interest ! Even Darwin has been gone for a month !—the last to go. But I had the pleasure of meeting him yesterday in Cadogan Place, having returned the night before. To give you the most striking illustration that occurs to me of the desert state of things ; I saw the other day a little girl of six years old playing her hoop in the centre of Piccadilly ! ! A cab *did* come at last and as nearly as possible ran over her—but skipping from under the horse's belly, literally, she recommenced her hoop-playing, with the same assiduity as before. And within doors is not a whit more gay I can assure you than without. Carlyle returned, as usual from his journeyings in quest of health, as bilious and out of sorts as he went away. Blue pill with castor oil " and the usual trimmings " had to be taken at the very outset, then by the time the distress of *that* was over it was time to be feeling the intolerable influences of—London !

The house was approved of as much as I had flattered myself it would be—and between ourselves he would have been a monster if he had not exhibited some admiration more or less at my magnificent improvements effected at such small cost— *to him*. The upstairs room is now a really beautiful little drawing room with a sofa—easy chair—ottoman—cushions— stools—every conceivable luxury !—all covered—and all the chairs covered also—with a buff and red chintz made by my own hands ! ! ! Mrs. Carlyle's picture is over the mantel- piece—but then yours and my uncle's are on the mid wall with Jean Paul between—and you cannot think how beautiful you both look on the pretty new paper.

All this and his own bedroom new carpeted and smartened up amazingly—to say nothing of the old big press in the china closet transformed by the female genius into a glorious re- splendent Chinese-cabinet ! could not fail to yield him " a certain " satisfaction and obtain me some meed of praise—but —also alas—never can one get out of the shadow of that *but !*— but after two or three days he began to find " there was no getting on in that upstairs room for want of the closet or some equivalent to fling one's confusion in " ! !—" best to accumulate no confusion " said I—" Oh there must be a place for keeping all sorts of papers for *a year* or so, till one has made up one's mind what to burn and what not " ! This was a first ground for quarrel with the room—and then—oh then—one day when he had been home about [a] week Miss Lambert took a fit of playing—the *first*—but that only made it more intolerable—for he had fallen into a false security through her prolonged silence. The next day again she played half an hour in the morning which was sufficient to set all his nerves up for the rest of the day—and it was solemnly declared that " no life of Cromwell or any other book could ever be written alongside of that damnable noise." Then Mr. Chancellor's cock had awoke him, he said, at six for two mornings, (he had not however come down to breakfast till ten) and " that bedroom was uninhabitable "—" Could one get a piece of ground to build some *crib of a* house upon at the Isle of Wight, did I think ? "—In fact just all the old eternal story commenced again !—I must fetch back Pearson to *consult* about the possibility of excluding noise—etc., etc., in the meanwhile.

Accordingly Pearson was here yesterday—kept in consultation for *three* hours ! the whole result being plenty of *possibilities*—and a positive order for a pair of window boards to be all stuffed with cotton ! to fasten on the back windows or the front (viz. in *your* room) at pleasure—and as these will prevent the sleeping with windows *open*, zinc pipes are to be introduced thro' the walls to let in a sufficiency of fresh air ! You are to observe by the way that it is only when the windows are wide open that this distant cock ever makes itself heard and—that the simple expedient which Pearson suggested— of *shutting the window* and *opening the door* would have solved the problem effectively and much more cheaply than all this apparatus of stuffed shutters and zinc pipes ! But then if the shutting make even the front room quiet enough for *him* to sleep in—and the zinc pipe brings in air enough for *him* to breathe ; the piano-problem is also solved ! for his present bedroom where alone the piano-noise is not clearly audible, is to be converted into his study—the partition taken down between the two front rooms, that the *two* four-posted beds may have room to stand up *there !* Until we can get a lease of the house (which is not procurable) and then a *silent* room, *twenty feet long, lighted from above*, is to be built on the roof ! ! ! *—

* This silent room was actually built in September, 1853.

So here is a quite other prospect than that of quiet order which I was looking forward to for the next twelve months at least ! And I assure you it is with a heart-rending sigh that I resign myself to the thought of lifting and altering all the carpets again, before they have been well down, and having carpenters plasterers and white-washers as before, besides the inconvenience of having one's spare room as it were annihilated—for could *you* for instance sleep in a double-bedded room with Carlyle ? However there may be many plans before the definite one gets *carried into effect*—and anyhow I cannot help it—and at least as Darwin says I " have always the consolation of knowing that he will need some *new* arrangements in six months or so ! "—But indeed Babbie if you saw how pretty the upstairs floor is in its actual state and knew all the toil and scheming I had in bringing it into such order you would not wonder that I am fretted. Your room too with the blue carpet from his bedroom (his had got the drawing room one) and the position of the bed altered looked so like the Templand bedroom —all the little things in it arranged as they were *there*—that one could almost deceive oneself into its being the same—and all this to be overturned. Well well, I cannot help it and what *is* the use of talking—*such* woes are but very petty ones after all !

My darling I wonder how you *really* are—I get the most thorough conviction from your letters that you are in one of two states—either much better in health than ever you have been *since I knew you* or—in the preparatory stage of a severe illness. God grant the former may be the truth—but when I consider how certainly all this new-found activity—all this sensibility to natural objects—in fact all this development of *gass in the blood* would in my own case be symptomatic of approaching illness, I cannot be quite easy about you.

How strange it is for me to fancy you all in Scotland—my uncle in Edin. !—strange and sad—I feel so as if I should be there too—to welcome you—and yet I would not be there for the world. . . . Give Helen a hearty kiss for me—and tell her that I love her all the same as if I were writing to her every day—I will never as long as I live forget her kind and considerate management for me under circumstances in which

M

and readjusted the things and to-day I have nailed down all the stair and passage carpets—at last.   There is still a good piece of work for me in the front bedroom which will be all the fitter for your and our visitors' reception in consequence of what it has undergone—but if he had only allowed me to do these things when I was about it in the summer it would have spared a world of fash—and such a sickening feeling towards household good ! ! as I do not remember ever in my life before to have experienced.   I am physically ill of the long continued discomfort and the cinderella labours in which I have had to put forth the activity of a maid of all-work—along with improvisation and inventive faculty of a woman of genius.

The fact is I have spoiled Mr. C.—I have accustomed him to have all wants supplied " without visible means " until he has forgotten how much head and hands it takes to supply the common resource of a good round outlay of money.   When one had not any money—it was all well—I never grudged my work—but now that we have enough to live on it would be good sense in him to say " get in a carpenter to nail your carpets " and a few other such considerate suggestions—no matter.   I shall get my hands kept clean and put into mitts for a time so soon as I have patched together a carpet for the new bedroom— and will lie on the sofa by heaven for two weeks and read French novels !

It was not that I was so *eternally* in motion from morning till night that I could not write to you—one can always find a half hour during which it is possible to sit still if one looks for it, but my temper was so bad that I could not compose it to write even to you—and as I have said my health has been bad as well as my temper—indeed these two things with me pretty invariably go with one another.

I will tell you of all the rest—that is about people &c. &c. next time.   Write you little false hearted gipsy.   Love to them all

Ever your affectionate

JANE CARLYLE.

62. *To Jeannie Welsh*

The aftermath of a double " earthquake "—The piano players
finally quelled—John in lodgings—C.'s irritability under
" Cromwell."

Sunday (12th Nov., 1843).

OH MY OWN BABBIE,

An hour's talk with you were " welcome as flowers
in May "—or what were a more delicious novelty surely—tho'
no one says it—as flowers in *December !* Why the devil then
do I not write more diligently if I feel such need of talking—
to write is to speak after a sort—ay—but " with the reciprocity
all on *one* side " and that makes such an irksome difference !—
and another difference is that one cannot in writing eke out one's
words with tones of the voice—looks—gestures—an occasional
groan—an occasional kiss ! and speech reduced to bare words
is so inadequate for certain " *beings* "—like *me* ! Besides
talking comes *natural* to every woman—*writing* is an *acquire-
ment*—and between the exercise of one's natural and one's
acquired faculties there is no comparison in point of ease !
And oh if you knew what a grand object one's *ease* becomes for
one ; when there is absolutely *no ease* to be had for love or
money. It *may* be an egoistical exaggeration but I cannot help
thinking that I have been of late months one of the most *worried*
of modern wives. I do not mean the most *ill-used* by men or
things—thank Heaven no !—I have always the " consolation "
which " *No.* 3 " found so efficacious under the death of her
lover that " she knew several women who had been still more
afflicted by Providence than herself ! "—but I say the most
worried—the most teased with petty annoyances—not one of
which *singly* would seem worth the consideration of the
philosophic mind, but such an accumulation of them, like the
packthreads of the Lilliputians, induces " a certain " desperation ! Nor do I foresee when the worry will get itself fairly
ended—any more than when *the Life of Cromwell* will get itself
fairly begun ! All that has been done—and *that* is not little—
has not yet cleared away the *material* impediments to writing.
The little study at the top of the house with its wee curiosity

of a grate—with the writing table transferred to it—with a cast of Oliver Cromwell's face—taken after death—fixed up on the wall—is *admitted* to be "*warm—light—*and as *silent* as the heart of man can desire" *but* "it is an abominable confined hole of a place"—"one cannot have one's books about one there—one spends half one's time in running between it and the Library"—and then "*the paper* is a perfect solecism! it would need to be new *papered* in some reasonable way before one could feel it anything but the *last refuge of a poor reduced beggar!!*" "Well then let it be new papered!" "Oh no—that will have to lie over till *you* can get it done when *I* am away somewhere." In fact the cruelty of having no place in which a man can write is the burden of his morning and evening song—and the nice Library is only an eternal source of lamentation—"such a large comfortable room rendered perfectly uninhabitable by an accursed pianoforte!" And so we move up and down thro' the house—trying ourselves there and then trying it here—and nowhere can any adjustment be effected—a sort of domestic *wandering Jew* he is become!—

A gleam of hope has arisen for us since last night that it may finally be rendered possible for him to fix himself in the Library. The piano to say the truth has been nothing like so deadly as it was in the beginning. Ever since the protest was sent in, the Misses Lambert have testified a certain respect for our feelings, *trying*—with more or less success—to abstain from playing till two o'clock—which was the compromise he proposed to make with them. But they seem tempted as often as they pass the seductive "instrument" to tinkle out of it a *few* "*town*-notes wild" or run over a scale or two just as if in saying to themselves "*le bon temps viendra!*" If he had the confidence which results to most of us from repeated experience—he would rely on it by this time that their passion would lead them into no further excesses and could hardly feel disturbed by such transient aberrations. But he has an inveterate tendency that poor man, always to *hope the worst*—and so if "the accursed *thing*" sounds at all, he expects that it will go on sounding for hours, and when it terminates he expects that it will presently recommence—thus it is *fear* of the piano more than *the piano* that drives him into the " beggar's refuge " up stairs.   During a week however—they have scarcely except on Wednesday (lesson day) *committed any nuisance* before the appointed hour —not I believe that they have been more self-sacrificing than usual, but that they have been making more morning visits.

However it might be, a bright thought struck Carlyle that he would take this plausible moment for sending Miss Lambert a copy of his last book with a pretty letter of thanks for the attention she was showing to his wishes and an eloquent entreaty that she would go on with the same observance of the two o'clock system during his present labours.   To be such a single hearted man, he *can* word such things with a delicacy, an insinuating poetry of expression sure to reach the heart of a plump young damsel like Miss Lambert !—and so the same evening brought a note from her as ecstatic as his own —promising implicit observance.   I will enclose it here that you may see the foundation of the hope of a *settlement* which I said had dawned on our minds since last night.   The " *love* to Mrs. Carlyle " indicates a young lady still in the first enthusiasm of her faith in human nature !   She has spoken with Mrs. Carlyle just twice on this planet—one day the two sisters found me in a shoe shop, rushed up to me, as if minded to embrace me and decidedly—but it went no further than a shaking of hands—owing to my backwardness who in the darkness of the shop and the dazzle produced by their painted velvet scarves—could not at first tell the least in the world whom it was I was transacting even the lesser ceremony of shaking hands with.   " It was such a long time," they said, " since they had been dying to speak to me !—*Would* I call for them ? they should be so delighted ! "   I promised anything to get my boots fitted on in peace—but when it came to per-formance, as Homer says " terrible was the thought to me ! "—Determined to carry their point however about a week after finding I did not call on them they " took the *Initiative* " and called on *me*—fine *healthy chatty* girls !—I left a card for them one day in passing—*having seen them go out a little while before*—this is all the passages of friendship that have taken place betwixt us—a slender groundwork for *love* !   However I will accept

their love and even *do the impossible* to reciprocate it if they will
only be quiet in the mornings. Considering the clatter I make
about my troubles it is odd—is it not ? that I should not be
more liberal of *thanksgiving* when any of them is removed. I
have reflected several times with wonder at my own forget-
fulness that I had always in writing to you forgotten to say
a word to you of the blessed deliverance from John. He
established himself in a lodging near Gambardella's on the
morning of the day when Carlyle was to return from Scotland.
Plainly Carlyle and he had been getting on very badly together at
Scotsbrig, and he made it a point of honour to be in *a place of
his own* when they should meet again—for he never seemed to
think of any change till Carlyle had fixed his day—*me* he seemed
to consider as there entirely for his convenience so long as he
pleased—which I was glad of on the whole—for ill as I liked to
have him I should have liked worse had he taken such a grand
step during *my* incumbency. As it was ; Carlyle saw in his
sudden removal " a natural shame of facing *him* again on that
absurd principle after all his magnanimous assertions of being
able to manage his own life without help or advice from
anyone "—and was moreover heartily glad to find the coast
clear—for he did not know any more than I had done how
another spell of him in his actual *distracted* state was to have been
endured. He comes here very seldom—and never stays long—
flaps about in the old fashion among indifferent people—seems
to me a very absurd figure in God's working world—but
so long as he keeps his absurdity so well out of our road we have
no business to interfere with him. If he does not choose to
practise his profession or do any but study his own bachelor
comforts and *eat the dinners which Carlyle declines*—for that
seems to be the principle on which he is invited out—" since
we cannot get Carlyle we may always have his *brother*," one may
regret that a man of some talent—and certainly without any *vice*
should so waste himself—but he is not a child that he should
be lectured for it—so enough of him.

I had a nice letter from Maggie the other day for which I
was duly thankful—Pray do write to me oftener when you are
at home again. This winter is going to be for me what I

predicted the last would be and was not—a time of dreadful
tribulation with that book.   Already he is beginning to get up
and smoke during the nights and his irritability and unsettled-
ness in that state of nerves is something that cannot be figured
but by those who have witnessed it.   However I hope I am
more *seasoned* now than I was during the writing of *the French
Revolution*—thank God, tho' we have now our November fogs
and the air is intensely cold I keep free of coughs hitherto and
can come down to breakfast *at any hour*—neither have I any
pain in my side—but *well?*   Ach Gott, that were too much
to ask ! bad nights and a continual malaise thro' the day keep
my spirits in a state of depression which the less that I say or
think about the better.

. . . Oh I have plenty more to say—but there is enough
for one time—Bless you my good Babbie—love and a kiss to
Helen—

Ever your affectionate

J. C.

63.   *To Helen Welsh*

Babbie's delays in writing—Illness; Carlyle's engrossment in Cromwell—Different kinds of writing—Caricatures of Geraldine—
The Mudies—Gambardella—Old Sterling improves.

Friday (early Dec., 1843).

DEAREST HELEN,

I will try *you* with a letter this time and see whether
you will not have the grace to answer, a thought sooner than that
little villainous Babbie has answered my last !—She is sure that
" my kind heart will find excuses for her "—the pretty phrase !
—the insinuating faithless Babbie !—My *kind heart* you may
say feels flattered by her good opinion, but has too much rational
work laid out for it, that it should dream of expanding itself in
quixotisms like that !   Far from finding excuses for *her*, I find
in her shortcomings excuses for all *my own* shortcomings of a
similar sort, past present and to come !   I say to myself with the
mild injured self-dignity of a Pecksniff, " when *I* fail in writing
it is because I am sick, or because I am over-worked or because
(as Edward Irving once wrote to me) ' the Lord has other views

with his servant, than that he should write so many letters of
human love as in the bygone time ' " !—it is never because I am
amusing myself—the fact being that *I* never amuse myself by
any chance !—moi !

I daresay however I should not be so implacable were it not
that I have been feeling so horribly in need of letters just at
the particular time thro' which Babbie's have failed me. For
I have been quite ill for a week or two—with that anomalous
thing which to save trouble we call Influenza—and you who have
always lived in a family can have no notion what a dreary thing
it is to lie all day in bed with no company but one's own, which
is little better than a death's head under such circumstances.
About *thrice* a day—on the average—Carlyle pops in his head
between the curtains and asks firstly " how are you now,
Jane ? " Secondly ; " have you had anything to eat ? "
Thirdly, " you are not thinking of getting up yet ? "—then off
to his Cromwell in which he lives, moves, and has his being at
present—as is always the way with him when he is writing
a book. Oh dear me, if all book writers took up the business
as he does, fidgeting and flurrying about all the while like a hen
in the distraction of laying its first egg, and writing down every
word as with his heart's blood ;—what a world of printed
nonsense would be spared to a long suffering public ! What a
host of *distinguished* Mr.'s and Mrs.'s and Misses would to the
great relief of Society be eating their victuals in resigned
obscurity !—Harriet Martineau used to talk of *writing* being
such a *pleasure* to her. In this house we should as soon dream
of calling the bearing of children " *such* a pleasure "—but
betwixt *writing* and *writing* there is a difference, as betwixt
the ease with which a butterfly is born into the world and the
pangs that attend a man-child ! Well ! the Cromwell will be
got fairly under way by and by ! and in fulness of time will by
God's blessing be got on the shelf. And meanwhile I am
recovered from my Influenza as well perhaps without any
making of as with it.

I had a precious batch of caricatures from Mrs. Paulet
lately professing to be " *illustrations of Miss Jewsbury's late
matrimonial speculation* "—in my life I have seen none cleverer,

they would have made old Petrucci himself " in the character
of *Heraclitus* " (vide Babbie) burst into laughter !—They
were sent at Geraldine's own request—which was infinitely
creditable to her good-nature—for a more absurd little *tick*
of a creature than she is represented thro'out never figured in
truth or fiction.   I will ask Mrs. Paulet to let me show them to
you—but she charged me " to keep them from all stranger
eyes "—she lives always in a dreadful *apprehension of consequences*,
that dear woman, which is odd in a person who nevertheless
seems not to conform to les règles in any one particular.
Geraldine had been staying there and is now gone back to
Manchester—she writes to me with an assiduity and disinterestedness that verge on the superhuman. I do not
remember whether I told Babbie that one of my *Mudies*, the
one last despatched, had been returned on our hands as wholly
inapplicable to any practical purpose—the drop which made
the cup of her Mistress's anger overflow was her having sewed
a *black* apron with *white* thread—whereupon her Mistress
remonstrated " very mildly " and the young person " threw
herself on the kitchen floor and kicked and screamed "—of
course her immediate dismissal was the result. The other
(Juliet) is conducting herself to one's heart's content. Her
Mistress, a Mrs. Hervey of Strangeways Hall (?), wrote me a
very pleasant and pleased letter about her some weeks ago—
so that one saved is all the percentage out of this destitute
family which Christian benevolence has to congratulate itself
upon—I am told it is as much as Christian benevolence usually
gets.

I do not hear a word of Gambardella—I suppose he never
goes to Maryland Street which proves decidedly that he is not
in " a state of grace." A pity !—one of those heaps of excellent
good bricks which one sees here and there on this earth which
for want of some sort of lime to build them together remain to
the end of the chapter—*rubbish !*

But here is the Sterling carriage come to take me a drive—
it seems kept up just now more for my use than anyone else's,
that dainty little *Brougham !*—And the old fellow himself has
mended his manners lately—indeed there was only one day he

expanded into such a munificence that I feared he was going to die ! only think of his buying me in one shop a packet of wax lights (which by the way I put in the pocket of his carriage and saw no more of) and a few minutes after at Howell & James's a couple of guinea pocket handkerchiefs !—a windfall really to *me* who never had a *dress*-pocket handkerchief in life except the little beauty that was given me by *you*.   And then he took me home by *Grange's* * (vide Babbie again) and gave me hot jelly and cake and the offer of cherry bounce ! but I *must* go—a kiss to you dear and to my still dear tho' reprehensible Babbie.

Ever your affectionate,

J. CARLYLE.

64.   *To John Welsh, Esq.   Me's Uncle*

On keeping Christmas—Dickens' *Christmas Carol*—An ingenious matchbox and extinguisher (*cb*. N.L. i. 133).

A pair of these same extinguishers was sent to Mrs. Russell of Thornhill ; it is curious to compare the description here with that in N.L. i. 133 : the same ideas and humours, but with, often, a different turn of phrase as they are dashed off.

Father Mathew, a great apostle of temperance.

(23rd Dec., 1843.)

MY DEAREST UNCLE,

It is not everyone that can *keep the Christmas* after the most approved fashion ;—in gormandizing over roast-beef and plumpudding, and defying Father Mathew in bumpers. For some of us the Drs. prescribe to " eat *abstemiously* " and to " drink *not at all* " while for others, " poverty, penury, needcessity and want " (as the Scotch preacher had it) enforce the same or a still severer discipline.   I fancy you and little *me* will dine on Christmas-day with the usual simplicity ; at least I am sure we ought *to* !   And should Mirth even dance on the crown of its head round about us, I do not see that *we* need be unusually *merry*, nor indeed how we could manage to be so if there *were* need—either you or I, dear Uncle !   It is all very well for those who are still young and hopeful to " *put up* the

---

* Cp. L.M. i. 269.   Grange's was the Gunter's of the period.

Christmas " and keep it *merry*, and go jigging out the old year into the new one, as if they were playing at blind man's buff ! But when one is arrived at *this* with one's life ; to be pretty certain beforehand that new-years will " come with *the rake* and not with *the shule* " and to be morally certain that, whatever they come with, not all their best possible bringings can compensate for what the old years have taken away from one— *then*, it is not with *mirth* that one can welcome the new year any more ! One may still *welcome* it as of God's sending,—as another year of *life* at all events, and " while there is life there is hope "—of one sort or other. But there is no use in pretending to be *merry* over it or indeed other than very sad ! Is it not so, dear Uncle ? *You* will not call me *unsocial*, " *misanthropic*," and the like, because " *I*, as *one* solitary individual " (my husband's favourite expression) prefer to remain quietly by my own fireside on the Christmas-day, and all such days ; keeping them, not *merry* but *holy*—in the silence of my own thoughts, with *all* whom I have loved on this earth for company, instead of *one* little, noisy party ! Whether far or near, living or dead, infinite Thought can bring them all round me to give my new year their blessing ! but for this I should break my heart in looking round me on the actual, and missing so much that has been !

My husband sends you the last literary novelty—a Christmas-*Carol*, no less !—It is really a kind-hearted, almost poetical little thing, well worth any Lady or gentleman's perusal— somewhat too much imbued with the Cockney-admiration of *The Eatable*, but as Dickens writes for " the greatest happiness of the greatest number " (of Cockneys) he could not be expected to gainsay their taste in that particular.

I also have a book to send you but I am afraid not by this parcel, the bookseller having " failed in his truth "—if it do not come in time to-day however you shall get it on new year's day. At all events behold a match-box of the latest pattern and of course out of sight the best ! the force of improvement one would say could no further go ! but we shall see ! You draw the matches against a side of their little cell in pulling them out and they come forth *lighted* without more ado—and in this state of separation they do not contract damp—which has been the ruin of so many matches. When the box needs to be replenished you open it *at the bottom*—and put the matches in with the un-brimstoned end foremost. This for the *production* of light—for the contrary purpose behold a *Nun* and *a Jesuit* hollowed out into *extinguishers ! !* Whether this novelty, which is having " a great success," indicates a growing favour for Catholicism, or a certain burlesque of it—whether the inventor be a *Puseyite* or *Anti-puseyite* or *what* he be, I can form no positive theory. " *The new extinguisher* " is plainly enough " significative of much " ! but of *what ?* " God knows " (as the universal Cockney answer runs). It is no easy matter to read in the deep brain of a Cockney-Inventor, especially when he commits himself to the sphere of the " *Symbolical* " ! He wanders in *Idea* through the whole universe of things at his own sweet will—collects, combines, confounds, with such a glorious indifference to fitness, probability and common-sense, and such a stoical disregard of *consequences ;* that one stands amazed before him and his works " as in presence of the Infinite " !

But oh my dear Uncle I am hard up for time, and I wont write to you a great deal longer ! Take twenty or even a hundred kisses to make up the difference between my wishes and my inability—And God send you a *good* New Year !

Your ever affectionate
JANE WELSH CARLYLE.

65. *To Jeannie Welsh*

Improvised dinner parties—Nina Macready's birthday party—
Dickens as conjurer—A dance with Forster—The pleasantest
company according to Burns.

Thursday (23rd *Dec.*, 1843).

A thousand thanks my darling for your long good Christmas letter and also for the *prospective foot-stools*, anything like a *worthy* answer you have small chance of getting from me to-day or any day *this* week. I have just had to swallow a bumper of my uncle's Madeira (which *is* capital drink !) to nerve me for writing at all ! A huge boxful of dead animals from the Welshman * arriving late on Saturday night together with the visions of *Scrooge*—had so worked on Carlyle's nervous organization that he has been seized with a perfect *convulsion* of hospitality, and has actually insisted on *improvising two* dinner parties with only a day between—now the *improvisation* of dinner parties is all very well for the parties who have to *eat* them simply, but for those who have to *organise* them and *help to cook them c'est autre chose ma chère !* I do not remember that I have ever sustained a moment of greater embarrassment in life than yesterday when Helen suggested to me that *I* had better *stuff the turkey*—as she had *forgotten* all about it ! *I* had never *known* " about it " ! but as I make it a rule never to exhibit *ignorance* on *any* subject " *devant les domestiques* " for fear of losing their respect—I proceeded to *stuff* the turkey with the same air of calm self dependence with which I told her some time ago, when she applied to me, the whole history of the Scotch free-church dissensions—which up to this hour I have never been able to *take in !* " Fortune favours the brave "— the *stuffing* proved pleasanter to the taste than any stuffing I ever remember to have eaten—perhaps it was made with quite new ingredients !—I do not know ! Yesterday I had hare soup —*the* Turkey—stewed mutton—a bread pudding and mince-pies—with Mrs. Allan Cunningham, Miss Cunningham—and Major Burns (son of the Poet) to eat thereof. On Monday hare soup—roasted *Welsh* mutton, stewed beef, ditto pudding, ditto pies—with Robertson, and John Carlyle, and *the disappointment* of Darwin—and all *that* day, to add to my difficulties, I had a headache—so bad that I should have been in bed if I had not had to stay up to help Helen—whose faculties get rusted by disuse. On Tuesday evening I was engaged to assist at Nina Macready's birthday party—but felt so little up to gaieties on the Monday that I had resolved to send an apology *as usual* when voilà—on the morning of the appointed day arrives a note from Mrs. Macready *imploring* me almost with tears in its eyes not to disappoint her and her " poor little daughter " by sending an apology—that a well aired *bed* was

* Mr. Redwood.

prepared for me &c. &c.—this forestalling of my cruel purpose was successful—I felt that I *must* go *for once*—so after spending the day in writing—not to *you*—but to people who, not having the reason you have to believe in my love, needed more than you to have a visible sign from me—I dressed myself and sat down to await *the fly*—" my dear," says Carlyle, " I think I never saw you look more bilious ; your face is *green* and your eyes all *blood-shot !* " fine comfort when one was about to make a public appearance ! " the first time this season." In fact I was very ill—had been *off* my sleep for a week and felt as if this night must almost finish me. But little does one know in this world what will *finish* them or what will *set them up* again. I question if a long course of mercury would have acted so beneficially on my liver as this party which I had gone to with a sacred shudder ! But then it was the *very* most agreeable party that ever I was at in London—everybody there seemed animated with one purpose to make up to Mrs. Macready and her children for the absence of " the Tragic Actor " and so amiable a purpose produced the most joyous results. Dickens and Forster above all exerted themselves till the perspiration was pouring down and they seemed *drunk* with their efforts ! Only think of that excellent Dickens playing the *conjuror* for one whole hour—the *best* conjuror I ever saw—(and I have paid money to see several)—and Forster acting as his servant. This part of the entertainment concluded with a plum pudding made out of raw flour, raw eggs—all the raw usual ingredients—boiled in a gentleman's hat—and tumbled out reeking—all in one minute before the eyes of the astonished children and astonished grown people ! that trick—and his other of changing ladies' pocket handkerchiefs into comfits—and a box full of bran into a box full of—a live guinea-pig ! would enable him to make a handsome subsistence let the bookseller trade go as it please— ! Then the dancing—old Major Burns with his one eye—old Jerdan of the Literary Gazette, (escaped out of the Rules of the Queen's Bench for the great occasion !) the gigantic Thackeray &c. &c. all capering like *Maenades ! !* Dickens did all but go down on his knees to make *me*—waltz with him ! But I thought I did my part well enough in talking the maddest nonsense with *him*, Forster, Thackeray and Maclise—without attempting the Impossible—however *after supper* when we were all madder than ever with the pulling of crackers, the drinking of champagne, and the making of speeches ; a universal country dance was proposed—and Forster *seizing me round the waist*, whirled me into the thick of it, and *made* me dance ! ! like a person in the tread-mill who must move forward or be crushed to death ! Once I cried out " oh for the love of Heaven let me go ! you are going to dash my brains out against the folding doors ! " to which he answered—(you can fancy his tone)—" your *brains ! !* who cares about their brains *here ? let them go !* "

In fact the thing was rising into something not unlike the *rape of the Sabines !* (*Mrs. Reid* was happily gone some time) when somebody looked [at] her watch and exclaimed " twelve o'clock ! " Whereupon we all rushed to the cloak-room—and *there* and in the lobby and up to the last moment the mirth raged on—Dickens took home Thackeray and Forster with him and his wife " *to finish the night there* " and a *royal* night they would have of it I fancy !—ending perhaps with a visit to the watch-house.

After all—the pleasantest company, as Burns thought, *are* the *blackguards !*—that is ; those who have just a sufficient dash of blackguardism in them to make them snap their fingers at *ceremony* and " all that sort of thing." I question if there was as much witty speech uttered in all the aristocratic, conventional drawing rooms thro'out London that night as among us little knot of blackguardist literary people who felt ourselves above all rules, and independent of the universe ! Well, and the result ? Why the result my dear was, that I went to bed on my return and—slept like a top ! ! ! ! plainly proving that *excitement* is *my rest !* To be sure my head ached a little next morning but the coffee cleared it—and I went about the dinner for Mrs. Cunningham without much physical inconvenience.

See what a letter I have written !—and such writing !— but I must stop now for the post hour is at hand. . . .

Your own

J. C.

N

66. *To Jeannie Welsh*

Babbie as Consuelo—Carlyle's tobacco—Mazzini as " first foot "—
Helen goes to a party—New Year's letters—Gifts from Helen
and Carlyle.

Tuesday (2nd Jan., 1844).

I am glad to see dearest Babbie that there is *a revival* in
your moral *department* since you got back into the atmosphere of
home—that you write to me oftener and longer—and more
like a Babbie whose wits had not all gone " a wool-gathering "
—in a windy day !   But you must continue in this praiseworthy
course for a while to come ; before I can recover that implicit
belief in your virtue (for virtue is writing to *me*, is it not ?)
which made you so long the comfort of my life—my *Consuelo !*

This is washing-day ; and further the ground is covered
with snow and further I have a headache. Better to have
waited till to-morrow so far as you are concerned. But
Carlyle told me last night " to be sure *when I wrote to Liverpool
to-morrow* (he supposes I write every day it would seem) to
send a message for Walter MacGregor—it went much against
his conscience to plague Walter, *in the midst of complexities
which seemed to be thickening and darkening around him, with
speech about tobacco*—but really it was essential to the comfort
of his (Carlyle's) existence that Walter should be made aware
that his good tobacco was *entirely done* and none to be got here
for money which was fit for a human being to smoke—ergo,
if Walter would send him some of the right sort as soon as
convenient (anglicé : *possible*) it would be esteemed the highest
favour—he was not to wait for opportunities but send it
by railway at once "—" damn the expense " of carriage where
anything so *vital* as tobacco is concerned. Now will you
give this message to Walter not in the phraseology in which I
have given it but courteously and modestly as your sweet lips
will know how.*

---

* Of this we hear again on January 20 : " I must not leave out C.'s
message to Walter M. ' the box of tobacco arrived all *exquisitely correct* '—
except for one little omision—*the bill*—which he (C.) had expressly requested
might be sent—but he hopes to have soon an opportunity of settling with
himself here at Chelsea."

We had a most quiet New Year day. I saw nobody but Mazzini who came thro' the snow to be my *first foot*—and my first words of thanks were—" What on earth could tempt you to come out in a day like this " ! He looked most pitiable with big drops of sleet hanging from the ends of his mustache. *Helen* went to a party in the evening ! At Chalmers's—There were *twenty* to dine with the family—(in a room the same size as ours !) and nine friends of the servants in the kitchen !—ecco la combinazione ! I asked Helen what they did—Oh says she " it was just a sort of *guddle* of a thing—all eating and drinking and no fun at all "—a pretty good description of most dinners—" three of the servants' visitors were kept all the time washing and *polishing* glasses for upstairs " ! I ought in gratitude to say however that even I who am superstitious about the beginnings of new years—who watch all their outs and ins as the Roman Augurs did the flight of birds, had reason to be satisfied with yesterday—it brought me *nobody* but Mazzini—it brought me a good long letter from my Babbie with another as long from Miss Donaldson bearing a great post-mark Haddington—so plain and large that one would have said it had been stamped in that particular way for *my* express behoof—and in the morning when I sprung out of bed half asleep—the room all dark—on hearing Carlyle go down, I was received into the arms of—Helen !—saluted with two hearty smacks on my two cheeks ! while an immense ginger-bread cake—which she had had baked more gingery than usual to suit my taste, was thrust into the breast of my night shift—and my whole room was filled with a most savoury smell of ginger-bread. From this *delicate attention* you will perceive she is very good just now—indeed since the fright she got last spring she has done her uttermost to keep a guard on her temper—and has *on the whole* behaved very well. Then on my toilet I found a hair-brush and *redd* (as they call it in Annandale, *anglicé* Comb) placed there the night before by Carlyle—but such a brush and comb as never were in my possession before—they are best described in Helen's words who declared them to be " *most noble*." The comb is tortoise-shell —the brush—oh Heavens !—it is the size and shape of an ordinary pancake—might have been made on purpose for Goliath of Gath !—the bristles are at least an inch and half deep—and you would say at first sight that it was some instrument of torture !   I do wish it had been about one fourth of the size, but Carlyle has just one rule in buying anything, to buy what is the *best* that is the *dearest*, and his meaning was so kind that I must show my sense of it in learning to wield this tremendous implement.

I am glad of the hope you hold out of our seeing Walter—tell him to be sure and come straight here—and to warn me that I may have his bed well warmed.   Love to them all—my head is very bad—and I *must* stop.

Your affectionate

J. C.

67.   *To Helen Welsh* *

Mrs. A. Sterling's *idée fixe*.

Mrs. Anthony Sterling, who had for some time suffered from nervous derangement, now conceived an *idée fixe* that her husband was in love with Mrs. Carlyle.

(9th Jan., 1844.)

MY DEAREST HELEN,
   . . . Mrs. Sterling is grown very peaceable, her Husband says—" takes everything now by the soft handle "—but there is no reason to believe that her private feelings towards *me* have undergone any favourable change.   Since her Doctor *commanded* her to cease from railing at me she has obeyed—but one day there occurred a little incident which showed her silence was mere compulsory.   She was dressing the hair of one of her little nieces and the boy, Edward, who was looking on (just come home for holidays) exclaimed (surely inspired by the Devil !) " Oh, that is very pretty ! that is just the way Mrs. Carlyle wears her hair ! "   Whereupon his aunt threw down the comb and said sharply " We do not speak of

---

* The undated letter printed as No. 120 on p. 284, should probably precede this No. 67.

that person here." Afterwards, on the children leaving the room, she said to their Governess, " Just think of *that !*—even that boy must talk about her ! " She professes to be grown so fond of her husband again that she cannot suffer him a minute out of her sight—" which," says Anthony, " is really *excessively* tiresome," but besides the *fondness* he fancies she is always in fear of his coming here. And so he comes rarely—and by *stealth*—without carriage or servants—like a man going to rob a hen-roost !—which I consider a quite *false position* in which to place either himself or me. He ought decidedly either to come in the face of day—to say to the woman " these people are my friends and I *will* go to see them reasonably—and there is no wrong in my going—and so *you* had better just reconcile yourself to the idea of it, or go mad again, if you like that way of it better "—or else if he considers *humouring her* to be his properest course, he ought to come here and say— " you see how I am oppressed by a distracted wife—she is my wife, however, and I must consult her whims before all else—and so since I cannot see you any more without pain to her, farewell and God bless you "—either of these courses would beseem him—but the middle course—coming here *in secret*—beseems none of us, and if he do not get to find this out for himself pretty soon, I shall tell him or make Carlyle tell him to stay away. I have plenty more mad work to tell you of but I am tired for to-day. I am still confined to the house—my cough is very obstinate this time, tho' I eat *raisins* for it world without end—I really think they tend to make me *sleep ! !* . . .

Love and kisses in profusion.

Ever your own

J. C.

68.   *To Jeannie Welsh*

No free moments—American visitors; James; Gen. Baird;
Coleman; Greig—Craik and Helps—Robertson's letter and Miss
Swanwick—Dinner catastrophe at Liverpool; Gambardella—
Mrs. Reid and Dickens' child—Mazzini's looks; his visit and
Eliz. Pepoli.

Miss Anna Swanwick is the Greek scholar, translator of
Æschylus.

(Jan., 1844 ?)

Oh Babbie Babbie ! " I am a-weary a-weary," as ever was
" *Mariana of the Moated Grange !* " Every day I pray to
Heaven for just two things, *quiet* and *the free use of my faculties*,
and Heaven turns a deaf ear !   If any approximation to outward
quiet be granted I am sure to have along with it a headache or
" real mental agony in my own inside " (as Helen phrases it)
or if both *my head* and " *mysel* " be comparatively easy, then
there are a hundred and one interruptions to snatch me up,
like a feather borne on the wind and whirl me away, far away,
out of my little sphere of industrial projects and good intentions.
Till Cromwell is finished I am not to be held " responsible."

Last Sunday I had thought to write you such a letter, as
long as my arm—and as interesting " as—as—anything ! "
But " The Countess " * came and made me go out with her
" against my sensations," and I came in so chilled that I had to
warm myself with brandy and nestle on the sofa under that
big shawl ; that I might be resuscitated for a party of Americans
that was to take effect the same evening—and the wretches all
came—and there was such a drawling and sir-ing—I would
have given a crown that you had been there for " it was *strange*
upon *my* honour ! "   There was a Mr. James with a wife and
wife's-sister, " not a bad man " (as C. would say) " nor altogether a fool," but he had only one leg !—that is to say only one
real available leg, the other, tho' the fellow of it in appearance
consisting entirely of cork—Now a man may be as agreeable
with one leg or three legs as with *two* but he needs to take certain

* Elizabeth Pepoli.

precautions. The one-legged man is bound in mercy to all people with merely ordinary nerves to use some sort of *stick* instead of trusting to Providence as this Mr. James does, so that every time he moves in the room it is as if " a blind destiny " had been set a-going and one awaits in horror to see him rush down amongst the tea-cups, or walk out thro' the window-glass or pitch himself headforemost into the grate ! from which and the like imminent dangers he is only preserved by a continual miracle ! For *me* with *my* nerves you may fancy the awfulness of such a visitor ! Of his two women what could anybody say ? Unless that they giggled incessantly, and wore *black* stockings with light colour dresses. Then there was an American " General " !—General Baird—the very image of Mr. Pecksniff, without the shyness. His ample breast was covered with a white waistcoat—open very far down to shew the *brooch* in his shirt—hair set round with pearls—the whole thing about the size of a five-shilling piece ! He seemed then, as a living confirmation of Dickens's satires on the American *great men* and several times I burst out laughing in his face. *The General* was brought by a Mr. Coleman who was sent us last summer by John Greig—an exceptional Yankee !—so full of life and glee, tho' turned of sixty ! A sort of man one feels tempted to *kiss*, so benevolent and *good* without any cant about it—and with such affectionate eyes—I daresay I *shall* kiss him some day—the other night I found to my surprise that I had got the length of standing with one of my arms round his neck ! ! which must have been a cruel sight for Creek who was also of the party—*brought* by Arthur Helps and his beautiful little atom of a wife in their carriage. He had been dining with them the promoted Creek ! and they had asked my leave to come and *see* the Americans and " took the liberty of bringing Mr. Craik along with them." He behaves very well now, the " poor fellow " !—does not come above once in the two months —and still his devotion survives even this self-inflicted absence —if I fling him one civil word he looks as if he would fall down and kiss my great toe ! and answers in the plaintive tone of a love-lorn shepherd in the Poetry of the Middle Ages. I begin to be *wae* for " poor Creek "! Such unrequited devotion

I have not found in all Israel! " That minds me " of a most
absurd little incident which befell a week or two ago which I
must tell you if my pen will hold out—for the general amusement
of your breakfast table.*

I received one day *by post* a letter the handwriting of which
was not new to me—but I could not recollect in the first
minutes whose it was—I read the first line—" Oh those bright
sweet eyes " !—I stood amazed " as in presence of the Infinite " !
What man had gone out of his wits ? What year of grace was
I in ? What *was* it at all ? I looked for a signature—there
was none ! I read on—" There is no escaping their bewitching
influence " ! " Idiot " ! said I " whoever you be " ! (having
now *got up* a due matronly rage) " to write such stale nonsense
to me ! *and to send it by* post " ! But I read on—" It is impossible but that such eyes must be accompanied by a feeling
heart—could you not use your influence with their possessor
on my behalf ? The time of young ladies is in general so
uselessly employed that I really think you would be doing—
Miss Swanwick a kindness in persuading her to—translate for
me those *French laws of pawnbroking* " ! ! ! Now it was
all clear—and I had the ridicule of finding that my virtuous
married-woman blushes had been entirely thrown away !
The " bright sweet eyes " were not *mine* but Miss Swanwick's
and the writer of the letter was Robertson, who had repeatedly
raved to me about those Swanwick-eyes to a weariness ! But
have you often in your life heard of anything more absurd—
more stupid (even for an Author) than this beginning of a
letter to one woman with an apostrophe to the eyes of another !
And when I told him afterwards the misconception thereby
occasioned, instead of feeling ashamed of himself he only
laughed till the tears ran down !

Oh what an awful adventure—a dinner party of eighteen
and a cook with a cut vein ! I can never understand how people
outlive such things—had I been the *Mistress* in such a case I
would have immediately *sailed for America*, or gone up to the
housetop and suspended myself from a rafter ! Remember me
to Gambardella since he has emerged again into the sphere of

* Cp. No. 32.

visibility. You may tell him I met his Mrs. Reid at that Birthday party *—and had the honour of being regarded by her with a marked terror and dislike—happily she went away soon—you would have laughed to have heard her as I did trying to indoctrinate one of Dickens's small children with *Socinian benevolence*—the child about the size of a quartern loaf was sitting on a low chair gazing in awestruck delight at the reeking plum-pudding which its Father had just produced out of " a gentleman's hat." Mrs. Reid leaning tenderly over her (as benevolent gentlewomen understand how to lean over youth) said in a soft voice *professedly* for *its* ear, but loud enough for mine and everybody else's within three yards' distance— " Would not you like that there was such a nice pudding as that in every house in London to-night ? I am sure *I* would ! " The shrinking uncomprehending look which the little blouzy face cast up to her was inimitable—a whole page of protest against *twaddle !* if she could but have read it !

Mazzini was here yesterday so *bright* as I hardly ever remember to have seen him. I saw one sunny flash in his eyes which might have been the first waking to life of Pygmalion's statue ! his face is all but well now. But besides that, some " change has come over the spirit of his dream "—I know not what it is—I know only that he looked almost dazzlingly beautiful yesterday and that this beauty was plainly the expression of some inward new-found joy ! Elizabeth came in— " the white face with which I had left her on Sunday had haunted her all the afternoon and she could not be easy till she knew how I was "—" but I see " said she with a peculiar look and tone " that you are QUITE *well* now." The fact was, Mazzini and I had just been regaling ourselves with wine *figs* and gingerbread, and when the rap came to the door I bade him put away the glasses and he put them into—*my writing desk !* so that when she opened the room door we both presented an unusual appearance of discomposure which Elizabeth, whose head is always running on " what shall I say—strange things upon my honour "—interpreted doubtless into " a delicate embarrassment." Elizabeth to have been always *virtuous*,

* See letter of December 23, 1843, No. 65.

as I am sure she has been, has really a curious incapacity of comprehending the simplest *liaison* between man and woman. She would not *sit* down—but having quite *looked us thro' and thro'* (as she thought) went home " to write letters." . . .

Ever your own

J. C.

69. *To Jeannie Welsh*

A mistake about blue pills—A reshuffled dinner party.

(*20th Jan.*, 1844.)

DEAREST BABBIE,

I said that I would write yesterday *God willing* but God was *not willing* and the manner of it was thus—on the preceding night I had *five grains of mercury* (*!*) introduced into my interior *by mistake*—instead of *one half grain* the quantity I am in the habit of taking at one time—and which is quite *enough* " *for anything*." So much for my husband's *false refinement !* I had been wretchedly bilious for some days and sent him to Alsop's for *my* blue pills—*he* also being in the practice of getting pills there—of *five grains*—which he swallows from time to time " in werra desperation " (as you know) and in fellowship with an ocean of castor oil—the pills came and I swallowed one ; merely wondering why they had sent me only *three* instead of my customary *dozen*—but ten minutes after when I became deadly sick I understood at once how it was. Carlyle frankly admitted it was quite likely there had been a mistake—" when he went into the shop a gentleman was with Alsop and he *did not like* to say *send the blue pills for Mrs. Carlyle* but said instead send the blue pills *for our house*." Alsop of course had preferred the *masculine gender* as grammatically bound to do—and so was *delicacy* another person's " own reward." All yesterday I was sick enough you may fancy— for I felt too weak to deliver myself from the confounded stuff thro' a great dose of physic—I thought it safest to let it work away there in the unfortunate *interior* of me until it had its humour out. Carlyle comforted himself and tried to comfort me, by suggesting that " it might possibly do me *a great deal*

of good in the long run ! " It may be " strongly doubted "
(as they say in Edin.)—anyhow it has not begun to do me
good *yet*—for to-day I am still passably *sick* and the pill and the
new onslaught of frost at the same moment—are making me as
miserable as Mrs. Anthony Sterling (my only enemy) could
wish ! But I write not to seem a promise-breaker, so long as
I can help myself.

Well my Dear just think of my having had a dinner-party
last Sunday ! the botheration of which was in fact the cause of
feeling the *besoin* of blue pill. John Fergus and Miss Jessy
were in town and Carlyle asked them " quite promiscuously "
to dine. Miss Jessy " had a cold " but John would come
" with pleasure." I was very much shocked—*under the circumstances*—but proceeded to meet the emergency as I best
could—schemed *a dinner*, had the ingredients provided—and
asked Darwin *for party*. The *acceptance* of Darwin arrived on
Saturday along with John Fergus's *excuse*. He had bethought
him, like a good soul as he is, that I was not well enough to be
plagued with a dinner and so, on the plea of next to nothing, he
wrote that he could not come to dine but that he and Miss Jessy
would come in the evening—if I would not give myself the
smallest trouble for them. The *trouble* alas was already under
way—the dinner had been *got in* and Darwin asked and coming
—so " who was to be got to meet Darwin ? "—" perfectly
unnecessary to get anybody " said I—but no, Carlyle had a
fixed idea of *giving a dinner*—exactly at the wrong moment—
and so at ten o'clock of Saturday night Helen was despatched
with an invitation to Arthur Helps—worse and worse—for
Arthur Helps *does his* dinners in eminent style—and the idea
of dining him was rather awful for me. He accepted *of
course*—then people came without intermission from one o'clock
on Sunday until the dinner hour five—so that I could not so
much as get the room cleared for the dinner table to be set out
*until half an hour after Darwin and Helps were come to eat
their dinner* and at the last moment Carlyle invited John and
Monckton Milnes of all people in the world to stay and assist
at the dinner which seemed never likely to be served up ! I
was never so nearly upset by a household complication in my

life before—and how Helen got thro' with it even with the aid of *Martha* (*!*) * I have no comprehension—everybody did get dined at last better or worse—and the novelty of *the style* I daresay rather charmed Milnes and Helps blasés on *fine* dinners. Certainly Milnes tho' I have seen him give himself the most insolent airs at great people's tables was modesty's self here. And as Carlyle feeling the whole thing to be his own most voluntary act *talked* like an Angel—and there was always my uncle's *Madeira* excellent ; whatever else might be humanly imperfect—the whole thing went off like a sort of firework—crackers of wit exploding in every direction—Darwin spoke only in epigrams—Carlyle in flights of genius—Milnes in poetical paradoxes—Helps in witticisms, rather small, but perfectly well turned—and John Carlyle did his best to resemble *Solomon*. As for myself—you may fancy what the preliminary fret made of me !—Shu-ping-sing was a *spoony* in comparison—every opening of my lips was sensibly felt—and Miss Jessy must have gone away with the feeling that she had seen for the first time in her life a woman of superhuman intelligence ! Pity that one can only be superhumanly intelligent in *dadding* one's nerves *a-abreed !*—I went to bed feeling a decided tendency to fly—and lay *the whole night thro'* without *once* closing my eyes. By breakfast time I had got instead of the inclination to fly, a horrible headache—and so I have been bilious ever since—and needed blue pill—and got it !

There is no paper in the house so I am writing on backs of notes and have written already more than seemed possible when I commenced—I have something to tell you—what shall I say —strange ! upon *my* honour—but not at this writing for several reasons—Love to all—kisses especially to my uncle—

Ever your own
J. C

> For thee no gaudy, monumental shrine ;
> Hester, a Husband's riven Heart, be thine—

Old Sterling's epitaph on his poor wife ! ! !

* Martha—" a child, whom Jeannie knows to her sorrow "—who used to be called in to help in emergencies, no one more efficient being available.

70. *To Jeannie Welsh*

James Baillie—Plattnauer away—Mazzini and his new plans.

Saturday (*27th Jan.*, 1844).

. . . The subject of extravagance leads me in turn to those documents I sent you belonging to our elegant cousin *—you take no notice of them, which is highly discreditable to your nice sense of family-honour.

How he ever could seek me again after I had refused him two sovereigns !—and having been allowed to come, how he could immediately propose to me a transaction at a pawn-shop ! —and such a vile transaction—for this picture of his son (illegitimate of course and worse than illegitimate—the poor child being *there* merely in virtue of its mother's small annuity) was *swindled* out of the hands of the painter in the first instance and pawned by *themselves*—and his object in getting *me* to buy it back was simply to get two sovereigns out of me by a roundabout process. All this, with my natural talent for sounding into the mysteries of rascaldom, I have *preciséed* at the pawnshop and at the Painter's—and have of course taken no notice of the beggarly commission and seen nothing of him since, except out of Sterling's carriage one day on the street. If I had been as rich as William Cunningham perhaps I would have taken the image of the poor child out of the pawnshop window where it still stands, and *kept* it—merely that nobody with one drop of my blood in his veins should occupy such an ignominious position—but as it is, I did not feel myself justified in preserving *intact* the family honour at the large outlay of *two sovereigns*.

Plattnauer is still at Brighton with the Ailesburys which is a great loss to my Sundays. I might replace him with Arthur Helps or Count Krasinski † —but it goes against my feelings to fill up living blanks. Mazzini keeps better and has *much need ;* for he expects, with " a faith the like of which is not in all Israel " (nor to be wished that it were) to lead a new " Savoy's expedition " into Italy as early as the end of this February ! ! ! (Keep this from the knowledge of Gambardella, of course.)

---

* Captain James Baillie. See Letter 11. † See p. 187.

I listen to his *programme* and miraculous hopes with an *indifference* that drives him to despair—for I have a modest reliance on Providence and " *the Laws of Nature* " that if he *does* cross the Channel with his tail of enthusiastic shoemakers and tailors and *Balloon* Inventors and what not ; he will be " turned back " as on the former occasion (according to Carlyle) " *at the first toll-bar*." To be sure there is chance enough of his being laid hold of and sent to meditate on his folly in the *Spielberg* or at " *the bottom of a well* " in St. Leo, for the remainder of his life—but as *he* is quite indifferent as to that, I do not see why I need get into any worry about it—indeed, I feel so downright angry at his delirium that I cannot care just now what becomes of him, the madman that he is !

And now, goodbye, dear child, I must proceed to " walk for my health," that most toilsome of sublunary duties. Love to all

Your own
JANE CARLYLE.

71.　*To Jeannie Welsh*

Babbie and Andrew Chrystal.

Tuesday (7th Feb., 1844).

MY VERY PRETTY BABBIE,

. . . Walter * spoke of being married in the course of a month—but I do not think he had any care about my *assisting* at the sacrifice, at least he expressed none—his chief motive in getting me to Liverpool seemed to be a generous anxiety about—you ! !—who he seems to have *a fixed idea* are always in need of my *Shu-ping-sing* faculty of seeing thro' stone walls and setting all sorts of entanglements to rights. *Now*, it seems that you are *spoken of* with Andrew Chrystal—and he (Walter) " does not know what to think of it," and whatever he (Walter) does not know what to think of there is a need that *I* should think of, and descend as a *Deus ex machina* (a god out of a machine, since you have no *Latin* you poor child !) into the thick of ! Now really dear Babbie granted that you are

---

* W. Macgregor, who had been in London.

becoming as great a bore with the number of your " suitors "
as Penelope was ; I do not feel sure, that even if I were there,
transported by *a wishing cap* or other miraculous means applic-
able to my circumstances, with all my eyes and ears opened as
wide as wide could be and my " Shu-ping-sing faculty " to
back them out ; I do not feel at all sure that I could penetrate
the " *grande mistero* "—inasmuch as I am still in a state of
modest doubt whether there *be* one to penetrate—and suppose
I could, did ever young lady since the world began take counsel
with the flesh and blood of her cousin on the private affairs of
her heart—she will regulate *these* by her own discretion or
*in*discretion let the sapient cousin say or sing what she likes.
And really as *she* is the person chiefly implicated therein one
cannot take it ill of her !—*This* however my good little girl I
beg of you to lay to heart, that if I find at any time that you
have been getting up a little matrimonial transaction without
(not asking my *advice* which of course you would not follow)
but without letting *me* into a secret which I am so much
interested in, from the very first moment in which it assumed
an *utterable* shape, I shall think you a very graceless Babbie and
shall tell you no more *secrets* of mine !—By which arrangement
you are likely to be a prodigious loser.

In sober sadness Babbie of my heart *are* you thinking to
marry this Mr. Chrystal—or even thinking of thinking to marry
him ? " Why not ? "—I am sure for my part I see no good
reason unless it be that neither of you ever happened to conceive
the wish—In *that* case it were certainly inadvisable but otherwise ? Mr. Chrystal could keep your bit soul and body together could he not ? he is as Carlyle would express it " *not*
a *fool* nor a *bad man* "—is he not ? And if these conditions
be fulfilled—why should not Babbie marry Mr. Chrystal and
Mr. Chrystal marry Babbie if they be both of that mind ?
You observe that I do not know him the least in the world all
the while—I once I think met him on your upper stair—but
I have not even the faintest recollection how he looked. Now
do like a good child write me a letter *to the point*—if to that
point and *some other points* included you would be doing me a
sensible kindness, for I cannot help giving a certain attention

to these *on dit's* when anything so precious to me as *your* future is in question. Tho' I do not make much complaint on the subject I may just as well take this occasion to tell you frankly, that these letters which contain all sorts of things, except just the things in your own heart and the very things I want to be told about, if they do not anger me do always *afflict* me more or less. The wearing of one's heart on one's sleeve is a thing which I neither admire nor practise, but the utterly shrouding it up and hanging it over with all sorts of frivolous disguises, with the person who perhaps is in the whole wide world the likeliest to understand it and sympathize with it, does seem to me a piece of unwisdom, a wilful rejecting of " the good the gods have provided " one ! Do *I* tell you all that make *me* ill just now and the time look " out of joint " ?—No—but only because a word to the wise—that is, to the *sympathizing*, is enough—and I have spoken enough of these *words* to *you*, for enabling you always to *divine* all that I keep to myself. But *you* have yet given *me* no such talismanic *word*—or else I have not been *wise* enough to *make it do*.

Now you see dear this is a sort of *preaching*—or rather *praying* letter, and I will even let it stand for such without attempting to make the *amende honorable* by tacking any extraneous matter in the shape of news to the end of it—I am still very *sick* in spite of my *airing* yesterday and I write with *effort* tho' with infinite facility of good will.

Mazzini was very glad of your letter tho' he did complain that you had evidently " *mended your pen* at *one place* " a proceeding which I felt to be inconsistent with a due trustfulness of friendship.

My kindest love to them all—and say yes I will come and cover them all with kisses but *not yet*—Bless thee my dear little good Babbie with many suitors—

Your own

JANE CARLYLE.

72. *To Jeannie Welsh*

A matter of handwriting—Proportionable sympathy in illness—
  Sterling's carriage — Bores and complaints, an unequal
  division—A *faux pas* of Thackeray's—Andrew Chrystal—Miss
  Jewsbury's rewritten MS.

(*15th Feb.*, 1844.)

DEAREST BABBIE,

If I had not given some sign of life at Maryland
Street before receiving your last ; I would have written on the
instant to explain the phenomenon of the unknown address,
which had caused your sympathizing little soul a quite needless
disturbance. But oh Babbie to think of your mistaking the
handwriting of a cousin-german to the last reigning King of
Poland—ci devant Chamberlain to the Emperor of Russia—
Author of various *works* including a *History of the Reformation*
in three volumes—a Polish noble, and popular member of the
most aristocratic English society, for *Helen's !* the maid-of-all-
work's !—Babbie, where were your eyes, not to see in those
sprawling characters of his the carelessness of a *Noble* and
Author—instead of the incapacity of a *maid-of-all-work ?*—
Just as I had finished my letter to you that day two events
came upon me within the same five minutes—Count Krasinski
and a basin of soup—the latter being *decidedly* the most
essential at the moment I told Krasinski by way of taking
his attention from my physical operation, to fold and seal the
letter for me—which done ; he proposed with great glee to
address it also—and I foreseeing nothing but a little pleasant
stimulant to your curiosity, assented at the first word—

> So this is the history,
> Of the wonderful mystery !

For the rest I do not ever give way—moi—like Harriet
Martineau (in her *Life in a sick room*) to dreadful qualms of
conscience on the ground that people " overrate my physical
sufferings and give me more sympathy than I am in strict
justice entitled to " ! !—I am always very thankful for sympathy
and pocket all I get as my due, without *calculation*, or the

O

slightest touch of remorse. And so the sympathy you bestowed
on me under the idea of my having become too sick to address
my own letter—may stand for my having been too sick to get
any good of my life ever since the writing of it and for a good
while before—with *no children* whatsoever, I am quite as puzzled
as *Goody two shoes* " *what to do* " ? How to make myself go
to sleep before three or four in the morning—and then only
for a few minutes at a stretch—or how to get up the necessary
appetite for keeping soul and body together—I have the most
perfect conviction that no medical advice could set me to rights
—only time may do it if it like—but meanwhile—I am a-weary
a-weary. Sterling's carriage—a *close* one now, and very comfortable, is a great temporal consolation to me under the existing
circumstances. He comes almost every day and gives me the
option of driving out with him—and *worries* me as little as is
" in *the nature of the Beast* " to do. Indeed he is much quieter
generally, since he returned to putting out his superfluous
energy in *Times-Thundering*. All the while, I have to do the
amiable to company as usual, and take all the principal *bores* off
Carlyle and go about indoors as if nothing ailed me—for as
Carlyle has long since appropriated the chief right to raise an
outcry—and put all his miseries into poetic language and as
possession is nine points of law—it were in vain for *me* to
take the field as a *complainer*, even if much relief were to be found
in that line, which I don't believe to be the case. So I say as
little about *my* " Interior " as need be—only indulging myself
in an occasional *miserere* like the present to you—and sometimes
a brief protest against " things in general " to Elizabeth.
Mazzini sets one such an *awful* example of stoicism in the
physical that with all the confidence in the world of his
sympathetic nature one has not the face to say—" to be *sick* is
miserable " in *his* presence. I have not seen *him* for a week
and am anxious that he may come to-day—for his " *affairs* "
were to be deciding themselves about this time—" *Savoy's*
expedition " to be or not to be.

As I am really too stupid to write you either an amusing
or edifying letter this day I send you a note from Dickens which
is decidedly the former—and which you must return to me

without showing it to anyone out of your own house—for it is in the highest degree *indiscreet* (God bless him)—the matter it alludes to was an absurd mistake of Thackeray's who put five shillings into Robertson's hand one night in the idea that he was reduced to the last " extremity of Fate " ! ! and then (what was much more inexcusable) told Dickens and myself of the transaction before witnesses in Mrs. Macready's drawing room ! The real fact of how the money was put into R.'s hands with certain mysterious words—and how R. stared after " the odd mortal " as he ran away, in total bewilderment as to what Thackeray designed him *to do* with the said shillings ! and how he called next day to return them and ask the meaning—and found him " *out* "—and on the next day again and found him " gone to Paris "—all that coming to my knowledge after, thro' the *unconscious alms-receiver* (!) himself—I thought it but fair towards him to set his case in the right light to Dickens who along with myself had heard the extraordinary *charge*— This note is his answer—

Well I will not mind any more of Walter's clatters—but you are wrong I think in supposing he would have *liked* you to marry Mr. Chrystal—he seemed to me to think you would be *thrown away* on that hypothesis *also*.

I have all Geraldine's MS. now and by the powers it is a wonderful book !—Decidedly the *cleverest* Englishwoman's-book I ever remember to have read.

Ever your own

J. C.

73. *To Jeannie Welsh*

A persecuted woman—Practical sympathy.

The *cause célèbre* of *Fraser* v. *Bagley* lasted four days, from Monday, February 19, to ten at night on Thursday, February 22, 1844, when the verdict for the defendant, exonerating Mrs. Fraser, was received with loud cheers in court. The dashing Fraser, who had married a well-to-do widow, it seems, for her money, went bankrupt in 1837 after speculating wildly, and departed to other fields of activity, bidding his oldest friend, a barrister like himself, look after the interests of his deserted wife. The friend did his best, and was rewarded by this action based upon the flimsy evidence of dishonest servants. John Carlyle, who had attended his old acquaintance, Mrs. Fraser, was called as a medical witness in the case.

Bay House, Alverstoke.
(*End Feb.*, 1844.)

DEAREST BABBIE,

Before I forget will you tell my Uncle with a kiss that I consider him the most *virtuous* father of a family I have ever known, and that having thus a whole " *Society for the Suppression of Vice* " within his own breast, there is every ground to believe that his Daughters will pass thro' life like *living snow-drops ! !* And do not you embezzle *this* message because you cannot understand it—to my uncle it will be quite as intelligible as *his* message was to me.

For the rest Babbie you must be content with a small return this day for your two long letters. All the last week I was kept in a very violent state of nervous excitement about a thing which you will think lay a good way out of *my* road. But when one is disposed to be excited it makes little difference whether the immediate cause be personal or no—and so my blood has been kept at the boiling point all last week by a—*crim. con. process* before the Guildhall—in which I was neither a principal nor even a witness—but John was a witness and *I* made it my own affair—from *esprit de corps* Carlyle says.

There never was I believe a more infernal prosecution raised against any woman than this which occupied the Guildhall Court for four whole days of last week and has been filling many columns of the daily Papers. Did you ever hear us speak of a William Fraser—it was he of whom John said so many times over that " with the best intentions he was always unfortunate " —till the phrase became a by-word in our house. Now and for a long while back he has been worse than unfortunate with good intentions—having performed one atrocity after another till he has consummated all by a crim. con. process against the best friend he ever had in the world and his own ill-used long since deserted wife.

I cannot enter into the details of the transaction—if you were to read the papers the impression left on your mind would probably be that Mrs. Fraser was *guilty* but with *such* extenuating circumstances that no really just and humane person could lay his hand on his heart and say that she was really very blameable for having been guilty—but Carlyle, John, all the men and women who have known personally the sort of woman she is, and the sort of life she has led, firmly believe her innocent in spite of all the perjured circumstantial evidence brought against her which after all was only inferential.   Think of its being made *criminal* to say to a man who for years had been dining four or five times a week in the house by her husband's invitation " my dear will you ring the bell " ! ! Merciful Heaven—what criminalities have *I* walked over the top of without knowing it ! At length on Thursday night she had a verdict in her favour—and tho' from what passed in Court it seemed to have been due to the evidence of her husband's monstrous usage of her rather than to that of her own innocence—it was received with " tremendous cheers " in the Court house and all along the street.   John had been in Court all the four days and sent me a daily bulletin of the proceedings—always, like a Job's comforter as he is, winding up with " that in spite of internal heartfelt convictions, there was every chance of its going against her."   And then Sterling sent me daily the *Times*—and there I sat fuming— wishing to be in the Court to show up misstatements which nobody seemed to notice, to draw palpable inferences which nobody seemed to draw, or at all rates to be with the poor woman comforting her—but as I had never seen her but once in my life just after my first coming to London I feared she would not receive me while she was enduring the horrible uncertainty.

" So soon as it *is* decided " I said to Darwin " I will go and nobody shall prevent me."—" Whichever way it goes ? " said Darwin—" Yes " said I " and all the faster if it goes against her "—" Bravo " ! said he—with a benignant smile—" Oh " said Carlyle " the woman is not that sort of woman at all—if you knew her you could not for a moment believe her to have done anything beyond *imprudences*—such as calling people *my Dear* and all that " (looking significantly at poor me)—" Ah !

—for my share " says Darwin " I cannot even see the *imprudences !* "—" Thank you for that " exclaimed I with effusion !—The day after the verdict I had meant to go—having sent her word before by John that I *must* see her—but that day I had my hands full at home; from six in the morning till six at night I carried on one incessant alternation of fainting, retching, screaming, even Cromwell had to give place to me !—and Carlyle was out and in fifty times during the day—not with the usual " how are you now Jane "—but—" merciful heaven what *is* this ?—what *can* I do for you ? " These *superlative* headaches coming back with " a certain " regularity are " a bad outlook " as Helen says. I have had as bad many years ago but then I had more stuff in me for resisting them—and they were in some measure compensated by having a perfectly clear head during the intervals—which is not the case now—for they leave me all beaten into impalpable pulp—to speak figuratively. Next day however by help of Sterling's carriage I got to the poor woman—whom I found in bed—in such a state as you may fancy a modest woman to be reduced to who had just been dragged before the public is such a shameful way. To-morrow I go to her after breakfast to stay all day and Carlyle God bless him will come to fetch me home. So soon as she is able I will fetch her here for a few days and if anybody thinks it " an improper connection," they are at liberty to cut my acquaintance. I really see no such natural way of showing my gratitude to Providence for having had my own reputation always mercifully preserved, [as] in affording the countenance of it to one who has been less fortunate. I will tell you all about *her* next time, at present I have written as much as is prudent—for my physical state—bless you all.

Your own

J. C.

I have seen nothing of the Walters—except a most *poisonous* looking piece of Bride cake, which came in a little box from a Liverpool confectioner.

DR. JOHN CARLYLE.
From a photograph.

MISS GERALDINE JEWSBURY.
From a photograph by C. A. Duval.

74. *To Jeannie Welsh*

On inability to write—Finds a publisher for Geraldine in return for
    help about the Mudies—Notable books and their reward—
    Accident with Carlyle's hot-water bottle.

(16*th March*, 1844.)

DARLING,

I write just a line to-day to prevent you fancying that
I have lost either my life or my senses.   *You* are not one of those
unimaginative characters who cannot believe in *inability to
write* unless it be attended with the outward visible sign of
confinement to bed—and so I need not fear your turning away
your sweet face from me with an incredulous and unsympathiz-
ing smile, when I declare that my silence has really been the
result of *inability*, though I have been all the last week on my
legs—yesterday however I sat down to write to you at last a
long letter—when behold the Sterling carriage drove to the
door—" *without encumbrance* " putting itself at my orders for
the forenoon—and as I very much needed to go to the Strand
to enquire the result of Chapman & Hall's cogitations as to
Geraldine's Manuscript which has been laid on my arms and
left there (!) very much as the baby which the gentleman in the
omnibus incautiously undertook the holding of, while the mother
stept out—I judged this an opportunity of getting that business
transacted *without fatigue* which in my present feeble condition
I ought not to neglect.   You know that with all my laziness
when there is *real business* to be done, I make it a point of honour
never to let it linger or miscarry for want of exertion.   Geraldine
was extremely helpful to me about my *Mudies*—I owe her
a service " decidedly "—and besides by putting her into the
way of getting her " superfluous activity " vented in printed
books I consider that I shall have done a real act of charity—
what is to come of her when she is old—without ties, without
purposes, unless she apply herself to this *trade?* and how is
she even to have a *subsistence* otherwise, should her Brother take
it into his head to marry ?   All these considerations have made
me very anxious to find a Publisher for her *first book ;* and
contrary to Carlyle's prognostications—beyond almost my own
hopes I yesterday found that her MS. was *accepted*.   (Do not

speak of this publicly, for it will be some time yet before the book *gets out*)—Certainly it is a very remarkable book, and well worth being tried—but when I think how John Mill's Logic which he spent *ten* years over—and Carlyle's *Sartor* a real " *work of Genius* "—had to hawk themselves about thro' all the *trade* before they could so much as get printed *free of cost*— I do wonder at my good luck and *hers* in having this philosophical novel accepted by the first man I offered it to—on the principle of *half profits*. Their counsellor as to the publishing of new works—whoever he may be—told them that it had " taken hold of him with a grasp of iron." Think of little Geraldine having a *grasp* like *that* in her ! Well, this morning as in duty bound I have had to write her the good news and now I am too wearied after all the " *explaining and expounding* " of my letter to *her* to write another letter of any magnitude even to my Babbie. Last night my incautious husband shoved *his* stone bottle of warm water over the bed—and the thump which it made on the floor just over my head in the dead watches of the night—just when after weary hours of tossing about I was fall-ing into sleep, of course put all ideas of sleeping far from me— and I have risen after a horrid night in a condition more dead than alive—curious coincidence of *bottles !*—there has also been a curious coincidence of *rings*. Two days after my last headache I missed a little ring from my finger which I wear constantly—one that was my Aunt Jeanie's—I made a strict search for it and finally had to give it up for lost—when Carlyle putting his hand into *the inside pocket* of *his dressing-gown* felt something and drew out in wonder the ring !—in my agony that day my hands were clutching at every thing within their reach and had clutched it seemed into his pockets and left the ring there ! But I trust in heaven there will not be a coincidence of *chimneys*—here the *disgrace* is the least of it, for we have to pay a fine of *five pounds* ! . . .

Oh my good Babbie what a wretched scrawl to put thee off with—but indeed I am good for nothing just now.

God bless you all—

Your own
J. C.

75.   *To Jeannie Welsh*

The Lion's wife—Deals with the bores—Mazzini and his disappointments—Carlyle, Cromwell and staying in London—A Glasgow
servant for Liverpool.

(13*th April*, 1844.)

DEAREST BABBIE,

I am sitting here to wait my Lord Jeffrey who came
to town yesterday—he may be here in five minutes or not for a
couple of hours—anyhow I may as well be turning my hand
with the fleeting moments as they pass, tho' under the circumstances you are likely to find me " very much detached."

Often in these weeks I have had *accesses* of Carlyle's mania
or " a house in some perfect solitude " (only *not* Craigenputtock) : there are so many interruptions to fritter away one's
time in this No. 5 Cheyne Row that my serious conscience
begins to protest against them. " When the Devil was sick,
the Devil a Monk would be ; the Devil got well and the Devil
a monk was he." But *I*—have not got well yet, and do not
feel as if I should ever get well enough to relish my existence
of Lion's-wife—especially so long as the Lion's self will not
take *his* part on his own shoulders but rolls over that also on
mine. Decidedly I begin to be weary of *doing* all the *bores*—
while if ever perchance an exceptional human being drops in
that one is carried off to smoke in the garden or talk tête à tête
in the Library ! Last night for example we had here the
Captain Mackenzie who played such a distinguished part in
the Afghanistan affairs—a real *Hero* and no mistake—and along
with him his wife and wife's sister. It is like listening to the
Mysteries of Udolpho in the first blush of one's youthful
enthusiasm to hear that Mackenzie telling " the dangers he
had passed "—but not a word of this was I privileged with
hearing last night—while Carlyle talked with him and John
Carlyle with the clever little wife's sister I was left with the
deaf young wife " all to myself "—who adds to the misfortune
of being exceptionally deaf a perpetual need of hearing what
is going on, so that by the time they were all got out of the house,
my throat was too sore " for anything." . . .

Nobody of mine is thriving just now. . . . Mazzini look
as if he had been boiled in tea leaves, and is *sad* beyond all word
to say.   These disturbances in Italy, that *will* not cease and *ca*
not come to anything worth while, keep him in a perpetua
slow fever.   He has been for the last two months ready to sta
at a moment's notice to throw himself into any part of th
movement where anything *positive*, no matter with what *succes*
seemed in the way of being done, but these prospects of revolu
tion so magnificent at a few weeks' distance always melt int
nonentity like the garden of Adonis on a nearer approach
Meanwhile he is to be deeply pitied, for however useless hi
feelings may be to himself or his country they are *nature*
and *noble*. . . .

Carlyle works away at his Cromwell without a word sai
of the *country* as yet.   Of course we shall have a vast deal c
mental locomotion before any *material* mile is travelled.   Nav
I should not wonder if after his last year experiences he shoul
decide on staying in London this summer—it is possible, th
more so that I am so eager to be out of it. . . .

I trust in heaven that small specimen of Glasgow humanit
which I have sent you will turn out a good bargain in the lon
run.   Make her my compliments and say that I hope to fin
her going on bravely when I come—it is good to keep up expecta
tions of that innocent and affectionate sort.   I found mos
of my hopes of her on the power of *attaching* herself which
read in her face and voice and in the few words that fell from
her when I gave her my parting benediction.   If you *exploit*
that judiciously, I think you will be able to teach her youn
idea to shoot any way you would have.

Bless you, dearest love.   Tea comes.   Love to them all.

> Your own
> JANE CARLYLE.

76. *To Jeannie Welsh*

Cavaignac's story and a visit to the Indians—Plattnauer shocked
by Jeffrey—James Baillie in prison.

Mr. Empson had married Jeffrey's daughter Charlotte.

Tuesday (23rd *April*, 1844)

DEAREST BABBIE,

. . . Then I went another day quite alone, in sober
sadness, to see *the Indians*. And another day with Mrs. A.
Sterling to see Tom Thumb—Tom Thumb I had the greatest
possible wish to steal away in my pocket. The Indians were
below my ideal of Indians—but I shook hands with them as all
the hundreds of people present did, and can now say thro'
all coming time when asked " have you seen the Indians ? "
" Yes I have seen them ! " The cause of my going there,
and alone, was that—Cavaignac is again writing in the *Revue
Indépendante !* You may not see the connexion at first sight—
but the one thing followed out of the other *quite naturally* I
assure you. Mazzini had told me that Cavaignac was becoming
decidedly a literary man—that he had an *Algerine Tale* in the
last number of that Review, exhibiting " a *calm* and *spiritualism*
—as opposed to *action* "—which he, Mazzini, considered to be
proof positive of his being " a *lost* man "—but which he
doubted not *I* would find " the right frame of mind for a
Demi-god "—" while even *he* " must confess that the thing as
a *literary composition* far surpassed anything he had read of his
before. The story was of a Father who had an only son " in
whom *the soul* had not awaked ; " the Father, however, confident
that the boy *has* a soul, could it only be *got at*, tries all means
natural and magical to inspire him. The first part of the Tale
ends in his trying the influence of an adorable woman upon the
youth " but *that* " said Mazzini " *even* that does nothing at
awaking his soul "—and there the Tale stops for the present.
Now as I saw in this curious idea a design on C.'s part to
produce his own *confession of faith* under an allegorical form, I
was most impatient to read it for myself and set off early next
morning to get a sight of the Review in the Reading Room of the

London Library—but the Revue Indépendante was just the only French Review which they did *not* have. So being there so early, tired, disappointed, not knowing what to make of myself for the rest of the forenoon—(a walk in the morning always unsettles me for doing any work at home) being thus circumstanced I could think of nothing so suitable as to turn in and take a look at the wild Indians! Their war-whoops would probably harmonize with my discordant feelings better than the human speech of anybody I might go to call upon!

My dear I would have given something considerable that you had been here last Sunday morning to have seen Plattnauer's face—while a much more fiery trial was appointed him than that of having to *wash his hands* before Ladies—while we were sitting very peaceably together Lord Jeffrey and Mr. Empson were announced—I sprang up delighted of course to see Jeffrey who had not warned me *this time* of his being come back to town. As it was not our first meeting however, and I had kissed him sufficiently when he came ten days ago, *I* was not thinking of going thro' *that* ceremony—but *he* having a strong natural tendency for *cuddling* people (without the slightest earthly harm in it) and taking advantage of his being now near seventy years of age to indulge this *innocent* taste to the fullest extent, took me all in his arms *as usual*—regardless of the presence of Plattnauer, Empson and *Helen* (as indeed he would have done the same before twenty starched Dowagers) and gave me one kiss after another, not " *on the brow* " or any of those delicate spots, but *plump on my lips !*—calling me " my darling Jeanie !—my sweet child ! my dear Love ! ! ! " and then when we had got over *the brunt* of the business and sat down on the sofa he ceased not a moment from kissing my hands, stroking my hair, patting my face—and saying the tenderest things in the tenderest tones ! Now all this was nothing at all for Empson or myself, or anyone that knows Jeffrey's *ways* and that knows *his age*—and that knows the sort of *Paternal* affection he has entertained for me upwards of fifteen years. But if you will just look at it with Plattnauer's eyes ! My attention was attracted towards him by his *convulsive* snatching up of a newspaper—over which he stooped is head, blushing !—Oh merciful heaven *how* he was blushing he poor young man !—He seemed only to sit witnessing such uperhuman indecorums from the total inability into which is astonishment threw him of going away !—At last he *reeled* cross the floor and bade me good morning with a look " significative of much ! " I have since heard that he went rom here to Elizabeth to compliment her on the extraordinary character of *Scotch salutations* as illustrated in the meeting he ad just witnessed betwixt Lord Jeffrey and Mrs. Carlyle.

Elizabeth begged him for God's sake " not to take the practices of Lord Jeffrey and Mrs. Carlyle as a specimen of *he national manner* "—but said she " I tried to comfort him by he assurance that Lord Jeffrey was 70 which he would not owever believe for *he* was quite *struck with his handsome-uess* " *!* *!* *!* Certainly if he had got *that view of the subject* he procedure was perfectly awful ! * . . .

James Baillie writes to me again in spite of all my hard-eartedness—and this time I *must* answer for he writes *in Prison* —I will send his letter next time—I wish he would give me up or—merely to hear of his troubles which I cannot help him ut of—which only God can help him out of by putting some sense and principle into him, makes me very uncomfortable vithout doing *him* any good. I would take any pains to find some situation for him if there *were* any situation for which he s fit—save that of *Marker to a Billiard Table* (!)—which I have o interest to procure him—but as to lending him trifles of noney merely to keep him afloat from day to day, he had better at once blow his brains out—Love to them all and kisses—Be sure to tell me of little Glasgow.†

Ever your own

J. C.

* The story continues in Letter 78.
† The Scotch servant at Maryland Street, who had been found for the Welshes by Mrs. Carlyle. See p. 196.

77. *To Jeannie Welsh*

Madness in the air—Garnier and his delusions—Mazzini and an impertinence from Sterling—Robertson and Helps—A letter to E. Pepoli from the Welshes' servant (see p. 212)—Mrs. Crowe.

(? *6th May*, 1844.)

DEAREST BABBIE,

My life for some days back has been " as good as a play " (to use *Mrs. Macready's* favourite simile) or one might even compare it to a novel by Mrs. Crowe—futile in the extreme, but so full of plot that the *interest* (such as it is) has never been allowed to flag. Take Friday forenoon for *speciment* (Robert Macturk). I sat down to write to you and while I was still seeking a pen that *would* write, " there came to pass " a knock long, lugubrious, distracted, which, skilled as I am in the physiognomy of door-knocks, I knew not what to make of. On the door being opened " a heavy body " walked in, of which I heard Helen inquire " your name if you please Sir ? " " I *have* no name," was the answer in a sepulchral voice—" *sarv'd her right* " ; for she knew it well enough without asking—as appeared by her flinging the door open and announcing " *Mr. Garnier*." I rose to give him a cordial welcome for I had not seen poor Garnier these many months and heard in the interim a vague rumour of his being in Prison. But when I saw the figure he was I could scarcely swallow down a scream. He looked *bigger* than ever—*blown up* in fact—his grizzled hair hung horrible about his head like a mop—his face, hands, and clothes were in the last stage of dirtiness—his shirt all open in the breast disclosed " what shall I say ? strange things upon *my* honour ! "—and the rolling of his eyes clearly indicated him to be as mad as a March hare ! I concealed my dismay as well as I could and bade him sit down and began asking him the usual questions. If his look had frightened me his speech frightened still more—" He had discovered a *nest of murderers* in the court where he lived, he knew of *twelve* who had been murdered by them—' it was quite a Burking business '—he had heard the screams of a woman in the night, had looked from his window and seen the murderers *of whom his Landlord was*

e chief, hide the dead body in a dilapidated house—there were
ood stains on the floor next morning and in spite of all this the
uthorities would not inquire into it—disbelieved his word—
s—damnation, he who in his own country had fought *twenty-
ve duels* to preserve his honour from stain (that's a fact) was
be insulted with impunity by the English—no by God—he
ad sworn to be revenged—the blood of the whole English
ation should wash out his disgrace ! (pleasant talking !)
enceforth he was the deadly foe of every Englishman ! "—
Well " said I trying to seem unconcerned tho' my eyes were
tently watching his least *movement*—" I am not an *Englishman*,
at a *Scotch-woman*, so you need not look so furious at *me* ! "
I have *done for* Mazzini however " said he—" and that is so
r good ! ! ! " then suddenly turning on me the most benevolent
es in the world he said with a quite *paternal* tenderness " you
ok *better* than when I saw you last ! a *little* better, but always
le ! " No wonder that I was pale just then !—and then
e tears rushed over his face and he turned his face quite
vay from me as if I were awakening some consciousness in
m which he could not endure. After half an hour of the
oodiest talk (during which I had the fortitude *not* to send for
arlyle—his mad fury seeming to have *men* rather than *women*
r its object—and my heart really quaking at what might happen
I brought a *man* to my rescue) he rose and stalked to the
oor—there he stopt and held out his hand to me turning his
ead in the opposite direction—I gave him my hand boldly—
hich *I* had soon reason to repent for he *crushed* it in his as if
meant to reduce it to a jelly. I screamed and fell half
inting over his arm—and tho' I cried several times " oh for
od's sake ! " he held it at least a minute in this horrible grasp.
hen he quitted it I held it up all red and swelled—He looked
it for a moment with a devilish satisfaction—then his expres-
on suddenly changing he said kindly " oh you are hurt—well
am sorry—but *it was necessary !* " then he walked slowly
vay—Heaven preserve me from any more such *necessities* !
y hand could *take no hold* of anything for many hours after
id it is not quite right yet.
    He had not been gone ten minutes when Mazzini came

to show that he had not been " *done for* " in the worst sense
the words—and while we were still gravely discussing po
Garnier's state and consulting what could be done for him
in the way of discovering his mother—or getting him put u
before he does any mischief which he is in the fair of—O
Sterling came—and finding M. here and something *gra*
going on betwixt us *He* was seized with a fit of " tempora
insanity " in which he permitted himself to utter *an impertinenc*
whereupon my humour being already jarred I told him that I
was an old fool and had better get about his business—n
exactly *in these words*, but that was the purport.   So with a lo
which Mazzini said was like that of a wild beast—I was n
heeding for my part how he looked—he started up and to
what was intended to sound—as an everlasting farewell !

"Will he ever come back ? " said M. ; as the door w
slammed behind the irritated John *—" Yes," said I, " the d
after to-morrow at furthest—he will rage out to-day—su
to-morrow—and come back on his knees (figuratively speakin
the day after "—and so it was—or rather he did better for I
sent me the carriage yesterday with a touching message th
he was too ill to write or go out—but sent me the carriage f
my own use—of course I sent it back again unused—for I do n
forgive him all at once in these cases and besides when it can
—Plattnauer was here.

Then after Sterling, came Robertson whose *normal* sta
is a *certain* insanity.   I rung for boiling water and made mys
some Brandy negus to brace my shattered nerves—then I we
out with Mazzini and him seeing they were determined to s
each other out, and not choosing to remain quietly the victi
of this conspiracy—on coming in there was a boy leading abo
a horse before the door and I found Arthur Helps lying on n
sofa asleep ! ! !

And so on ! the air is full of madness at present—I cou
give you more extraordinary instances than the above out
my own experience—but one cannot *write* everything.   Y
have read in the newspaper *our* murder I hope—you cann

---

* The familiar name of John Sterling slips from Mrs. Carlyle's p
instead of Edward.

ink how much more interesting a murder becomes from being
mmitted at one's own door.

I saw a letter from your house the other day to Elizabeth. It
as to the following effect :

> " *Cowntess Puplow*
>
> " I am arrived here saf I hope you did not tak it amis that
> i have not written to you—i have been very busy since I
> cam to this town—I am very comfortable—*thy* are very kind
> to me—but I have a good deal of wark. Tell Cownt
> Sartoriow that I will write to him when I can find time—
> Your obliged
>
> MARGARET "—

e hand was strong—and flowing—Elizabeth dreaded that
was *a man's*—but I comforted her with the assurance that the
elling which I have not at all done justice to could be nobody's
t the girl's own.

I was glad to hear that you had a prospect of seeing
rs. Paulet again. I was just going to have asked if she had
elted into thin air.

But I must conclude for several reasons—the best that
y letter is already long enough. Kindest love and kisses to
em all

Ever your own
affectionate JANE CARLYLE.

. . . I forgot the address Margaret gave Cowntess Puplow
Mr. Welsh's 20 MERYLAND *Street*.

78. *To Jeannie Welsh*

A sequel to the scene with Jeffrey (No. 76).

Tuesday night (15th *May*, 1844).

. . . Plattnauer *did* come back—(I saw him out of the
riage to-day that is why I [am] bringing him in so oddly)—
told me that Elizabeth, when he was expressing his astonish-
nt to her—turned to Pepoli who is going with her to Kirkaldy
July—and said in an encouraging way—" I assure you Carlo

P

you may travel from one end of Scotland to the other withou
meeting anything of the sort "—great comfort for the *modes*
Carlo *no doubt !*   He told me also being unusually communi
cative that on his remarking that Count Krasinski was pre
posterously fond of Mrs. Carlyle Elizabeth said dryly " oh al
the men are *that ! !* "   Slightly splenetic don't you think
and monstrously stupid if it was meant to *warn* Plattnauer— . .

79. *To Jeannie Welsh*

Carlyle's exacting ways—Miss Bölte goes at last—Anthony Sterlin
follows the rest of his family.

Miss Bölte was a German governess, whose devotion to Mr
Carlyle outweighed her occasional obtuseness.   Mrs. Carly
had taken her in, for " ' that damned thing called the milk o
human kindness ' is not *all* drained out of me yet " (15.v.44
the sea captain's phrase, as in L.M. ii. 324.

Kirkcaldy Helen had taken a holiday : Maria, the substitut
was sadly flustered by Carlyle's exigent little ways.

For Theresa see p. 7.

Friday (31*st May*, 1844

. *As she is* she [' the new woman '] might be gone on quit
comfortably with in any other house but this, where it is cor
sidered the sin against the Holy Ghost to set a chair or a pla
two inches off the spot they have been used to stand on ! an
where the servant of a week is required to know all the *ou*
and ins of the house as currently as the servant of seven years
Men are very unreasonable really and this man in particula
is enough to turn one's head—at times. . . .

Just fancy Bölte staying on thro' all my difficulties, fro
week to week, and when I had only offered her a bed for tw
days betwixt her coming to town and Mrs. Buller's.   Indee
her stay was assuming an air of *permanency* which made my bloc
run cold, and not only *mine* but everyone's that frequents th
house—for you know her way of sitting gazing at one's visito
without ever speaking a word—Anthony Sterling requeste
as a particular favour that I would " marry her to Plattnau

nd so set the two pairs of gazing German eyes to gaze at one
nother ! " She is gone now however " *thanks* God ! " is
ngaged to Sir James Graham at a salary of a hundred guineas
year ! Mrs. Buller told Lady Graham that she was recom-
nended by *me*, and that *she* had considered all other recom-
nendation perfectly superfluous—whereupon Lady Graham
as pleased to say " oh certainly ! Mrs. Carlyle's recommenda-
on is to be received as *conclusive !* " So " the first chapters
f Genesis " are silenced for ever !—and now having done my
uty of general humanity so successfully by her, I recommend
er to Destiny and her own deserving—for I really *am* sick of
y protegée !—She is an excellent governess ; the miraculous
nprovement she had wrought on Theresa proves *that* beyond
ll doubt—But for a companion to *me !* the cat is an angel in
omparison !

. . . Somebody has just sent me the present of a new sort
f coffee pot—I fancy it must be Anthony Sterling, who is
aking up the *family-feelings* towards me—he gave me a *large
ug* the other day !—bless you my darling. Pray for me. . . .

Ever your own

Postscript in Mazzini's hand, at the head of the first sheet :

Read approved and confirmed. Jos. Mazzini. May 31.
want to write a long epistle to you, and will do so one of these
days. I believe, from approximative calculations, that you
vant a fresh supply of *progressive* paper for your curls. Mean-
vhile have the homage and good wishes of Your devd. J. M.

80.   *To Jeannie Welsh*

Need of consolation—The Cromwell atmosphere—Inspires devotion in
her servants.

(After the 10th June, 1844, the date of the enclosure.)

Yes Babbie ! I *do* need to " have my hair combed "—
need it horribly ! and—by the Lord Harry your hands shall
lo it before I am much older !—there now ! that sounds like
a positive promise I think, and the next thing will be to get it
accomplished—I have put off writing till I could bring my

longings and purposings to something like a fixed determinatio
and now I tell you, that so far as one can make sure of anythin
in this Destiny-ruled world I make sure of seeing you in
fortnight or so from this date. What a pleasure to kiss my ow
Babbie again ! to kiss everybody !—If I had once got over th
journey—the going into your house *again*—and all which wi
at first remind me too sadly of my last fearful visit ; I sha
be very happy I am sure !—as happy as *I* can be under an
possible circumstances.

You see my dear " the Reign of Terror " *is* raging itsel
wild here now ! and I begin to be weary of it—moi ! and i
begins to look a stupidity rather than a heroism in me to sta
till my life is crushed out in it—seeing that my life is precious t
many deserving persons besides myself. And then where o
earth should I fly to, but just into the " bosom of my family "—
of all that is left of family for me here on earth ?

My uncle's " *tell her to come at once* " has sounded *in th
ears of my heart* ever since I heard it—And then it is so plainl
" *a duty* " to go !—for I shall return after a week or two of you
kindness, and of abnegation of worries, in a much more philo
sophic temper of mind, and more up to the necessary effort
and endurances of my lot of *Man-of-Genius's-wife*. . . .

Helen arrived last night betwixt eleven and twelve—
. . . She seems as glad to get back as the other is sorry t
go away—Poor Maria ! she had been *crying* off and on for th
last two days—certainly I have a wonderful luck for inspirin
fervent *passions* to servant-maids ! She is going to Blount th
Chemist in Cheyne Walk, this Maria, which I am really glad of
I should have quite suffered to see her bundling off with he
bits of bundles and boxes into unknown space ! There I shal
have my eye upon her and be cheered occasionally with th
sight of her innocent good humoured face— . . .

81. *To Jeannie Welsh*

Sir James Graham and Mazzini's letters.

On June 14 Mazzini's complaint that his letters were bein
opened in the post was brought up in the House of Commons
Sir James Graham admitted his responsibility. He ha

cted as other Home Secretaries before him under a statute f Anne. But with his genius for being unconciliatory he id not proceed to explain that in this case he had only acted t the request of Lord Aberdeen, who thought it right as 'oreign Secretary to discover if plots were hatched in England gainst foreign Governments. The matter was referred to secret committee of nine, who reported fully to the House p. 209).

(*19th June*, 1844.)

DEAREST BABBIE,

I have fixed my day—and mean to keep it—on Monday next, God willing, I shall be deposited in your arms— ransmitted by railway in better or worse condition—I cannot et specify the hour in the evening.

Meanwhile I am " very much excited "—more than ever eeding to have my hair combed—if you have been casting our serious eyes on the Public Prints you may have seen the ffair of " *Mazzini's letters* "—I will tell you all about it when come—it is no news to *me* for I have been in the secret for aonths—but it is news for this *free* country of England— isgraceful news—and the thing which is setting up my blood ıst now is the cool way in which Englishmen take the acknow- dgment of a fact which *before* it was acknowledged they eclared to be *too bad for being credited* !

Carlyle has written a glorious letter to the " Times " on the ıbject—but the " Times " with its accustomed personal rejudices will possibly decline inserting it.

Darwin advises me " to apply for copies of all *my* letters to I. at the Home Office "—but my letters have a long while ack been written more for the Austrian embassy than for the erson they were addressed to—nay I lately said at the end of a ote requiring despatch that " Mrs. Carlyle would be par- cularly obliged to the embassy to lose no time in forwarding ! " God bless you all—I have no patience for *writing* now—

Your own,

J. C.

82. *To Jeannie Welsh*

Geraldine's " tiger jealousy "—Other guests—The Bandieri.

Seaforth House.
Friday (12*th July*, 1844

DEAREST BABBIE,

Thanks for your letter,—doubly welcome that I wa
not expecting it—for the *justice* of the matter was clearly tha
I should write rather than *you*. My cold is not *quite* gone—a
least I do not feel it safe to take the smallest liberty with myse
—durst no more, for instance, drink two tumblers of porte
and two glasses of champagne and a glass of Madeira all i
one day than eat fire ; but I am able to keep out of bed and g
a little into the open air which is here very *open* indeed—an
am no longer the miserable being I was in the first days.

I have had another trial of temper however substituted fc
the cold in my head—an out-break—in *practical* form of wh
Geraldine *rightly* termed her *tiger-jealousy*—I will tell you a
about it when I come on Monday, suffice to say meanwhi
that Mrs. Jordan in *The Jealous Wife* acted no more astoundir
vagaries than Geraldine has been treating us to here for th
last twenty-four hours. *Thanks God*—my temper happene
to be in an *unusually* placid state—and the thing has been g
put down without any poisonings or suicides tho' not withou
great annoyance to Mrs. Paulet and the whole househol
Really the *fondly cares* of those who love us are more agreeab
proofs of their *passion* than *tiger jealousies*.

Frank Jewsbury and the Spaniard Montero were her
last night and the Spaniard played on the guitar and sang-
fandagos and ' all that sort of thing "—I take him to be som
what of a pinchbeck Hero, this Spaniard ; but he does ve
well *for the provinces*—Mrs. Ames was here also yesterda
forenoon, and sang like an angel and talked " like—like
anything ! "—I never heard such talking since I was born-
it is quite a thing worth hearing once and away, just to kno
what a woman, merely human, *can* do in that line !

I am very sad about Mazzini; the two young Bandieri
are shot! God help their poor Mother.

Love to you all and kisses—till Monday—adieu—

Ever your affectionate

JANE CARLYLE.

83. *To Jeannie Welsh*

Friday (26*th July*, 1844).

MY GOOD CHILD,

It is not to-day that I can answer your most welcome
letter as it deserves—I must keep myself *very* quiet to-day
" *morally* and physically." But I *will* write a few lines just to
certify you that I *do* love you as well as before—perhaps even
better—for I feel more *sorry* for you than before. Take that
consolation, such as it is. . . .

Mazzini came the first morning—I asked him " how he
knew ? " He shrugged his shoulders and said " the wonder
would rather have been if I had *not* known "—I find him looking
better than I expected. He awaits the decision of the secret
committee with supreme indifference. On Lord Brougham's
great idea of the " *Gaming house* " he remarked that he wondered
so imaginative a character as Brougham had not rather accused
him of having " kept a cook-shop of human flesh ! " If any
attacks are made on his character in their *Report* he will make a
public justification of himself—and the Editor of the " Westminster Review " has been applying to him for particulars of
all the " *murders* " he has committed and projected that he
may have a vindicatory article upon him in his next number.
There are plenty of honest people now to take up his cause.
But all that is as nothing for him compared with the troubles in
Italy—the Bandieri are not certainly *known* to be taken—far
less " *shot* "—all that stuff in the newspapers was *un*official—
and *he* has had no private communications as yet—but still
he has grounds enough to fear the worst. *Lady Harriet* has been

making new advances to him—which for a Tory woman of her distinction connected with the enemy as she is, does infinite " credit to her head and *hort*." He was engaged to her last night and she had brought divers persons in authority to meet him and Carlyle was there *of course*. But Mazzini will not be caught by that syren—the insensible man that he is !—He did not come ! ! !—It must be strange for the Lady Harriet to have found *one* man that can resist her fascinations and refuse her invitations.

But I must stop, Babbie, I am doing myself hurt by writing even this sort of babble—God bless you my own Babbie—only beware of marrying Mr. B—— and all will be well *some time*. But *that would* be a fatal step if I have any spirit of divination in me ! I dislike that man *at once* and *for ever*—ask me not why—for I cannot tell you—only he is antipathetical for me. My first look into his eyes satisfied me that he would never make a deserving husband for my own *upright* gentle Babbie.

Kiss my uncle for me—alas—that I should need a proxy for so pleasant a duty—and give my kindest love to all the rest

Yours ever affectionately

JANE CARLYLE.

84. *To Jeannie Welsh*

Method in self-improvement—Lady Harriet's fascinations (C. and Mazzini)

(1st *Aug.*, 1844.)

. . . I have been in a most dejected state all these days and have been holding on like grim death by the *safety-rope* of *method* amidst the general shipwreck of my powers of body and mind—doing certain *small things*—such as one *can* still do— with a certain regularity and a certain determination of purpose is I always find the best resource in these conditions. If one attempt anything *great*—or exerts oneself only by fits and starts —nothing comes of it but failure and deeper discouragement. Of a heap of letters that had accumulated on my conscience I have been making it a law for myself to write *just one* each day—and each day I have hemmed two towels ! ! and each day

ead two *articles* in Jeffrey's miscellanies. This is very *humble*
ork certainly but with so much headache and sickness it is a
air conquest from the *Inane*.

Yesterday I ate *the wing of a chicken*—and received the
ongratulations of the house thereupon—on the strength of
his I am writing longer than usual to-day.

Carlyle is to dine with Lady Harriet again to-day—and this
ime poor Mazzini *must* go—I begin to have a real *admiration*
or that woman—her *fascination* of Carlyle proves her to be the
most masterly coquette of Modern Times !—A hundred kisses
o my Uncle—I shall never get that *paying for my seat* out of
my head—there was something so *very* unclish—so *fatherly*
most, in the way it was done . . .

And so God keep you my Babbie.

Ever your affectionate

J. C.

85. *To Jeannie Welsh*

roportionable sympathy for illness (again)—Improving health and
occupations—Geraldine and her publisher—"Loves with the
Painter "—Servants back at Liverpool.

Margaret, the Welshes' servant, had just lost her mother.

Monday (*Aug.*, 1844 (?)).

Dear,

Harriet Martineau has clearly shown in her *Life
a Sick Room* that to accept more sympathy than one's
curate due is a turpitude little short of stealing a purse.* I
asten to tell you then, that I am now in *my usual*, can *eat* and
ep again in a reasonable sort of way, and if there be any
uth in looking-glasses, have changed my colour from sea-
een to a modest yellow. *At last* I shall receive those compli-
ents on my " *improved looks* " which even the force of habit
respecting persons who have had " *change of air* " has not
t obtained for me from an observant public. But then,
as, " *the wished-for comes too late* " now, as always, for the
blic is all gone or going " into the country." Only two or
ree scattered individuals still remain to one, left by the ebb of

* Cp. Letter 72.

fashion like weeds on the beach ! *tant mieux*, for *moral* purpose;
The soul gets leisure to listen to itself in this silence, and t
form " good intentions "—if it could but keep to them !

With my improved health the standard of my occupation
has proportionately elevated itself. I sat down the other da
to a determined critical reading of Voss's *Homer*—the onl
translation which gives a person ignorant of the Greek an
adequate idea of the real Homer. I am horribly rusted i
my German I find, so that I get on with it very slowly, but th
task is very well worth the pains. *That* employs two or thre
hours in the morning. Then I am translating—or to spea
accurately—I have *bought foolscap for translating* somethin
which I did one half of years ago and which I should like
see in print before I die. Then I am making extensive an
enlightened repairs of the household linen !—I *mean* to hav
a piano !—and *I think* a great deal ! Perhaps like the ol
woman at Haddington, I also " *repent* a great deal." But I c
not *cultivate* that branch of morality. I have always indee
considered *remorse* the most wasteful of all the virtues, devourir
a great deal of good faculty which might be turned to practic
account.

I have written to Geraldine since my return but had
letter from her. I suppose she is over head and ears with h
manuscript and her *Loves with the Painter*—who was to be
Manchester at this time. Her Publisher has just been he
with me for two hours—unmerciful human being ; boring n
about alterations to be made ! I had better have written th
book all over myself than have had so much intermediation
transact !

I am very glad that poor Margaret is back with you agai
and that the cook looks promising. Give my kind regards
Margaret and say I have deeply sympathised in her afflictio
I will look when I go up stairs for some little thing to send h
just to show her my goodwill.

Love to them all. Kisses.

Your own
J. C.

86. *To Jeannie Welsh*

The rescue of poor Plattnauer.

(*12th Aug.*, 1844.)

DEAREST BABBIE,

I have been reading no German *Homer* last week—mending no linen—and my *method* has been scattered to the winds ! Still I have been much and actively employed with a matter which has indeed taken up much of my thoughts ever since I returned to London. A person whom I am deeply interested in—(I will not *name* him as connected with such circumstances—you may *divine* him perhaps—and if you do, I desire that you will keep his name secret—as it would be of the worst consequence to him in every sense that the facts I am about to tell you should be spread about concerning him)—Well this person had disappeared out of my sphere in the most perplexing manner. A letter from him lying on the mantel-piece for me at my return showed him to be got into some very questionable state of mind—laid hold of *all on a sudden* by some of these " new ideas " that are infecting this lower world in these days. He talked of being " completely regenerated so far as he could see," of being now become from the most wretched the happiest of human beings &c. &c.—and " what mostly occupied him in these days was how he could *be of use* to *me* and *Mr. Carlyle !* "—" but alas," said he " with regard to the latter I fear his hour is not yet come—if it ever will come ! "—he concluded with stating his intention to return to London the following day and to see me immediately on *my* return—to which end he begged me to write to him at his usual London address, saying when he might come.

I wrote to him accordingly to come the first morning he could before one o'clock—adding that I had read his letter three times over and did not know what to think of it the last time any more than the first—but that I looked to *him* for helping me to the solution—That I congratulated him on having arrived at Happiness by whatsoever inconceivable means, but wished he would name that word as little as possible—" *for I*

always heard it with a superstitious shudder—Happiness if ther
was such a thing at all seeming to me of the nature of those delicat
spirits which vanish when one pronounces their name"—Th
sequel has shown that I wrote those words in the true spirit o
prophecy ! It *did* cross my mind that he might be falling int
insanity—but I struggled against the idea as too horrible—
Still it was a strange letter from a man not given to foolis
enthusiasms and who has the utmost detestation for all sorts o
cant and humbug.

Day after day passed on and he did not come—neithe
write any more. At the week's end I wrote again expressin
my fears that he was ill—and begging that if such were the cas
he would either write or make somebody write for him—N
answer—Thoroughly alarmed I wrote again reproaching hi
for his indifference to my anxieties and entreating him " *as*
favour " to make me understand what all this meant—Silenc
as of death !—This was more than I could sit still under. Bu
for the English ideas of propriety as recently illustrated i
the case of Mrs. Fraser I should have got at once into a stree
cab and driven to his house to inquire after him. This I wa
regretting in the presence of Theresa * could not be don
—and the child exclaimed " you shall take Godpapa's carriag
and Godpapa himself and the servants—and *then there will b*
no impropriety ! "—And off she ran, and came back in tw
minutes, and told me all this precautionary equipage would b
at my orders in half an hour—clever Child ! off then I went—
Old Mr. Buller driving me *thro' the rain*, and having with som
difficulty found his lodging, some five miles off, I made Esco
inquire if he were *returned* and *well*—No—he had not returned—
he had written that he was coming and then again that h
" would not come any more ! "—" And his letters ? "—" Ha
all been punctually forwarded to him "—" Then they coul
give me his actual address ? " The servant went to inquir
and returned presently with a slip of paper on which wa
written

Accordium

Ham Common, Surrey

* The Bullers' godchild. See pp. 7, 204.

his in itself was a revelation—The name—and situation
aken together suggested to me at once one of those dreadful
egetable, *fraternal*, *universal-religion* establishments, which
lcott and the like of him have originated on this long suffering
arth !

Well, I thought, it might have been worse—no wonder
aat he dared not confess to *me* he had become a member of
ach an establishment !—To be sure for the time being it is
ad—pitiable—but he is too manly a person to be long hum-
ugged by such creatures and too *honest* to live in a humbug a
aoment after he has recognised it as such. So I set myself
own in forced composure " *to await*."

And I might have *awaited* long enough had not a letter come
om a mutual friend asking " can you tell me what on earth
as happened to —— I hear something dreadful has happened
» him—it is too horrible—they say he has become *insane !* "
'here then was the horrid word put into so many letters for
ae by another !—All my own vague fears turned almost into
artainties by being given back to me by another !—

My tongue and my feet were at once loosened by this
ord as from a sort of enchantment. I went immediately to
arlyle and told him something *must* be done—" Well," said
e, " I will go to Ham Common myself and see after him
xt week if you can get nobody else to do it or *do not like to*
» *yourself* (*!*)—or perhaps I will go to-morrow "—I could not
ait till " *next week* " nor yet on the strength of a " *perhaps* "
·I put on my bonnet and set off to—Craik ! That man
esired no better even than to be *suffered* to do me service—
.d in such an emergency I felt no delicacy in using him.
s I expected ; Craik being informed of such particulars as I
uld give him flung by his work and set out on the instant for
am Common, from thence to one place after another, and
me back to me here between ten and eleven at night with a
ear and full account of the whole sad affair—*He* had at the
ne mentioned, entered the *Accordium*—which he had been
siting occasionally for some weeks before. For two or three
ys he worked *in the garden* and appeared well enough—but
on he began to reproach them that they *did not carry out their*

own principles (noble detestation of humbug surviving even i
the wreck of reason !)—The *Pater* as he calls himself wa
angry and resisted his disciple's innovations—whereupon —
burst into frightful violence and proceeded to strike at them al
and break everything within his reach. The Pater as th
easiest way of ridding himself of the poor young man—got
Magistrate's warrant and had him conveyed to the nearest gac
where he passed the night in a dark cell and was found in th
morning raging mad. This the wretch himself did not confes
but Craik thinking he was holding back something hunte
about in the neighbourhood till he found one that could te
him. A young man of fortune, who had recently made ——'
acquaintance in their mutual walks and taken a great fancy t
him, heard tell of the thing—got him out of the prison an
conveyed to a private house in Richmond—but what to d
next ?—There was nobody who knew anything about him ther
—and how to discover his friends if he had any ?—He ha
torn the letters he received into such small pieces that they coul
not put two words of them together—the last which came, whe
he was no longer in a state to read it the young man venture
to open—and found it *without date* (of course, being *min*
and signed only with *initials*. There was no light to be g
from *it*—except that I had mentioned *one* name—which nan
they had traced to its owner and thence the letter *I* had receive
—Meanwhile his madness continuing too violent for ar
individual person to manage he was conveyed to Wandswor
Lunatic Asylum—as a person belonging to nobody !—

What I felt in hearing all these particulars you may *part*
conceive—I wished it were morning—to *do* something—th
what I knew not—all night I thought and thought. To go
the Asylum and *see* the locality and his doctor to get hi
proper medical assistance—if the advice he had seemed inef
cient—to discover the address of his relations and write to the
in case of the worst—to discover also the address of his or
intimate friend that I knew of in London and communica
with him—*to see himself* if the Dr. would suffer it—all th
things at least were clearly enough to be done—and I g
up with an agitated mind to do them. Craik again kindly und

ok to go in quest of the gentleman I wished to see—and
scovered him—or rather the place where he had been—for
e was gone to France for some weeks. I myself having
ritten some letters of questions—in the midst of which came
Lady to pester me about James Baillie for more than an
our—went off to Wandsworth *via* Marlbro' Street which
precisely in the opposite direction to pick up Darwin's
rriage and himself—that I might go with such an appearance
respectability as would impress the people favourably as to
— and ensure me lucid answers at all events *civil* ones.

I fortunately found the consulting physician there at the
me—and one look into his face carried the consolatory
surance along with it that my poor friend had fallen into
ccellent hands—And he told me—oh God bless him for the
omfort !—that he had no doubt but my friend would soon be
uite cured—that all this phrenzy had been merely the
onsummation of long neglected physical disorder.

From all that I saw and heard it was clear that he could
ot possibly be better than just where he is—And the hope of
s soon being well again !—and that we shall talk over all these
oes together *as past !* Oh what an unspeakable relief was
at visit to the Asylum.

But I must stop—for I am writing myself into *delirium*
emens.

They will wonder what all this writing can be about—
you do not tell—so I do not forbid you to communicate the
rcumstances—it is only the *individuality* that I would keep
oncealed.

Ever your own

J. C.

87. *To Jeannie Welsh*

Babbie's illness—Plattnauer, the third scene.

Sir Alexander Morison, M.D., was a leading authority
n mental disease, and from 1835 physician to Bethlehem
ospital. The Marchioness of Ailesbury was the mother of
attnauer's pupil.

(22nd Aug., 1844

Poor dear Babbie !

Sitting there a martyr to toothache and *all that*—an
not even receiving the slender consolation of frequent letter
from *me* ! But oh my Babbie tho' I have had no toothache
nor any *physical* thing absolutely forbidding me to write ; stil
I have not been " at ease in Zion " *moi*. I have had so mucl
writing to do about that poor man, and worse than any con
ceivable amount of writing so much mortal anxiety about him—
that my conscience really does not reproach me for havin
failed in writing to *you*— . . .

For my poor friend ; thank God he is saved !—and th
Blessing of Heaven be on the head of that good old Sir Alexande
Morison, who has treated him so skilfully and so humanely—
in other hands I have not a doubt but that he would have bee
driven into permanent insanity—for this man is the only *rea
physician* I have seen since I lost my own Father ! and *th*
case was most critical. How so many of his friends had dis
covered his state of mind—and yet not *one* of them discovere
till *I* did where he was, I am perfectly at a loss to comprehend—
especially as they are all at a distance—not a soul interested i
him left in London at this moment except myself—but the fac
is that one after another has written in the most feveris
anxiety to *me*—one, the most truly concerned to judge from he
letters, had been referred to me by a gentleman now in Dublin
To *her* only of these unknown persons have I written wit
perfect openness—for I judge her by her letters to me in spit
of her emblazoned coats of arms and all her magnificences to b
a really warm hearted, helpful woman, a *very woman* tho'
Marchioness ! (hush). With the others I have staved off " th
particulars " which they asked, and confined myself to assur
ances of his being under the best care and rapidly recovering
But no sooner do I answer than they write again—and—I ar
tired in fact.

But he will soon be able to answer their inquiries himself—
Already he has written to *me* a long excellent noble letter !—
And what is more I have *seen* him !—When I went to th
Asylum the day before yesterday—the Dr. invited me to judg

f his improvement for myself—declaring that he would *now* be
ne better for seeing me—I wondered if the Dr. knew well
hat he was saying—but I followed him into the garden,
usting in God,—where my poor friend was sitting on a bench
part from all the other patients. He recognised me a great
ay off—further off than *I* could possibly have recognised *him*
xcept by his starting up, *passing his fingers thro' his hair* (the
nly little movement of human weakness he betrayed)—and
nen with a free erect air hastening towards me—no awkward-
ess—hardly any surprise—but such joy !—He was dreadfully
ale and in the uncouth dress of the Establishment so that
ne first look was sad enough—but in a minute we were walking
rm in arm thro' the garden as if we had met after our long
eparation under the most natural circumstances in the world.
During all the half hour that I staid with him he was perfectly
ntional and composed (more so I am afraid than myself for
was " too happy for anything ")—recognising his actual
osition with a mixture of stoicism and humour—which
endered it rather *absurd* than *horrible*—nothing could be more
nanly and dignified than his whole way of taking the thing—
ven to his last action—insisting *dressed as he was*—in attending
ne to the carriage in which he *knew* Darwin was waiting for
ne, and apologizing to him in the most courteous manner for
aving detained me so long.

You may fancy Darwin's astonishment !—And now having
old you this good news I must answer a letter from Anthony
terling at present in the Isle of Wight. The Dr. promises
nat my friend will be *dismissed cured* very shortly—but he
eeds at present to be kept where he is till the *excitability*
emaining from his illness be calmed down—love to all and
isses—My dear Uncle why cannot I give him one myself—

88. *To Jeannie Welsh*

The rescue of Plattnauer (*continued*).

The authoress of *The City of the Sultan*, is the vivacious
Miss Julia Pardoe, a copious novelist and memoir writer,
hose knowledge of Turkey was unequalled by any woman

Q

since Lady Mary Wortley Montagu. She was afraid
Plattnauer.

(After 22nd Aug., 184

DEAREST,

You may well say *in this instance at least* that whi
others talk I act. Certainly I have been *acting*—with a ve
geance ! You will wonder if I have not become insane mys
when I tell you *the sequel*—would to Heaven I could call
the solution ! Last Sunday evening Carlyle and I had ju
finished an early dinner preparatory to setting off on a Cockne
Sunday-excursion to the Regent's Park to be helped out wi
tea at Mrs. Macready's—when I heard a gentleman's voi
at the door inquiring for *me*. I had heard that voice only on
before in my life but I recognized it instantly as Sir Alexand
Morison's. What on earth had brought so busy a man to n
own house ?—Was he come to tell me that *He* had committ
suicide or *escaped ?* I rushed upstairs to him as white as milk
tearing my muslin gown by the way to an extent that wou
have tried even the temper of Ann Jane.—With an impassi
air, that operated like a shower-bath on me at the moment, t
good old Doctor delivered me a letter from my friend—stati
that he had appeared before the Committee on the previo
day, been pronounced *cured* and now only waited till son
friend should " *take him out* "—a formality it seemed whi
could not be dispensed with. Would I *send someone ?* I to
Sir Alexander of course that I would come myself next morni
if C. could not leave his work. But what then ?—suff
him so soon as I had emancipated him to rush out into spa
under the first excitement natural to recovered liberty—an
without either money or plan from all I could learn ? The thi
was not to be thought of, so when Sir Alexander asked : " B
where will he go ? " I looked imploringly at Carlyle who, go
as he always is on *great* occasions, said directly " Oh he mu
come *here* for a while till he sees what is to be done next." An
so it was settled and I had no difficulty in bringing *himself*
consent to the arrangement ! !

Thro' unavoidable hindrances I was obliged to spen
nearly *the whole day* in the Lunatic Asylum and a *happier* d

hardly ever passed [in] my life. At seven at night I landed
im here in *a fly* and here he has been ever since and will be
or some time yet. Whether it be the consciousness of having
one a good action—or that he discovers a faculty and nobleness
f Character in him which he had before not allowed himself
pportunity to discover ; I cannot say—but the fact is that
arlyle seems to take to him most *lovingly* and shows him the
ttermost kindness ! ! Still I have much to keep me anxious
or not only does his future lie most perplexedly before us but—
hatever the Drs. and Committee have judged, *I* do not con-
der him by any means *sane*. He is horribly excitable—and
as many wild whims in his head which might at any moment
y injudicious treatment be exploded into madness—and his
hole bearing and manner of speech is quite changed—*for
e better* so far as that goes—never did he seem half so clever
r noble or highbred—but this very superiority alarms me.
know that *I* can keep him from any new crisis so long as he is
eside *me*—my influence over him is without limit—but then
e cannot be *always* with *me*—and I tremble at the thought of
hat will become of him when left to himself. God knows—
erhaps I frighten myself needlessly and his present state is
ut the *natural* consequence of the past five weeks.

Mrs. Buller is worrying herself to death with the fear
f his killing me—in these days of *insane* murders. Just
Jeffrey used to warn me against William Glen but no madman
ill ever hurt a hair of *my* head. I have too much *affinity*
ith them.

You will understand now it is not easy for me to write
these days. There is still a deal of writing to be carried on
ith the Marchioness—the authoress of *The City of the Sultan*
d others—which is merely *boring me* without doing the
ightest practical good to *him*. And then Lord bless you he
as torn all his linen entirely to rags, as he did all the ropes
ey bound him with. It is somewhat awful to hear him say
the midst of a calm tête à tête—such a thing crossed his
ind when they were " carrying him to such a place *in chains* "
-or " when they had chained him down on the floor of *the
ouse of Correction !* "—He remembers accurately everything

that happened only fancies that *he* was all the while quite i
his right mind and merely that the other people were " s
stupid." But I was saying his clothes are all in rags and as I hav
constituted myself his sister for the present I am kept ver
busy repairing them. What things I have done for him to t
sure ! in the way of *familiarity*. Poor poor Soul his body is sti
all lacerated with those infernal chains, and Sir A. Moriso
assured me that had any judicious Dr. or friend been besi(
him at the commencement nothing of all that need ever hav
been !

But there is his rap at the door so I must conclude for th
present.

I cannot help regretting that monster was *not* hanged i
spite of all my sympathy with his children.

Love and kisses to all,

> Ever your affectionate
> JANE CARLYLE.

89. *To Jeannie Welsh*

Carlyle visiting Lady Harriet—Mrs. C. cleaning house and attendir
to Plattnauer, still very mad.

(12th (?) Sept., 184

DEAREST,

Carlyle is gone on a visit to Lord Ashburton's i
Hampshire—Lord Ashburton being the father-in-law of La(
Harriet who with her husband is now residing there, and as tl
Lady Harriet like the Queen must have her Court about h
wherever she goes or stays, she has summoned Carlyle down 1
The Grange for a week at the least—and *he never* by any chan
refuses a wish of *hers*—the clever woman that she is !—So 1
went last Tuesday morning leaving me as many things to (
in his absence as if he were going to stay till Christmas—h
dressing room to be papered—various paintings to be done—
new carpet to be got and put down in the two rooms—h
Library to be cleared out, and all the books *dusted* oh heavens !-
with ever so much more—and all the while a madman to atter
to !—who needs to be cared for more than the most impatie:
of spoiled children—who gets quite beside himself when I eve

lk long to anyone else in his presence. Strange is it not that
arlyle should never have looked at the fact of *his* being here
the light of an impediment to his own going ?—Everybody
se was *terrified* for my being left alone in the house with him.
ut C. has no idle apprehensions ; he paid me the compliment
f supposing that I had presence of mind and clearness enough
manage perfectly well without any protection—and I am
uite of his opinion.*

How long you ask is this going to last—not very long I
aresay for as Darwin says, such eternal solicitude will make *me*
mad as himself in process of time. He gets no better—his
adness is far deeper in him and more complicated than we at
rst suspected—*I* cannot *cure* him I can only keep him safe
ntil his natural friends take him under their own care—
wrote ten days ago—telling all the sad truth to the Count of
eichenbach † and begging him to come directly to England—
ngaging for his safety in the meanwhile—it will be a week
nger at the shortest before we can possibly get an answer.
le is wanting to start, so soon as Carlyle returns, on his travels !
-out of this house for three days, alone, in his actual state,
d again he would need to be *chained !*—Carlyle is as sure of
iis as I am and will on no account suffer him to go till some
nswer arrive from his Brother-in-law. With all this you will
xcuse my rare letters—the occupation and the anxiety eat
p my whole thoughts between them.

Love to them all, God bless you—*He* desired me to " give
s love to *Jeanie* "—adding—" how this world seems to be
l full of Jeanies ! "

Ever your own

J. C.

* In L.M. i. 292, T. C. notes, " Plattnauer she had just rescued from a
adhouse, and was (with heroic and successful charity) quite taming here
to his normal state ; our perfectly peaceable guest for about a fortnight !
ismissed, launched again, with outfit, etc., after my return."
† Plattnauer's brother-in-law.

90. *To Helen Welsh*

Weariness—Mrs. Paulet's visit : impression left on Mazzini and
   Sterling—Her feeling for the Welshes—A " bed-talk " : impossibl
   at Cheyne Row.

Monday (7th Oct., 1844)

DEAREST HELEN,

. . . " Thanks God " however there has been n
new tragedy in my life since I wrote to you—only excessiv
worry and hurry—in the midst of this, rendered more *wearin*
by a long spell of sleeplessness, there walked in on Wednesda
morning last Mrs. Paulet with her husband and daughter—
they staid three days in London and good part of the tim
she passed with me—I wished I had been in better trim fo
her—but such as I was I still got good of her sunny looks an
stirring words.

She saw here Mazzini much to her contentment—and
think also to *his*—I have not seen him since to hear all he though
of her but I am sure he liked her by this token—that h
talked to her a good deal instead of sitting staring at he
with his great black eyes—the only notice which he usuall
bestows on *new* people. Nay, Heaven knows how, they fel
within the first ten minutes into an animated discussion o
Love—of all topics ! I taking a trifling part, according t
ability—I am not aware that any *new* light was thrown by an
of us on this interesting subject—tho' many pertinent observa
tions were made—as for example this of Mazzini " *woman* i
always desiring *to be loved*, man rather *to love* "—if so one ca
but admit that *man* has chosen the better part, " upon m
honour." She saw also old Sterling, Bishop Terrot and th
Count Krasinski—all of whom I must candidly confess seeme
rather *startled* than *charmed* with the beautiful Phenomenon
Old Sterling indeed passed the subsequent night as he after
wards informed me in questioning himself " how it was tha
being indisputably pretty, witty, good humoured, and gracious
one nevertheless *could not* fall in love with her ? " The reaso
I should have fancied plain enough—without need of th
clairvoyance of a sleepless night—and to lie simply in " *one's*
seventy-four years of age !—with the additional fact that havin

st lost by death the noblest of sons * " *one* " might have had
mething else to think of than falling in love with other men's
ives—but he flattered himself to have found a more com-
ortable solution of the *grande mistero* and what think you it
as ?—" her face was too *exclusively intellectual* " *! !* Oh
e thrice grained goose ! as if any *woman's* face was ever too
xclusively intellectual, and as if Mrs. Paulet's particular face
ad not—what shall I say ?—decidedly a dash of the *improper*—
ery lovable " improper " I admit—but still something that
ould bid a man who loved her—in spite of the glaring fact
f a *Mr.* Paulet—not utterly despair—provided he were a
an after her own heart—which being not easy to find—poor
Ir. Paulet may keep himself easy.   Darwin is come back—
issed her by half an hour which was a pity—one likes a person
ne likes to know the people one likes—till that is the case there
 always a certain extraneousness about them—the *new* friend
 mean.

   By the way—or rather by the direct—Mrs. Paulet seems to
ave a real hearty regard for *you*.   Babbie also she likes—but
ou I think suit her best—Babbie's *stillness* has indeed no
ffinity with her animated manner of being and she admires
er accordingly as one admires " the sleeping beauty " of the
airy tale.   I tell you this not as a mere insipid piece of com-
liment—but as a practical hint—one can always get on better
vith people when we have a clear notion how they feel towards
s.   And now tho' late, thanks for your speedy and amusing
etter—another will be gratefully received. . . .

   God keep you dearest Helen and all of you—I wonder when
 shall have another long bed-talk with you—not in *this* house
vill *that* ever take place—for *here* no one must stir or whisper
ven, after being deposited in their own rooms.   If Carlyle
vere even to suspect you were *combing your hair* after *he* was
one to bed he would not be able to go to sleep—not he—he
vould rise and smoke !   But you will accommodate yourself
o the caprices of a *house of Genius !*

   But there is four striking—adieu—

                                    Your affectionate
                                         J. C.

          * John Sterling died September 18.

91. *To Jeannie Welsh at Auchtertool*

A stiff neck—Receives visitors in the black scarf—Darwin's accident—
  His new house—The Pepolis' visit to Scotland—A letter from
  Plattnauer—Babbie getting demoralised.

(21st Oct., 1844.

DEAREST BABBIE,

I have had a " *crisis* "—not such as the Italian exiles
are liable to, which means neither more nor less than what we
term in the Scotch dialect " cleanness of teeth "—but a bilious
crisis—*dans sa plus simple expression*—viz ! violent rheumatism
in the head and neck—for five mortal days had I to lie on the
flat of my back, incapable of turning this way or that except
with my eyes ! a spectacle of " heartrending interest " to all
beholders—for I *would* be beheld—moi ! would lie on the sofa
rather than in my bed—that red bed is such a horrid sojourn
for me in the day time !—so associated with " all things most
unpleasant in life ! " Of course I mounted the black scarf—
nay even a *new* black scarf—instead of the *night-cap* customary
in such cases—and so escaped having as Fanny Kemble would
have said, " a ba-wd *effect*." The reverse of that—I was told—
by Mazzini—who never lies that I had the effect of —— the
Priestess in *Norma*. So everything has you see its *compensations*
—as we are religiously instructed—even that most inconsolable
looking thing a stiff neck.

Meanwhile Darwin let " a piece of iron heavy and sharp "
fall upon his foot—and will have to " lose a nail " and was
without hope of getting a boot on for two months—but he was
here yesterday in *a sandal*—or rather to speak without flattery
with his *foot* in a black silk handkerchief neatly tied round with
ribbons. He Darwin is about to remove into a new house—
which he calls " *the baby-house* "—not that there is the faintest
shadow of an idea of its ever being applied to the purposes of
baby-hood—but because of its exceedingly diminutive size.
I cannot imagine what is inducing him to cram himself into
such a Melusina's box—it would make you quite uncomfortable to see him touching the dining room ceiling with his
forefinger—and stepping the floor at three strides. And for
this crib of a place, dark too being overshadowed by the houses

opposite, he is to pay a hundred a year—but then says Miss
Darwin, " it is near Hyde Park—and he will not have half the
number of barrel-organs." He says, poor soul, that " he is
sure I will view it with more favourable eyes, after having eaten
a nice little dinner in it." And he has already got the
programme of this proportionable dinner in his head—" one
smelt, one patty, and one pigeon, with a little bottle of Canary."
But surely that would have suited the little Helpses better
than him.

The Pepolis are returned to Felsina Cottage more than a
week ago, I have seen her just once and that only two days ago,
she having been *doing* a cold while I was laid up with my neck.
She talks much of her enjoyment of Scotland, but in that
indescribable tone, with which Mr. Alcott used to tell us that
" *he* was always *serene* and *happy* "—and which made it
impossible for us [to] believe him tho' he had sworn it on the
Bible ! Pepoli she also says " enjoyed himself very tolerably."
But I take his own postscript in a letter of Elizabeth's to
Plattnauer as a more truthful picture of his feelings—After
praising " *Scotzia melanconica* " he adds " *fa freddo* " and that
was in the heat of summer mind you.

[Plattnauer writes sanely but for mental restlessness.]
What *is* to be done for him if he return to England as he left
it ?—But sufficient for the day is the evil thereof.

By the way Babbie—talking of evil it seems to me you are
demoralizing more and more. When I smiled at your promises
of energetic exertions to rehabilitate your spirit, if you were only
somewhere else than just where you were—you looked rather
piqued and said " you don't believe me ; but you shall see."
Well ! now I have seen !—I told you that the great things which
were to be done *when this or the other change in one's circum-*
stances took place—never so far as I could speak from experience
came to much—" *Here* or *nowhere* is America ; " must one say
to oneself if one is not (to) be turned back by the first difficulty
or disgust. There you are now " in the Country "—are " with
Walter "—and stocked with German books and all sorts of
preparations I doubt not for " *making your soul* " (as the poor
Irish say)—And what is the result ?—visitings—among people

the propriety that ever she had which was not *much* to begin
with.

Carlyle went to dine at Mr. Chadwick's the other day and
I not being yet equal to a dinner altho' I was asked to " come
in a blanket and stay all night " ! had made up my mind for a
nice long quiet evening of *looking into the fire*, when I heard a
carriage drive up, and men's voices asking questions, and then
the carriage was sent away ! and the men proved to be Alfred
Tennyson of all people and his friend Mr. Moxon—Alfred
lives in the country and only comes to London rarely and for
a few days so that I was overwhelmed with the sense of Carlyle's
misfortune in having missed the man he likes best, for stupid
Chadwicks, especially as he had gone against his will at *my*
earnest persuasion. Alfred is dreadfully embarrassed with
women alone—for he entertains at one and the same moment
a feeling of almost adoration for them and an ineffable contempt ! adoration I suppose for what they *might be*—contempt
for what they *are !*   The only chance of my getting any right
good of him was to make him forget my womanness—so I did
just as Carlyle would have done, had he been there ; got out
pipes and *tobacco*—and *brandy and water*—with a deluge of *tea*
over and above.—The effect of these accessories was miraculous
—he *professed* to be *ashamed* of polluting my room, " felt " he
said " as if he were stealing cups and sacred vessels in the
Temple "—but he smoked on all the same—for *three* mortal
hours !—talking like an angel—only exactly as if he were talking
with a clever *man*—which—being a thing I am not used to—
men always *adapting* their conversation to what they *take
to be* a woman's taste—strained me to a terrible pitch of
intellectuality.

When Carlyle came home at twelve and found me all
alone in an atmosphere of tobacco so thick that you might
have cut it with a knife his astonishment was considerable !—
Twenty kisses for your long amusing letter—the books came
perfectly safe—love to all.

Your own affectionate
JANE CARLYLE.

93.   *To Jeannie Welsh*

On feeling the need to write—Men friends more attentive than women
   when she is kept to the house—Plattnauer like Byron's bear—
   Miss Jewsbury's novel—Her publishers' fears—Appreciation
   in unexpected quarters—The " Darwin hand-shake " again—
   A learned Egyptian—Improvement in Geraldine—"Cromwell"
   desperation.

Mr. Fleming was something of a society fribble, who danced
attendance upon the Bullers and others.

Thursday (*6th Feb.*, 1845).

I pray thee dear Babbie, do not get into the " *apologetic* "
vein—when there is a real grievance apologies mend nothing—
when there is no real grievance they are uncalled for ; so that
in any case apology-making is sheer waste of human faculty.
Write to me when you like and can, and be sure that to no one
are your letters more dearly welcome—provided always that
they be written on " the voluntary principle," but do not take
up writing to me as a *duty ;* nor accuse yourself of " *ingratitude* "
or any other vice when you have preferred doing other things
than writing to me or even preferred doing nothing at all.
When I am pained by your silence ; it is not because you *have
not written* but because you *have felt no need to write* and the
worst I think of you in that case is, that (as they say in Scotland
of certain human imperfections) " it is the waur for yoursell."
To exact of you that you should *feel a need to write* were exacting
that which does not lie in your own power.   Such needs grow
up by grace of God—like the lilies—and ourselves can neither
make nor unmake them—if we obey their impulse when there,
it is all that can be reasonably required of us.   Perhaps too
we may do a little towards the blossoming of such good *needs*
by attending to the general culture of the soil—as we may
promote in ourselves wholesome tastes in diet by " attending
to our general health " (as the medical phrase is).   But when
one sees a person eating raw vegetables or *chalk* even—and
leaving his nourishing broth or roast meat—one does not
dream of calling him *ungrateful* or any other bad word—one
says merely that he will certainly do himself a mischief

and that it is a pity he should not know better what is good for him.

I have been attending to *my* " general health " here in the literal sense of the term, till I am become thoroughly sick of the occupation and doubtful whether keeping alive is worth all the fuss one makes about it. All the last week I have again been confined to the house and breakfasting in bed—the extreme cold threatening to bring back my cough—in fact have only been *four* times out in all for the last nine or ten weeks *—and then never further than Sloane Square. It is in such seasons that I find the advantage of having numerous *lovers* (*!*) The women, to their shame be it spoken, like me best when I am *well*, and when there is a chance of getting me to their stupid parties. But all *my men* vie with each other in delicate attentions to me when I am shut up—and I have really more society then than at other times, so that I can but keep out of my bedroom where it would be judged improper for an *English* woman to *receive*. There is *one* however whose attentions I would gladly deliver myself from if I only knew how with *safety*, I mean poor Plattnauer who is not only severe trial to my own nerves whenever he comes †—but positive terror to the rest. Arthur Helps was saying the other day that I seemed to " keep that madman to frighten people away as Lord Byron used to keep a *bear* for that purpose." It is not anything that he does or says that inspire apprehension so much as an idea which seems to haunt the mind of everyone who sees him even as it haunts my own mind that he will do some dreadful mischief before all's done. quite despair now of his ever being quite recovered—the madness looks to have got *ingrained* in him, and the best to be hoped is that he may subside into a half-sane half-fatuous state like Mr. C——. But it will depend I think on his life going on much more smoothly than is at all likely, that he do not make a second outbreak—and the second I am sure will make him a maniac for life. So no wonder that I *fear* to drive him away or do anything to hasten this horrid possibility

---

* She continued ill another three or four weeks.
† He had returned from Paris in January.

Sometimes he will transact the whole visit without *saying* anything that would give a stranger the impression he was mad, but there is an everlasting *chase* of strange *expressions* over his face and his manner has lost all its calm and courtesy. Last Sunday Mr. Fleming came while he was here, and very soon he gave indications of thinking that his (Mr. F.'s) visit was prolonging itself needlessly. He started from his chair at last, seized the *Cat*—danced her in the air a while like a Baby—then pitched her on the floor—and asked if he might go upstairs for some of his books still here. I said by all means—and he went off—*not* upstairs but down to the kitchen where he marched to and fro smoking and talking very loud to Helen.

I am certain in my private mind that he went away because he felt that if he stayed he would do Mr. Fleming a mischief. He told me once already how *tempted* he had been to " seize the poker and dash out the brains " of a little Aberdeen man who sat " talking the horridest stuff to me, which no woman but myself could have listened to ; for three deadly hours " ! Oh for a good inspiration how to put a *peaceable* end to these visits, the chief indeed sole interest of which has come to be the question ever in my mind ; will he or will he not to-day or some other day do to myself or one of the others some mortal harm ? Poor Mr. Fleming ! he is the greatest coward, that man, out of petticoats ! . . . So there he sat all in a *tremble* perceptibly to the naked eye—and then hurried off an hour before he would have gone in the course of nature.

Geraldine's Publisher has just been here and said he would apply to *me* to *bail* him if he were taken up for bringing out Zoe ! —divers individuals, among the rest Mrs. C. Hall (Geraldine's *kind friend*) having told him that it would do him no good as a publisher, that it was " a most dangerous book *shaking the foundations* of all sound doctrine ! " I engaged to bail him with *my head* against the book's having any serious consequences *of any sort*. He seemed all the while content with its success so far—it is talked about and that is the great point—for a pub-lisher ; whether for praise or blame is a secondary question—besides it has been more praised than blamed as yet. Among

those who have read it of my own acquaintance its warmes
admirers are just the two whom I should have said would hat
it most—Darwin and Arthur Helps—Darwin who is what yo
know—the type of *English* gentleman, the " Sir Brown
(*Indiana's* Ralph) in real life—Arthur Helps again is a man o
the *deadly sensible* sort, *moral* to the finger-ends, holding muc
by all the existing *respectabilities*—he is the author of *Interva*
of Business—*Claims of Labour* and two Tragedies remarkabl
for their *prosaic rationality*. Mr. A. X.— (to satisfy you
idle curiosity) is No. 2—and I suppose you are none the wise
for I believe you never saw either him or his pretty little butto
of a wife. By the way *who* was the other who " once befor
remarked on my manner of shaking hands with Darwin "—
have quite forgotten. But don't you see that there *must* b
something " *truly* " extraordinary (as Elizabeth Pepoli woul
say) in this Darwin-hand-shake ! Since Mr. X. *complaine*
of it, Plattnauer has said to me ; that I " shook hands wit
Darwin as if I wished to show all others how little I cared fo
them " ! ! ! And poor good Darwin never himself to hav
noticed this " the least in the world " ! like the Shepherds i
Virgil " too happy in not knowing his happiness " !

Geraldine is to send me this week a learned Egyptian o
all things in the world ! actually a living, breathing follower o
Mahomet, who has at home in Egypt a harem and all that so
of thing, and is a man of many virtues and talents, *sel*
Geraldine. He is to bring something that she has made o
rather *got somebody to make* to keep my feet warm. I mu
say so far as *I* am concerned she has been showing to advantag
of late months. In the fuss and flurry of finding herself ju
emerged into publicity, and busy too as busy can be, in tran
lating a pamphlet for Mazzini who has not allowed her ha
time enough ; she has nevertheless not failed a single time
send me the long *weekly* letter which a while ago she made
a fixed rule with herself to write me every Sunday—and th
best of it is that she never so much as speaks of expecting a
answer ! If I give her one letter for four or five she thinks
have done well. When Mazzini saw her last half dozen litt
sheets he held up one hand and said quite touched—" but n

ERASMUS ALVEY DARWIN.
From a photograph.

THOMAS CARLYLE.
From the lithograph of a daguerreotype (1848) in the possession of Mr. Alexander Carlyle. Photographed by Macnab, Glasgow.

Dear, that is *goodness !* that is *more clever* than Zoe ! for upon my honour I have sent her last week work enough to leave her not time to eat, and it is all done " !

Mazzini thinks Zoe full of talent, and the *boldness* which may be fault for " *an English* " is for him " rather *good* "—but he dislikes the book for its want of *womanness*—" it is the book of what shall I say—a *man* upon *my* honour ! "

Carlyle is now got about as deep in the *Hell* of his Cromwell as he is likely to get—there is a certain point of irritability, and gloom which when attained I say to myself " now soul take my ease—such ease as thou canst get—for nothing worse can well be ! " Desperation in that case induces a sort of content. Still I wish the Spring would make haste and favour my getting out of doors—for the (moral) atmosphere within doors is far too *sulphury* and *brimstoneish*. . . .

Ever yours

J. C.

94. *To Jeannie Welsh*

Carlyle and Cromwell—John's futile advice.

(*21st Feb.*, 1845.)

. . . Carlyle is very much out of sorts—nervous and a man sorrows *not* acquainted with *silence*—tho' he *does* love it *platonically* " *—in fact his book is lasting too long for his strength—so that we are a grim pair—and I feel a rather irksome necessity of being *patient* under my own illness and saying as little about it in the house as possible. I do not think he has the smallest idea how ill I am—at least never for above a few good moments together. As for John !—he sees me here coughing and suffering month after month and the only advice he has given was to " make a point of getting out a little—not of course while my cold lasts—but so soon as it is gone " ! ! ! if it were *gone* I should not need *his* sapient advice or anybody else's. . . .

* So Mazzini remarked.

R

95. *To Jeannie Welsh*

Geraldine's book and its improprieties—A love affair springing
from it.

(26th *Feb.*, 1845

. . . It is quite curious to see the horror excited in som
people (and these the least moral) by Geraldine's book while th
moralest people of my acquaintance either like it or are not a
the pains to abuse it. Even Miss Wilson to whom I dared t
lend it—tho' she confessed to never having " ventured o
reading a line of George Sand in her life " brought it back t
me with *a certain equanimity*—" It is *avowedly* the book of a
audacious *esprit forte*, and so of course you did not expect *m
to *approve* of it, nor do I, but I think it very clever and amusing
—voilà tout ! While old and young *roués* of the Reform Clu
almost go off in hysterics over—its *indecency*. The oddes
thing of all is that Geraldine seems to me in the fair way o
getting a Husband by it ! ! !—Q. in a fit of distraction took t
writing her letters of criticism about it which have led hin
already further than he thought—and she—has taken or
fast taking " *a fit* " to him—and both I can perceive contem
plate a lawful catastrophe. *There* is encouragement to your
ladies to write *improper* books—dearest love to my Uncle an
the rest. Write soon, it will help to keep your soul warm
your poor body must take its chance.

Your own

J. C.

96. *To Jeannie Welsh*

Ill—Miss Fox's portrait of Carlyle—Book I. next spring—Publishe
call.

(*Feb.* (?), 184

DEAREST BABBIE,
Both yesterday and to-day I am so sick—Elizabe
Pepoli might say *so* " *truly* " sick ! that I absolutely cann
set myself to write a handsome letter such as your mer
entitle you to expect. But I send you meanwhile somethi
to keep your heart up—a scrap of my execrable handwriting

and a sight of Miss Fox's horror which she calls Carlyle ! I say *a sight* for it is my positive will and pleasure that when you have laughed your fill over it and all the rest have enjoyed the same " questionable " pleasure you are to lay it on the coals and there consume it until it be dead—the only fate which beseems such a chimera ! If you do not contrive to lay yourself up with a bad cold by means of all these temptings of providence with white muslin I shall consider you quite an exceptional little girl.

Carlyle's *first* book * will be ready for printing in the Spring—he is getting on like a house on fire—there is even a prospect of their giving him a little money for this one.   Twice during the last week " we have had the visit " (as Mazzini phrases of it) of *Mr. Chapman and Hall* (Helen announced him so) to *propose*—I may mention at the same time that Moxon another bookseller took the opportunity of coming here with Alfred Tennyson and has since sent a magnificent *present of books*, his new editions of Shakespear, Ben Jonson—Massinger and Ford—Beaumont and Fletcher—Wycherly Congreve etc.— Curiosities of Literature—Miscellanies of Literature—Charles Lamb's works—Cicero ! ! ! Does it not look as if the Millennium were at hand—attentions from Booksellers are more infallible proof of *rise in the world*, for people in our line than whole string of coroneted carriages at the door.

Oh what a disgusting world it is after all ! especially with one's inside all in a worry from continual blue pills. Bless you my darling

Yours   J. C.

97.   *To Jeannie Welsh*

Geraldine's " affaire."

(*8th March*, 1845.)

DEAREST BABBIE,
          I ought to have returned thanksgiving for the improved state of the weather in writing to my natural friends— but if you knew the worry of correspondence I have been engaged in ! I am absolutely sick of the sight of paper and

* Of *Cromwell*.

ink. My dear there has been the Devil to pay in Manchester—
that was my secret—now however I feel at liberty to speak of
it to *you* and *Helen*, so little discretion having been observed by
the parties themselves.

A fortnight ago Q. went off to see Geraldine who had
already accepted him or to speak more accurately I believe
offered herself to him on paper ! ! I had from the very starting
of the correspondence warned them *both* against committing
themselves, and declined so much as *forming an opinion* as to
the feasibleness of the match—so that I had no occasion to
have been dragged into their mad doings as I have been. But
" the living—on earth have much to bear." * A few days
after Q.'s departure came a letter from Frank Jewsbury—
entreating me to interfere to stop proceedings or at least to
give recognisances as to Q.—and every day since ; I have had
at least *two* letters on the subject from the several parties—
yesterday there were four—two in the morning and ditto at
night—this morning I have *three* and heaven knows what the
evening post may bring. To all these letters from Frank—
Geraldine—Q. and Mrs. Paulet—with whom Q. now is—
answer as briefly as possible—in the spirit of Cassandra, tellin
them they are all mad—and yet they grow none the wiser.
would not answer at all ; if it were not that there is always i
their distracted letters some practical question to be answere
or some assertion to be refuted. Such letters were never
think since the Minerva Press began showered on the head of
any rational woman !

Q.—a very goodnatured somewhat chicken-hearted fello
has been *doing* the Mirabeau of Zoe, thinking I suppose that h
could not make love to Geraldine more agreeably than after
her own ideal of Love—Frank Jewsbury has suddenly r
vealed himself as a second Geraldine—full of " madness "-
" ready to die " in fact reduced to such conditions by h
sister's precipitate resolve as man never was before—Geraldi
went off in great style as a Heroine of the first magnitude b
that spaened † very shortly and has been looking of late da

* See p. 327.
† A Lowland Scots word meaning to " wean "—and so " change."

less like a Heroine than a bladder with the wind let out of it. Poor Mrs. Paulet " dreams they have both gone mad " and has had her quiet Seaforth turned into a Bedlam—Q. demanded explanations of Patten—and Patten " rung the Hall Bell " to *the rescue.*

Q. has told Mrs. Paulet last letter that he must *return to me* (oh poor me) who have so many times comforted him when no one else could !

Frank Jewsbury concludes his last with " Please to write to me and *comfort me if you can !* " (comfort *thee* thou poor Manchester dud !)—I do not exercise my *mission* so indis-criminately as that comes to !—Geraldine writes " oh write to me *can* I break off ; for I am *frightened* out of all *love.*" " Cer-ainly—I answer, only fools marry for the sheer sake of keeping heir promise."

Thus Babbie my head is a mess of Manchester *diablerie*—moreover I am getting well—and the first stage of wellness for me is always a long spell of headaches—that will wear off however now that I can walk out a little and in consequence get sleep. I have not been down to breakfast yet—have not breakfasted with Carlyle (except during a few warm days in the middle of January) for *four* whole months—I mean to try to-morrow.

Did you not feel that dedicatory letter of Mazzini's to Giacopo Ruffini to be the heavenliest thing you ever read in his world ? . . .

Ever your affectionate

JANE CARLYLE.

98. *To Jeannie Welsh*

Health—Domestic employment as reaction against Manchester—Geraldine's affair ; continued—Sir J. Graham and Mazzini's letters.

(*5th April*, 1845.)

DEAREST BABBIE,

Expect no comfortable letter from me this day ther. . . . I should like to have a feeling of being well again

tho' it were only for five minutes—I feel as if I should be able
to *do* such wonderful things, if I had only the physical force
and freedom from physical depression which so many people
enjoy without knowing their happiness—but there's no use
wishing—I " should be thankful " as the Annandale man
suggested " that I am *not* in Purgatory "—I wonder after all
if Purgatory be much worse than the sort of thing one has to
go on with here week after week, month after month—year
after year—heigh-ho !

. . . Actually since Monday I have made covers for the
large sofa, four pillows, the two easy chairs and one footstool !
not before they were needed, but what set me on them just
this week with such particular vengeance was a sort of reactionary movement against all that Minerva press nonsense
which has been transacting itself at Manchester.

The whole affair is blown up—for the present—but I am
greatly mistaken if Geraldine so soon as she finds that the man
takes no further notice of her, do not be at him again—and he
is *such* a simpleton poor Q., that anybody with half Geraldine's
art might wheedle him into anything.

Frank Jewsbury has conducted himself like " a mad " thro
the whole business, and his two last letters to me were not the
least mad part of his behaviour. Seeing there was no likelihood
of his ceasing to pester *me* with his nonsense I poured out a
few drops of vitriol on him last Saturday which brought him
to his senses with a suddenness !—Also on Geraldine a few
drops of vitriol, which brought *her* to her senses so far *as*
was concerned—by Monday's post I had a letter from Frank
Jew, making *humble apologies*—from Geraldine Jew, making
impossible justifications, from Q. goodnaturedly regretting " th
immense botheration he had given *me* who so little needed it,
but the greatest consolation of all has been a packet of *caricature*
from Mrs. Paulet which made me laugh till the tears ran down
I have seen poor Q. twice since then and have brought *him*
pretty well to his senses—*his* " madness " is the only *excusab*
madness among them—for besides that it was really a mortify
ing thing for the man to have a *second* marriage break down wit
him within *two months*, a marriage too which was none of h

wn seeking—he has poor fellow a *constitutional* tendency of
lood to the head which when anything *excites* him violently
roduces a sort of *brain-fever.*

Geraldine's conduct thro the affair has been that of an arrant
ool, tho' she should have written not one, but twenty clever
ooks. Now she is off to Paris to get the cobwebs blown out
f her brain—off with Frank and the—Egyptian ! ! I am
isgusted upon *my* honour, and she judged well not to see me
n her way but to defer that pleasure " till my provocation had
ubsided."

Have you been reading the " debates " on the Mazzini
question ? Good heavens what a *dirty* animal that Sir J.
Graham is ! he does things which a street sweeper would not
toop to !—*The Murderer* takes it all *calmly calmly*—as is his
sual—and we his friends can also afford to take it calmly
nowing what a man he is !

Ever your own

J. C.

99. *To Jeannie Welsh*

Uncle Robert's son, John Welsh—Geraldine improved.

(*10th June*, 1845.)

DEAREST BABBIE,

. . . The very day [Miss Bölte] went arrived my Uncle
Robert's eldest son from Edinburgh *—He wrote me a letter
good number of weeks ago—taking me on my weak side
—exploiting our relationship and saying very pretty things
n the tone of regret that he should know me only by name.
He might perhaps " run up to London for a few days in June,"
when he had undergone his law-trials and " wished to know
he would find us then here." You know I had not seen him
ince he was in petticoats—and I detest his Mother—but my
wn Father's nephew—I *must* be kind to him at all *risks.* So
asked Carlyle in fear and trembling if it would bother him
much should the Boy come here to stay during " the few
ays " he talked of—" Oh, I suppose you will sedulously keep

* Cp. N.L.M. i. 160, where this young man's visit is very briefly touched
pon.

him out of *my* road " said C. " and in that case he can do me n
particular harm "—And so I asked him to come here at onc
instead of going to a lodging—an invitation seized on wit
avidity—and which was of course the *aim* of his sudde
development of " natural affection " for me his unsee
cousin.

It is now near *a fortnight* that he has been here, turning th
house, at least all one's regularity and quietness, upside down—
and then he is not one of those lovable people for whom on
can resign oneself to be put about. He is a long sprawling ill-pi
together youth—with a low brow, a long nose and hangin
jaw a sort of cross betwixt a man and a greyhound !—He neve
sits—and his boots always creak as if they had a Devil. He :
argumentative and self-complacent beyond anything that on
can conceive out of Edin. Not a bad fellow absolutely—with
certain *shrewdness* and a certain *honesty* and even *naiveté*—bu
so disagreeable ! And then *of course* he is out every night :
some theatre or other devilry—and I never get to bed ti
far on in the morning—and then he cannot be got wakened i
time for *our* breakfast but after repeated assaults on " the woode
guardian of his privacy " which he carefully *locks* every nigl
as if he were a delicate virgin—he comes sprawling down :
ten or eleven o'clock and needs a second breakfast made fc
him—and in the same manner he runs after *sights* at our dinne
time and needs a second *dinner* made for him—and all th:
fuss in such hot weather drives me to despair. I sincerel
hope he will be got home to Edinburgh next week—where h
had better remain for the future—Carlyle could almost *ki*
him I see—but there is no help for it now. If you heard hii
spouting off his Edinr. Logic on Carlyle !—with no moi
respect for his superior years and wisdom than if himself wei
the Archangel Michael ! or if you had seen him the oth
night dashing in with the rudest questionings and contradic
tions into the talk of Lady Harriet who unluckily had come t
tea *—you would wonder we have let him continue to breath
so long ! One comfort is that he is in the fair way of goin
home with what he calls his *Principles* entirely subverted—fc

* An earlier date for the acquaintance than is given in N.L.M. i. 184.

the first few days I was bored to death with the *free kirk*—and the *respectabilities* and " the three thousand punctualities "— and now—to-day for example—*Sunday* (the better day the better deed) he is stretched out *on the green* (thank God) reading—*Zoe !*—with intense enthusiasm—feeling he says as if it were " to constitute a new era in his spiritual existence." He saw Geraldine on her way thro' and *she* gave by her *profane talk* the first shock to his *principles*, but *the Book* is still more effectual—I told him a few minutes ago that " having ascertained the slight tenure by which he held these respect-abilities of his ; it was to be hoped he would henceforth cease from *twaddling* about them ! " and he took the advice quite gaily. Geraldine was two days in London and spent most of her time here while the Brother and Sister-in-law went after sights—I received her very coldly but there is no quarrelling with that creature ! Before she had been in five minutes she sat down on the floor at my feet and untied my shoe-strings— " What are you doing ? " I asked—" Why my dear I am merely going to rub your feet—you look starved—I am sure your feet have not got well rubbed since I did it myself last year ! ! " and all the two days she did not leave off rubbing my feet whether I would or no for a quarter of an hour together. I never saw her look so well—she actually looked like a *woman*— not as formerly like a little boy in petticoats. Whether it be her love affair that has developed some new thing in her I cannot say ; but there was now and then a gleam on her face that was attractive—I could now fancy a *man* marrying her ! . . .

Ever your own,

J. C.

100. *To Jeannie Welsh*

The Scotch cousin, John, proceeds to Liverpool.

Thursday (19*th June*, 1845).

DEAREST BABBIE,

Orson alias *The Grampus* alias *Leviathan*—alias ur rural friend (Carlyle's various names for my unexampled cotch cousin) departed this morning to *do* Oxford—from

Oxford he goes to Liverpool to-morrow, and home in the steamer on Saturday night. I was swithering whether to introduce him to you or no—it seemed odd to let a cousin of mine pass by you unseen—and then again he is such a floundering blockhead! that question was however settled for me by his own modest assurance in plumply *asking* me for a note of introduction, which I had not the moral courage to refuse. So he goes provided with my card and some books for Maryland Street—that eternal *Camp of Refuge* which Helen never could find for my Uncle and some erudite little volumes for Sophy to enlighten her innocent mind. Do not bother yourself with him " the least in the world." He will ask what is *to be seen* in Liverpool—*suggest* the Docks and *voilà tout* —By the way I may as well mention that he professes to be " extremely susceptible " " falling in love with almost every goodlooking girl he sees—and in that way being often very much in love with several at one time "—so that if he testifie any sudden raptures towards you or Maggie you need not be too much alarmed.

My house is in ineffable disorder and my soul—what with one devilry and another I have not had an hour's peace these three weeks—and the night has been about as bad as the day—for this youth goes after *sights* at nights also and of course had to sit up for him—the crowning grace of the business has been that all the while he was professing the uttermost weariness of this sight-seeing—was *doing* it wholly from *a sense of duty*— that *sense of duty* is the devil— . . .

101. *To John Welsh*

Encounter with James Baillie—Mrs. Ames—Visit to the Opera—
A Carlylese letter from Glasgow—William Gibson.

William Gibson " was a massive, easy, friendly, dull person physically one of the best washed I ever saw ; American merchant, ' who had made, and again lost, three fortunes ' originally a Nithsdale pedlar boy ' Black Wull,' by title

Silver-headed Packman,' he was often called here."   (T. C. in
.M. i. 36 ; again in N.L. i. 80)—" to the last he was loyalty's
elf to all that held of Walter Welsh or Family."

5, Cheyne Row,
(28th June, 1845).

DEAREST UNCLE,

  I have a small piece of family news, and " I feel it
ny duty " (as Sir James Graham says when stating the most
uperfluous things) " to communicate it " to the Head of the
amily direct.   Finding myself the other day tired of my life
nd in need of what Helen calls " a fine change," I flung myself
ito an omnibus to be carried away into the remote regions of
ne City, where I might get out and enjoy a *solitary* walk,
or the solitude of the peat bog at Craigenputtock was hardly
nore *solitary* than that of a great never-ending thoroughfare
here there is not a human being to be met with that one ever
aw before or that knows or cares the least in the world about
neself.   I had myself set down beyond the Royal Exchange
n which I had never set eyes till that day, and was sauntering
ong " in maiden meditation fancy-free," casting an occasional
lance at shop windows ; when suddenly a male person placed
imself right before me in an elegant attitude, and hoped he
w me well.   In the first surprise of the thing I let him take
y hand, but so soon as I had time to think I drew it away and
id, " Indeed James " (for it was our scamp of a cousin
mself), " I *cannot* speak to you, will absolutely have nothing
 do with you."   " Pooh Pooh," said he, looking a very
carnation of *the cool of the morning*, " but you *shall* speak to
e, you shall not go till you have said that you forgive me for
at blockhead of a letter I sent you.   You must know, my little
ousin, if you do not know it already, that I am *mad* at times,
d what can a poor devil who is mad do but madnesses—Come,
is not *my* fault if I am out of Bedlam and scandalizing sensible
ople like you."   And so he rattled on looking so confoundedly
odnatured that I could not be disdainful to him as he deserved
it actually stood some quarter of an hour listening to his recent
story, which was of course all lies, tho' I could not but
e that the passersby all stared at us, in wonder what such a

decent looking woman as myself could have to say to a membe
of the swell mob—for decidedly that is the style of man he i
grown into—the shabbiest of done up Dandies! He wa
living at Greenwich he said with "a splendid prospect from
his window, but deuced little to eat occasionally"—expectin
some windfall of money from some "*settlement of his affairs*" (
(I fancy his *affairs* are pretty well *settled* by this time) perhap
too some of his friends might find him "something unde
government. He would take a situation on the railways—
anything." "It was confoundedly difficult, he found, for
man to live in London without money—*in honesty*." Begir
ning to fear that our lengthened colloquy was exciting th
attention of the Police, I told him he might walk a little way bac
with me, but must absolutely leave me before I got into know
territory—which he did quite cheerily—asking nothing of n
but that I "would not be sorry for having stumbled on hir
and forgiven him *after a sort*."

I wonder if he could not get an engagement at any of th
minor Theatres? What is to become of him "in honesty
—were hard to say—a man whose word cannot be believed, ar
who has come thro' so much, without ever discovering th
what he calls *misfortunes* are the natural consequences of h
misconduct, cannot be recommended to anything. One da
not charge oneself with the responsibility of recommending hir
How he lives at present is however as great a mystery as ho
he *shall* live—if he be managing it *in honesty* now, why then l
may for anything one sees carry on to the end of the chapter—
in living on air as in walking without one's head it is only t.
first step which is the difficulty.

I wish he were not so *good natured* for there seems r
possibility of ever getting quarrelled with him.

We had Mrs. Ames here last evening singing like a lint
Carlyle liked her very much, thanks to my management
keeping her *singing* so as to allow her no leisure to *talk*.
have had rather more of singing however than I can well dige
I was taken to the opera the night before with Lady Harri
Baring—my *debut* in fashionable life—and a very fatigui
piece of pleasure it was, which left a headache and a

uncomfortableness which I have not got rid of till this hour. Carlyle too was at the Opera, God help us !—went to ride in the Park at the fashionable hour then returned and dressed for the Opera ! ! Nobody knows what he can do till he tries ! or rather till a Lady Harriet tries ! This morning I thought I would begin the day with an energetic effort of virtue which *of course* has not been " its own reward." I got up ill and took a shower bath to make myself well *par vive force*—but these efforts of virtue never succeed with me so my headache is getting worse and worse, and this note to you which the spirit moved me to write, instead of darning the family stockings, is probably all the activity that will be got out of me for the day.

Thanks to Babbie for her long letter—the Orson writes from Port Glasgow that he was " greatly delighted with my *cousins* " and " wished the weather had permitted of his taking home some *shrimps !* " His note was in such a Carlyleish style that I could hardly understand the rest of it—a certain Bishop he mentions as " a hopelessly mendacious phenomenon, and entirely supernumerary biped on this earth "—upon *my* honour this is coming it a little too strong " even for the Provinces " (as Babbie remarked). I forgot to tell that some weeks ago William Gibson walked in out of a deluge of rain, the old man to the minutest hair of his clean-scrubbed head. He was complaining that in Jersey sugars was " *rizz* " and that Mr. Wilson was very disappointing in his " *remittances.*"

God bless you, dear Uncle,

Your affectionate,
JANE CARLYLE.

102.　*To Jeannie Welsh*

Wednesday (9th July, 1845).

DEAREST BABBIE,

Heaven be praised for all its mercies ! except for those recognised in the Annandale man's grace " the blessings

my affairs.   This will be easily managed—altogether pleasant—
and I know I shall get as much good of it as of a more laboriou
expedition.

All the rest I will tell you when I come.

I enclose a letter which came this morning (can you imagin
anything more heartbreaking than that address)—you are t
give it to my Uncle—and ask him if the person it is from i
a proper person to help—she seems so from her letter—i
there is no reason to disbelieve her story I will send her fiv
pounds—and be very glad of an opportunity to do a kindnes
which *she* assuredly would have done.   Answer me thi
immediately—for the letter has been long on the road doubtles
Oh it had far to seek !   I have seen John Greig too who crie
like a child—oh me I wish I could sleep for six months.

Send me back the letter.

J. C.

103.   *To Jeannie Welsh at Burnside, Helensburgh*

Refreshing indolence at Seaforth—Geraldine still improves.

Seaforth.
Tuesday (19th August, 1845

DEAREST BABBIE,

After all it is but a fortnight past on Friday that
have been here, and it was the end of the first week when
got your letter.   Not that I would justify myself the least i
the world.   When one is from home—out of one's usu
routine the weeks look like months and this for *me* as well :
for you—so that I have been thinking my own silence as lor
as you have done.   The fact is simply that I have been indulgir
in a quite oriental fit of indolence—" consulting my sensations
all day long—and so forwarding the great object of my bei
here, viz : *accumulating atoms*—and getting my nerve-strin
screwed up to something like *living*-pitch.   I come down
breakfast betwixt eight and nine—dinner is at half past one
that I may dine at such an early hour without doing violen
to my stomach I have to take plenty of exercise before
indeed it is wasting the goods of Providence to be in the mid

" *Nature* " without running about in it at all hours, so I have
ways to take a drive in the gig, or a walk on the shore, or
mewhere, before half past one—and as the post leaves at
vo my writing must be done *immediately* after breakfast and
ust not take up too much time in the doing—and just consider
at I am bound by my marriage obligations to write to my
usband almost every day ! ! After dinner we—*speculate !*
Geraldine being still here) and I get my feet rubbed—and I
unter on the lawn inhaling " change of air " and I glance into
rench novels—do anything rather than write—then after
a at half past five comes music and chess—and we are all in
ed by *ten ! ! !*

This life is not very industrious but it is very favourable
the accumulation of atoms ; accordingly the fatness which I
t at Hoylake has been growing more and more solid—nay
eraldine and Mrs. Paulet have even fancied to perceive a
wn of *colour* in my cheeks—but *that* I must say seems to me
mere fancy. Certainly I feel much better than when I left
ondon—and have a " wholesome desire " (as Carlyle would
y) to continue my present life for the next six months—nothing
n exceed Mrs. Paulet's kindness which is as judicious as it is
rdial—and Geraldine is very nice this year—much *calmer*
an I ever saw her. Decidedly that explosion of folly with
. has done her good—I protest against company and am
lowed to have my way in that as in everything else. . . .

My gold pen is intolerably *stiff* this day—the paper does not
it it. Carlyle sees no chance of getting away before the
t of September—I shall probably stay here till he comes and
ve up all idea of Wales—I am not a hunter of the Picturesque—
d in all other respects I fancy Seaforth more after my heart
an that Welsh mansion would be—and I shall have oppor-
nity of cultivating my " everlasting friendship " with
iss Wynn* in London—a hundred kisses to my own dear
ncle—

Ever your affectionate
JANE CARLYLE.

* Charlotte Williams Wynn, a literary light in the Baring and other
cles, who is said to have added to her other distinctions by **refusing three**
kes.

S

104. *To Jeannie Welsh at Burnside, Helensburgh*

" Earthquaking "—Private theatricals by Dickens and Forster–
    A call from Tennyson—The " earthquake " drives out Joh
    Carlyle—First visit to Lady Harriet in town—A long visit urged–
    Lady H. does not really like her.

" Hell and Tommy," T. C. explains (L.M. i. 345) ɛ
" Buller's definition to me of a Martin picture (engravin
rather) on Macready's staircase one gala night. Pictui
mad—mad as Bedlam, all, and with one ' small figure
(' Tommy ') notably prominent."

Monday night (30th Sept., 1845

Well, Babbie dear ! You do not fancy that I am waitin
on here, in the romantic expectation of receiving *anoth*
letter from you ! Oh no ! *that* were *too* romantic " *for any*
thing ! " I know that your *epistolary* benevolence at lea.
has limits, and these, for the time being, of the narrowes
So I resign myself, with such grace of resignation as is given m
to let our correspondence stand " on the broad basis " of "
suitable return " (as William Gibson * would say). " Blesse
are they who do not hope ; for they shall not be disappointed
—at my years, it is time to have laid in a tolerable winter-stoc
of *that blessedness*, such as it is—and I cannot accuse myse
of want of providence.

I have been and am busy, as " little ant or honey bee th
speedily away doth flee "—turning up my whole house fro
top to bottom, *painting*, sweeping chimneys, beating carpet
making the house into " Hell and Tommy " (I " *Tommy*
and when it will be all subsided into its normal state lies beyo
my immediate sphere of contemplation. To complicate n
household difficulties, I found on my return two wool-ma
tresses perfectly swarming with *moths !* had all the wool
boil and *dry*—and the heavens constantly pouring down rai
Did you ever see the wool of a large mattress all afloat ?
not ; pray the superior powers that you never may ! it is

* See p. 244.

ight before which the female human mind is struck stupid
with a sense of *the Impossible !* Moreover I have had an
immense letter-debt, at first almost as hopeless looking as the
National Debt, to discharge—in addition to the letter *every
second day*, required of me by Carlyle. Happily I am not
much taken up with visitors—" nobody in town "—at least
nobody *ought* to be *in town* at this season ; still stray human
beings do occasionally drop in upon me—enough to keep me
in mind that I am still in an inhabited world—a still more
forcible reminiscence of the same was our recent " Amateur
Play " *—the " realized Ideal " of Forster and Dickens. It
was—what shall I say—best perhaps characterized by Helen's
favourite phrase of admiration " *Oh how expensive !* " The
" fule-creturs " † must have spent a mint of money on it—a
public Theatre engaged for the occasion—scenes painted by
Stanfield—costumes according to the strictly historical style
of Macready—*cost* " no object." In fact Macready himself
could not have *got up* the *material* of the thing any more
sumptuously—and all this for *one* night. " To think of *the
waves* Babbie " that their frolic might have supplied to " the
poor people ! " " the working classes eating boiled dog " !
For the *acting ;* it is much praised in the newspapers—much
praised by the majority but there is a small *minority* of *one*
at least that thinks it was nothing " to speak of." There were
six or seven hundred people invited and there present by
Heaven knows what amount of locomotion *at this season of
the year !* from hundreds of miles they came—among them
were many of the leading aristocracy ; *I was told*—but to my
matter of fact eye they looked rather *a rum set.* To be sure the
Duke of Devonshire *did* sit opposite to me, with his nose
looking towards Damascus," and old Lady Holland graced it
(not the nose but the play) with her hideous presence. I must
confess " as one solitary Individual " that it needed me to be
always reminding myself " all these *actors* were once *men !* " ‡

---

* Performed September 21, 1845.
† Definition of poetry, " Pack o' lies, that fuil craitures write for diver-
sion." (T. C. in L.M. i. 206.)
‡ Speech of a very young Wedgwood at a Woolwich review, " Ah,
pa, all these soldiers were once men ? " (T. C.'s note in L.M. i. 341.)

to keep myself from being shamefully bored. With John Carlyle for my only companion, it would have needed a rather unexampled excellence of acting to have awakened me into anything like enthusiasm. I saw Alfred Tennyson in the lobby—and *that* was the best of it! And better still he came to take tea, and talk, and *smoke* with me—me—by myself me—the following evening—such at least was his *intention*, not a little flattering to my vanity considering his normal state of indolence—but the result was, that he found *Creek*, and *John* and *they* made a mess of it—" The Devil fly away with them both!" In fact the Devil *has* flown away with one of them (John) within the last few days. I fairly *painted him out* blessings on my powers of invention! There he was; waiting to " see his way clearly " and never so much as wiping his spectacles—babbling and boring, and holding oyster-like to the external accommodations of one's house—without a thought beyond! an element of confusion hindering all my efforts at order! But never let a living woman despair—I wielded the Earthquake in my small right hand, and one morning he awoke and found himself " in his old lodging "—where there was no vestige of a reason why he should not have been all this while Carlyle has not fixed a time for his return but says in every letter " it will not be long." Lady Harriet is unexpectedly in town for two days—" too ill to go out." She sent me a note to that effect and the carriage to take me to see her. More than *gracious! incomprehensible* upon *my* honour! She insisted that I had promised to " give her *my whole winter* at Alverstoke! "—and yet I have an unconquerable persuasion that she does not and never can like me! Well by and by I shall (like John) " see my way clearly." A bushel of kisses to my own Uncle—with so many daughters all taught the art of writing—pity that I can hear of him so seldom.

Ever your affectionate,

J. C.

105.   *To Jeannie Welsh*

Difficulties of letter-writing.

(*November*, 1845.)

It seems to me I must have a volume of things to tell you
by this time, but my head is of the muddiest at present, & I
have no facilities for writing such as I used to have.   Carlyle
sits always in the same room with me since he returned, with
no work on hand, & you know I cannot write in the presence
of a fellow creature, especially one who is apt to say when I
have finished a letter : " Now read it to me ! "   When he
walks before dinner some one is sure to come in & take up
the happy moment.

106.   *To Jeannie Welsh*

Description of Bay House, Alverstoke—The Paulet difficulty solved
    —Lady Harriet's charm and its limits—Plattnauer and the
    letters to his relations.

Mrs. Paulet was bringing her husband to London for an
operation on his eyes, and Mrs. Carlyle was unwilling to leave
her friend alone.

Bay House, Alverstoke.
Sunday (16th *Nov*., 1845).

DEAREST BABBIE,

I must not leave you so good a pretext for not
writing to me as doubt about my actual address.   Of course
a letter addressed to Cheyne Row would be sent after me
even to Timbuctoo—but these simple ideas are slow of suggesting themselves to those who find the state of uncertainty
favour their natural tendency to sit still, with their hands
gracefully crossed in Indian-God-like adoration of the Forces
of Circumstances.   Know then, to leave you without excuse,
that I am *here*—very accessible to letters—and much in want of
them—here being—Bay House—a large fantastical looking
New Building on the shore of the Sea, belonging to Lord
Ashburton but made over for this Winter to Lady Harriet.

It is not *in* the Isle of Wight as I had fancied but opposite to
it. I daresay it is a charming place in Summer but in Winter
all that body of cold water which immense ranges of windows
look out on makes me feel like William Gibson " rather chilly '
—and then the gardens about it have lost their bloom for this
year and the *woods* are as yet prospective—more like nursery-
grounds than anything else. Inside, it is warm enough and
magnificent as money and taste can make it—Carlyle and I
have *two* rooms * which I stipulated for before I would undertake
to come at all—and the first principle of living comfortably
in another person's house is granted one amply viz : one is
" well let alone "—may do as one likes within reasonable
limits. But the grand happiness of friendly intercourse—
viz : leave to be " as ugly and stupid and disagreeable as
one likes," *that* of course is out of the question here—*tanto
peggio per me !*

My cold thanks God was considerably abated before I
left home—and is no worse for the " fine change " (as Helen
would say)—and I was cut out of my complication with
Mrs. Paulet in the most unexpected manner. As I had feared
just when we were on the eve of setting off they arrived in
London for the operation !—giving me just twelve hours
notice. I was in the horriblest quandary ; to go away and
leave them alone there with their troubles was impossible
for me—to renounce the visit here equally *impossible*—in another
sense—I meditated a sort of compromise between the two
impossibles—to let Carlyle go without me and follow in a
week or two—but the following morning in rushed Mrs. Paulet
fresh and rosy like a lump of coral and told me they were all
to go back the road they had come that very day—the eyes
were not ready to be operated on. Instead of sympathizing
in their provocation I was heartily thankful that all that money
had been spent and trouble undertaken for no end—by the
time they return I hope that I also shall be returned—in a
month or six weeks she said. Lady Harriet insists we are to
stay here " all the winter "—to stay " till parliament meets in
February "—but I fancy Carlyle's need to be ugly and stupid

* Cp. N.L. i. 183. (October 10, 1845—" all to myself.")

nd disagreeable without restraint (never to speak of my own)
vill send us back to London in a month or so.

I feel as if I should get on here in an even, middlingly
pleasant sort of a way. I am not in the horribly excitable
tate I was in when I went to Addiscombe *—I take things
low very calmly — almost coolly. Lady Harriet seems a
voman of *good sense* and perfect good breeding—and with
 person of that sort one need not, unless one be a fool one-
elf have any *collisions*—at the same time she seems to me so
ystematic and *superior* to her *natural feelings* that however long
nd pleasantly I may live beside her I am sure I shall never
eel *warm affection* for her nor inspire her with warm affection—
er intercourse will remain *an honour for me*, never be a heartfelt
elight—as it might be if she were as loving as she is charming—
nd Bay House will consequently not suit me as well as Seaforth
Iouse.

Plattnauer returned from Germany some weeks ago—*not
hanged* the least in the world—except that he is now entirely
n his natural senses. He had in rummaging in a Cabinet of
is Brother-in-law come upon all my letters about his madness ! !
ead them—and even " taken a copy of one of them "—his
exation had been considerable—especially over my " excessive
agerness to have him kept in Germany for the rest of his life "
—but he spoke even of this *contretemps* with a courtesy and
ustness which proved as much as anything his sane state of
nind—he brought me a beautifully embroidered card case
rom his sister—it might have been done by Titania Queen of
he Fairies !

And now it will behoove me to go and dress for dinner—at
even in these days instead of *four* Lady Harriet's usual hour—
ut after to-morrow thank goodness we are to return to christian
abits. A Mr. Senior who is here causes the present
ormalities. . . .

Love and kisses to all of them—no—only to my Uncle the
est are undeserving of remembrance.

Ever yours
J. C.

* See p. 248.

107. *To Jeannie Welsh*

Later in the month gaiety palls.

November, 1845. The last week however has sadly abate
my courage for eight o'clock dinners, and dressings, and sitting
in state. I look round on my snug little room here with a sigh
& am not so grateful to Providence as might be expected fo
having opened to me the Golden Gates of the Aristocrati
Paradise, such as it is !

108. *To Jeannie Welsh*

The charm of Lady Harriet—And of life at Alverstoke—Reason
for staying on.

Bay House.
(*4th December*, 1845

DEAREST BABBIE,

I snatch one quarter of an hour " out of the Blac
Dog's jaw "—the *Black Dog* at present being the Genius c
" strenuous Idleness," tutelary Deity of this Place,—just t
tell you that I am still alive and experiencing, as Darwin wishe
for me at parting, " as few *disagreeablenesses* as could reasonabl
be expected."

Lady Harriet is kind as possible and has not done said o
looked a single thing since I have lived beside her to justif
the character for haughtiness and caprice which she bears i
Society—in fact a woman more perfectly regardless of *ran*
I never happened to see. *Strength* is what she goes upon
a *weak* Prince of the blood she would treat with undisguise
scorn, and would behave herself quite *sisterly* towards a *stron*
street sweeper. In fact she is a *grand* woman every inch c
her—and *not* " a coquette " the least in the world—if all th
men go out of their sober senses beside her how can she hel
that ? Meanwhile she is not so well employed as she migl
be—but floats along on the top of things in a rather *ignis fatur*
sort of way. She is making a great *fly* at German however—an
as looking in the Dictionary hurts her eyes I am serving her ¡

room of *a Dictionary*, then there are occasionally outbreaks into battledore and shuttlecock, and—in the evenings an almost normal state of chess playing. All this carries off my day, before I know where I am—or get anything done towards my own individual affairs.

There is no talk of going home—but I *must* go—*alone* if necessary when the Paulets return to London *—which will be *before* the eighth of January I fancy—the soonest that Lady Harriet will hear of our going !—Now that I am fairly settled into the thing I feel no haste to encounter London winter—if the sea *be* " somewhat chilly " it is at least very *clean* to look out upon—and to be relieved from all charge of *material* things in cold weather is a great preservative from colds. And really there is as little of burdensome *state* here as can possibly be made to do—not so much *dressing* as *you* have to transact in Maryland Street—rational hours—and no strain on one's wits—for Lady Harriet *does* all the wit herself ; and nobody " feels that it is his duty " to amuse—if it lie in his way to do so well and good—but things will go on briskly enough without him. . . .

When I had written so far Lady Harriet opened my bedroom door and asked me to come into her dressing room to hear great news—*not* the repeal of the corn laws—but that *snow* had fallen to-day near Winchester—whilst here we have had almost summer sunshine—another reason she says why I should " write to Mrs. Paulet on no account to let her husband have his eyes operated upon till after the eighth of January." Meanwhile Mr. Baring returning from Gosport brought your letter—thanks for your movement of the spirit. Pray do muster your energies and actually *go* out to Seaforth—that woman has heart and soul enough in her to fit out a whole regiment of the sort of women I see about you and you let her lie unused !— It is a pity that you get so little good of her—a still greater pity that you do not *care* to get such.

My kindest love and warmest kisses to my Uncle—none of the rest deserve a kiss from me idle as they are.

* Mr. and Mrs. Carlyle returned on December 27.

109. *To Jeannie Welsh*

A grateful Christmas gift—Trouble over a new edition of Cromwell.

> 5, Cheyne Row.
> *Sunday evening (29th Dec., 1845).*

DEAREST BABBIE,

Your letter and the beautiful purse were a great god-send to me on the Christmas morning—it was my only letter—and away there *—amongst entirely new people and new things I felt dreary to death on that day, so unlike any Christmas day that I had ever lived before ; and your letter was a link between past and present that I could have ill dispensed with. . . .

I will write by and by God willing at more leisure than I have been able to command these many weeks, meanwhile my conscience is not easy till I have written a simple acknowledgment of your kind remembrance.

Carlyle is as cross as the Devil since we came back because— they already want a new edition of his Cromwell—the whole twelve hundred being almost sold off ! ! An odd thing to be cross about one would say—inasmuch as a new edition will bring him in some three hundred pounds—but he abhors the *trouble* of new correcting of proofs. There is no satisfying of that man. Bless you—love to all

> Your own,
>
> J. C.

* At Bay House.

110. *To Jeannie Welsh*

Plattnauer tormenting—Geraldine and Miss Cushman—Lady
Harriet pleasant : asks her to Rome—Carlyle and a house in
the country—Ann Summers.

After telling how she cares for the Paulets in Hanover
Street after the operation on Mr. Paulet's eyes, and describing
pretty little Julia's ball dress, Mrs. Carlyle continues :—

Monday (19*th Jan.*, 1846).

DEAREST BABBIE,

. . . Plattnauer was very crazy some weeks ago—but
is considerably subsided again—I suppose he will continue off
and on in this sort of fashion to the end of his life. Mazzini
does not go mad—but I do not know whether it would not be
better for him if he could—these long many years of failed hopes
and destroyed illusions seem to be taking effect on him—not on
his health—or sanity—but on his *temper*—he is grown so
captious and *silently irritable* that one knows not what to make
of him—every word one says provokes a contradiction or a
reproach—and it does not help the matter that like Geraldine
he *torments me simply because he loves me so much.* I prefer
people's love for me should *stop* just at the point where it
becomes *tormenting*.

Geraldine by the way is all in a blaze of enthusiasm about
Miss Cushman the Actress—with whom she swore everlasting friendship at Manchester just when she had got jealous
of me and Mrs. Paulet. Ever since her letters have been filled
with lyrics about this woman—till I could stand it no longer—
and have written her such a screed of my mind as she never
got before—and which will probably terminate our corre-
pondence—at least till the finale of her friendship for
Miss Cushman. Lady Harriet returns to town on the
2nd February. Meanwhile she writes me very nice letters.
Lady Ashburton sent me a huge pot of honey the other day
and some game and a kind little note *—so that I do not seem
at all events to have kicked the bottom out of my " new position "
yet !

* Subsequently sent for Babbie's inspection.

in the way of attaching much importance to Helen's descrip
tions. What chiefly interested me was the thought of wha
I should do with them—*ask them to dinner of course*, as Joh
Sterling says * " when you want to be civil to anybody *natur
prompts* you to ask them to dinner." Easy to say—but in th
present afflicted state of this household a dinner even *dans s
plus simple expression* is the fearfulest of bores. I have no
strength or fortitude enough to take even the slight handful o
it which I am in the way of taking—Helen left all to hersel
goes to nonsense and Carlyle, " gloomy and disconsolate '
as *he* is at present for ever and ever, looks like a chained tiger
when doomed to sit stuck up with company especially when i
is *my* company not of his own asking—and there I sit i
momentary expectation of Helen coming to a *dead stand*, o
of Carlyle brandishing the carving knife and ordering hi
guests to " vanish in God or the Devil's name lest a worse thin
befal them " ! In virtue of being like the Pigs " used to it '
I preserve an outward calm through these scenes of trial whicl
might lead people to fancy me either the most obtuse or mos
philosophical woman that ever sat at the head of a table—n
matter which, so long as my pretended impassivity has mucl
the same effect as Caleb Balderston's impudence—viz. that o
making people doubt the evidence of their senses—and keepin
them from rushing wildly into the street to dine on a passin
muffin or on nothing at all, rather than under the singular con
ditions that attend the dinners of a man of Genius—when th
Devil has taken him and his under his own particular patronage

At all *risks* however the New-marrieds must be invited—
and this conclusion was hastened rather than otherwise by
note from Walter, which came a few hours after his call, invitin
us to dine with *them*—preposterous ! *that* would have been sti
worse, if it had not been *impossible*. So I asked them for on
of three days and they accepted for Saturday. I called i
Sterling's carriage but missed them again, so left the not
which I had provided myself with in case of such contingency
To provide them with some entertainment such as lay withi
my peculiar sphere I asked a *Lioness* to come in the evening—

* Mrs. Carlyle speaks of this familiar friend as if he were still living.

he *last new Lioness*—a rare creature indeed—the Miss Rigby who wrote *Letters from the Baltic* etc., and who is now setting ire to the Thames as a Quarterly Reviewer. Besides being a Woman of Genius she is a world's wonder for *personal* attractions—six feet high ! but so beautifully proportioned that you ould not wish her a cubit less—with the most magnificent tatuesque head—the expression of a Corinne, and the graceulest manners. When I told Carlyle that I had done this hing he was like to go out of his senses—" what *could* Miss Rigby make of the Macgregors or they of her ? "—" he had ever seen me guilty of such a piece of pure distraction, many s were the distracted things I had done in the way of bringing ncompatible people together ! " There was no end to his esperations—for Miss Rigby appeared to have taken an nmense place in his (Carlyle's) imagination. It was *done* owever—" with the best intentions always unfortunate ; " nd so now " I must ask anybody, everybody, to *dilute* the orrible combination." So I asked just everybody I saw and he produce was John Carlyle at dinner—Old Sterling, and rthur Helps and his wife in the evening besides the awful Miss Rigby. You may figure what sort of *anxious* affair it vas for *me*—and I was never thankfuler than when the door losed on the last of them and I could reflect that after all here were no lives lost.

The Macs came at four—to dine at five—if they had been en minutes later they must have arrived drenched to the skin or they had got into a wrong *omnibus* (!) and had to walk from loane Square—and it came such a torrent of rain just after nat Carlyle had to come home in a cab. The first look of he Bride did not shock me much—I was prepared for someing unprepossessing and she looked rather better than I ad expected—but when she had laid off her things and sat own on a chair as if she were nailed to it—with her lean little gure without so much as a handkerchief to break its angularity -and when she spoke—in that acrid brusque tone of hers -my dislike grew every moment stronger till I was absolutely raid of looking Walter in the face, I was so sure that he must ad there " merciful heaven how *could* you sell yourself for

that woman's thousands ? " It is impossible Walter can *love*
that woman—" *amiable ?* " she is *not* amiable—she is a limited
splenetic, dirty little thing—" an ignoble rat-trap "—a
" insufferable little wild cat," as Carlyle among many othe
eloquent denunciations said of her. Carlyle has never cease
since lamenting over " poor Macgregor's fate." Walter himsel
was not so agreeable as he used to be *here*—he was too noisy-
too excited—very affectionate—poor fellow—and trying t
look content with *her*—but if he were really happy just no
he would not take such pains to persuade people of it.

As the Devil would have it Miss Rigby sat alongside c
Mrs. Macgregor on the same sofa and if I had taken pains ho
to contrive a mortification for Walter I could not I am sur
have fallen upon a greater than showing him the two wome
in such near contrast. And then Mrs. Arthur Helps is lik
Titania Queen of the fairies ! as lovely in her diminutive pr
portions as Miss Rigby is beautiful in her gigantic ones
But when a man marries such a woman as that he must hav
abjured forever his faculty of drawing comparisons, or hav
privately pre-determined to *take a mistress !* Now do n
think I am attaching absurd importance to looks—I care le
for *beauty* so called than most people—indeed I am certa
that the women most truly and passionately loved are ve
rarely if ever regular beauties—but it is the expression of
mean meagre *soul* that is stamped on Mrs. Macgregor's fa
and manners and whole bearing which I cannot abide and
am the more vexed at Walter having chosen such a wife becau
I am persuaded he was at a turning point in his own inwa
life—and that this new influence which he has subjected hir
self to will prevent all the good aspirations that lay in him fro
ever working themselves into a practical shape. Hencefor
he is doomed to *ambitious mediocrity*—the pitiablest state
nature. I ought to say however that John Carlyle thin
" Walter has got a *pretty* little woman for a wife ! ! "

And now my dear I have written myself into such a passi
on a subject which I have really after all no special conce
with—that I must leave the better things I had to say t
another opportunity.

I saw Mrs. Fraser on Saturday forenoon. She was out of
bed on a sofa—but still very feeble and dreadfully excited.
She had heard that her husband was ill—had also been delirious
for some days after the trial—and absolutely you would have
said that she was dying to go to him and comfort him ! She
loves the man passionately—there is not a doubt of it—after
all the woe he has wrought her ! And in this moral slavery
lies the fearfulest prospect for her. It would make anybody
weep to hear how she defends him—finds out excuses for
him—always ending with " Oh poor William !—God pity
him ! where *can* he wander ? " They are selling prints of
him about the streets under the name of *the handsome
Husband*.

Again thanks and kisses to the Morning Star and your
sweet self and love to them all and do not think me ill-natured
to your new kinswoman. You will find when she returns that
the aversion is quite mutual or I am greatly mistaken.

Your own,

JANE CARLYLE.

112. *To Jeannie Welsh*

Sleeplessness and drugs—A month at Addiscombe—Lady Harriet
"a bit of fascination"—The Paulets delayed—Pressure of
Carlyle's work—William Chrystal (a brother of Andrew).

Tuesday (*10th March*, 1846).

Here goes Dearest Babbie ! just to *try* whether the Devil
or I shall be strongest to-day, in the matter of writing to you
—how often *he* has had the upper hand of late, to the utter
suppression of the many things I have wished to say to you,
I am ashamed to think ! for if one cannot make head against
the Devil in a world where one meets him at every turn, one
may as well take a little arsenic at once and spare oneself the
sin and sorrow of being nothing but a Spooney in God's
Universe. For ten days I was nearly out of my wits with want
of sleep—and I say this not *figuratively* nor even *exaggeratively*
but in simple truth. Four nights in one week I never *once*
closed my eyes, and *henbane* even in large quantities of no

T

more use to me than cold water. The consequence was such
a state of nervous excitation as nobody ever saw in me before
—Carlyle declares me to have been " quite mad " for half an
hour—and I can well believe him—I have for a long while
back been dreadfully haunted with the apprehension of going
mad some day—and I am only too thankful to have got off
with " half an hour " of it thus far. For the last week I have
been sleeping—and in the reactionary state—that is to say
dead stupid. Oh ! the blessedness of *stupidity* at times ! I feel
as if I would not make " a wit " just now for fifty guineas.

On the 20th I am going with Lady Harriet to Addiscomb
for a month—and that will be good for me I suppose. Carlyle
is so hard at work that he will not miss me—besides if he take
a notion of seeing me at any time he can be there by railway in
half an hour. We two *women* go alone. Mr. Baring and
Charles Buller of course—will be there on the Saturdays and
Sundays—and we are to come up to town once a week for
two hours, her Ladyship to take a Drawing lesson (!) I to bless
my family with a sight of me and regulate the week's account
If all proceeds according to Programme it will be a pleasant
month ; but I cannot fancy Lady Harriet anywhere leading
a life of privacy ; however she may propose it to herself. She
needs the excitement of company, imagining all the while that
she is bored with it—and so many people are ready to follow
her into Siberia—if she chose to take her flight even there
She is " a bit of fascination " (as the Countrymen said
" *Tagg*lioni ") * a very *large bit*. I profess never to this hour
to have arrived at a complete understanding of her—but *that*
I fancy is just a part of her fascination—the insoluble psycho
logical puzzle which she is and bids fair to remain for me !

The Paulet servants and children go off home to-day
Mr. and Mrs. Paulet must wait a few days longer till Alexander
is pleased to give them leave. He had fixed this day a week
ago—and in consequence the house was given up, which
the reason of despatching part of the family. Now he says

---

* " Two London mechanics paused at a print-shop window where
was. ' Ha ! ' said one to the other in a jaunty knowing tone. *Tag-li-o*
Bit of fascination there.' " (T.C. in L.M. i. 314.)

† The oculist.

etter wait " a few days longer "—and so they have had to
hift into a new lodging. I am vexed to death I could not
nsist on their coming here for these remaining days—but
Carlyle is in such a fuss with his work and so nervous and
bilious in consequence—that altho' he would have *submitted*
to my bringing them I know such an interruption of the *silence*
he needs about him would have driven him to despair. This
ewriting of Cromwell has been very hard on him—and on me
oo—we thought to have washed our hands and hearts of it
or ever and a day when the first Edition went to the bookseller.

Only think, I was sitting here with Mazzini one day, when
n walked Mr. William Chrystal ! looking as pleased as Punch—
vidently considering he was giving me the most joyful sur-
rise ! Alas it was not *joyful* the least in the world ! I have
' mads " enough on hand without taking up *him*—even if
were disposed from benevolence to be civil to him, I could
ot get it done—for C. no sooner heard of his visit than he
xclaimed in imperative terror—" I desire my Dear that you
vill absolutely bring no more mad people about this house ! "
Ie (Mr. Chrystal) informed me that he lived in Knightsbridge
alas too near !) and left his card with an invitation that when
' I felt tired I should come in and rest myself and take a glass
f wine "—Helas ! . . . Dearest love to my Uncle and the rest.

Ever your affectionate

JANE CARLYLE.

113. *To Jeannie Welsh* *

ady Harriet's sincere affection—Getting-on in Society—William
Chrystal again—Mazzini and the children.

Thursday (1846).

. . . Lady Harriet is returned and seems disposed to keep up
ur country intimacy—she sends her carriage for me often in
he evenings and sends me back—treats me in all respects
vith *a consideration* for which I cannot but be grateful to her.
he never *says* to anyone that she likes them—she goes upon

* It seems that this letter should be dated May, and therefore should
ollow No. 114.

the silent system as to all the thoughts of her *heart*—it is only the thoughts of her *head* which she gives one the benefit of—and so she has never *said* what one could call a *kind* word to *me*—but she proves by all her behaviour that she is rather fond of me—the mere fact of her having *kissed* me at parting and meeting again proves more affection for me than twenty reams of protestations from a Geraldine would do—for her Ladyship is *sincere* to death—and would think much less of boxing the ears of a person indifferent to her than of kissing her ! for my part I *love* her now as much as I *admired* her in the beginning. She is the only woman of *genius* I have found amongst all our pretenders to it—I only wish I had got to know her twenty years ago when I was better capable of enjoying the advantages of such an acquaintance—the " getting on-in-Society " part of it looks to me often enough a practical irony at this time of day rather than a good fortune to thank my stars for.

You would be amused to see the increase of charm I have for the smaller gentry since Lady Harriet took me up ! I could not help answering a *kind* note I had from Lady Monteagle the other day *after a twelve-months' silence*—in a tone of very *frank sarcasm*. . . .

I had almost forgotten to tell you that some weeks ago walking thro' Piccadilly one day I came bang against—William Chrystal,—our eyes met—so I saw nothing for it but to speak. He told me in a pettish sort of way that he " did not know me " and when I laughed at that, he asked " how are your friends up there " nodding towards Hyde Park Corner ! I supposed he meant at Liverpool and answered accordingly. When we had gone our several ways Mazzini who was with me asked " who is he ? " " A distracted lover of my two Cousins " said I— " Are these his children ? " said Mazzini. " *What* children ? " " The two little, little things—so high "—pointing to his knee —" and dressed both alike, whom he was leading when you stopt him—and whom he joined again." " I tell you, said I, the man is a lover of Jeanie's—was not married before that I know of—how then can *he* have little things dressed both alike ? " " Oh, said Mazzini, I did not know—I thought perhaps by your laws *poligamy* might be allowed to a *Mad*."

Do *you* understand about these " little things "—it certainly had a suspicious appearance.

God bless thee Babbie, a kiss—a hundred of them to my
Uncle—love to Maggie. I felt rather jealous the other day
when Mrs. Russell wrote to me that *they* got newspapers
addressed *in my Uncle's own hand*. Write soon again I
need it.

Ever your affectionate

J. C.

114. *To Jeannie Welsh at Auchtertool, Fife*

Home quiet after Addiscombe—A present of " Lady's work "—
    Plattnauer invades Buckingham Palace—His new delusions—
    Addiscombe : the Charteris—Heavy depression.

" Came to pass." " A poor Italian painter, protégé of
Mazzini's, living in some back street of Chelsea, had by ill
luck set his chimney on fire ; but, by superhuman efforts,
to escape the penalty, got it quenched in time. Still, in time,
as he hoped ; ' when,' said Mazzini, reporting in Mazzini
English, ' there came to pass a sweep ' who smelt the soot of
him, and extorted from him still a guinea of hush-money—the
greedy knave." (T. C. in L.M. i. 278.)

5, Cheyne Row.
Wednesday (22nd April, 1846).

Dearest Babbie,

You are saying to yourself with as much of a sarcastic
smile as your good little face is capable of ; that I must have
been full of occupation indeed, if *this* be the " first *possible
hour* " for writing that has come to me. I do not however
take my stand on a position so little tenable—several hours
or at least quarters of hours " came to pass " (like Mazzini's
sweep) during my last week at Addiscombe in which I *might*
have written to an indulgent Babbie—but only with a mind
all churned into froth, and since Monday evening that I have
been here again in my own quiet establishment, I have pur-
posely put off, that my letter might get double welcome by
reaching you on your Birthday—good luck to it (the Birthday)
my dear Babbie ! and may the " good resolutions " which
are *sure* to come up in you on its advent not go altogether to

the paving of the Place that is nameless ! but some little
fraction of them go to the building of a tight little wind-and-
weather-proof house for the Babbie's soul to live in long and
happily. And here is a piece of *Lady's work*—of all things
in the world—to remind you that " all is vanity "—I confess
I do not see much other *use* it is for ; but it is very beautiful
is it not ? Is it the fruit of my intercourse with fine people i
—have *I* at last taken into this sort of thing ? Thanks God
No !—I did not work a stitch of it—and yet you may regard
it as the proof of my active virtue or virtuous activity which
you like—for it was the *reward* sent by the Gräfin von Reichenbach for my kindnesses to her Brother ! *—which Brother, by
the way, is again entirely distracted—and what is some comfor
—his insanity has now taken a form which greatly diminishes
one's interest in him—the form, namely oft botomless *vanity*
The day before I went to Addiscombe—a gentleman with
whom we were dining at Lord Ashburton's mentioned as the
news of the day that a young Prussian—Plattnauer by name
had just been forcing his way into Buckingham Palace and
when laid hold of, and asked his business by Lord Somebody
had said " the Queen was just going to be confined and had
sent for *him !* " The Police had to be called in to remove
him and he was carried away to the Marlborough Station
House. I looked in all the newspapers for some days to see
the issue of the business—to strike into it *practically* with the
prospect of figuring in Police-reports was more than human
friendship felt *up to*—besides the Government takes excellen
care of the *insane* destitute however it may leave the *sane* to
shift for themselves, only they must *seem* to have *no friends*—
otherwise the Government washes its hands of them. So that
unless I meant to take the charge of him again myself, I was
doing best for his interest in leaving him in the hands into
which he had fallen. Somebody however must I suppose have
interfered for the case did not appear in the newspapers. A
week ago Mr. Fleming met him on the street " looking extremely
ill and dreadfully dirty—his hat broken in the brim—he said
he had just come from Paris the day before, for the purpose

* Plattnauer.

f superseding Peel and that he was to return to Paris next
ay to settle Poland " ! A Lady of his friends writes to me
1at she had had a letter from him wanting money to carry
n his political affairs in which he stated that " during the
receding week he had been in *several* Asylums and Prisons
1 France." I doubt however if he has ever been out of
,ondon—probably in some Public Asylum *here*—and dreaming
ll his travels. Fortunately for *me* I provoked him so much the
1st day he was here by *putting down* his pretensions that he
vent away in great wrath—and is not I think likely to come
ear me while this fit lasts.

My visit to Addiscombe went off quite well. Her Ladyship
vas as usual without caprices or any sort of questionabilities
or me. Carlyle came every Saturday and staid till Monday
—Charles Buller and Mr. Baring did the same—and besides
here were other incidental visitors—on the other days Lady
Harriet and I were tête-à-tête—but for ten days at the end—
he Easter Holydays—the house was quite full. It was very
interesting to me to make acquaintance *there* with a young
Grandee from my own East Lothian—Mr. Charteris *—pro-
pective Earl of Wemyss—he has the beautifulest young creature
or wife I ever set my eyes on—and as good seemingly as
beautiful. I took quite a liking to the pair, and it seemed to
be reciprocal for Mr. Charteris painted a picture of me ! ! and
Lady Anne promised to come and see me so soon as she had
finished *Zoe* which I lent her—so my aristocratic *connexion*
goes on extending itself. *Ach Gott !* if I had not such an
eternal hundredweight of leaden thoughts on my heart I might
live *pleasantly* as other people do, but once for all, life is *not
pleasant* for me and the best I see in it is that it does not last
very long.

Ever your loving Cousin.

* Francis, afterwards Lord Elcho and Earl of Wemyss ; married, 1843
Anna Frederica, daughter of 1st Earl of Lichfield (born 1818, died 1914).

115. *To Jeannie Welsh at Auchtertool*

Death of Mr. Liddle—Thoughts on dying young—Escape from suffering and disillusion—Conceals her own feelings—Is congratulated on perpetual cheerfulness by Mrs. Macready—Her talents are deserting her—Plattnauer's escapades: is in Paris—Has become a bore as well as dangerous.

Tuesday (19*th May*, 1846

DEAREST BABBIE,

Few deaths could have surprised me more than Mr Liddle's ; he had so little the look of one born to die young I can well believe that all who were in habits of intimacy with him will long mourn the loss of such a cheerful kindly soul For me, I am got to that with it now, that I can no longer feel sorry for the one who *dies* but only for the friends he leaves behind to miss him—one escapes so much suffering by dying young !—all the good one *could possibly* have enjoyed in longer life is not it seems to me to be put in the balance against the evil which one *must necessarily* have suffered, surviving one after another of all one loved—one after another of all one's beautiful illusions and even most reasonable hopes, surviving in short one's original self ! You cannot understand *yet* how life may grow to look no such blessing—even for those who have no claim to be considered exceptionally unfortunate—long may it be before you feel this as I do ! it is a weary, dreary feeling almost making one regret the feelings of acute sorrow out of which it grows. And yet it is well to be prepared for it—that one may have it in as gentle a degree as possible by beginning early to pitch one's hopes from the world rather low—and by laying in as many good thoughts and good actions as one possibly can to look back upon for comfort, when one ceases to feel any comfort in looking forward. I have not got into a Socinian zeal for the " *pleasures of a good conscience* " tho' the foregoing sentence might lead you to that idea. I do not pretend to know by experience what the " pleasures of a good conscience " may really be—but I fancy them like all other *pleasures* that I *have* experience of, a feeble refuge against the pressure of existence as it hardens gradually into old age—stript of all its early poetical illusions—but without any Socinian self-conceit.

I *may* say to you of my own knowledge that the natural sadness of the latter part of one's life may be cruelly *embittered* by the reflection that one's best years, which might perhaps have produced something good have been suffered to run to waste, fertile only of tares and nettles !—But enough of moralizing.

I have not been well—as Mrs. Paulet said—but not more ill than when Mrs. Paulet spread such fine news of my improved looks !—People must talk—about other people's looks and much else that comes readiest—but what they say *for talking's sake* is not worth a minute's recollection. Ach Gott ! how little even those who like one, *divine* of one's actual state— unless one *put oneself into words* and hardly even then can the generality of one's friends tell whether one is glad or sorrowful —feeling pain or pleasure ! I called at the Macreadys' the other day—in a humour that a person under sentence of death need hardly have envied. For days and weeks a cheerful feeling had not been in my mind—but of course one does not make calls to show oneself as *a spectacle of woe*. I talked talked—about the feats of Carlyle's horse &c.—and they laughed till their tears ran down. *I* could not *laugh*—but no matter—perhaps my own gravity made the things I was saying only more amusing by contrast. By and by Mrs. Macready who is in the family-way began to talk of the dreadful " depres- sion of spirits " she occasionally laboured under. " Ah said I, everyone I suppose has their own fits of depression to bear up against if the truth were told." " Do you say so ? " said Miss Macready. " Oh no surely ! some people are never out of spirits—*yourself* for example, I really believe you do not know what it is to be ever sad for a minute ! ! ! one never sees you that you do not keep one in fits of laughter ! " I made no answer—but congratulated myself on having played my part so well. I wish I could find some hard work I *could* do—and saw any sense in doing. If I do not soon it will be the worse for me.

Meanwhile all *around* me goes on as usual—C. is just getting done with *his* work—speculating about " where to go." The usual people come about ; but seldomer I think—seeing that I am less disposed to amuse them—new people come—

but I have lost my talent for " swearing everlasting friendships."
All my talents seem to be going one after another.

Did I ever tell you that Plattnauer had gone quite mad
again—committed follies rather dangerous—for her Sacred
Majesty the Queen—and finally been obliged to leave the
country. I hear he is in Paris—still *at large*, the very man for
actually shooting Louis Philippe !—God grant he may not
come back here anyhow—he had become *really dangerous* and
what I considered worse to tolerate—a dreadful bore from his
fatuous vanity.

God bless thee Babbie, love me while you can.

Ever your affectionate

JANE CARLYLE.

Kind regards to Walter.

116. *To Helen Welsh*

The burdens of High Life—Lady Harriet a perfect ornament to
Society—In the valley of the shadow of Cromwell—A threatened
move—Babbie's dawdling courtship—Lady Harriet's acts of
affection—Character of Mrs. Paulet—Geraldine's proofs—
Miss Bölte's " new ideas " from Germany.

Friday (26th *June*, 1846).

DEAREST HELEN,

I would have answered your letter in *the enthusiasm
of the moment* if the moment had not been needed for more
practical purposes. There was much to be put straight on
my return *morally* as well as *materially*, and I had not even
my *normal* amount of force either moral or material to bring
to the work : for the excitement of a houseful of the most
exciting and excited people during the last ten days had been
a prodigious overbalance to the " *pure* air " and other advantages
of Addiscombe. The more I see of aristocratic life, the more
I wonder how people with the same system of nerves as oneself
and with the same human needs, can keep themselves alive in
it—and *sane !* Lady Harriet especially, who is the woman of
largest intellect I have ever seen—how *she* can reconcile herself
to a life which is after all a mere dramatic representation, however successful, fills me with astonishment and *a certain* sorrow

But like the pigs they "are used to it," and nobody, I fancy,
knows till he try how difficult it is to tear himself loose from
the network of Lilliputian pack-threads in which our nobility
grow up from their earliest days. A *poor* woman has enough
of serious occupation cut out for her by the nature of things
—sometimes *more* than is good for her—and therein lies *her*
grievance—we in *our* sphere have also something given us to
do—how far it may suit our taste is another question and a
secondary one—we see at least how our activity may be turned
to account better or worse. But a great Lady—should *she*
take a notion to wrap herself in a blanket and go to sleep like
Beauty for a hundred years ; what would stand still that needs
to go forwards ? Only herself ! And should she take the
better notion to put away Great-Lady-things and lead a rational
useful life, how is she to set about it ? How extricate herself
from the imposed *do-nothingism* of her *position?* As Lady
Harriet herself once said to me " one would have to begin by
quarrelling with all one's husband's relations and one's own "
—a beginning that one may be excused for finding rather
questionable !—No ! it is not *easy* for a Great Lady in these
days to be anything but " an ornament to Society in every
direction," and *that* her Ladyship succeeds in being—to
perfection ! The old illustration of the camel passing thro'
the eye of a needle still holds good. Let those who are not in
the camel's shoes, among whom are you and I—be thankful—
tho' cooks may sometimes give one a deal of trouble—and
holed stockings may accumulate into a small Ben Lomond
while one is away on a visit—and other the like nuisances
render one's career of household activity often enough anything but a *pleasurable* one !—Now, what has tempted me into
this moral-essay style, I have not the slightest conception !—
When I sat down to write I did not feel at all *preachingly*
disposed. But I am in the habit of letting my pen go its own
way, and this is the way it has gone.

The Cromwell-turmoil is again subsiding and the second
edition will be out in a few weeks. " *Thanks* God ! " and now
I hope we shall really be done with that man ! if he had been
my husband's own Father he could not have gone thro' more

hardship for him ! We have lived " in the valley of th
shadow " of Cromwell now, as of Death, for some three years
But everything comes to an end if one have patience. What i
to come next Heaven knows. We have been enquiring al
about for houses in the country—without, it seems to me
much chance or even *much intention* of a practical result. Some
times—in desperately bilious days Carlyle speaks of returning
to Scotland and living *there* " in seclusion for his few remaining
years." I do not look for much practical result to *that* ide
either. Still this perpetual talk of moving takes away all one'
pleasure (such as it was) in Chelsea—I feel myself no longe
in a *home* but in a *tent* to be struck any day that the commanding
officer is sufficiently bilious.

When the warm weather comes and it is coming fast—th
present restlessness will mount into a crisis of some sort—
journey somewhere. But as yet I do not see a fortnight befor
my nose. . . .

What *is* Jeanie about with Andrew Chrystal ? I do no
like these dawdling courtships at all—in the Laird of Noloss'
phraseology " they are a great off-put of time." If people d
not know what they would be at in love they may depend o
it what they *call* love is no authentic love or it would tell them
The most important thing that has *happened* to me since m
return has been the gift of a splendid Indian scarf (from Lad
Harriet) almost " *too* splendid *for anything*." But I was greatl
pleased with it because of its being the facsimile of one she ha
got for herself. She rails at *sentiment* and never puts any int
her *words*, but it peeps out often enough in her *actions*. Sh
would not put an *affectionate* sentence in her letters for th
world but she will put *violets*—leaves of the *flowers one like*
—sometimes sends me envelopes by post containing nothin
else ! ! What a contrast I often think betwixt that woma
and Geraldine ! the opposite poles of woman-nature ! . . .

Ever your own,

JANE CARLYLE.

(26/6/46.)

[Half page torn off.]

. . . . .

ölte is returned from Germany all agog with *something* that
he calls " *the new ideas* "—above all quite rabid against
marriage. Varnhagen, Bettina, all the *Thinkers* of Germany
he says have arrived at the conclusion that *marriage* is a highly
nmoral Institution as well as a dreadfully disagreeable one—
nd that the only possible . . . [incomplete.]

117. *To Helen Welsh (a Fragment)*

Geraldine helpful.

In the summer of 1846, Mrs. Carlyle's long-continued
l health appears to have reached a critical point with a ner-
ous breakdown.   On July 4 she went to seek quiet with
Irs. Paulet at Seaforth, where Carlyle joined her from July 23
) August 6, on the way to Scotland and Ireland.   Then she
ent to stay with Miss Jewsbury, returning to the Welshes at
iverpool until she went home in September.   She was
nequal to joining Carlyle in the short Scotch trip with the
arings, which followed his visit to Scotsbrig.   In L.M. i. 370
er husband exclaims of her " ill spirits, ill health," he himself
aving left for Scotsbrig, Ireland and Liverpool " sorrowfully
nough, but not guessing at all how ill she was.   She had gone
) Geraldine's quiet place in Manchester, rather as in duty
ound than with much hope of solacement or even of greater
uietude there ; both of which, however, she found, so
eautiful was Geraldine's affectionate skill with her, delicacy,
lent sympathy and unwearied assiduity (coming by surprise
o) for which she never forgot Geraldine."

This is borne out by the present letters, however briefly
ey tell of her stay in Manchester, which lasted two weeks
istead of two days.   (*Cf.* N.L. i. 209.)   Thereafter Geraldine
inked high among her friends, although a further outbreak
f jealous sulks is recorded in May, 1847 (N.L. i. 227), besides
er " want of common sense in her new book," January, 1848
N.L. i. 238 and 242).

Manchester.
(*16th August*, 1846.

My dear Helen,

I " find myself in a new position," not knowing my
own mind !—so much has Manchester fascinated me ! I
am not going to-morrow either—Geraldine arranged a pleasure
excursion for me to-morrow to the house of Bamford " *The
Radical* " * and my love of punctuality was not equal to putting
a veto on it, and then for Thursday the Brother Tom settled
that I was to be shown a foundry and a ware-room. In fact
the pains taken to keep me and amuse me is something that
exceeds my comprehension, considering how little I feel myself
capable of making what William Gibson would call " an
adequate return." I am certainly, however, much better since
I came here, so their virtue has had its reward in one way.
will never more think of Geraldine as an unpractical woman—
the practical good she has done me since I came under her
roof is something to be grateful for as long as I live. I mean
to go on Wednesday but she entreats me not to say this in my
note to-day ; but merely that I will write again before . . .

118. *To Helen Welsh*

Geraldine a real help in suffering—The Scotch expedition will
not restore health—Home best.

Wednesday (probably 19*th Aug.*, 1846.

Dearest Helen,

Geraldine will not hear of my going to-morrow
nor do I feel, *myself*, in any desperate haste to leave her. This
noiseless, well-ordered little house of hers—the very pink of
Martha-Tidyism—is so calming-down after Seaforth and
herself so good and *quiet* and *sensible !* I should like to see
the perfectly *rational proper* Mrs. Ellis of a woman that could
have managed as well with me as this poor little authoress of
a questionable *Zoe* has done in these days. People who are a

* Samuel Bamford (1788–1872) the weaver-poet, " a fine sturdy old
fellow," tried to relieve the workers from trade oppression, but without
violence, and was imprisoned for his pacific share in the Peterloo meeting.
Mrs. Carlyle appreciated his recent book, " Passages in the Life of a
Radical." See p. 98.

ease in Zion—I myself when I have been so to a certain extent
—may have found Geraldine very teazing and absurd—but
let one be ill—suffering—especially *morbidly* suffering—and
then one knows what Geraldine is ! All the intelligent sympathy and real practical good that lies in her !

I shall return on Monday and beyond that I have no certain
purpose. The Scotch expedition grows to look more difficult
for me every day—and the wisdom of squandering a quantity
of money and bodily fatigue on it more doubtful. If I were sure
of having my health mended by it I should think *that* to be
attained at all costs and risks—but I am sure of no such thing
—and think sometimes that my own house at Chelsea were
by far the fittest and *safest* place for me in my present state.
I shall get to *some* conclusion before many days are over—and
this much is certain that I shall be with *you* in Maryland Street
on Monday—God willing.

Love to them all and to Isabella.

Ever your affectionate,

JANE CARLYLE.

119. *To Helen Welsh*

Depressed state after returning from Manchester visit—The sort
of woman Carlyle should have married—Stimulates the moral
as well as the physical circulation—Helen Mitchell leaves to
join her brother.

After two years, Helen Mitchell's arrangement with her
brother terminated ingloriously. Then, as her admirable
successor, Anne Brown, was leaving to get married, she begged
to be taken back, but returned only to relapse into drunken
ways. See Letters 150, 156.

Tuesday (Sept., 1846).

DEAREST HELEN,

Two letters for one is a windfall that never came to
me out of Maryland Street before—and claiming double
thanks—for the *novelty* of the thing as well as for its *generosity*.
I would have written sooner if I had had anything *pleasant*
to say : but to tell you that I was down at *Zero* again, seemed a

thing there was no haste about communicating. I came
home wearied and gloomy—with no work to fall to—nothing to
do but ray out darkness on all *my* human attempts at occupation
or amusement—and these alas! are never so energetic now-
a-days that they should make any long stand against that sort
of thing. C. should have had " a strong-minded woman "
for wife, with a perfectly sound liver, plenty of *solid fat*, and
mirth and good-humour world without end—men do best with
their opposites. *I* am too like himself in some things—
especially as to the state of our livers, and so we aggravate one
another's tendencies to despair! But there is no altering of all
that now—nothing to be done but make the best of it—which
I candidly confess I am far from doing. I do *try* however to
the best of my humble ability—and having found small profit
hitherto in mending and tinkering at my *soul*, I am for the
moment modestly directing my faculties to the repairing of
my *body*—trusting that the soul may be ultimately reached
thro' that outwork. Every morning I take the shower-bath—
quite cold—and three pailfuls of it! The shock is indescribable! and whether it strengthens or shatters me I have
not yet made up my mind! but at all events when I have taken
it, I feel to have accomplished a very decided *act of volition*—
and *that* makes my *moral* blood circulate a little; however it
may be with the physical! then I *eat* all that ever I can and
drink *bottled porter*—not so good as *yours* by any means—but
tolerable—and I *walk* as if the Devil were in me—and so,
fancy he *is*—six and seven miles in the day on an average.
I also try, to be neither *solitary* nor *idle*—which old Burton
recommends as the grand cure of " melancholy." Still
must not put too much reliance on these laudable efforts.
Whenever one gets into the self-complacent idea of being able
to *put down Destiny* by *one's own Deserving*—then, if ever, is
one sure of being " made to *eat dirt!* "—more of it than one
has the power of digesting.

I was wondering one day what effect a great *practical*
misfortune would have on me—for instance being burnt
out of house and home and reduced to work for my bread! and
twenty four hours after Providence kindly gave promise of

ratifying my curiosity—in a small way—prepared as pretty *little* practical misfortune for me as one could have imagined :

Helen came with tears in her eyes and smiles on her lips to tell me she was going away! Never could such news have found me less prepared for it—or less disposed. Her conduct has been so exemplary of late that, I saw no more danger of *needing* to put her away, and her attachment to me seeming greater than ever, and her matrimonial chances none to speak of, I had no apprehension of her going of her own accord. But Helen also, insignificant as she looks, has *a destiny!*—is liable to great Events!—and what is most extraordinary of all, is going to be an exceptional instance of *virtue* really *getting* its own reward! At least one hopes so!—A brother in Dublin—a pushing sort of fellow—has got into trade on his own basis—manufactures *coach-fringe* for which there is immense consumption at present on the Railways—and so well has he prospered (by his own showing) that he has now three hundred girls in his employment—a *genteel house* and plenty to keep it with! *Himself* however (for I saw him the other night) remaining a particularly *un*-genteel man. He never did anything for Helen hitherto beyond calling on her for *quarter of an hour* when his business brought him to London— never gave her to the value of a farthing in his life—tho' sometimes asking her if she would like that he brought her a poplin gown!! "Don't you wish you may get it!" Now however he is seized with a sudden fit of brotherly love and invites her to come and be his housekeeper and *mistress*" and she has of course accepted at the first word. I wish it may end well for her—the man looks to me a flustering incredible sort of man— and very selfish with the two black eyes set close together in his head! His conduct hitherto has been so unbrotherly!— that I cannot help fancying he merely wants a *good servant* in Helen on his own terms. Then he may marry shortly and turn her adrift—"tho' he does *promise* in that case to settle a handsome provision on her," but *will* he?—On the whole I wish for her own sake that Helen had taken a little time to investigate and reflect. It is not I, however, who having a manifest interest in retaining her can urge prudence with any

U

effect. So go she must and take her chance. " Poor thing,'
says C. " perhaps she may get married to some decent man ir
Dublin and become mother ' of a mighty Nation ' " *—the las
part of the possibility I should think in the highest degree
improbable ! . . . It will be a while anyhow before anothe
can suit me as well as this one who has been with me ten o
eleven years—but as John Carlyle says " there is no use ir
rebelling against Providence." You may believe I am rathe
unsettled for the moment. Nor do I know more of our *own*
plans than when I left you. Lady Harriet is not returned and
nothing has been said about Alverstoke. But all will arrang
itself by and by better or worse—and some time within winter o
spring *you* will come and help to cheer me up. . . .

120. *To Helen Welsh* †

Helen's promptitude in action—Margaret scalded—Mrs. Anthon
 Sterling's jealous monomania—Another similar case—Carlyle
 chaff of her " profligate life."

Tuesda

DEAREST HELEN,
 If your letter had not been so long or so amusing
if it had been in fact less " creditable to your head and *hort* "
the chances are it would have been answered sooner. I shoul
have flashed you off a few lines " at the earliest opportunity
—but being a meritorious letter, I wished as poor Willia
Gibson used to phrase it, " to make a suitable *return* "—an
for *that*, one has to await the " convenient season." Thus yo
see, my dear young lady, there is always " something very pa
ticular " occurring " *here down* " (*che che*) to prevent virtu
having its " own reward " ! There is one touch in your lett
which has filled me with genuine admiration. You were n
at all aware I daresay (for merit is ever *unconscious*) when yo
historically mentioned the fact ; of the importance I w
likely to attach to it, and the favourable inferences I shou
draw from it respecting the general state of your soul. Yo
said that on being told how Margaret had poured boiling so
" all over her " you *ran for cotton*, and *then* down stairs etc., et
Now *that* is what I call having one's wits about one, *that*

---

* A Carlyle family saying.
 † This undated letter, formerly assigned to 1846, should probably pr
cede No. 67 (p. 174).

:ally being a *useful* member of society. There is not one of a
undred young Ladies who would have *run for cotton* FIRST,
ho would not have run to see the state of the accident first—
ad so lost time which is always precious but never so precious
s in cases of burning. I make you my compliments on your
alm ready helpfulness my gentle cousin—it would be well if
here were more of that sort of helpfulness circulating in this
ussy little world. And when I meet with an accident—
' happen a misfortune " as my first London servant used to
ay—I hope you may be at hand to help me—you—with your
little cry and *much* WOOL ! "

If I had not been very busy in these weeks, I really think I
hould have been tempted to send for sixpenny-worth of
rsenic—and put myself out of pain. Everlasting rain—
he air a solution of soot—the universe one abominable " *clart* "
—no possibility of taking outdoors exercise, and no faculty of
eeping without it—and everybody that comes in, sworn
 one might think) in a general conspiracy, to tell one something
agical or disagreeable. I really do think sometimes that a
ort of things occur to ME which occur to no one else, at least
hey occur with a *frequency* which has no parallel. There is
nother of my intimate acquaintances gone mad ! madder
han twenty March hares—and as if *I* must needs be mixed
p with all the madness that occurs in my sphere—*the idea*
' her *monomania* is, that her husband is my Lover ! ! The
oor creature (Mrs. Anthony Sterling) has done nothing—
absolutely nothing—these many years but read novels—and now
suppose we are witnessing the *consummation* of her futile
xistence ! It is more than a fortnight ago, that hearing
ccidentally she was *ill*, I put on my things like a good Samaritan,
nd went off in the rain, to see whether I could be of any help.
he servants looked *strange* at me—the Master looked *strange*—
e whole house had an atmosphere of *strangeness*, which puzzled
y unsuspecting mind. Anthony shut the door of the Library
autiously on himself and me—and then told me his wife was
out of her wits simply and shortly." " Good gracious ! "
asked, " do you seriously mean that she is gone mad ? "
Yes," said he—" she is at present in a decided state of

monomania—which the Drs. say the slightest contradiction
may drive into *Hysterical-phrenzy*." " Monomania ? " said
I, " and what is her particular *idea?* " " Her ' particular
idea,' " said Anthony with all the *military* composure in the
world, " is, that I have fallen in love with *you*—that *you* are a
dreadful person and that I ruin myself in making you presents ! '
Actually the poor wretch was raving one day about his
(Anthony's) having *given me my new dining room carpet and
new piano*—" She was sure it was *he ! ! !* "   And all these base
visions growing out of the one poor little fact of her husband's
having once given me *a crockery jug ! !*   You may fancy if I
sat very comfortable in my chair after this *revelation*. He
offered me wine, which I declined tho' really *needing* it—as I
also declined his offer to send the carriage home with me
tho' I should have been the better of that too—in short I
conducted myself like an angel of *discretion* and *came away*
with all despatch—but MY *discretion* never *succeeds*, the unhappy
woman was told by one of John's children that I had been there
and forthwith fell into the *phrenzy* which the Drs. apprehended
For several days the poor Husband's state was truly pitiable—
he could not leave her room a moment without her shrieking
out that he was " going to walk with Mrs. Carlyle "—and
flinging *the poker* all about. At last she suddenly took a
violent *dislike to him* and would not suffer his presence, which
was so far good. . . . Anthony tells me this jealousy has been
an affair of some standing—tho' neither of us can recall a
single circumstance that could have given a rational or even
irrational ground for it. . . . Happily I never liked her much
so that I can bear her misfortune *like a Christian*—and her
madness is of such a very repulsive sort that one cannot feel
any *tender* sympathy with it. . . .

Curiously enough—another married lady of my acquaintance
—*not* mad—has just at this moment—misfortunes never
coming single—taken up a rabid jealousy of poor innocent *me*
Has done such absurd things in evidence thereof and made her
husband do such absurd things that even Carlyle " has no longer
a doubt of it."   He, Carlyle, is making himself very merry a
what he calls " *the judgement* come upon me " and calls m

·ftener than "Jane" or "my Dear" " *Destroyer of the peace
f families!*" This morning as I was sitting very half-awake
ver my coffee, he suddenly exclaimed—"just to look at you
here, looking as if butter would not melt in your mouth, and
think of the profligate life you lead!" As John Carlyle would
say "it is *very* absurd."

He—John Carlyle—is expected to arrive here this evening—
God's will be done! . . .

And now with kisses world without end to all and several
—I bid you adieu.

Your affectionate cousin,

JANE CARLYLE.

Send this letter on to Babbie. She has not had many
ately—nor long ones—and I forgot to tell her of Mrs. Anthony
Sterling.

121. *To Jeannie Welsh at Auchtertool*

nhomeliness of life at the Grange—Her false position there, only
appreciated by Carlyle—Lady Harriet is kind in her own way—
New feelings drive out all native shyness—The place and the
people—Family prayers : not attended by Mrs. Carlyle, Rogers,
or Lady Harriet—Lady Bath.

Old Rogers is the poet, famous also for his breakfast parties.
Mr. Byng—the man of fashion, nicknamed "Poodle,"
who was so shocked at discovering that the second Lady
Ashburton had a woman cook instead of a chef. (N.L. ii. 258.)
Whether the "false position" in which Mrs. Carlyle finds
herself refers to the incongruity of her frivolous surroundings
: to the beginnings of her *idée fixe* about Lady Harriet Baring,
uncertain. Certain it is that her physical health was "very
feeble," as T. C. says in L.M. i. 391. Returning home she was
prostrated by the domestic hurly-burly caused by the new
servant from Edinburgh, Isabella. Old Betty of Haddington
had recommended her—as being of perfect Free Kirk orthodoxy.
But if grace abounded, work did not, and she earned the title
Pessima. In the unhappy three weeks between her departure
and the coming of the faithful Anne Brown, who stayed till
her marriage two years later, Mrs. Carlyle was a wreck, mostly
keeping her bed. Fortunately Helen Welsh had come on a
visit (see next letter) and helped to smooth out things.

The Grange,
Friday (30th Oct., 184

DEAREST BABBIE,

I have no prospect of being able to write you
deliberate letter even at this late date. Tho', for the momen
I have not a room merely but a suite of rooms all to mysel
where no one may come to molest me—still my soul is in
state of hurry-scurry which makes *deliberate* writing qui
impossible. The very look of this bedroom with its immen
dimensions, its vaulted and carved ceiling, its princely ma
nificence of every sort makes me ill at ease—I feel to have g
out of my latitude—as much as if I were hanging on to th
horns of the moon ! and then the recollection of all the id
restless people under the same roof with me—whose idlene
and restlessness is so contagious ! In fact *this* is " a count
house " with a vengeance ! and I do not find that my Destin
has done amiss in casting *my* lot amongst " *the poorer orders*
We are here professedly on a visit to the Ashburtons—*virtuall*
at least so far as C. is concerned, on a visit to Lady Harriet-
and besides Lady Harriet and Mr. Baring, there are son
dozen visitors, the Marchioness of Bath, Lord Ashburton
eldest daughter, with two tiny ladyships and their Frenc
governess—Old Rogers—an Honble. Mr. Byng—a beautif
Miss Dalton—a rich Mr. Portal etc., etc. In all *my* life
never drew my breath in such a racket ! Some of the Peop
go to-morrow and then others will come. It is the rulin
Principle of the Host and Hostess to keep the house alwa
full. *We* shall remain till the end of next week and by th
time I shall have had enough of it I fancy. The Ashburto
one and all of them are excellent people—very *homely*—a
very kind—they make me as much at home as it is possible fo
fish to be in the *air*. Lady H. also continues *kind* to me aft
her fashion. But, as you can easily conceive, I feel myself
a false position—and find it very difficult to guide myself in
I have always however the consolation of feeling quite su
that nobody knows nor can divine my difficulties except C.
who since I make no noise about them is bound to recogni
them with respectful toleration. " One fire," they say, " driv
out another ! " or (another version of it) " one devil drives o

another "—and *that* at least is something to be thankful for ! My natural shyness and over-modesty (of which I have a great deal, tho' neither you nor anyone else perhaps ever found it out) has entirely given place to more powerful feelings—so that I have no more care than a cat about things that would have fussed me once on a time. I used to be apprehensive that my toilette might look defective, that my manner might look *gauche*—that my speech might sound flat—amongst sumptuous, self-possessed, brilliant people. Now I am so entirely absorbed in thoughts far away from all outward *appearances* that if I had been brought up at court all the days of my life I could not feel more perfectly regardless on these points.

But it were more amusing for you to hear something of the Place and People than of *my* feelings towards them. The Place is like, not *one*, but a conglomeration of Greek Temples set down in a magnificent wooded Park some five miles in length. The inside is magnificent to death—the ceilings all painted in fresco—some dozen public rooms on the ground floor all hung with magnificent paintings—and fitted up like rooms in an Arabian night's entertainment—but the finest part of it is the entrance hall and staircases—which present a view of columns, frescos and carved wood and Turkey carpet—that one might guess at a quarter of a mile long ! In the Hall which indeed resembles a church Lord A. reads prayers every morning to a numerous congregation consisting of men and women-servants ranged on opposite sides and his own wife and daughters kneeling beside him. The *effect* as seen from the *gallery above* is very pretty ! ! but I did not meddle with it personally further than looking over the balustrade—and I saw old Rogers this morning doing the same. They are very *good* in the religious sense of the word—the whole family of them—except of course Lady Harriet—who *goes* on nothing of that sort—but they are not bigotted and let one hold one's own opinions. They have had their own trials poor people—a favourite daughter the beauty and genius of the family—when grown to womanhood was burnt to death in Italy some years ago—and the Marquis of Bath *drank* himself to death—this poor Lady now here . . . has still such a suffering patient look ! And this morning she was maintaining against me the Beauty and holiness of *marriage* even in these days ! ! ! Every mortal woman I fancy is born to be made miserable thro' one cause or other. And with this moral reflection I will conclude.

Ever your affectionate,

J. C.

122. *To Helen Welsh*

An invitation to Chelsea—Visits to Lady Harriet—Helen leaving.

(7th November, 1846.)

DEAREST HELEN,

I am just returned from the Grange—*that* is *one* good job over—and I may calculate now on being let alone till after Christmas—so I write to urge with all solemnity that you should *immediately* fling some clothes into a trunk and come off to me. The programme is that after Christmas we shall go for a month to Bay House where we were the last year. *So* the Lady Harriet wills *at present*—and her Ladyship's will is become the law of this house !—even her *whims* are as imperative as the ten commandments ! In March she will be at Addiscombe—only twelve miles from here—and if she wish us to amuse her ennui there also, of course, it will be so arranged—then in April what Darwin calls " the 5 Cheyne-Row-spring-fever " begins—frantic speculations about where to go—etc. etc. So that it seems to me on the whole, there is no time so good as the present. We have six clear weeks till Christmas—if you start immediately you may have a tolerable view of London in that time. So let me have a letter by return of post to say what day you will be here—the journey is the simplest thing in nature—nothing in the shape of *escort* need be waited for. You have only to bid a Policeman at the station get you a cab—(meeting people is *impossible* in Euston Square) and you will be fetched safe here without a word spoken. I am too much occupied with the prospect of seeing you to enter into any detail of my visit—it was *grand* to Death !— people with eighty thousand a year can *afford* to do things in style. I will tell you things that will amuse you when we meet.

Helen does not go till the 20th when I expect a new woman from Edin.—but the change will not put *you* about—who are used to changes. Say to my uncle that I bought with his five pounds a beautiful plaid shawl, boa and fur cuffs—a whole equipment for winter !

Ever your affectionate
J. CARLYLE.

123. *To Helen Welsh*

Belated Christmas correspondence and its surprises—Carlyle evades
her prohibition of New Year's gifts.

Carlyle's " kind and considerate motive " for now giving his wife birthday and New Year presents was to fill the gap left by the death of her Mother, who had always sent presents on those anniversaries. The pathetic remembrances they wakened sometimes made her weep over her husband's gifts. (L.M. i. 150.)

Friday (1st Jan., 1847).

DEAREST HELEN,

Your kind letter and gift along with a packet from Babbie were brought up to me in bed *yesterday* morning with my breakfast—at an hour when there is no post from either Liverpool or Scotland ! To-day I have ascertained the meaning —your's had been *missent to Camberwell !* and, the postmen having half a holiday on Christmas, Babbie's packet having arrived by the afternoon post was not delivered till the following morning. Provoking enough that my dear little cousins should have been thus hindered in their good thought to enliven my Christmas day—but so far as myself was concerned I am not sure that I was not a gainer by having the pleasure arrive so *promiscuously.*" Kindness is kindness on the 26th of December all the same as on the 25th, and at that unusual hour of the morning it came with the additional charm of a most *complete surprise.* . . .

I had another surprise—very great—on the Christmas day—almost " too great *for anything* " in fact. You know I daresay Carlyle's sacred horror of shopping. To such an extent had he brought it, that he could never be induced to order even his own coats and trowsers at the tailor's until

three or four years ago, that having sent me to get him a coat
I ordered one *sky blue* with *yellow buttons* which made him
" an ornament to Society in every direction "—and quite
shook his faith in my judgement (he told me) " So far as the
dressing of him was concerned." You may imagine then what
a thing it must be for a man thus puzzled to buy his own
indispensables when he has not only to buy but devise *a present*
for someone. Accordingly he never dreamt of making me
presents till in these last three years that a most kind and
considerate motive has induced him to *give me something* on
birthdays and new years' days—but the pleasure of receiving
his little gifts is always spoiled for me by thinking of the plague
he must have had in realizing them—with such a habit of
mind ! So I asked him the other day to promise that he would
do what I asked without knowing what it was—on assurance
that the thing was easy and rational—and then when he had
promised—I told him he was not *to give me anything on new*
year's day ! He laughed very much and repeated that he would
not. But to reconcile his promise with his wish to show his
kindness—what does he do but sally forth and buy me a present
for Christmas, and in a fit of audacity almost incredible the
thing he chose to buy was—a cloak !—a woman's cloak !—
and when he came in on Christmas morning to ask how I was
he cunningly slipt it down on the chair at the bottom of my
bed where I first noticed it when I was putting on my clothes
at midday. It happened that just at that moment I was
thinking of the warm dressing gown which used to be sent
him every Christmas by *her*—and all the flannel petticoats
and night-caps and thoughtful things of her own making for
myself ; my heart was full of sorrow—and just then I saw on
the chair what seemed a new dressing-gown—like the former
ones—there was something perfectly bewildering in the vision.
I stood staring at the thing uncertain if I was going mad and
merely *fancying to see it*, at last in a sort of desperation I laid
hold of it and found it was a woman's cloak—and then I
understood the whole matter—but I was made horribly sad
and nervous by it for the whole day. Poor Carlyle ! his gift
deserved to have excited gladder feelings—however I did not

best to *look glad* over it before him—and he was much consoled by my assurance that *it could be worn*. He had bought it " by gas light " he said and " felt quite desperate about it when he saw it in the morning." But it is a wonderful cloak for *him* to have bought—warm, and not *very* ugly—and a good shape— only entirely unsuitable to the rest of my habiliments ! being a brownish colour with *orange spots* and a brown velvet collar ! !

But oh the head of me does ache to-day. So I *must* have done. Love and kisses.

124. *To Helen Welsh*

To Bay House despite illness—Lady Harriet's consideration—Length of stay—Lady H. gives up German—Her parrot : the " green chimera "—Her cleverness : even manages Mrs. C.—Lady Ann Charteris—Alternation of splendour and squalor—Leaves the mind in its even tenor.

Honble. W. B. Baring,
Bay House,
Alverstoke, Hants.
Wednesday (20*th or* 27*th Jan.,* 1847).

DEAREST HELEN,

Here I am then—not dead—nor dying—just yet. On the whole better *every way* than I had room to expect. My nervousness at starting was " rather exquisite." Everybody had taken such *solemn* leave of me that I felt much as tho' getting into a fly for the purpose of going to be executed. Then the feeling of a *bonnet* on my head etc., etc., all that was so new to me—and the thought of what would become of me if I arrived unable to keep up appearances and the thought—worst of all alas !—how things would go on *in another department !* But all has gone better than I expected. My black blanket coat-cloak—with the woolen jacket under it effectually kept all cold from my body and my *respirator* hindered any from entering in. In fact before I had been half an hour on the railway—what with the movement and what with being worn out by *the violence of my emotions* I fell fast asleep and slept to the station ! ! I who could not sleep like a Christian in my own comfortable bed bed !

I arrived here hardly so tired as I have been on getting up from the sofa of late weeks to make tea.

Lady H. received me most kindly with a certain recognition of my *weak* state—hardly to have been hoped from her. She actually ordered me some hot soup—*before* dinner—and had assigned *me* the largest bedroom this time and C. my old little one. There is no soul here but herself. Lady Anne Charteris is in the neighbouring house and comes in *during* the heat of the day—but she is a prisoner after sunset. . . .

I do not go out here either—it feels quite as cold as in London and I have got some cold *in my head*, but that is nothing to cold in my *left lung*. Nothing could exceed Lady H's *tact* so far—and I feel very grateful to her—as I am not *up to* much *agitation* just now. . . . I do not know how long we shall stay, Lady H. does not mean to go to Town till the 1st of March—and " really *does* hope that now I *am* here, I will stay—and *let Mr. C. go back by himself if he wishes it—he might really spare me a while for my good*." She will read no German with him. "Now that her health is so improved she has no longer any pretence for giving up society—and she cannot carry on *that* and find time for studying languages.' Moreover she has got a green parrot—to which she pays the most marked attentions even in spite of his calling it a *green chimera*. And the Parrot does not mind interrupting *him* when he is speaking—does not fear to *speak thro' him* (as the phrase is) and her Ladyship *listens to the parrot*—even when C. is saying the most sensible things! By Heaven she is *the very cleverest* woman I ever saw or heard of. *She can* do what she wills with her own—I am perfectly certain there is not a created being alive whom she could not gain within twenty-four hours after she set her mind to it. Just witness myself —how she plies *me* round her little finger whenever she sees I am taking a reactionary turn.

Lady Anne is a dear little soul—*true* to the backbone—and so beautiful! How ridiculous my life is as a whole! such shifting scenes—such incongruities—material splendour alternating with material squalor. One time unable to get a cup of tea without two or three men-servants mixing themselves with the concern—another day advertising in *The Times* for a maid-of-all-work—and thankful to get one who can boil a

ettle ! Ach Gott ! I like more " even tenor " in one's life—
t requires a versatility of genius to adapt oneself to these
brupt changes—which *if I have it*—I should prefer not being
equired to use it. My *mind* at all events keeps in the even
enor of its way—always with more *weight* on it than it can
vell bear, always enveloped in London fog (figuratively
peaking). . . .

125. *To Jeannie Welsh at Auchtertool*

The journey to Alverstoke—Lady Harriet a successful diplomatist.

Bay House.
Thursday (28*th Jan.*, 1847).

DEAREST BABBIE,
        . . . The idea of setting out for this Place to lead
he life of last winter—in my actual state of weakness—to fall
ll perhaps, and be laid up in bed here ! was too awful—never-
heless after several refusals I had to give in—for the Lady
•eing all alone in the House for most part (Mr. Baring only
oming down—with Charles Buller and others for the Satur-
lays and Sundays) she could not have C. to stay with her alone
•y them two selves without *me*—and when she gave him so to
nderstand he made a sort of point of *my* going—and I was too
roud to stand in the way with my sickness or anything else.
•o here we are ! I walked straight out of my two hot rooms
ito a *fly* which deposited me at the Railway and Lady H.'s
arriage met me at the end and brought me safe here. For the
rst two or three days I thought I had reason to congratulate
nyself on having caught no new cold and on having had
othing to encounter which I was not quite *up to*. When Lady H.
kes to *manage* me she is always able to do so—and a greater
•roof of her diplomacy could not be given than the fact that
he can wind *me* about as she pleases—even now— . . .

. . . Best write to Chelsea in any case as my letters are
orwarded from there the same day.

Ever your affectionate
J. C.

126. *To Helen Welsh*

The bad throat and Sir J. Richardson—Neglectful attendance : a
helpful footman—Dr. Christie : empty sympathy of the great—
Impending visitors : Clanricardes, Buller, Lansdowne, Clarendon
—A Cabinet meeting adjusted for dinner—The parrot—Lady H.
appears to " play Mrs. C.'s cards for her."

Sir John Richardson, famous as Arctic explorer and
naturalist, was at this time physician to Haslar Hospital, and
therefore not far from Alverstoke. It was on Franklin's first
Polar expedition in 1820 that he was compelled in self-defence
to shoot an Iroquois voyageur, Michel, who had murdered
Robert Hood, a midshipman.

Bay House.
Friday night (5th Feb., 1847).

DEAREST HELEN,

    . . . I had a sore bout of illness after I last wrote to
you—was confined to bed several days with a feverish sore throat
—so ill that Carlyle fetched Sir J. Richardson (the man who shot
the Indian) to see me. If he had prescribed that I should be
carried out and flung into the sea, I would not have offered the
least resistance, for in my life I never felt more desolate than
lying here in my exposed French bed—at the mercy of the
housemaids who did not find it " in their department " to
attend to sick visitors. Lady H. of course never once came
near me—and it was by a sort of continual interposition of
Providence that I could get a cup of tea or anything I needed—
one morning my breakfast was brought in and placed on my bed
by one of the footmen ! ! ! who had been entreated by C. to
see after it, and who could not find any woman servant at
leisure ! But when I got down to the drawing room again—
which of course I did as soon as *possible*—nothing could be
more gracious than the Lady's reception of me—and in a few
days she managed by her kind manner to make me quite
impute her neglect to the *manners of her sphere*. Thank Heaven
I was not born in a sphere where it is made a point to *ignore*
all sickness and sorrow so long as they do not touch oneself
Poor Dr. Christie ! Mr. Hawes " has no more work for him "
and his poor wife died last Monday—I have had the sorrowfulest
letters from him. What to try next I know not. I got Lady

. to write to C. Buller about some Custom-house or other
ork—but C. Buller replies he is " *obliged* to save all his
nfluence for his own constituents." I talked to Mr. Charteris
bout him till *tears came into his eyes ;* but none of these great
ch people dream of *doing* anything for anybody—except their
own *constituents* " (literally or figuratively speaking). And
ll that *I* can do is to lend or give him some money. Ah me.

We continue very quiet—Mr. Baring mostly in London.
ut to-morrow there will be an influx of people which will last
ll Monday. Certain daughters of the Marchioness of
Clanricarde (very dowdy young ladies) come to lunch—then
y the evening train Mr. Baring—Buller, the Marquis of
Lansdowne and Earl of Clarendon. They were to " get over a
Cabinet early so that they might be here to dinner "—if the
ation knew how its affairs are managed ! The " green
himera " continues much in C.'s way—and he meets with
ther little contradictions which I cannot pretend to be sorry
or—I cannot make out what Lady H. is after—but to look at
er one would say she was systematically *playing my cards for
e.* Please do not read *that* aloud. . . .

Ever your affectionate

J. C.

127. *To Helen Welsh*

bout to leave Bay House—Works purse for Mazzini's bazaar—
Mrs. Bancroft's *faux pas* about Lady Palmerston's children.

Bay House, Alverstoke.
Wednesday (17th Feb., 1847).

. . . Lady H. has been really very kind to me—and I feel
xtremely obliged to her *in every way*—as well for what she
as *not* done as for what she has done. I do not pretend to
nderstand her better than heretofore—but this much is quite
ertain that from one motive or other—systematically or
nvoluntarily she had *staved off* a deal of vexation from me which
ight easily have attended my visit and made it very wretched.

Thanks for the silk which I have already worked up into a
urse for Mazzini's Bazaar. . . . Lady Anne is working for
Scotch Bazaar and Lady Joscelin for an Irish one. Lady

Joscelin you may remember is that daughter of Lady Palmersto
who had Count Giuliano for Father—and is living close by he
with her Husband for sea air. Since they came she has bee
over almost every day—and I must tell you an absurd thir
that took place. Your acquaintance Mrs. Bancroft was dinir
one day at the Palmerstons'—and the discourse turning c
children Lady Palmerston observed that sons general
resembled the Mother much more than the Father—whereupo
Mrs. Bancroft, not aware that Lady P. had been marrie
before, and that she had professedly *no* children by Lor
Palmerston—only *two* of *Lord Cowper's children being Lo
Palmerston's,* exclaimed " Well I am quite astonished that you
Ladyship does not see the most wonderful likeness in you
second son to Lord Palmerston ! ! ! " And at a party afterware
where some of the Palmerston people were the poor fool sai
publicly—" is it not strange that Lady P. sees no likenes
in her second son to his Father ? " ! ! Lady Harriet had bee
telling me this story in presence of Mr. Charteris. We
one day that Lady Joscelin was here and Mr. Charteris an
Lady Anne at the same time—Lady Anne said something c
being unable to get on with Bancroft's book—whereupo
Charteris exclaimed to Lady H. " what was that good stor
you were telling me of Mrs. Bancroft ?—Some dreadfull
stupid thing she said somewhere ? " Lady H. being rigl
opposite to Lady Joscelin could make no sign to him—merel
said confusedly " I don't remember "—and he continue
insisting about it till Lady Anne took hold of his arm an
gave him a dreadful pinch. Afterwards *he* went away and
went upstairs—and Lady Harriet sitting with only Lad
Joscelin and Lady Anne fancied somehow that the strange
were gone and that she was left with Lady Anne and *me*—an
began " I really think Frank is going mad ! did you eve
hear the like of that about Mrs. Bancroft ? " ! ! and the
Lady J. turning a look of inquiry on her she came to herse
and had to get off the matter as she best could. . . .

God bless you all.

Ever your affectionate

J. C.

128. *To Jeannie Welsh*

Mazzini a true friend.

Mazzini, whose letter was enclosed, had written to inquire anxiously after Uncle John Welsh.

(22nd Feb., 1847.)

MY DEAREST BABBIE,

Yes Mazzini is a friend worth having—one that is always best in the hour of need. If he had heard of the illness of his mother in Italy he could not have been more anxious than he has been in these days to learn the last news from Liverpool. He has a power of *identifying* himself with those he loves—at least in their *sorrows*, which I never saw equalled.

129. *To Jeannie Welsh at Auchtertool*

Exchange of letters—Plattnauer returned "no madder than most" says John—Praised by Carlyle—Does not mind his latent madness : a faithful friend—Mazzini and the Ashursts—Geraldine is engrossed with new friends, but will come back.

Saturday (24th April, 1847).

DEAREST BABBIE,

If you really desired to hear from me again, you did well to write—for, upon *my* honour, I had made up my wicked mind that if *I* at *my* time of life, with *my* miserable health, and *my* endless botherations was to be held to letter for letter by you, I would once for all " *protest* and appeal to *posterity.*" * When people treat me *better* than I deserve, I am still capable of being roused into a wish to justify their faith, but when they give me my bare due—or less—I leave them to receive their recompense from the sense of their own accurate justice. My *due* is so little in fact that they may keep *that* too if they like and I shall hardly feel myself poorer. . . .

Did I tell you ever that Plattnauer was returned to England —half a year ago ? . . . He gives no signs of derangement *at present ;* unless his almost superhuman insight and elevation can be called *derangement.* He comes here about once a week —or seldomer and it does me good to talk with him. He

* " *Vous êtes des injustes,*" said a drunken man, whom boys were annoying ; "*je m'en appelle à la posterité !*" (One of Cavaignac's stories. T. C. in L.M. i. 169.)

X

goes also a good deal to John Carlyle who has fallen int
profound admiration of his character and "transcenden
eloquence" and will not admit the possibility of his being sti
mad—hardly will he admit that he has ever *been* mad—"tha
is to say any madder than the generality of people are." Eve
Carlyle is greatly struck with his "earnestness" and "kee
intellect." But they may all say what they like, the *madness i*
lying in him the same as ever, only deep down—ready to burs
up any day. *That* I know—but I also do not mind it—hav
got to regard his fits of insanity much as other people's fits o
biliousness—or influenza. And one cannot but feel well dis
posed towards a man who absent or present, mad or sane, locke
up or at large, never alters in his feelings towards oneself.

Mazzini is pretty well—very busy as usual with hi
benevolent schemes—not so solitary as he used to be—havin
got up to the ears in a *good* twadly family of the name o
Ashurst—who have plenty of money—and help "his things
and *toady* him till I think it has rather gone to his head. .
Miss Eliza Ashhurst *—who does strange things—made h
acquaintance first—by going to his house to drink tea wit
him all alone, &c. &c.!! and when she had got him to he
house she introduced him into innumerable other houses o
her kindred—and the women of them paint his picture—an
send him flowers, and *work* for his bazaar, and make verse
about him, and Heaven knows what all—while the men giv
capital towards his *Institutions* and adopt "the new ideas
at his bidding. . . . Miss Ashurst has been staying wit
Geraldine in Manchester and G. is coming to London with he
She is not in her "choicest mood" towards *me* at presen
as always happens when new "everlasting friendships" ar
getting sworn—but I know her ways now, and can let her tal
her swing sure that she will right herself at last. . . .

Ever your own

J. C.

* Miss Ashurst was a daughter of the Radical reformer W. H. Ashurs
whose friendship with Mazzini sprang from indignation at the opening of h
letters by the Post Office in 1844. In 1851 he founded the society of th
"Friends of Italy,"

THOMAS CARLYLE.
From a photograph by Elliott & Fry.

130. *To Helen Welsh*

sleepless night and its occupations—Visit from the Duke of
Saxe Weimar—Miniature of Mrs. Carlyle, recovered from
Seaforth—Mr. Fairie.

Monday (Spring, 1847).

DEAREST HELEN,

. . . If it had not been for my plenty of headaches ; I would have sent you sooner, for the benefit of my
uncle chiefly, a penny-a-line account of the Grand-Duke's
visit to Cheyne Row—and now it looks an old story, and I
cannot get up even penny-a-line-steam about it.   Here however
the fact of the business.   Saturday gone a week the Secretary
announced in official style, that " his Royal Highness Reigning
Duke of Saxe Weimar " would call for Mr. Carlyle next day
at twelve *if convenient*—and received of course an affirmative
reply.   On Sunday morning I *dusted all my little things* very
accurately—put clean water to some flowers I already had—
saw that Ann bloomed out into her best gown—(for Ann
unless expressly ordered would not dress herself *out of the
usual time* for Queen Victoria never to speak of a foreign
Highness)—and then I walked off into space !   Had I staid
at home I was going to have felt myself " in *a false position* "
—either I must have been put *au secret* in my own house—or
invited down to my own sitting room, as an ineffable condescension—and I did not feel any *besoin* of the *condescension* of anybody.   With Carlyle it was all right—the Prince had to do with
him—and the visit was honourable to both parties—but I should
only have embarrassed his Highness and he me—and so I
went up to Mrs. Buller's.   She insisted on my staying till her
driving hour, when she would take me home.   I came in half an
hour after the dinner hour expecting to be reproved—but C.'s
first words were " you have just missed these people by ten
minutes ! "—" From twelve till twenty minutes after five " ?
what a frightful royal visit I thought ; but it had not been so
bad as that.   At twelve the little Secretary had arrived " all in
a sweat " to say the Queen Dowager (*our visitor's* aunt) had
insisted on his going to church with her ! ! so it was hoped an
hour or two later would make no difference.   About four they
came, that is to say the Prince his Chamberlain and Secretary,

in a handsome open carriage with two servants behind, wh
excited Ann's admiration by their "genteel dress—plain blac
coats, blue breeches, and white silk stockings—nothing th
least *fine* about them except their—gold garters!" Anothe
thing seemed to have struck her rather forcibly. "So soon a
the carriage stopt the Prince took off his hat and then all th
rest did the same—and at going away they all remained bare
headed till the Prince put on *his* hat after he had sat down i
the carriage." And all this uncovering of heads I really believ
Ann considered honour paid to—her Master! In which blesse
illusion I allowed her to remain, as a new reason for cookin
his chops to the best of her power! C. liked the Prince ver
well—but who would not like a Prince that comes to pay or
a morning visit?—he is only some four or five and twenty—ver
handsome C. said, "with beautiful blue eyes" "extremel
aristocratic looking"—(who is to look aristocratic if not King
and Queens?)—"the most dignified German" C. had eve
seen. "*More* dignified than Plattnauer?" I asked. "Why—
no—the indestructible dignity of Plattnauer *in all sorts of coa*
is what one *never* sees the like of." When they arrived C. wa
doing *a Yankee* of all things—introduced by Emerson, but I
had him upstairs and dismissed him summarily, with apologi
—the Yankee loitered, and seemed to think it strange th
he should not be invited to assist at the interview.

When C. came down to the low room he found his Highne
standing with the other two men. He apologised for *intrudi*
on his retired habits &c. &c. then said looking about that I
could fancy himself at home in Weimar here; so man
reminiscences of Goethe and of Germany—then he went abo
looking at the various portraits of Goethe and finally seate
himself on the sofa and *invited* C. to be seated. *That* was one
the prospective etiquettes that scared me *out*—having to sta
till I was permitted to sit down on my own chair! He sta
some hour and quarter talking "intelligently enough" an
being talked to I imagine *emphatically* enough. He invite
C. to Weimar—promised to show him various things—promise
to send him a scarce book they had talked of—begged that "I
would not forget him"—(how touching! and I should thi
superfluous) and then went in peace.

I have heard nothing of Geraldine for many days, she is very busy finishing her book down there. By the way I had to write to Mrs. Paulet the other day that I must have back my miniature—when she got it I told her it was C.'s property—but a chance if he would remember anything about it till after my death when she was to be sure and restore it.

The long Mr. Fairie—is going North—in search of two things—neither of which do I think he will ever find—for lack of a strong enough *wish*—an occupation—and a wife ! I gave him your address in case——

Pray send this letter on to Babbie—I will write to herself in a day or two—about the Bazaar.

Ever your affectionate J. C.

131. *To Helen Welsh*

A spell of calm—Geraldine's second visit : makes up for the first by taking her to many parties—A " situation " at Monckton Milnes' breakfast—Geraldine too expansive for John—Her aim at marriage—Lady Harriet has other people to amuse her in town.

DEAREST HELEN,   (*15th June*, 1847.)

At length I have a day of *calm*—not a day of *leisure* yet ; for I have much to do in the way of what you used to call " *siding* things " and making up accounts etc.—my natural love of order having for the last fortnight succumbed to force of circumstances. But I am relieved from the worry of having to be amiable and *lively* all day long—and need not go to any party or public place for a month to come unless it be my own good pleasure. It is a fortnight past last Wednesday since Geraldine removed hither from her Ashursts—and ever since I have " lived and had my being " in a racket very foreign to my habits and tastes. Being *up to* going about however, so far as physical strength was required, and vexed by the recollection of the wretched time *you* had of it in winter—and the failure of Geraldine's first visit also—and never forgetting the endless pains she took to keep me comfortable and amused last year in Manchester I " felt it my duty " to accept for her behoof all the invitations that turned up—the more that on the strength of *Zoe* people whom I could hardly have intruded

her upon before—were now quite glad to have her at their
parties as a new specimen for their several *menageries*. Upon
my honour I believe if a *Lady* had been tried for murder, so
that she only escaped hanging or transportation; she would
have a better chance of " getting on " in society here than one
of whom nothing had been *talked*. Geraldine was a much
more lively and agreeable person in company, when I knew
her first—*before* her book—than now—but there was hardly
a house in London *then*, to which I could have used the freedom
of taking her along with me—and now because she has put her
cleverness into a *book*—above all a book accused of immorality
(quite a new sort of distinction for a young Englishwoman)
there is no house I visit at where the people would not *thank*
me for giving them a sight of her and an opportunity of *exhibiting* her to their friends. *She* feels no misgivings about all this
—she is *received—politely*—complimented on her book—and
thinks the people are very kind, and it is all right. But *I* as
her *Chaperon* have had considerable qualms I can tell you!
Especially at Breakfast at Richard Milnes's the other morning
—got up on purpose for us two—Carlyle was not asked—and
tho' he might have gone if he liked would not go—so I had to
be responsible not only for myself but for Geraldine. I
thought the first entrance would be the worst of it—but figure
my consternation on finding ourselves in a room with eight
men! and not one woman! " Lady Duff Gordon had fallen
sick." I never made such a comfortless breakfast in my life
—the situation would just have suited Lady Harriet, but me
it was too *strong* for—obliged to make conversation with all
these men brought to meet us—and obliged at the same time
to keep an ear open to what Geraldine was saying to her next
neighbour lest she should get on dangerous ground. *She*
enjoyed herself immensely and was astonished afterwards to
find I had been *put about*! She " thought it queerish for the
first moment, but when she remarked the perfect tranquillity
and aplomb with which I was going thro' the thing she supposed
it was all *quite natural* " ! So little do one's most intimate
friends see into one's heart—provided one have self-command
enough to keep clear of hysterics and such like outward visible

signs. I did not tell her that the chief apprehension which haunted me—was lest I should be mixed up in the minds of these men with *the Chapel scene* and certain other question-abilities in *Zoe*. We breakfasted another morning at Rogers's and dined at the Macreadys' with Jenny Lind of all people—and attended *a ball* at Mrs. Procter's—in fact I am sick of gaieties and very thankful that Geraldine is gone into Essex to her Miss Darby. John *did* most of the sight-seeing with her—for a few days it looked almost as if he were trying to work himself up into a matrimonial sentiment for her. But she did not play her cards well—she made him take her to too many Plays etc.,—and John dislikes paying out shillings on all hands—she was becoming rather expensive—and his incipient sentiment was too weakly for bearing up against con-stant demands on his purse. On the whole I rather imagine no man will ever be found so constituted as to fall in love with Geraldine and think of her as a Wife—which is a pity—as her heart seems to me set on being married to any sort of a male biped who could maintain her—at all risks ! Tell me of Sophy. There is no talk yet of summer schemes—nor will be while C.'s *aristocratic* friends are all in town. *I* see very little of *the* Lady—as usual when she is in her town-house—with plenty of other people to keep her from weariness.

I must be quiet for some weeks to come for I am required to give some heed to a large tumour on my throat—a result J. Carlyle says of " extreme physical irritation "—nobody knows of it but John—as I can cover it with the black lace I wear round my neck. . . . I have said nothing about it even to Carlyle. *Speculating* about it will not help to *absorb* it—and a *tumour* is not an interesting phase of human ailment. Besides as I have been able to hold my peace on the physical suffering which has produced this beautiful little *dumpling* in my throat—I may surely hold my peace on a symptom which is not painful. I tell *you*—because should it turn to anything serious you would think it *unnatural* that I should have made a secret of it.

And now I must off to my housewifery.

Love and kisses to my Uncle.

Ever your affectionate,   J. C.

132. *To Jeannie Welsh*

" Real " letters—Misses Alverstoke—John thoughtful.

5, Cheyne Row.
(12*th Feb.*, 1848.)

DEAREST BABBIE,

This last is the only letter I have had from you for an age that I have felt a *besoin* to answer *at once*, I would have written yesterday had not my head been too bad for writing. Perhaps you wonder what was in *this* letter to make it particularly acceptable—but no—you cannot but have an inward sense that it was *the real transcript of your mind at the moment* which your letters have long ceased to be—I have had letters of many *sheets* from you—not " *stupid* " letters by any means —as *kindly phrased* too as I had any business to expect— which I have nevertheless thrown into the fire the minute after reading them, with a feeling of the most profound disappointment and chagrin—because they contained no one word that seemed to have come out of any deeper source than your ink bottle—were not in fact letters from *you* to *me*, but such as might stand labelled in the *Ready letter writer letter from a young Lady residing in the country to a female cousin in town*—letters written *not* to *communicate* your real thoughts but to *conceal* them. And yet who is there who can understand all that is in your heart—even the saddest of it, and what you may feel to be the least creditable to you—your discontents with yourself—your circumstances &c. so well as just I who have passed my whole existence in that sort of thing—and to whom there is no sorrow in life, no weakness in human nature that is not intelligible thro' my own experience ! You may say my own letters are as little written out of the heart as yours —certainly ! I am very sensitive—morbidly so—and I can only be confidential where I am met by confidence—besides *my* inward life is connected with outward *facts* on which I am bound to be silent—so that I could not always let you see into my heart without exposing myself to cruel misconstructions. Still were you less shut up—I should never have got

o *inarticulate* for you as I have long been. But it is a truth
ou say ; friends should see one another from time to time, if
hey would go on understanding one another. And yet—the
ast time we saw each other were we any better for it in the
natter of understanding ?

I wish we could carry *the Switzerland project* into effect
—be together awhile somewhere quite far away from all
nterference.

I have got over the Alverstoke visit this year most unex-
ectedly. We were to have gone the beginning of January
or five or six weeks, but I fell ill—*really* ill just the night
efore—and after waiting for me a few days C. went alone—
or a fortnight while confined to my bedroom with a dreadful
ough and the usual accompaniments—never getting a wink
f sleep except by means of Morphia, I was every day written
o " when will you be well ? When are you coming ? "—and
fixed time after time ; to oblige them—which when arrived
as found impossible—at length I believe I should really
ave gone to be done with it—ill as I was—and *got done with*
once for all had not C., I *must* say *happily*, taken a cold *there*,
hich he felt no hope to get rid of in a houseful of company
ith seven o'clock dinners, French beds &c. and so he came
ome himself instead of insisting any longer on my going. . . .

John was very attentive to me both in this last illness and the
ne I had after my return from Yorkshire. He is much *subsided*
nd improved since he got his *Book* * under weigh—especially
 regard for *me* he is singularly improved. Yes I can see it
l at Maryland Street. Give them my love a kiss most warm
 my Uncle.

Ever your affectionate
JANE C.

[NOTE.—A long passage omitted from No. 133 again wel-
mes a " real letter," though self-styled an " unsatisfactory
rap," which carries " one word out of Babbie's own heart."
Write me always *such scraps*—write to me when you are sad
—when you are out of humour—when the Devil is in you, if
u like—I love you all the same, whatever is *in* you."]

* Translation of Dante.

133. *To Jeannie Welsh at Auchtertool*

Mazzini leaving England—Her feelings towards him unconcerned—
Gifts : her small possessions—Plattnauer.

Monday (20*th March*, 1848)

DEAREST BABBIE

. . . Mazzini will be here in a few minutes *to take leave*
He went to Paris so soon as Louis Philippe decamped—to
see I suppose if anything could be arranged for a new " Savoy"
Expedition " ; the distinct prospect of being permitted to
return to Genoa " *in peace* " being *extremely distressing* to
him ! ! He had no time to come before he went—merely
wrote—and since his return I have not yet seen him. He
wrote that he would be here to-day at two o'clock ; and was
going off again to Paris on Wednesday—probably not to return
—I shall hear if he got your note. I take the prospect of his
final departure with a *calm* that would surprise you. Whether
it be that my *feelings* have got extremely chilled by years and
suffering—or that *he* has worn them out—perhaps both causes
have operated towards making me tolerably unconcerned
God bless you Babbie.

Ever your affectionate

J. C.

Not one word said of the beautiful little *mats !* and one of
them all the while before my eyes—in the tray that holds my
" details." Thanks—it is curious how these net-things have
always come just at the right moment. I had got a beautiful
amber-box from Capt. Sterling which I was afraid of getting
chipped in a *hard* tray—and was thinking what sort of round
thing I could make to lay in the tray—when voilà ! these ! the
little one—the beauty—lies in the little black Templand tray in
my bedroom which holds my watch. While I was ill I made
my bedroom so pretty with all the pictures and little things
belonging to the Past that I set most store on, Cavaignac
medallion amongst the rest—I thought I should like to die
amidst all these things.

Plattnauer is still in Ireland—still keeps *sane* in spite of
these Revolutions—so far as I can judge from his letters—he
is a noble man—and true as death ! Love to Walter.

134. *To Helen Welsh*

The gaieties of the season—Young girls cured of shyness—Chopin's
playing—Cavaignac.

(*After* 14*th July*, 1848.)

MY DEAREST HELEN,

. . . I have been very *gay* of late weeks ! Nobody unless
the paralytic Miss Chorley, I should think, has been going
more *resolutely* " a-head " in " the gaieties of the season "
(*so-called*)—with *my body*—that is to say—for my soul has
been at quite other work.

We dined at Mrs. Norton's * one day ! we grow very *compatible* don't you think ?   Well she is a beautiful witty graceful
woman—whatever else, then a dinner at the Macreadys' where
was Count D'Orsay ! and old Lady Morgan " naked as robins
half way down "—age seventy-five !—and Lady Duff Gordon
and an American Mrs. Jay. . . . Then we had another dinner at
the Procters'—where were Adelaide Kemble and her husband
—and a morning music party at Lady Eddisbury's—" the
beautiful Mrs. Stanley "—that was †—Darwin's " *Moonface* " ‡
—young girls *very* young and pretty—sang with the self-
possession of Grisis to an immense concourse of Ladies and
(more to the purpose) of *young marriageable Lords* one of whom
(Lord Dufferin) said to me—" a charming way of passing a
morning this !—and such a capital thing—don't you think,
for *curing them* of all sort of shyness ? " Decidedly ! There
was one girl a real beauty—the daughter of Sir James Graham
—about seventeen—with the most innocent modest *face* in
the world and there she stood with her face to the company
—trilling and quavering with *the smile* of a consummate opera
singer ! It seemed to me really *bad* all this !

But I went to hear Chopin too—once in private and once
at a morning Concert and Chopin has been *here ! !* I never
heard the piano played before—could not have believed the

* The Hon. Mrs. Norton, Lady Dufferin's sister, was famous as a poetess
and for her matrimonial troubles, especially her husband's suit, perhaps
politically inspired, against Lord Melbourne in 1836.

† Here begins a fresh sheet of grey notepaper, headed " no more good
paper, alas."

‡ Mrs. Stanley was a Dillon. Her husband was created Lord Eddisbury
in 1848, and later became the second Lord Stanley of Alderley.

capabilities that be in it. Quantities of more things of the same nature I have *done*—I was going to say *in my sleep*—but *in a bad dream* were nearer the truth.

The one earthly thing that I have been getting any real satisfaction out of has been something very far away from all that—the wise and valorous conduct of General Cavaignac—and the admiration he has won from all parties. If I had been his sister I could not have watched his progress with more interest. . . .

And now I must really make an end.

Love and a kiss to my Uncle.

Ever your affectionate

Jane Carlyle.

135. *To Jeannie Welsh*

Proposed cottage on the Ashburton estate—Lady Ashburton and her guests—Two new friends: one, Aubrey de Vere.

(Addiscombe, 28th Sept., 1848.)

Dearest Babbie,

. . . The Parlours are painted and papered I understand —and it is to be hoped will not smell *too* bad when we return in *ten days* I expect. "All's well that ends well." For this time nothing is settled or even strongly proposed about "The intellectual *gate*." Lord A.* finds so many unexpected drains on his fortune—large as it is—just at the first coming into possession that they are not indulging in any *fancies* this year —and other years it is to be hoped will bring their own requirements—it is much more agreeable for *me* that the project should sink away thus than that *I* should have put a veto on it or *he* for *my* consolation. But anyhow he could never have been mad enough to dream of letting that farm house be fitted up for him !—as unless the genii could have carried it a quarter of a mile from its offices and farm yard—sleep for *him*—never to say for *me*—would be perfectly impossible there—it is no *poetical* farm—with the farming left out—but the place where all the cocks and hens and geese and ducks and pigs and cows and horses and carts requisite for the maintenance of this immense household are kept—and the noise is something too

* Mr. Baring succeeded his father as Lord Ashburton, 13 May, 1848.

dreadful! I question if that which greeted the ears of Adam amidst the first Creation of animals came up to it.

Lady A. got a bad cold in going up to London last week to see her Dr., and could not return next day as she proposed, and only came the day after to go to bed ; where she remained, at least in her bedroom, for several days—even now she is only a few hours in the day in the Drawing-room—does not dine with us—but I play chess and talk with her in her private sitting-room—which is the beautifulest room you can imagine and opening into a large conservatory with a glass door. Most of the company were gone or going when she fell ill—and there now only remains her mother Lady Sandwich—who is *very* agreeable and a good sort of woman to my notion tho' her daughter can hardly endure her. *She* goes on Saturday and Lady A. proposes that next Monday she should take Mr. C. and me to *Freshwater* in the Isle of Wight for a week while Lord Ashburton is *doing* his yeomanry in Winchester. After that I rather expect we shall be *allowed* to go home—as she has a great houseful of people coming on the 16 of October and will need a few days of *Alverstoke* to put her up to them. . . .

I have made two new acquaintances whom I mean to keep up in London—a male and female acquaintance—the female one has already reached its culmination—and no more can come of it than has come—pleasant superficial intercourse—with the male one it is better—that may develop itself into a real friendship—the name is romantic enough, Aubrey de Vere—and the man who bears it romantic enough—very handsome—young—*religious*—to the extent even of eating fish on Fridays and fasting in Lent. A Poet—highly accomplished every way, despising " *wits* " (wonderfulest of all) and in short a rare mortal as men go. But I must stop—" Her Ladyship expects me in her sitting room." God bless you my Babbie.

Ever yours.

136. *To Jeannie Welsh*
Reconciliation with Mrs. Anthony Sterling.

Millbank was the first of our new-model prisons, finished in 1821. The system was continued at Pentonville, opened in 1842 ; Mr. and Mrs. Carlyle visited this on January 2, 1851 (see L.M. ii. 144), and Mr. C. was taken over the King's Bench prison in 1835 (L.M. i. 43).

(*Autumn*, 1848.)

DEAREST BABBIE,

Is he gone yet?—are you at leisure to listen to me? for I have today actually something to tell! I have had a visit which threw me into perfect—or to speak quite veraciously —into *comparative* beatitude for several hours—guess from whom!—but you never could come within a hundred miles of her!—for it *is* a *her*—so I must just tell you. I have had a visit—indeed *two* visits from—Mrs. Anthony Sterling!! I cannot tell you how it pleased me to be no longer however unintentionally a cause of misery to that poor woman! She came voluntarily—" would have come long ago if she could have believed I would receive her." Nothing could be more beautiful than her behaviour—she came alone—stopt " on the mat " (Helen said) until I said she might come in, and then came forward with meek and brave words of apology—which you may be sure I cut short with kisses. Poor soul, I almost fainted myself from putting myself into her situation. I begin to think I must have some sympathy after all. She said " I must be *an angel* to receive her as I did after her conduct " —but it was *she* who was the angel this time—I in her place could not have gone thro' the thing as well as she did—and after all what had I to forgive her poor woman? the suffering to *herself* which attended her mistake about *me* was proof enough of its *involuntariness*. Oh don't I know what she has suffered?—too hard punishment for her error of judgment! That was Saturday. I had received a note from Anthony in the morning telling me not to be surprised if she came—but there had been some talk of the same thing before—and it ended in smoke, so I could hardly expect her till the carriage drove up—had just thought it so far possible as to put myself into a cap and shawl to make out a decided case of *an old woman!* for her better opinion in case she *did* come.—Would any mortal have thought of *that* but myself?—Of course I did all I could to raise her up in her own esteem again and make her aware that she had not sunk but infinitely risen in mine. I wrote

er the most encouraging letter, after, that I could *invent* to
meet the reaction which I feared would follow her magnanimous
ct—and she has answered so sweetly. To-day she came again
—with Anthony to get me to go to Headley * for a few days—
She would not believe I had quite forgiven her till I came to
Headley."—Perhaps I will go. I would do anything to help
er with her life—but it looks a sad mess to me. Anthony
nd she grate on each other like a couple of files—she proud
nd petulant towards *him* and he cold and contradictory
owards *her*—since seeing them together this morning I almost
espair of ever being able to make them better friends. But
I have great influence over him of a *moral* sort—and I will *get*
nfluence over her too or the devil is in it—seeing I have set
ny heart on reconciling them.

Yesterday I went over Tothillfields prison † with Forster and
Mr. C. and we dined with Forster after and were filled half
drunk with champagne as usual. The Prison must remain
ver for another letter for I perceive to my horror it is twenty
ninutes past four—ten for sealing and posting ! Only I must
ell you I saw and received a curtsey from Annette Meyers
he sauciest looking commonplace little creature that ever
layed the part of a [illegible] criminal.

Love and kisses.

Ever your,   J. C.

137. *To Jeannie Welsh*

sad Christmas letter—Death of Charles Buller : a visit to his
Mother—Lady Ashburton's grief—Lady Sandwich and other
friends—Devotion of the Sterlings.

Charles Buller died November 29, 1848 : six months after
is father. Mrs. Buller died broken-hearted on March 13, 1849.

Saturday (23rd or 30th Dec., 1848).

DEAREST BABBIE,

The notion of its being Christmas time when people
re, or ought to be, all " merry " complicates my difficulties

---

* Headley Grove, his farm on the downs near Betchworth.
† *I.e.* Millbank. The girl they saw had in March been sentenced to
eath, but with a recommendation to mercy, for shooting the young soldier
ho had betrayed and swindled her.

in writing letters—for a *merry* letter such as would beseem th
season is wholly above the reach of my imaginative power
And therefore do I write to *you* instead of to my Uncle
whom my heart most devoutly wishes all the good wishes tha
one is in the habit of giving voice or ink to on the approac
of a new year. You are to kiss him for me, and tell him th
I hope to kiss him myself before another year is done—an
that he is to wish this good wish for me—that if I live to h
age I may be found then *as good a man* as he is, God bless hir

Since I got your last I have been two days in bed—wit
that eternal *sickness*—and three days and two nights on a vis
to Mrs. Buller at the other side of Hyde Park. This locali
for her is extremely inconvenient for *me*—in the short co
days and I have to go seldomer and stay longer. On Frid
gone a week she sent a miserable letter beseeching me to con
for some days as Fleming was gone to the Grange—and
could do no otherwise than go. "Very mad" Mr. C. calle
my going—for I had not slept for two nights and was ill enoug
—but John said I could not, at her house, "sleep worse tha
none—and perhaps the change might do me some good"-
and so it did—I felt a great calm come over me when I l
down in that new bed—and in spite of carriages rushing b
all night, and a housemaid snoring in the next room—I g
the best sleep I had had for many weeks.

She is a sad spectacle and every time I see her I feel mo
desperate of being any help to her. It is not her *grief* that
saddest in it—that is nothing like so violent as one might ha
anticipated—and her health seems to me rather better than
has been for years—but it is the complete giving up of hersε
to the sensations of the moment, her complete want of sε
denial when a momentary indulgence brings prolonged suffe
ing—her recklessness about expense where the merest whi
is concerned—all *that* is miserable to see; for it overlays h
great sorrow with the meanest troubles and difficulties—aι
will drive away from her much sympathy and many consolε
tions that might have cheered her remaining years.

Lady A. is with her husband at the Grange. Fleming writ
that he left her on Monday in much better health and spiri

—but her last letter—to Mr. C.—was sad as death—as sorrowful a letter as *I* could have written. Mr. C. is unwearied in writing consolations, and sending her books and doing everything that in him lies to comfort her, and she seems extremely grateful for his kindness. Lady Sandwich goes to her on Tuesday— but *that* will be no comfort. Meanwhile Lady S. will be rather a loss to *me*, for she is the pleasantest person I have here just now to go off and talk with when I am too bad company for myself. She seems very fond of me, and she who was always represented to me as the most insolent of English Peeresses is precisely the only one of them I have known with whom I feel entirely free to say what I like, and whom I can run in to with as little ceremony as I could do to any old woman living on a hundred a year. Miss Wynn who was my most constant visitor last winter, and for whom my friendship always increases the longer I know her, has got some lingering illness that makes me rather anxious and is sent out of London for the present. Bölte is still at Brighton. Capt. S. still at Headley—but he comes to town every week and calls both in coming and going —and brings me flowers—the beautifulest hothouse flowers tho' it is winter now—and if he could bring me health and happiness there is no man who would sooner do it. I wonder what strange attraction lies in me for all of the blood of Sterling ? For Father and Mother and *both* sons I have been more than any other woman—not married to them. There is no understanding these things. I am sure I have taken a hundred times more pains to please some others who never took to me at all. . . .

Write soon.

Ever your
affectionate J. C.

You will take heart about your handwriting when you see his scrawling—but you are a young lady, my dear, and are not permitted to be illegible as I am.

138. *To Helen Welsh*

A child's visit.

Saturday (20th *Jan.*, 1849).

DEAREST HELEN,

What a shame! The only real business I have " *here down* " (as Mazzini used to say) seems to be writing to the people who like to hear from me—and see how I bestir myself in *that*! The fact is ; nobody that is much caring to do ever the " things that they *ought* to do " and even the things they *intend* to do should live in London—even on the most domestic principles ; there being here a *parti pris* on the side of *the pigs* to " run thro' " all one's " best laid schemes " ! I have been interrupted dreadfully these two weeks, but the wonderfulest " *go* " of all has been *a child!* Yes indeed ! I have had a child—to keep,—to sit at meat with, and sleep with (good God !) and dress dolls for, and wash and comb and all that sort of thing—and also (—most fatiguing of all—) to *protect* it from Mr. C. who gave manifest indications of a tendency to wring its neck ! Where did I pick the creature up ? —Ah my dear ! the creature picked up *me*—" quite promiscuously "—I went some six weeks ago to call at the Macreadys' —and dined at the children's dinner and was reminded that I had a godchild, *by seeing it.** Not one godmotherly thing had I ever done towards the child ! and really it was a godchild to be proud of, so now I took it on my knee and kissed it and like a fool, asked " will you go with *me* ? " " I should like it very much " said the child. " *That she would* " said the mother, " and you need not be afraid of her misconducting herself for she is a good child." I saw the thing had been taken *on the serious* so I backed out of it as well as I could, " some time we shall see !—when I come again *with a carriage*." Well ten days ago I went there again with Anthony Sterling—and was asked gravely by the eldest daughter if I " meant to take Jane Lydia back with me ? " " She had never ceased talking about *her visit* since I had been there." I was in for it ! so I said " not to-day ; " (it was necessary to prepare C.'s mind a

* She became godmother to another Macready child also (p. 332).

well as my own) " but if her mother would bring her any day she liked to name I should do my best with her." So Saturday was named—and the little creature delivered over to me in a transport of joy, (hardly mutual) to stay " as long as I could be troubled to keep her." I modestly suggested that three days and three nights—just the time that Jonah was in the whale's belly—would probably be enough of it for *her* as well as for me —and the mother went and I remained alone—with a child of six years—very *stirring* and very small and delicate ! during the first day I " ran horses " at her bidding, and performed my new functions with a determined energy—but the night came, I durst not put her to sleep in the spare room—for fear of her crying in the night—and awaking Mr. C., and being herself very miserable, so after infinite perplexity in getting off her clothes (all *sewed* together) I laid her in my own bed, where she soon commenced—singing !—after an hour's waiting upon her I left her still awake—when I went up again she was asleep but lying right *across* the bed—at twelve I placed her properly, and went into bed myself, but of course not to sleep : all night long she pitched into my breast with her active little heels— and when she awoke at seven and threw her arms about my neck calling out " Oh I am so glad to be here ! " I had not once closed my eyes, and in this state to have to wash and dress her and play at horses again ! it was a strange and severe penalty for being a Godmother. Next night I put her in the spare bed at all risks—with a good fire and trusted in Providence—and she did very well there—but I had got some cold by the job and the idea of being *laid up* in such a cause after having got so far thro' the winter on foot—was very vexatious. So I kept the house a few days and when the child's time came Anthony Sterling took her home for me ! ! I have a great quantity more to tell you about this " *go* " and other things— but Mr. C. has been bothering ever since I began to write about helping him to pack a boxful of old clothes and things for Scotsbrig—and in an hour I have to be off to Mrs. Buller so I will finish this letter to Babbie. God bless you all

Your affectionate

JANE WELSH.

139. *To Jeannie Welsh*

Apologies needless—Society without a carriage—Duty with Mrs
  Buller ; pleasure with Lady Sandwich—Lady Ashburton
  makes a generous gift—Hides grief for C. Buller—Carlyle wil
  never make her " more earnest "—A. Sterling and his wife—
  G. H. Lewes described—The Schwabes and Cobdens—Robertson
  and the death of Cavaignac.

Monday (5*th Feb.*, 1849

DEAREST BABBIE,

Thanks for your letter, *notwithstanding* the apologies
Bless your life, my child, we are got long beyond apologie
you and I ! I should as soon think of returning into *tucker*
and bead-necklaces for my part—I have been and am, and look
as (if) I should continue to be *pressed for time.*

" Oh my ! "—Really the business of *Society* gets to be quit
business enough for me without *aiming* at any other—so long
at least as I have no *carriage* to help me thro' it. . . .

My chief social occupations however have been Mrs. Buller
and Lady Sandwich. The former I go to from a sense of duty
the latter because I like it—for Lady S. amuses me more than
any woman I ever heard speak, more than even her daughter.
She is going off to Paris again however presently, and there wil
be an end of *that*. The Ashburtons have been in town for
week, returned to-day to the Grange for another week and then
back to London for *the season*. Lady A. came to see me on he
arrival with an *armful of shawl* which she laid into my
arms, saying " there, dear Mrs. Carlyle—there is my *late* new
year to you—at new year's day we had so much to think of
else ! " and she kissed me. It was well and graciously *done*—
still, *valuable* presents for which I can make no return, distress
me always from that quarter—there are people from whom
can take things without any *spoiling* sense of obligation, but
then I feel that I can repay them with love—now Lady A. can
do perfectly well *without* love of mine—love from *me* beyond
a certain point would bore her rather than otherwise. She
looked quite herself again—all her wild grief over C. Buller
crushed down out of sight into the bottom of her heart, or
perhaps *out of it* altogether. She spoke of him with *supreme*

* Lady Ashburton.

omposure—and was in a racket of company all the time of her
tay. Poor Mr. C. will never succeed in making her " more
earnest," dear, gay hearted, high spirited woman that she is !
God bless her for her seeming determination *not* to be " *earnest* "
for *his* pleasure, or anyone else's, but to be just what God has
made her, the enemy of *cant* and lover of all mirthful things.
t is a great faculty that of being able to throw off grief—I
would not somehow care to have it, and yet I see well enough
how much better people, who have it, both enjoy their life and
contribute to the enjoyment of " others."

The Anthony Sterlings are living at the Knightsbridge
house at present—he intends that Mrs. S. should henceforth
remain there, and the children and Governess at Headley where
he will spend most of his days, out of the tear and wear of his
wife's *incompatibility*—it is a great pity she will not separate
from him—it would be better for herself as well as for him—
for he cannot conceal the worse than indifference which all
that is past between them has left in his mind towards her.
One cannot blame him—he was the most devoted husband for
sixteen years—and even her madness did not estrange him
from her—until she got into that horrid state in Rome . . .
no man's love could stand *that*—his died of it, and cannot be
brought to life again, and he is not a man to make believe what
he does not feel—and she hates him (naturally) because having
loved her so long and *passionately* he now shies away from her.
You may fancy the little *domestic hell* of all this ! A little of
" the new ideas " might really be introduced into English
married life with benefit.

But what I took up my pen to tell you is that little Lewes—
author of *Rose Blanche** &c., &c. is going to lecture in Liverpool
—one of these days and I have given him my card for you—
and you *must* try and introduce him to my Uncle ; for he is
the most amusing little fellow in the whole world—if you only
look over his unparalleled *impudence* which is not impudence
at all but man-of-genius-*bonhomie*—either you or Helen saw

* " Rose, Blanche and Violet," 1848. G. H. Lewes, brilliant in
philosophy and science, biography and criticism, was less successful as a
novelist. He had married Miss Jervis in 1840, but left her for George Eliot
in 1854.

him here—and his charming little wife. He is [the] best mimi
in the world and full of famous stories, and no spleen or envy
or *bad* thing in him, so see that you receive him with open arm
in spite of his immense ugliness. What nice people thes
Manchester Schwabes of Geraldine's turned out! I quit
took to the Lady and she to me. I had a kind letter from he
this morning " swearing everlasting friendship " and pressingl
inviting us to visit them. I will certainly go the next time
am in Lancashire. When that will be God knows. They wer
staying with the Cobdens here and Mrs. Cobden took th
opportunity of calling for me. I was out and when I returne
her visit to-day *she* was out. I suppose the next thing will b
an invitation to dinner—which will be accepted as Cobden i
not *absolutely nobody* for Mr. C.

Isn't it great work that I have not had the least bit of cough
or chest devilry this whole winter ?—and very few headaches—
really I seem to be " looking up " as they say of the funds.

Robertson who has again appeared on our horizon is t
bring Louis Blanc * to tea here on Friday night. He (Robertson
was trying to make me get up an interest about it, and when a
else failed, he said—" I am sure you will like him—he wa
talking to me to-day many things that would have intereste
even *you*. It was in *his* arms, he tells me, that Godefro
Cavaignac died ! "—I started as if he had shot me—the thin
took me so by surprise—and I could not answer one word—th
man was coming on Friday night ! I felt as if he would transm
to me even thus late Godefroi Cavaignac's last breath ! An
Robertson was watching the effect of his words ! I cared n
—why should I ? I had my boa gloves reticule &c. in my la
I flung them all violently on the floor—why, I don't know—
I could not help it ! Robertson went on to say that he, Lou
Blanc, talked of Godefroi as of a Divinity, that Genera
Cavaignac was very inferior to *him* in Blanc's opinion—and the
seeing that I was not even going to make an effort to convers
on this topic he stooped and gathered up my things saying with
significant look—" *that*, I *suppose*, is not the place where thes
articles are meant to remain, Mrs. Carlyle." I took them ou

* The French Revolutionary.

of his hands and left the room—I could have killed him—I cried a little upstairs then *dressed* myself, and returning to the parlour where C. had by this time joined Robertson, I said to the latter with proud defiance enough : " *now*, Mr. Robertson, I have *thrown off* my spattered gown and *everything* that made me unfit for enjoying your agreeable company." He looked hard at me with his *diabolical* look, and said " the metamorphosis is really astonishing ! I never saw you so magnificent before ! "   " Yes," said Mr. C., " *it is a smart gown !* "

I believe Robertson said that about Godefroi, in the devilish intention of watching its effect on me—I *know* he has been heard to speculate on my intimacy with him.   Well ! let him draw his inferences—it is no disgrace to *any* woman to be accused of having loved Godefroi Cavaignac, the only reproach to be made me is that I did not love him as well as he deserved.   But now he is dead I will not *deny him* before all the Robertsons alive !

. . . Love to them all.

Ever your affectionate
JANE C.

140. *To Jeannie Welsh*

Picnic visit to Headley—Consideration for Mrs. Anthony Sterling ; mad again—Exit Helen.

The final catastrophe of Helen is also told in L.M. ii. 37 and N.L. i. 251 ; this, however, is a livelier description than either of the others.

(*27th Feb.*, 1849.)

DEAREST BABBIE,

I have so much to tell and so little time to tell it in that I don't know where to begin—besides I have forgotten in the " hubbub wild and dire dismay " of late days where I left off in *my life*—that is to say the history of my life—outwardly speaking—but certainly when I wrote last I was not gone nor meaning to go to Headley—so I shall begin with that—Mr. C. surprisingly invited himself to Headley (Capt. S.'s country place) incited thereto by the charming description given of it by John Carlyle, who had gone down with Capt. S. for a couple of days —a beautiful country mansion, with " fresh air " and horses

to ride, and no *woman* in the house, or servant of any so
indoors, but one old Scotch cook—taking care of the premise
in the absence of Mrs. Sterling and the children now settle
at Knightsbridge—all *that* had charms for Mr. C.—and ther
being nobody in town just then that he cared to stay for, h
proposed to go down with Anthony on his next weekly visit t
the place—but Anthony had no notion of having *him* withou
me, and Mr. C. himself thought I should go, to " keep Anthon
off him and let him enjoy *the perfect* silence "—(as if *that* ma
could enjoy or yet *endure* perfect silence for one week !)—
liked the idea of going ; but would not agree till I had writte
to Mrs. Sterling about it, and asked *her* to go too ! It was a
very well to tell me she was fast going mad again, and that i
was determined she should *never* go back to Headley. All tha
was no concern of mine, no reason that I should cause he
annoyance. So I wrote and she answered me in the friendlies
manner—without mentioning the thing to her Husband—
declining to go to Headley " from the shades of which sh
was too happy to have just escaped " but " seeing no earthl
reason why I should not go with Mr. C. and Capt. S."
was so glad after that I had, as Mr. C. phrased it, " completel
attended to *the three thousand punctualities* with her," for if
had not, I could not have felt sure the irritation of our settling
such a thing without her knowledge, had not hastened the fina
explosion of the fit of mania hanging over her the last six weeks
It exploded *before* our visit took place—for a *fortnight* she wa
in a strait waistcoat occasionally ; but is now more quiet tho
still confined to a room with two mad-nurses. She has showr
no dislike of *me* this time—on the contrary seems to want tc
make *me* a party against her Husband—poor thing. But al
this of *her* is nothing new now. Her Husband takes it, as
a matter of course—and tries to keep " never minding." We
went to Headley on Tuesday gone a week, meaning to return
on Friday—but the curious gipsey life we led, on a *basis* of all
the comforts and luxuries of civilization—answered so well
that on Friday I came to town with Anthony (who had to go
and speak with mad-doctors) leaving Mr. C. in perfect bliss—
if *solitude be bliss*—and having provided changes of linen &c.

returned next morning to remain till Monday.   It was the most
successful visit I have made for long.   Anthony and I laid the
table, set wax candles &c. &c., the old woman cooked out of
sight what victuals were not brought ready from London—
and Mr. C. let himself be *waited upon* by us with an amiability ! !
Then He had four riding horses which he might by turns gallop
to death—and I had a pony which took me, as fast as Anthony
could *walk* at his head, over all the beautiful hills in the neighbourhood—and we sat and smoked in *the carpenter's shop*
Capt. S. has fitted up for himself—and I learned to *turn* and
shoot with a bow—and shot—*myself !* in the cheek !—as a
green mark can testify to this hour : and indeed indeed I felt
very like little Macready in its late three days' visit to myself—
with no end of wishes and whims and in childish surprise and
felicity to find them all immediately gratified.

Monday   came   however—and   we   *must*   return—the
Ashburtons were to come to town that day, and we were to
dine at Bath House Tuesday.   We drove to our own door
where Mr. C. and the luggage were to be deposited, I going on
to Knightsbridge with Anthony to settle about a governess
for him.   But Mr. C. knocked in vain for a good while and
we were speculating about breaking in at a window and storming
at Helen for having gone out when she knew we were coming
—when the door opened to a twentieth blow and an apparition
presented itself which I shall remember as long as I live.   There
stood Helen—her mouth all over blood, her brow and cheeks
white with chalk from the kitchen floor—like an excessively
ll got up stage-ghost ! her dark gown ditto—her hair hanging
in two wild streams down her neck—her crushed cap all awry—
and on her face a hideous smile of idiotic self-complacency !
Nothing *could* be more drunk !   We ordered her downstairs
but she refused to be " *used in that way* " so Mr. C. had to drag
her down !—and leave her on the kitchen floor.   I walked off,
with the *sublime calm* which always comes to me in purely
material trouble, followed by Anthony to Mrs. White to tell
her to come to the rescue—when we came in Mr. C. was on his
knees lighting the parlour fire.   Anthony then drove off coolly
remarking that " as I seemed to have affairs of my own to

attend to he could not expect me to come and settle his."
Mr. C. retired to his study—there was no fire in the kitchen
either. Mrs. White lighted one and proceeded to get dinner
cooked while the little beast stormed at her for " daring to do
her work." I tidied things upstairs—the whole house was
beastly—she had been drunk every day of our absence and
having *drinking parties* in the house. That it escaped being
either burnt or robbed is a miracle.

About five in the afternoon—(we came at one)—she got
her legs and rushed out into space for more drink—staggered
home at ten and fell insensible on the kitchen floor—she had
had *half a pint of rum*, and a quart of ale—in addition to the
half pint of gin she had taken in the morning. Mrs. White
got her into bed with difficulty, took away by my desire all
combustibles and bolted her in (as she believed). I was to
open the outer door to Mrs. White at seven in the morning
and barred and chained it for the night as usual. When I
came down at seven the bars and chain were all undone and
there was a sound as of an animal rolling on the kitchen stairs.
The little beast had been out ! with a bonnet and shawl on the
top of her night clothes and had more drink—at night she got
her senses again—and was told by Mrs. White that she must
get ready to leave the house next day—*I* would not see her
at all. Providence under the form of Miss Bölte had sent
a most promising looking servant here the very day we came
home. Miss Bölte knew nothing of the exigency but this
servant " had come in her way and she could not resist sending
her to me, to see if the sight of her would not tempt me to put
away that dirty little Helen." Did you ever know such luck !
I liked the girl *—found her character satisfactory and engaged
her to come as soon as I could get the little beast out of the
house. She tried her old despair and tears upon me—but
in vain this time—I had found her a shocking dirty stupid
servant ever since she came and now I knew why—she had been
all the time partially drunk. When I was not to be moved by
tears she took to bed, and swore she would not go. I told her
thro' Mrs. White—that I would take her at two on Friday in

* Elizabeth Sprague.

Capt. S.'s carriage to the house of her dearest friend—who lives at Camden Town and has a room to let or I would put her on board a Kirkaldy steamer and pay her expenses—whichever she liked—if she insisted on lying in bed I would send for a Policeman and have her taken to the Station. She saw there was no irresolution more, rose and dressed herself—and agreed to go to Camden Town. I spoke hardly ten words to her all the way—explained the circumstances to the woman of the house—put two sovereigns into *her* hands, that she might pay herself the present shelter afforded her—and came away desiring never to see her (Helen) again in this world. She may go to the Devil her own way—I have bothered myself enough in trying to hold her back.

The new servant came on Saturday—and bodes well to be an immense blessing to us. And now tho' I have not told you half what I had to tell I must make an end for the present—and try to walk off the headache I got at a dinner at Thackeray's last night where *you* were not—love to them all.

Your affectionate
J. CARLYLE.

141. *To Jeannie Welsh at Auchtertool*

Neglect and patience—Dinner with Dickens—Rogers's offensiveness about Carlyle and Lady Ashburton—Mazzini and the Roman rising—Portraits of Mrs. Carlyle by Laurence and a German.

Holy Thursday (1849).

DEAREST BABBIE,

Your *unreproachingness* is touching—upon my honour—almost equal to Mrs. Allan Cunningham's who, when I called for her the other evening, after having let her alone for some eighteen months, during which interval she had left two cards at this house, exclaimed, heartily clasping me in her large arms ; " Oh Mrs. Carlyle I'm ashamed to look you in the face ! " There is more human patience and goodness in the world, than I gave it credit for. And it is rational of you as well as patient and good, to believe that my silence has not been this time more than any other time the natural expression of my feelings towards you—the more I have to say to you always, the less I like to write—the things I have to say being

for most part Lamentations of Jeremiah, for which transient
human breath is only too good. To *write* Lamentations has
always you know been contrary to my ideas—and is.

I have had no more headaches since that dreadful one I
told Helen about—now that the weather is warmer I can stand
a pitcher of cold water on the back of my neck every morning
and that always agrees with me. I have been to several parties—
a dinner at Dickens's last Saturday where I never went before.
" A great fact ! " Forster might have called it. Such getting
up of the steam is unbecoming to a literary man who *ought* to
have his basis elsewhere than on what the old Annandale woman
called " Ornament and grander."* The dinner was served up
in the new fashion—not placed on the table at all—but handed
round—only the dessert on the table and quantities of *artificial*
flowers—but such an overloaded dessert ! pyramids of figs
raisins oranges—ach ! At the Ashburton dinner served on
those principles there were just *four cowslips* in china pots—
four silver shells containing sweets, and a silver filigree temple
in the middle ! but here the very candles rose each out of an
artificial rose ! Good God ! Mrs. Gaskell the Authoress
of *Mary Barton* was there—I had already seen her at my own
house, a natural unassuming woman whom they have been doing
their best to spoil by making a lioness of her. Before dinner,
old Rogers, who ought to have been buried long ago, so old
and ill-natured he is grown, said to me pointing to a chair
beside him, " sit down my Dear—I want to ask you ; is your
husband as much infatuated as ever with Lady Ashburton ? "
—" Oh of course " I said *laughing*, " why shouldn't he ? "—
" Now—do *you* like her—tell me honestly is she kind to *you*—
as kind as she is to your husband ? " " Why you know it is
impossible for *me* to know *how* kind she is to my husband ;
but I *can* say she is extremely kind to *me* and I should be stupid
and ungrateful if I did *not* like her." " Humph ! (disap-
pointedly) Well ! it is very good of you to like her when she
takes away all your husband's company from you—he is always
there isn't he ? " " Oh good gracious no ! (still laughing

* " ' What ornament and grandeur !' Indignant old sailor to me once
about his new binnacle in his new-fangled steamship." (T. C. in L.M. ii. 377.)

admirably) he writes and reads a great deal in his own study."
" But he spends all his evenings with her I am told ? "
" No—not all—for example you see he is *here* this evening."
" Yes," he said in a tone of vexation, " I *see* he is here *this*
evening—and *hear* him too—for he has done nothing but talk
across the room since he came in."   Very devilish old man !
but he got no satisfaction to his devilishness out of *me*—

> " On Earth the living
> Have much to bear ! " *

Poor dear Mazzini—all my affection for him has waked
up since I knew him in jeopardy and so gallantly fulfilling his
destiny—and not mine only—the public sympathy is fast going
over to his side—under the atrocious injustice of the French,
who one year ago loudly invited all nations to form republics
and now proceed to shoot lead into the only one that has obeyed
the call.   It will be the ruin of Napoleon's government this
work in Italy—I have had an *Italia del populo* sent me daily
since Mazzini started it in Rome—and you may fancy how
anxiously I expect it every morning—not sure whether its
discontinuance will not indicate that the French have overcome.
—I sometimes feel myself *up to* wishing that the Romans and
Mazzini included may let themselves be all blown to atoms and
their city made into a heap of ruins—it would be perhaps, that,
the last thing that could be done to rouse Italy into a right
fervour of patriotism.

And now I must like Mazzini " put on my bonnet " to go
off to Laurence—to—sit for my picture ! ! !   Actually I am
just now sitting to *two* artists—" by particular request " !
Bölte wants to possess my image—and that is natural enough
as she likes me dearly—and has employed a German painter,
under great obligations to her, to paint it—(*gratis* of course)
—but the other picture—or rather drawing for it is to be in
chalk—is a " *grande mistero*," Laurence wrote to *beg* I would
sit to him as a personal favour—as if I were simpleton enough
to believe that after having known me for twelve years he would
be suddenly now when I am so old and ugly seized with an

* From " Tieck's *Phantasms*, the trusty Eckart of my translating."   (T. C.
n L.M. ii. 388.)

enthusiasm for my face !—No, No ! Laurence has some othe
motive—most probably a *money motive*—somebody who wishe
my picture for the sake of my—what shall I say ?—*virtues*—
has employed him to draw me—not seeing any other way o
attaining the end. I *told* him I knew there was *a do* at th
bottom of the thing but I would oblige him by sitting all th
same—and he laughed and *blushed*. I think I *know who* i
fool enough to be up to giving fifteen guineas for a sketch o
my faded *charms*. It is too ridiculous ! And if you just sav
what a fright I am just now ! Kindest love to Walter. Goc
bless you dearest Babbie. Don't drop the system of writin
off a few lines at any *willing moment*.

Your affectionate

JANE CARLYLE.

142. *To Jeannie Welsh at Auchtertool*

Unitarianism and amiability—Addiscombe : after Charles Buller'
death—Death of Mrs. Buller—G. H. Lewes and his wife—Walter'
supposed gaiety.

Chelsea first, then Addiscombe.
(*1st and 4th April*, 1849.

Upon *my* honour, dearest Babbie, I am afraid you ar
growing into a—Unitarian !—you heap coals of fire on m
head with such an air of unconscious amiability !—not tha
unconsciousness of all things is a distinctive feature of unitarianisn
but the *amiability !*—it is *more* than Christian this writing awa
—all the same as if your letters got duly answered. Well
you do quite right—it is the only way of touching me in certai
periods of devil-possessedness—in which periods by the way
the most striking symptom is a horror at letter-writing, simila
to the horror mad-dogs conceive at water. You might hav
sulked at me in silence a good while yet, or you might hav
written me several letters of——

There's a fine go ! The above was written at Chelsea thre
days ago—I was interrupted by little Louis Blanc—interruptio
followed interruption—till here I am—at Addiscombe—fo
twenty four hours with my letter still just begun !

This visit is one of the things that has been unsettling me—

it was to have come off a fortnight ago—but Lady A. fell ill—
or rather fell worse—and could not move from London till
the weather softened.   I am alone with her hitherto—Lord A.
is in town and also Mr. C.—but the latter is asked to come on
Thursday and will not fail, and we shall then stay, both, till
Monday next.

It looks very sad here without Charles Buller—everything
reminds me of him—there are two foolish strings of beads
which he once brought to Lady A. from some fair—a red string
and a blue one, hanging about the china candlesticks of a
writing stand, that I could almost cry over—*me*—! but Lady A.
has recovered entire composure on that subject—speaks of
him as unconcernedly as I do.   And his poor mother is dead !
—better so—her life was miserable and she died without pain.
I was with her the night of her death till within half an hour
of her breathing her last—but the scene was shocking for me
in more ways than one—and I could do no good by remaining
as she was quite unconscious of my presence—so I kissed her
little cold hand and came away.   That and other things put
me on a tack of headaches—which I cannot at all get out of—
perhaps the week here may break the spell.

. . . Little Lewes came the other night with his little wife
—speaking gratefully of you all—but it is Julia Paulet who has
taken his soul captive ! ! he raves about her " dark luxurious
eyes " and " smooth firm flesh "— ! his wife asked " how did
he know ? had he been feeling it ? "   In fact his wife seems
rather *contemptuous* of his raptures about all the women he has
fallen in love with on this journey, which is the best way of
taking the thing—when one can.

I used to think these Leweses a perfect pair of love-birds
always cuddling together on the same perch—to speak figuratively—but the female love-bird appears to have hopped off
to some distance and to be now taking a somewhat critical
view of her little shaggy mate !

In the most honey-marriages one has only to *wait*—it is
all a question of time—sooner or later " reason resumes its em-
pire " as the phrase is.   Cultivate this new thought of writing
off six lines at me whenever you have movement that way.

I hear her Ladyship gone down—and must follow to tea. God bless you. This is as good as no letter tho' long enough—but I have not *settled down* here yet—indeed it is a while since I was settled down anywhere.

John Fergus * told me the other day that " Mr. Welsh was surely the gayest young Reverd. going—he constantly met him driving young ladies in gigs." I answered very coldly—" any man, even revd., might drive his sisters I supposed without a scandal "—he asked what relation he was to *me*—and when I said my cousin, he pretended surprise and repeated " What ? your whole cousin ? "—but I must go.

Ever your affectionate

J. C.

143. *To Jeannie Welsh at Auchtertool*

Ancestral gift of prophecy—Impending visit from Geraldine—Her superabundance of emotion—Copies out a correspondence—Friendships nipped by children—Another Macready godchild—Darwin in ill-health—A man uninteresting even in sorrow—Thackeray's practical joke—FitzGerald—Garnier—On being eaten up by little things, like Mazzini—Born to be a martyr.

Thursday evening (17th May, 1849)

DARLING,

Do you know, between ourselves, I am not at all sure that I have not got a little of—the spirit of prophecy ! And why not ? My Great Great Ancestor John Welsh the Covenanter had the gift of prophecy beyond all doubt—he displayed it on many remarkable occasions—once, I remember he foretold to a certain city in France which had used him scurvily that the plague would devour it in a few days—as it actually did—now why not fancy a little of a turn for prophecy to be still in the blood as well as a tendency to consumption &c. &c. ? Even Carlyle tells me sometimes that I have " the intelligence of *Schupingsing* " (you remember that Chinese young lady ?)—" who resembled a disembodied spirit " in the accuracy of her insight ; being able to tell always what her enemies were plotting on the other side of stone walls. The occasion on which my spirit of prophecy—or Shupingsing

* Of Kirkcaldy, Elizabeth Pepoli's brother.

intelligence—call it what you like—has just evinced itself, relates to you and your dose of physic—both Tuesday and Wednesday when I returned disappointed from the letter box I said to myself—" there is something strange in this—if it be not that she has worn herself out in Manchester, and has had to take physic since her return ! " When to-day I came to the *physic* in your letter I felt a sort of fear—of *myself*—really shuddered at the superhuman in me !

Along with your letter to-day came one from Geraldine which I allowed to repose on the mantel-piece till I had read yours all thro' ; and behold when I opened it the first words were that she would be here on Monday ! Good heavens and *this Thursday*—I feel as if I should have little enough time to get up the steam—I do not mean the *house-steam* for *that* you know will not be put out of its natural course, but my own internal steam. Carlyle now says " My dear I wish that girl may not fatigue you dreadfully ?—! it is needless to be getting up such apprehensions after the matter has reached its actual stage." " Oh I hope not " says I " Jeannie like the judicious little soul she always is, has told her that it will be best she should let me alone, and not fuss me when I am ailing." He reflected a moment and then asked—" would it not be better if *I* wrote to her myself and impressed the same thing on her before she arrived at all ? " Poor Geraldine ! I declined this considerate offer—for really I thought if *he* should write to that same effect, she might be driven to carry the letting alone system to an extreme—and I should be as much worried with her unnatural stillness as with her natural superabundance of emotion. Indeed I am so prepared for *the worst* that I do not think she will drive me out of my composure. At all events it is very absurd to ask her to come and then to take fright at the thought of it—the beautiful confidence of sixteen with [which] she is *rushing to my arms* on the first word—deserves a kinder return.

Now Babbie never pique yourself any more on the *crimping of that collar*—I grant you it was a *devoted* proof of affection but I flatter myself I have done as much, and more, for you in the copying of my whole correspondence with Robertson for

z

your delectation !—I who have an absolute horror of copying—
especially my own letters !—there it is nevertheless ! manuscript
enough to curl your hair with for a month—besides the " intellectual feast " it will be to you !—a feast, by the way, not
unlike that which was once set before me at a fine country-
town evening party where I happened to find myself in appetite
(I was young then, and not above feeling *hungry* at times)
well, supper came in due course, and each person received a
wine-glass heaped with white froth (of milk) with a teaspoonful
of red currant jelly at the bottom ! devil a thing else !

I can sympathize with you in your Manchester " miseries
of human life "—oh yes, I know the irritation of feeling oneself
entirely superseded in the heart and life of an old companion
by a little troublesome monkey of a child. I remember my
first visit to Agnes Vetch after she became a *haus-frau*—my
friend par excellence—as I considered her—before I knew what
the word *friend* meant—for one's first *friendships* are apt to be
as great *spooney*-isms as one's first *Loves ! That* does not
however hinder one from thinking them life-and-death matters
at the time, and so I had my heart quite crushed within me by
being made to feel at every turn, that the vilest squall of her
little slobbery red-coloured child was more precious music
to her ears than the most eloquent language of my long-tried
affection—but I learned as you will do—just to take back my
friendship from those who knew not the worth of it and to
bestow it on such as did. " *That minds me* " as Helen says—
I am going to be found in a child !—without personal inconvenience however and—without possibility of detriment to
my other affections. I am requested to be Godmother to the
new Macready ! *Jane* Welsh Macready ! ! * What a strange
combination—Tristram Shandy's Father might shake his
head portentously over the poor infant that is to be launched
in the world with such a name !

You have asked more than once about Darwin and K.
and never been answered. Darwin is better—not yet well—
he has only been once here these last three weeks—a bad account
of him—but I have been oftener than once to him. As for K.

* She was already godmother to Jane Lydia (p. 316).

our tender sympathies need not trouble your sleep on *his* account. A man *must* be *sorry* more or less for the death of his own child—but K. is as uninteresting in sorrow as out of it. He has been here several times and except that he has on black clothes, and minces his words a little more affectedly than usual can trace no difference in him. If you look narrowly at his countenance indeed—you find on it always a smile which seems to *challenge your warmest admiration* and *gets* your *heartiest disgust*—a smile which says as plainly as words—" look with what *manly cheerfulness* and *sublime resignation* I bear my trial—look and take example by me ! " Bah !—Cavaignac stamping on the floor, and repeating his awful " *ce n'est pas juste—mon Dieu !* " was not *a perfect sufferer* but was one that could sympathize with better than with this " *diffusion-of-useful-resignation* " Mr. K. ! !

Thackeray is returned from Paris ; he was here with Fitz-Gerald the other evening—I was upstairs when they came in—and on coming into the room went to Thackeray first, to shake hands *in enthusiasm*—as one does after a journey to Paris—but gave a loud scream on finding a small, cold, hard hand—as of a dead fairy—laid in mine—it was *your* hand which he had fastened at the end of his sleeve ! I declared the joke to be a *heartless* one which seemed to vex him greatly—he repeated a dozen times during the evening that he wished he had not done it !

FitzGerald had lost a good deal of his high colour and was very good and rational—I got to like him. Garnier was here last week—*saner* than I ever saw him in my life—he asked many questions about you and about *the German*. By the way my dear you will never do anything *effectual* in German or in things in general until you muster courage and determination enough to lock yourself up—in *a cupboard*,—if so be that you cannot be allowed a *room*, all to yourself. I see for ever before my eyes —in Mazzini—how little all the talents and *good intentions* in the world can avail—so long as one submits to be *eaten up* as it were, by *little things*—one, two, twenty of them could not tell on one's general results—but let them become infinite— by daily recurrence and like the pack-threads of the Lilliputians they make a mesh that the strong man cannot tear himself loose

from. Poor Mazzini ! I declare I could weep over him som
times—there in his enchanted Tancioni * Castle holding
free communication with the world he lives in—*just* as y
figured him in your dream !—and then I get angry—and scold
but it is of no use—he is born to make a martyr of himse
and *the great* not having accepted his sacrifice he offers hims
bound hand and foot, to *the little*—which always *accep*
Love and kisses to them all—I am out of humour w
Spiridione † entirely.

Your own

J. CARLYLE.

144. *To Jeannie Welsh*

On the way to Scotland—Visits to Lady Ashburton—The Neuber

" A good joy." So one of Leigh Hunt's children at si
of flowers (T. C. in L.M. i. 104).

Mr. Neuberg was a friend and literary helper of Carly
This agreeable description is a set-off to a depreciatory sa
of Mrs. Carlyle's elsewhere.

W. E. Forster, Esq.
Rawdon,
Leeds.

(*17th July*, 18.

DEAREST BABBIE,

It is " all right "—I am thus far on my road to yo
—have been waiting till I had settled *the day* in my own mi
before writing to you—that's all ! . . . Have I written at
since Mr. C. went ? I have been ever since in such a hu
that I positively can't recollect. I went to Addiscombe w
Lady A. three hours after Mr. C. started for Ireland and stay
three days—very *pleasantly*. On my return I had all sorts
things to do and was so beset with visitors as I never rememl
to have been before in all my life—*every* evening there was
improvised tea-party. At last I cut out of it all and reac
Nottingham at nine on Monday night, a week gone. And th
I remained till Friday—at least till Friday I was under the g
providence of these Neubergs—getting myself carried to t

---

* He lodged with some compatriots of this name.
† Gambardella.

lace and the other and kept in a perpetual series of " good
oys."   Germany must be a Heaven of a country to live in,
f this be the ordinary style of German hospitality ; but
Mr. Neuberg is a very exceptional man I fancy in *any* country
nd his sister is a little darling.

. . . Meanwhile kisses to you all—I will write again to
ix the day and hour.

Your own
J. C.

I dare hardly think that I am on the road to Scotland.

145. *To Helen Welsh*

"Shirley" and other novels—The Sketchleys—The Manning
murderers.

Mr. and Mrs. Manning were hanged in October, 1849,
or the murder of Mr. O'Connor.

The reference to them is an instance of the often morbid
interests which Sir James Crichton-Browne notes in this period
f Mrs. Carlyle's life. The part omitted tells of ill-health and
estlessness.

5, Cheyne Row.
Sunday (November ? 1849).

MY DEAREST HELEN,

. . . I have read several novels lately, Cooper's *Capt.
Spike*—clever but four-fifths of it unintelligible except for seamen
—*Shirley* *—The *Ogilvies* *—curious as being written by a
young Irish girl—twenty years old—with little knowledge of
anything, Society included—but it is full of Love " as an egg's
full of meat "—the old highflown romantic circulating Library
sort of love—which one looks at in these days of " the
new ideas " as one would look at a pair of peaked shoes or a
uff out of the reign of Elizabeth—and the plot goes ahead
amously. The young woman supports both herself and a
Brother by her literature.

I have seen no more of the Sketchleys—if Miss Pen don't
write a novel I am no prophet—she wants to distinguish
herself and that is the career open to female talent just now.

* Both published in 1849, " Shirley " on October 26. Miss Mulock,
ater of " John Halifax " fame, was then 23 years old.

And now I will thank you to write or make somebod
write about yourself—you have not ceased yet to be " a
object of interest " so you must pay the penalty.

Have you taken much interest in these " interesting bu
ferocious " beings the Mannings—the General Public has talke
of little else here—and even now that they are got well hange
out of the road " additional particulars " are turning up daily
I will send you their pictures.   *Maria* has a strange likeness t
(never tell it)—Lady Ashburton !   God bless you Dear, lov
to Walter and Jeanie.

> Ever your affectionate
>   JANE W. CARLYLE.

146. *To Jeannie Welsh*

Mrs. Carlyle as prototype if not author of " Shirley "—The Sketchley
   in London—Gambardella and the child—Carlyle rides
   velocipede—The Captain and the Actor—Plattnauer again.

The old velocipede for two riders, one at either end, ha
four wheels, and long treadles within like those on a sewin
machine or a portable grindstone.

Thursday night (November, 1849

DEAREST BABBIE,

A question if I should write *even now* had I such
mirror as that which Beauty had from the Beast, and might
by merely looking in it, inform myself of all your welfares an
Helen's in particular—who is at present the interesting membe
of the family.   In fact I do everything and anything just no
rather than write letters.   For the last two days I have bee
wholly occupied in reading—a novel !   *Shirley*—not that th
interest was so very " absorbing " but I had it from the Londo
Library in an *unlawful* manner on condition of returning it a
fast as possible—the fact that I made this effort to get a *nove*
was wonderful enough—but you see I get the credit with certai
critics in style of writing these Jane Eyre books myself—and
was curious to see whether the new one was up to my reputa
tion !—besides Anthony S. had told me *Shirley* (the *woman*
was so ridiculously like myself that the author must have draw

it from me feature by feature. I was curious to know what he
thought " ridiculously like me "—and have reason to be
satisfied ! especially with the *age* of my likeness. For the rest
I am not *satisfied* at all with anything in heaven or earth—unless
perhaps with the new black cat I have got which seems full of
good dispositions. Did I tell you I had a call from the
Sketchleys ? I laid by their card to send you—I fancy *it* so
" ridiculously like " the old Lady. Both Mother and Daughter
looked extremely well and in good spirits, the old Lady had
quite a " spicy " bonnet with a feather in it—*green* I think.
They have got a very pretty little house in a new square opposite
Elizabeth Pepoli's old house in Gloucester Road. When I
returned their visit *Miss* was out—*Mrs.* sewing window curtains
with a *great many* caps of different colours on her head. I sat
a good while and found her " a capital talker "—that is to say—
listener—she has the art of seeming *so* charmed with one's conversation. Gambardella and they might *blow kisses* to one another
from *their* several windows but catch him letting himself be
seen by *them*. Did I tell you moreover—I have forgotten all
about my last—that Mr. C. actually went with Gambardella
one day on the same *velocipede* to Wimbledon !—three hours
that strange pair were toiling along the Highways on a great
sprawling velocipede ! ! and one day Gambardella brought to
the door the loveliest phaeton and white pony and laced-hatted
tiger all as small as might have suited Queen Titania and in it
the loveliest—*child !* about 3—dressed like a miniature
Garibaldi—another *Spiridione* *—I suppose, not, it is to be
hoped to " *go to the undertaker* "—this one ?

Another thing I laid by in my head to tell you—I met one
day since my return the Capt. who lived with the Liverpool
Actor—no longer in the queer green and red carriage—no longer
side by side with the little Actor but walking sorrowfully along
in the deepest mourning—as for a wife—and a Lady in deep
mourning, whom I saw by her nose *must* be the Actor's sister
leaning sorrowfully on his arm. Whence I inferred that the
poor old foolish rich Actor must have passed away—and the
poor *companion* was left on his own sad basis.

* Gambardella's Christian name.

But the strangest thing of all—a rap came to the door one evening a week ago which I did *not* know—" that " I said to Mr. C. " is nobody that comes here at present but it *has been* here often." " What an odd faculty that is of remembering people's raps " said Mr. C.—and the door opening there walked in—Plattnauer. Mazzini would have surprised me much less ! I received him with a scream—of real terror. He had tired of his situation—been *unsettled* by seeing Mr. C. at Ballyan I think—had got some notions about *his time being come*—and suddenly left in spite of the *tears* of Lord George. He was to send a substitute—but has not succeeded in finding such—had had letters from Lord George and the little children that touched his heart. I have persuaded and remonstrated and finally he has written to Lord G. that he will return. Thank God—for tho' he appears quite sane—a little while's starving in London would soon have sent him to the Madhouse again. News of Helen please ?—Love to her and all of them.

Ever your affectionate

JANE CARLYLE.

147. *To Jeannie Welsh*

Geraldine's new MS.—Zoe began in a joint authorship—Delight in Nero—Latter-Day pamphlets—Sweet-briar cuttings.

Monday (4th March, 1850).

DEAREST BABBIE,

 . . . This last Chapter is a great improvement on the three or four previous ones. I cannot understand what Geraldine means by showing up Seaforth in this way. Mrs. P. and she are not such friends as they have been I think—still anything like a coldness between them would have as little *tempted* her as *justified* her for publishing anything that would annoy the Paulets—*ergo* she must either be perfectly unconscious that she is drawing these flagrant likenesses or perfectly satisfied that Mrs. P. will take no more of it to herself than will be *pleasing* to her. To do Geraldine justice she is extremely *noble* in her *quarrels*—and would be more *tied up* with a friend she had quarrelled with than one she was on the best terms with. What makes me think she can have no intention to

how up Mrs. P. nor fear of *her* fancying *that*, is that long ago
—Geraldine and Mrs. P. and I were to write *a book* among
us in the form of letters. I told them to start it and I would
take it up when I saw their scheme—they *did* send me a screed
of MS. which I augured no good of, it was so *stormy*—and so I
backed out of my engagement, and then Mrs. P. gave up out
of indolence—and Geraldine went on—and that beginning
after all sorts of manipulating and *repairing* in the Highland-
man's gun fashion, turned into *Zoe*—but I remember much
of *this* tale that seems bare-faced painting of Seaforth was in
these pages *they* wrote between them ! !

. . . My little dog continues to be the chief comfort of my
life—night and day he never leaves me, and it is something,
I can tell you, to have such a bit of live cheerfulness always
beside one.

Elizabeth [the servant] has been to Exeter for a fortnight
visiting her Parents and her sister Maria has been here in her
stead. For the rest, Mr. C. is very busy with his pamphlets all
the forenoons and in the evenings is generally at Bath House
or elsewhere. I have got to-day some slips of the sweet briar
and some others from Templand which I wrote to Mrs.
Russell for—the slips I got from the garden at Haddington
having taken root. Love to all.

148.   *To Jeannie Welsh*

Bad cold after Addiscombe—Nero tries to fly.

> 5, Cheyne Row.
> *Monday* (*25th March*, 1850).

DEAREST BABBIE,

I came back from Addiscombe on Thursday afternoon and ever since have been spending half my time in bed.
Of course I caught a bad cold, that house being *incapable* of
getting itself heated in cold weather—fortunately the mischief
lying in me did not *explode* until the day after my return—
there I kept up appearances well enough, and *here* I can get
my bed kept without annoyance to anybody, except perhaps

poor little Nero, who feels it his duty to remain there while
do, and has nobody to take him out for a run—besides missing
various lumps of sugar and occasional windfalls of that sor
which make life more of a pleasure to him when I am o
foot.

He has had another wonderful escape that dog! I begin
to think he " bears a charmed life." This time the danger
was entirely of his own seeking. Imagine his taking it into
his head that he could *fly*—like the birds—if he tried! and
actually trying it—out at the Library window! For a firs
attempt his success was not so bad ; for he fairly cleared th
area spikes—and tho' he *did* plash down on the pavement a
the feet of an astonished Boy he broke no bones, was onl
quite *stunned*. He gave us a horrid fright however. It wa
after breakfast, and he had been standing at the open window
watching the birds—one of his chief delights—while Elizabeth
was " dusting out " for Mr. C. Lying in my bed, I heard thro
the deal partition Elizabeth scream ; " oh God! oh Nero ! "
and rush downstairs like a strong wind out at the street door
I sat up in my bed aghast—waiting with a feeling as of th
Heavens falling till I heard her reascending the stairs and
then I sprang to meet her in my night shift. She was whit
as a sheet, ready to faint—could just say ; " oh *take* him !
the dog's *body* lay on her arm ! " *Is* he killed ? " I aske
with *terrible self possession*. " Not *quite*,—I think, all *but !* "

Mr. C. came down from his bedroom with his chin al
over soap and asked, " has anything happened to Nero ?
" Oh Sir he *must* have broken *all* his legs, he leapt out at *you*
window ! " " God bless me ! " said Mr. C. and returned t
finish his shaving. I sat down on the floor and laid m
insensible dog over my knees, but could see no *breakage*—onl
a stun. So I took him to bed with me—*under* the clothes—
and in an hour's time he was as brisk and active as ever.
wonder if he intends to persevere in learning to fly—for
don't think either my own or my maid's nerves can stand it !

MRS. CARLYLE.
From a photograph by W. Jeffrey.

THOMAS CARLYLE AND THE DOG "NERO"
IN THE GARDEN OF NO. 5, CHEYNE ROW.

149.   *To Jeannie Welsh at Auchtertool*

C. absorbed in Latter Day pamphlets—A " comfortable " visit
to Addiscombe—The story of a pimple on the nose—On resisting
hypochondriac tendencies—Consideration for friends in reduced
condition—Autographs—Sermons.

Saturday (? April, 1850).

DEAREST BABBIE,

This is the only sheet of paper I have in the world,
and I dare not interrupt Mr. C. at his *pamphlet*, to borrow
some, so I must write close and to the purpose. When I
wrote last I was in the thick of a cold caught at Addiscombe—
that wound itself up with a little fit of *cholera*, and then I went
back to Addiscombe to get up my strength ! ! Mr. C. going
this time for three days out of the six I stayed. Nobody else
was there but Miss Farrar whom I like well enough in other
people's houses—in my own she is too riotous. Lady A.
was *well* this time and in " *tearing* spirits " very kind and somehow I felt more *comfortable* than usual in most respects, but
there was one grand drawback quite fatal to my enjoyment—
in consequence of my cholera I suppose, there commenced the
very day I left home an outrageous pimple on the very top
of my nose, making me really " too ugly for anything " and so
painful that I *could* not get it forgotten if I had had philosophy
enough to forget it for a moment. Could there be a more
unsuitable position for transacting such a thing ? it only
reached its " culminating point " the day I came away—and has
since been gradually subsiding, but there is still a *redness*
very distressing to my own sense of the beautiful as well as to
other people's. The only person who put me at ease about it
was Anthony S. who when I told him how it had annoyed me
at Addiscombe exclaimed cordially—" Damn your nose ! for
a sensible woman you have really the *oddest* ideas ! as if
anybody *really attached* to you could love you an atom
less if you were all covered over with small-pox ! ! ! " I
should not like however to *try* human love with permanent
small-pox.

I wrote a scolding letter to Helen the other day—I had not

got a word from Maryland Street and can see that she is letting herself get *imprisoned* in the details of her own sick body. She had not written to Miss Sketchley either—very wrong to neglect the letters of a person fallen into poverty, and consequently more sensitive to attentions! * If anybody has a right to remonstrate with another for *giving up* to the egoistic temptations of long-continued ailment it is surely I who have felt them so strongly and have for so many many years *kept them under* by efforts like to tear the life out of me. If Helen could just *feel* for an hour the bodily sensation and consequent mental depression with which I go to most parties and do most of the things my hand finds to do, she would know that she is not entitled to occupy herself exclusively with the cares for herself. She *had* written however a nice long letter which crossed mine—and the next day came a good-natured note, really she had taken my hard sayings extremely well! My paper is getting filled. I send you *a royal invitation*—as a curiosity in " *the Provinces* " and to make you *great* in the eyes of Mr. Liddle! I should not wonder if he would like to *buy* it of you!—I will also send one of these days a vol. of sermons to Walter *as a model!* they are considered wonderfully fine, and were recommended to *me* by Thomas Erskine—but I cannot get up a sentiment for sermons.

. . . God bless you dear—Love to Walter—

Yours affectionate

JANE C.

150. *To Helen Welsh*

The ball at Bath House—An unaccustomed low dress—The Duke of Wellington—Week-end with young folk at Addiscombe—Death of Peel: effect on Carlyle—Geraldine and Fanny Lewald—Meets Charlotte Brontë.

Thursday (4th *July*, 1850).

DEAREST HELEN,

. . . The Bath House Ball threw me into a perfect fever for one week—as I had got no dress for it; not understanding

* Passages omitted from the preceding letters talk of the Sketchleys' impracticable gentility, and how Pen's friends employ her to make not very satisfactory copies of their existing portraits.

that I was to go—but Mr. C. was " quite determined for once in his life " to see an aristocratic Ball and " if I chose to be so peevish and ungracious as to stay away there was no help for me." I pleaded the want of a dress—he " would pay for any dress I chose to get ; " and then I fell back on the horror of *stripping* myself, of " being bare "—at my age after being muffled up so many years ! and that if I didn't I should be like no one else—to which he told me angrily—" true propriety consisted in conforming to other people's fashions ! ! ! and that Eve he supposed had as much sense of decency as I had and *she* wore no clothes at all ! ! ! " So I got a white silk dress—which first was made high and long-sleeved—and then on the very day of the ball was sent back to be cut down to the due pitch of indecency !—I could have gone into *fits* of crying when I began to put it on—but I looked so astonishingly well in it *by candle light*, and when I got into the fine rooms amongst the universally *bare* people I felt so much in *keeping*, that I forgot my neck and arms almost immediately. I was glad *after* that I went—not for any pleasure I had at the time, being past dancing, and knowing but few people—but it is an additional idea for life, to have seen such a party—all the Duchesses one ever heard tell of blazing in diamonds, all the young beauties of the season, all the distinguished statesmen &c., &c. were to be seen among the six or seven hundred people present—and the rooms all hung with artificial roses looked like an Arabian Nights entertainment—what pleased me best was the good look I got *into the eyes* of the old Duke of Wellington—one has no notion, seeing him on the streets, what a dear kind face he has. Lady Ashburton receiving all these people with her grand-Lady airs was also a sight worth seeing. On Saturday I went to Addiscombe with a party of *boys* and *girls* and returned on Monday night. Mr. C. and Thackeray came to dinner on Sunday but had to return at night every room being taken up. I can't imagine why Lady A. always asks *me* to help her with these flirting young Ladies and gentlemen. I feel more disposed to wring their necks than take part in their riotous nonsense.

Now ; all is changed in *that* quarter by the death of Peel.

Lady A. was deeply attached to him—she is off into the
country again to escape parties ; came here on her way, all
in tears, and asked Mr. C. to come by himself *this* week—as
one asks the Clergyman when one is in affliction !—indeed
this death has produced a greater dismay than any public
event of my time—not only among his own set but crowds of
working people pressed round his house all the time of his
illness demanding news which a constable lifted above their
heads tried to make heard in vain—and written bulletins were
finally hoisted up to be read by the crowd from hour to hour.
Mr. C. is mourning over him as I never saw him mourn
before—went to-day to look at the house where he lies dead !—

But no impression lasts long in London society—in a few
weeks they will all be visiting and " making wits " again as
if nothing had happened.

I have seen little of Geraldine, she comes pretty often but
has always engagements to hurry her away.   She has sworn
friendship with Fanny Lewald the German authoress who is
also lionizing in London at present—and gives me much of
her semi-articulate company.   I also met Jane Eyre (Miss
Brontë) one night at Thackeray's, a less figure than Geraldine
and extremely unimpressive to *look at*.

Write to me how you feel after your journey.   John wrote
that you seemed to him much better than last year.   Kindest
love to them all and kisses to my Uncle.

Ever your affectionate

J. C.

151.   *To Helen Welsh at Buxton*

Mazzini returns with a beard.

Sunday (25th Aug., 1850).

DEAREST HELEN,

. . . I was immensely glad the other day to receive—
Mazzini !   I did not think I *could* have felt so very glad.
He looks much better than I expected and is in excellent spirits
—he has a greyish *beard*—which is altogether a new feature—

before he wore only black mustachios—but this beard he begged me to believe was no *efflorescence of Republicanism* but *necessitated* in the first instance and then persevered in because found so convenient—' for you must recollect, my Dear, that in the old times I needed always to have a barber to shave me—and in the camp with Garibaldi, and flying for my life, I could not of course take everywhere with me a barber ! and so my beard had to grow and now and then be cut with a scissor.' " For the rest he looks much as he did —and is the same affectionate simple-hearted, high-souled creature—but immensely more agreeable—talks now as one who had the habit of being listened to—and has so much of interesting matter to tell. Imagine his going to live in a *mad-house* at Marseilles ! while waiting for a false passport—he " thought they would not seek him amongst *mads*, decidedly " —and another time at Geneva he lodged in the *same* house with the Magistrate who was empowered to discover him— sure that the magistrate would look for him in every house before his *own*—and they lived under the same roof for fifty days.

. . . I hope my dear Uncle is getting good of Buxton— pray tell me soon about you both. Give him the best kiss you can for me. Remember me kindly to Sophy.

Ever your affectionate,

JANE CARLYLE.

152. *To Helen Welsh* (?)

Not yet well—Stayed on at the Grange—Lady Ashburton has nothing to say.

5, Cheyne Row.
Sunday (Oct.–Nov., 1850).

Alas, my dear Cousin, my hostile star is still in the ascendant ! and hardly anything short of a strong impulse of *natural* affection could prevail on me to write a *letter* just now. But it looks so very long since I wrote, and *you* are so good in answering : that I *must* find half an hour's time and

a little composure of soul just to tell you briefly how it ha
been and is going with me here.

Your last long good letter found me still at the Grange—
where I remained three days beyond the appointed tim
Lady A. caught a cold at the end of the business and wa
in bed the day we were all to come away. Lord A. was n
yet returned from Spain where his wife had sent him for th
purpose of being made seasick in the Bay of Biscay—se
sickness being " extremely good for all that family." Amon
the *thirty* servants at the Grange there was not one in who
kind nursing her Ladyship seemed to trust—moreover sh
seemed a little afraid of being murdered by housebreakers !
So I offered to stay behind the rest till she was about agai
if it pleased her—and it did please her—tho' *why* were difficu
to tell, for—she would not have me sit with her above an hou
in the day while in bed, and when out of it, the third da
she had absolutely nothing to say to me ! I don't know wheth
she is always so when alone with women—but the longer w
know one another and the more we are intimate to outwar
appearance the less have we to say to one another *alone*. . . .

153. *To Jeannie Welsh*

Upset by a dose of morphia—Mazzini arrives—Engages a new servan
—Tenderness for her servant's infirmities.

5, Cheyne Row,
Wednesday (5*th March*, 185.

DEAREST BABBIE,

I am in poor case for writing, having been laid u
in bed for pretty well three days—I suppose it is an *unpro
nounced* cold—if not the effects of—*poison !* Not that
suppose my Life in any one's way—or have been attemptin
it myself—at least voluntarily. I merely wished to get myse
some sleep after having gone without it for three nights, an
took about four of the third morning a dose of Morphine whic
might or might *not* have been the right quantity—for the littl
black pills had melted and run all together and I had to divid

them with a penknife. All next day I felt quite *dead*—as if I were only kept going by galvanism. Mazzini dropt on me from the skies, and even the surprise did not *awake* me—and at night I took to fainting and having horrid spasms. It might be that the morphine, so useful sometimes, had merely on this occasion had a quarrel in me with the ailment, whatever it was, that had been taking away my sleep—certainly the effects of that must be quite over now—and I still feel sick and sore and miserably *all-overish*.

Yesterday I got up about four in the afternoon, and came down to—engage a new servant ! a thing very repugnant to me even in the perpendicular position—and horrible to think of on the flat of my back. I told you I think that the *last new one* had gone deaf on New Year's Day. She has never recovered yet and has been a very heavy handful latterly ; as I have had to do all the door-answering in the first instance, (having to go to seek *her* to *open* it). How It gets opened when I am out of the house I have no conception ! Then instead of exerting her other faculties to make up for the defect of hearing, she grows more and more nervous and helpless—not to be wondered at poor thing ! having a most delicate fine-lady organisation to begin with. Still I thought if *I* who was used to her and so hated new faces and new ways could not make shift to *go on* with her *who* would be likely to *begin* with her ? And nobody knows how long it would have been before I should have mustered inhumanity enough to give her warning on account of her deafness—to say nothing of courage enough to front another change. But a week ago she *took the initiative* and told me with the most placid indifference that she " meant to leave in a month " as she should certainly " die of grief " if she went on " *listening to bells and never hearing them !* " " But what will you do ? " I asked. " Oh ! (she had it all cut and dry) I will go into *a kitchen* where I shall have fellow servants to speak loud to me and, have nothing to do with the bells, or *the up-stairs*." I could not but approve her purpose—provided she get it " carried out ". So yesterday I was engaging another—equally refined—*less sensitive* looking but *more sentimental*—with I should say a great tendency to

2 A

" *George Sandism* and all that sort of thing." I remarked
that she did not look very strong—the answer was " perhaps
I look more delicate for being in mourning—mourning (for
her mother) is *such a denial* to a young person, everyone, I
think, looks best in colours." But she has a three years'
character and can cook—especially *fish* her mistress said—
" all sorts of fish in all sorts of ways "—pity we never *eat* fish
hardly—I suppose I shall get hardened to changes like other
people—certainly I am taking this one *easily*. To be sure there
has been no *row*—the general accompaniment of change—
and which puts one all bilious at the outset. I really *am* very
sick Babbie dear ! and must not begin another sheetkin.

Kindest love to Uncle and all the rest,

Your ever affectionate,

JANE CARLYLE.

154. *To Jeannie Welsh*

Volition weakened by ill-health—Recent letters could not be private
—Regrets Babbie's impending marriage—Further change of
servants—The Great Exhibition disappointing.

Sunday (11th *May*, 1851).

DEAREST BABBIE,

When I got your last note, I meant to answer it by
the next post ; but what I *mean* to do is precisely the last thing
I get done, anything, everything rather than *that !* Of course
the fault is in myself and not in my *contrairy* circumstances
—if I could rid myself of the weak notion that I am too bothered,
or too wearied out, for doing this or that, for *writing to you*,
for instance ; there is no such pressure of bother on me that
I might not write you at least a dozen lines every day of my life,
but *believe* that you haven't time nor strength and you haven't
them, tho', for the rest, you may be all the while yawning over
the fire, and up to walking ten miles were the temptation great
enough.

Don't suppose, like a dear Babbie as you are and will always
be for me, that there is anything more in these long silences
than a defective condition of my *volition*, the result in great
measure of general ill-health I am sure, for long ago, whatever

thing I had it in my mind to do, I *did* and the more hindrances, the more haste—and latterly there has been too a complication in our correspondence rendering my letters to *you* individually a *pro bono publico* affair, a sort of letters which I have no skill in writing, and *less than no* liking to write. If I was to be always keeping Helen in view in my letters—better, certainly *easier* it was, to write direct to herself, and so at the same time show her the little attention which is the privilege of invalids. Do *you* write to *me* as formerly ?—there is no invalid *here* keeping a sharp look out on all the letters that come to the house, and feeling aggrieved if they be not imparted to her ; and yet— what do you tell me but small nonsenses that you evidently fall half asleep over while you are writing them—for example you *had* to tell me in your last letter that Andrew had been a fortnight with you in Liverpool—and a good deal besides I should think—and what *did* you tell me ? Oh Babbie ! how I wish it had not been your *idea* to pitch your tent in this " valley of the shadow of *marriage* "—it is a very *relaxing air* I am sure and peculiarly unsuitable to *your* constitution. But certainly I am not the best authorized person to tell people how they should manage their lives under that head of Method—having made such a mess of my own life—God help me !

If you have heard from Liverpool in these days they would perhaps tell you that I am scheming to have Helen up for a week or two to see this eternal " Exhibition." If Mr. C. had only carried out his project of going off to Copenhagen the beginning of May, great things might have come off—in which *you* might have taken some part—but instead of what I had set my heart on I find myself more tied up even than usual—Mr. C. *here, correcting proofs* with no more tendency towards Denmark for the present—and oh horror ! the old story of a change of servants to be gone over again the week after next ! . . . I was not purposing to go near the Exhibition myself till I took *her* or someone to see it—I had not so much as gone to view the outside since it was roofed in. But the other day Forster offered us his Examiner-ticket * which admitted both Mr. C. and *a lady*—so we went and oh how—tired I was !

* *I.e.* a press ticket for his paper " The Examiner."

Not that it is not really a very beautiful sight—especially at the entrance ; the three large trees, *built in, because the people objected to their being cut down*, a crystal fountain, and a large blue canopy give one a momentary impression of a Bazaar in the *Arabian Nights Entertainments*—and such a lot of things of different kinds and of well dressed people—for the tickets were still 5/- —was rather imposing for a few minutes—but when you come to look at the wares in detail—there was nothing really worth looking at—at least that one could not have seen *samples* of in the shops. The big diamond indeed—worth a *million ! that* one could not have seen at any jeweller's—but oh Babbie what a disappointment ! for the big diamond—unset —looked precisely like a bit of crystal the size and shape of the first joint of your thumb ! And the fatigue of even the most cursory survey was indescribable and to tell you the God's truth I would not have given the pleasure of reading a good Fairy Tale for all the pleasure to be got from that " Fairy Scene " ! I have surely a great many things to tell you *not* about the *Exhibition*—but I have only a horrid steel pen and my paper appears to be scarce.

Write soon again, you demoralised little dear Babbie—and believe me your ever loving,

J. C.

155. *To Helen Welsh*

Thackeray's Lectures—Nero lost again—Her "superfluous sensibility."

Thackeray lectured on English Humorists, May 22–July 3, 1851.

5, Cheyne Row,
Thursday (? 5th June, 1851).

DEAREST HELEN,

Just one line to say that I find I miscounted by a day. I said the 12th. and it is on Wednesday which is the 11th. that I want you—Thursday is Thackeray's Lecture day, and I have a ticket waiting for you. The Lectures between you and me are no great things—as *Lectures*—but it is the fashion to find them " so amusing " ! and the *audience* is the most brilliant I ever saw in one room—unless in Bath House drawing-rooms. So I will expect you on Wednesday—about four—that is much the pleasantest hour for arriving—especially as going to meet you at the station would be perfectly useless—as I should certainly miss you in the crowd.

I am very dull this morning having again lost my dog. I went out to walk with Mr. C. last night (for a wonder) towards dark ; and at the top of Cook's Grounds, close by my own door, on returning, the poor little creature was snapt up by two men and run off with into space ! It is a very *cruel* sort of thieving that ! His name and address is on his collar, so they can bring him back if they like—but won't I fear unless I again advertise and offer a specific reward which I will *try hard* to keep myself from doing, miserable as I feel under his loss ; for there is no doubt of its being the regular gang that have got him this time, and if they find I am ready to buy him back at any price (as I am) they will be always stealing him—till I have not a penny left ! or else I should have to take him out only with a chain—and that is so sad a life for the poor dog. What his life is to-day I am afraid to conjecture.

I wish I had never *set up* a dog. I did not think there was so much superfluous sensibility left in me—that I should lose my sleep for the dog's absence out of my bed.

God bless you.

J. C.

156. *To Jeannie Welsh*

Carlyle returns from visiting the Ashburtons at Paris—Apparent slights from Lady Ashburton.

Wednesday (15th *Oct.*, 1851).

DEAREST BABBIE, . . .

. . . Mr. C. has been sleeping like a top and eating vigorously since his return from Paris—the Ashburtons were only two days behind him—a fact which threw some light on his return sooner than was expected. They (the Ashburtons) are now in town. She brought me a woollen scarf of *her own knitting* during their stay in Switzerland and a cornelian bracelet and—a similar scarf only smaller for Mr. C.—in fact I believe the dear woman would never have done all that knitting for *me* unless as a handsome preparation for doing the comforter for Mr. C.   She is really " what shall I say ?—*strange* upon *my* honour."   On her first arrival in London she staid only two hours and drove down here with these things.   I was gone out so she left them—with Mr. C. whom she saw—and then wrote me a note of invitation to the Grange—which I answered negatively—" being so wearied of visiting for the present " —but begged she would let me see her on her coming to town this week—I would go up to her at any hour morning or evening. After knitting me a scarf one might have supposed she would have *cared* to see me for ten minutes in six months and after having Mr. C. away in Paris she might have felt it *decent* to constrain herself to receive his wife whether she liked it or no. But not at all !   When Mr. C. who of course was there so soon as she arrived, and before I knew she was to arrive that day, asked " if she would be disengaged at any time so that I might see her " *she made no answer* he said, and on the following morning comes a note which I will enclose.

Because she must go to the Exhibition with Lady Sandwich one day she could not have me come to see her any of the three days she was to be in town ! and the very day this note came— and after reading it Mr. C. walked off and sat an hour with her and is off now again thro' a pouring rain to sit till dinner time.   And he " could not see what the devil business I had to find anything strange in that or to suppose that any slight was put on *me* "—on the contrary she " had spoken of the *impossibility* of receiving me *in the most goodnatured manner ! !* "

I suppose I ought to feel by this time quite resigned to such annoyances—or rather I ought to feel and to have always felt quite superior to them—but I am angry and sorrowful all the same.   It is not of course any caprice *she* can show to me that annoys me.   I have long given up the generous attempt at loving her.   But it is to see *him* always starting up to defend everything she does and says and no matter whether it be capricious behaviour towards his *wife*—so long as she flatters himself with delicate attentions.

This did not get finished in time for the post—thro' the Sterling girls coming to call—and while they were here your letter came—thanks for it dear Babbie—it is very kind of you to write at such length besides so often—when you must have your hands and head and heart all so busily employed. With your letter came a note from Lady A. to Mr. C. which turned out to be an invitation to *him* for this evening at 9 and after that another note came begging he would come at 8—and he is now off there again.   I will not write any more to-night being in rather a bitter mood and the best in such moments is if possible to consume one's own smoke—since one cannot help *smoking*.   God bless you all.

Your affectionate

J. CARLYLE.

157.   *To Helen Welsh*

Dressing dolls at the Grange—The servants' tyranny—Macaulay, Lord Grey, etc.—Will not stay if ill—Books to read—French affairs—Ledru Rollin.

The Grange,
Alresford,
Hants.

Saturday (6th Dec., 1851).

DEAREST HELEN,

Your note followed me here without delay and now here is the direct address for you.   Recollect moreover that when one is on a visit, the time seems always much longer than when in the monotonous routine of home—so by next week it will be seeming a month since I had news of my Uncle. Also to touch your heart as much as possible ; let me add ; that the very day after I arrived, I took cold which has been keeping me in-doors till I am grown quite *low*, and *imaginative*, after my bad fashion, to an even unusual degree.   Happily there are no visitors here except the old Countess of Sandwich, Lady Ashburton's Mother, and the days pass quite calmly in —dressing dolls !   If I had to sit thro' long dinners and take part in " *wits*," I could not hold out on my legs 24 hours.   But that doll-dressing suits me entirely.   There is to be a fine

Christmas tree for Lady A.'s school children and *seven* dolls form part of the gifts. These were bought *naked*, except for a wrappage of silkpaper and a piece of cotton wool on each of their noses to prevent damage to that interesting feature and Lady A., tho' not much given to a credulous faith in her fellow creatures, *actually* hoped that her Lady's maid and the House-keeper, and *their* numerous subordinates would *take an interest* in these dolls and dress or assist *her* to dress them. But not a bit—not only did they show themselves impassive in the dressing question but not a rag of ribbon or any sort of scrap would they produce so that Lady A had to *insist* on the Housekeeper giving some pieces of furniture chintz to make frocks for the dolls and to write to London, to her *ci devant* Lady's maid for some scraps ! !—The very footmen won't *carry the dolls* backwards and forwards ! When told to bring one or to desire Josephine (the Lady's maid) to bring one they simply disappear and no doll comes !—I remarked on this with some impatience yesterday, and Lady A. answered, " Perfectly true, Mrs. Carlyle—they *won't bring the doll !*—I know it as well as you do—but what would you have me do ?—turn all the servants men and women out of the house on account of these dolls ? for *it would* come to *that*—if I made a point of their *doing anything in the doll line !* Perhaps it would be the right thing to do—but then what should we do next week without servants when all the company come ? " Such is the slavery the grandest people live under *to what they call* their *" inferiors."*

Ask my Uncle " why does a duck put his head under water ? "

Answer—" For *diver's* reasons."

Lord Ashburton is gone into Devonshire till this day week when plenty of company comes—among the rest Mr. Carlyle and Mr. Twisleton.* Then we stay on together till after Christ-mas—betwixt the 18th. and 22nd. the house is to be as full as it can hold—Macaulay, the Chancellor of the Exchequer,

---

* Lawyer, politician and author—1809-1874. While investigating the authorship of the Letters of Junius, he employed Chabot, the handwriting expert, to examine the original MSS.

Lord and Lady Grey, the Humphrey Mildmays etc. etc. God grant my cold be gone before then. I have kept myself quiet hitherto by an internal resolution, that should I grow *too ill* for taking part in the treadmill of society,—have to go to bed and that sort of thing—on no account to do it *here*, but put myself on the railway *at all risks* and go straight home to my own house where I might at least die without being considered a bore. . . .

What work in France again. The President's *audacity* astonishes me—nothing else. I want Ledru Rollin to be President because he will withdraw the French troops from Italy—and because I have bet—five shillings with Lady Sandwich on his head. Send my address to Jeanie.

God bless you all,

Your affectionate,

J. C.

158. *To Helen Welsh*

Titania's ledger—Induced to stay on at the Grange—Cannot get presents there to send—The Christmas tree—Carlyle and the dissected map—Trifling presents to the school children— The Thackerays—Miss Farrar—Lady Airlie's confidences.

The Grange.
(27th Dec., 1851.)

DEAREST HELEN,

Your letter and the " tiny book "—that might have served as house-ledger to Titania the Fairy Queen—were none the less welcome that they came on the morning *after* Christmas day. I am very thankful to you for writing so often —but I do regret that I should be at such a distance from you all that I cannot *drop in* now and then, and get a kiss of my dear Uncle, and see how he is with my own eyes. Another regret is that I shall not now be able to get *The Romance of the Peerage* to him by new year's day as I intended *to*—for we are to stay here till Friday of next week. Had Lady A. confided to me when she begged me to stay, and help her to *do* the little Thackerays that both Miss Farrar and Emily Baring were to be here at the same time I should have kept to the original *programme* for *my* share—Miss Farrar having a fund of liveliness and good nature up to taking on her own shoulders the weight of any number of little Misses—but I was left to believe Lady A. should be *alone* with these children and her Mother, if I refused to stay ; and in that case there would have been a *certain* ungraciousness in refusing her request. It *puts me out* considerably however not being home before new year's day to send the little remembrances I am in the habit of sending to dear old Haddington Betty, Mrs. Russell and various others—*here*, there is absolutely nothing to be got. Alresford the nearest place has no decent shops in it, and besides I could no more get there than to London, being still a sort of prisoner—all my walking being a few turns on sunshiny days (which are few) on the sheltered side of the flower garden. I can *write* to them however in the meantime and send the ribbons &c. after I go back. Then too I will not forget my Uncle's book.

Our Christmas Tree came off with great success on Wednesday evening. It stood in the middle of the Servants' Hall which was profusely decorated with evergreens, and inscriptions written in red berries " *God* save the Queen "—" Long live Lord and Lady Ashburton &c. &c."—the tree was a fir tree six feet high—stuck quite full of apples and walnuts gilded with Dutch leaf—lighted coloured wax tapers—and little bundles of comfits—the presents, of which the seven dolls were much the finest, lay on a table erected all round the tree and covered with white cloths—the forty-eight children with their school mistress and Mothers and most of the servants, were ranged round while Lady A., attended by his Lordship, the Clergyman and his wife and two daughters, Mr. C. and myself, distributed the presents calling up each child by name and saying something graceful and witty along with the doll, top, or whatever it might be. Mr. C. had begged to have a map of the world in pieces given to *him*, which was done very cleverly. " Thomas Carlyle—the *Scholar*," shouted her Ladyship and the *Scholar* himself advanced. " *There* is a map of the world for *you*—see that you put it all together and make the pieces fit." *The scholar* made his bow, and looked as enchanted as any little boy or girl among them. There was afterwards some *mumming* executed before us by country lads in paper dresses—and then we came away leaving the children and their mothers to enjoy the mugs of tea with large junks of currant loaf spread for them on a long table. The whole thing had a very *fine effect*—and might have given occasion for a laudatory newspaper paragraph, but one reflection that I could not help making rather spoiled it for *me*—viz : that the whole *forty-eight* presents had cost just 2 pounds twelve and sixpence ; having been bought in the Lowther Arcade the most rubbishy place in London—with a *regard* of *expense* that would have been meritorious in the like of us but which seemed to me—what shall I say ?—*incomprehensible*—in a person with an income of £40,000 a year—and who gives balls at the cost of £700 each, or will spend £100 on a china jar !—I should have liked each child to have got at least *a frock* given it—when one was going to look munificent. But everyone has his own notions on spending money.

For the rest it has been what Miss Farrar would call " a dreadful *slow* Christmas " except for the servants who had a ball last night which lasted till six in the morning—we upstairs were in the reactionary state of our company spirits of last week. But Thackeray and Miss Farrar come to-day—and the steam must be got up again.

And now I must end having several other letters to write— to the young Countess amongst others (Blanche Airlie) who continues to send me letters *so* confidential, that I feel as if I were being constituted *dry nurse* to her soul !—without having been " trained to the business." Love to you all, kisses to my Uncle.

Your aff.

J. W. C.

159. *To Helen Welsh*

Lady Sandwich and evening dress—Recovering—Clough, Emily
   Baring, Lady Grey—Lady Alice Lambton—Invitation from
   Lord Lansdowne—Miss Sedgwick's book on England.

The Grange.
(*Monday*).

If it were not for the worry to yourself, dearest Helen, I
should rejoice at the little mistake which has procured me *two*
nice long letters from you instead of one—the other letter came
with its enclosure all right, nor did I even notice the misdirec-
tion.   Thanks very many for your prompt and *liberal* execution
of my little commission—the tinsel ribbon was quite an inspiration of Providence, it suits so beautifully the ornament to be
suspended round my neck and without which I could not wear
the only *low* dress I had brought with them—any *bareness*
being horribly against my feelings at this date tho' Lady
Sandwich who is turned 70 shows a whole neck and breast
much less presentable than mine, any day.   I have counted
sixteen splendid silk dresses in which that old Countess has
appeared since she emerged from her sick room !—the last was
white glacé with a low *polka* of the same profusely embroidered
with *white bugles !*   As for me I have just *two* decent gowns and
I put them on on alternate days.

For the rest, I am pretty well recovered now—tho' I have
only once gone further than the Conservatory *—so afraid
I am of getting fresh cold, our five visitors all went off this
morning—for a Cabinet meeting—leaving behind only
Mr. Clough (a Liverpool man) and Emily Baring Lord A.'s
sister.   Lady Grey who generally calls her husband " *my*
Earl " reminds me always of Mrs. Davidson at Haddington—
no great shakes of a *Lady*—and a young Lady Alice Lambton
whom she brought with her would in *our* circles be called a
little white Negro—but as the daughter of Lord Durham, she
passes for a " young person of very elegant manners and
great intelligence."   The old Marquis of Lansdowne was

* This conservatory, being one-thirty-sixth of a mile in length, made
a good promenade.

also here and, as a proof that my *private sufferings* did not make me *dull*—whatever else—he has invited *me* as well as Mr. C. to Bowood—a crowning grace of aristocratic favour—which may remind you of Miss Sedgwick's book on England, in which she mentions having " scaled the social ladder " beginning with tea at Thomas Carlyle's and ending at Lansdowne House. There is a good deal that is wearisome in it but also an interesting account of Jewish manners—and many eloquent and thoughtful pages.

I must stop—Dear—the meaning of this separate page I will tell you next time.

God bless you all.

Yours affectionately
JANE CARLYLE.

160. *To Helen Welsh*

Nero lost and found—Lady Ashburton's misfortunes on the way to Windsor—"That nose on a pillow!"—A cushion for Lady Ashburton.

Sunday (Feb., 1852)

DEAREST HELEN,

. . . Yesterday I went with Miss Farrar to buy some pots of flowers, and when she had terminated her bargaining with the man—(she has a mania for beating people down in their prices, that young Lady !) I perceived that I had lost—Nero ! After looking all about for him, I hurried back home and when the door was opened he bounded out into my arms. Ann said " he got a lady to knock at the door for him ! " " The lady said ' wasn't this our dog, she had found him very unhappy in the streets.' " I said to Miss Farrar, " I wonder he followed a stranger lady home." " Pooh," says Miss Farrar, " depend on it the lady followed *him* home, by way of looking obliging ! " The half-hour's fright however had given me what Ann called " quite a turn "—I could stand the creature's loss now less than ever. Tom Taylor has made a poor thing of the stealing of *Mrs. Baker's Pet*—Mrs. Baker is not half *miserable* enough—only very foolish. By the way how is Mary's blessed Tearem ? Her attachment to that I must say

not very lovely dog was quite beautiful, so superior to both abus
and ridicule. . . .

Lady Ashburton has been in town for a few days on he
way to Windsor to visit the Queen. She had just laid by
all her fine clothes till they should be needed for the Londor
season—the Company at the Grange being all over—and had
got a couple of gowns packed to go with to Addiscombe wher
the invitation arrived—the Carriage already at the door to
take them to the Train. So she left her French maid behind
to get out the necessary finery and came up to town without a
maid, and " drove about Islington all the forenoon seeking up
a former maid to help her in getting a new gown "—(as if she
hadn't enough) and next day the French woman arrived, having
left half of what was required behind her ! ! " The trouble.
that afflict the just " etc. The old Countess is also come to
town—going back to live at Paris, which I am sorry for—a
72 she is decidedly one of the very most entertaining and
agreeable people I know. I was talking to her of A. B., saying
I wondered that she didn't get married, with sixty thousand
pounds. " Married ! " said Lady Sandwich—" what *are* you
thinking of—who would marry anything so ugly ? " " But
really," I said, " she is not after all so very ugly. She is
Ladylike—has a very nice figure, a good skin and hair—is
not too old—is accomplished, amiable ; men don't need all
that usually to help them to marry sixty thousand pounds ! "
The old Countess sat staring at me till I had done and then
exclaimed almost indignantly—" Great God, Mrs. Carlyle
what nonsense you *are* talking ! just imagine *that nose* on a
pillow ! " But unless you had seen the nose you cannot enjoy
the fun of this speech. *That* is the style of the thing.

I had such a laughable note from Lord Ashburton the
other night which I will send you—but let me have it back
for it contains a *riddle* which I have not yet been able to solve—
where has he put my cushion? When I was at the Grange I
had some wool for *crocheting*—by way of drawingroom work,
after the *dolls* were dressed. I had chosen it myself and
nothing could well be uglier—everybody cried out " what
a frightful piece of work !—what *are* you going to make of it ? "

One night amidst the general reprobation I had spread it on my knee and was looking at it quite disheartened, when Lord A. who never attends to what is said or if he does, forgets it in an instant, said suddenly, " that is very pretty ! "   " You *really* think so ? "   " Yes, certainly ! "   " Then you shall have it ! I will finish it after all—for *you* ! "   He looked quite terrified —everybody laughed at him, and Lady A. said, " *Mouse*, I pity you with that cushion ! you will inevitably get it ! and whatever you are going to do with it Heaven only knows ! " A fortnight ago I made it up—and left it at Bath House for his coming—with a ridiculous note *inside* of the paper cover. When I saw him on Tuesday evening he said not a word of the cushion, and on Thursday night came this note.   Read it and tell me if you can *where has he put my cushion*.

And now I have written enough to make your eyes weary. Good night dear Helen.   Kisses to my Uncle and God bless you all.

Yours affectionately,
JANE CARLYLE.

161.   *To Helen Welsh*

No lawful claim to a letter—The " year in Germany " given up —C. stays during building alterations till the middle of the month—Builders less fatiguing than soirees.

Friday (*July*, 1852).

DEAREST HELEN,

I am well aware that I have no *lawful* claim to any letter from Auchtertool—and yet such is the natural injustice of me that I have been daily expecting one, and feel as if I were an injured woman.   Clearly none is coming, anyhow, until I shall have myself written, and so I write—tho' in circumstances of " distraction " making all reflection and even all grammar impossible.   Our " year in Germany " has ended, for the present at least, in a general repair of this house, worse than *repair* indeed, for certain alterations are being made that have thrown the whole first floor in *ruins*, and every day irruption is made into some room above or beneath rendering it necessary to catch up all the furniture in one's arms and rush away with it—one knows not where ! A week now has passed in this violent exertion and there may be some *three months* more of it for any hope I see to the contrary, and if you consider that the thermometer has been all the while standing at 83 in the shade—and also that Mr. C. exactly at the wrong moment has been seized with an invincible disposition to *stay where he is* you will readily figure that my situation is rather wonderful, and not favourable to letter-writing. If Mr. C. had but gone away, I should have had *his* bedroom, which is *only* to be papered and painted ; into which I might have stowed away myself and the furniture for a time—but he has had the little dressing room turned into a most delectable study for the occasion, and there he sits serene in the middle of a noise as of a battle of Waterloo, and universal chaos throughout the rest of the house—then of course *meals* and all that sort of thing must go on as usual, and cold baths ! and his floor must be kept constantly *watered*—and in short I have had to bring back my little girl to attend on *him* specially. For a week or two before the disturbance began I was every day running up and down to the City and elsewhere—after the *lease* and lawyers, and house-agents and architects and the devil knows what— and all the while not knowing whether Mr. C. would go or stay or whether I myself was not to go on the first of July to Homburg with the Ashburtons. Now, it seems pretty certain that I must stay here—at least till the painting begin, and then I must retire into the neighbourhood to superintend it— Mr. C. thinks it would be all botched if nobody looked to it— and I daresay it *would*. Lady A. offered me the use of Addiscombe whence I could come twice a week or so—but I shall *hardly* accept that magnificent retirement—if I can find any other.

Nero is very unhappy and I am uncomfortable enough— but like better being tired out in this way than in *soirees* etc., etc., —thanks God I keep clear of headache—and in spite of the intense heat my *sickness* is not so *continuous* this summer as the two or three previous ones.

Interrupted—

Best not miss a post.

162. *To Helen Welsh*

istressing neuralgia, result of a call on Miss Mulock—Lady Airlie
   and the authoress—Character of Lord Airlie—Letters and one's
   inmost feelings—The " year in Germany "—Geraldine's phases
   and " getting old "—The Sketchleys : use for a portrait by Pen—
   Ann.

Thursday (July? 1852).

DEAREST HELEN,

I cannot bear that you should think me slow in
nswering your kind and I cannot tell you how welcome letter,
 I sit down to write just risen out of my bed, and holding
y face with one hand ; being in severe pain with the face-
he.   It is four or five days that I have been in and out of bed,
neeling before chairs, walking desperately about the room,
ying all ways of bearing this gnawing pain which prevents me
om either eating or sleeping.   Lady Airlie (*Blanche Stanley*
hom you remember) made me go with her last Friday to
amden Town in an *open* carriage to call for Miss Mulock,
uthoress of *The Ogilvies, Head of the Family*, etc. from whom
e romantic and not very wise young Countess had taken it
to her head she could extract " *the secret of the Universe* " !
liss Mulock was much amused seemingly at this aristocratic
gary, *looked down* on the Lady Airlie who like all romantic
omen had chosen to sit on " a low seat " beside her, with an
xpression of *humouring condescension !* and answered her
uestions as if she had been some precocious *child !*   I keeping
lence till Blanche got on the subject of " Husbands who have
arried women of superior minds to their own "—and then I
ld Miss Mulock " not to let that young lady talk nonsense
out her husband to her—that her Husband was quite a
fferent person from what she led people to suppose " ! ! !

" Let us hear," said Blanche quite good-humouredly—
do tell us what he is ! ! ! "   " He is young and handsome and
ntlemanly " I said—" is very unpresuming, very affectionate-
oking, very silent and shy—but what he does say is sensible ! "
Dear me " interrupted Blanche, " I shall tell him all that—
 will be quite pleased ! "   Did you ever hear of such a foolish
eature ?

2 B

On the way home she put her arm round my neck and
begged me " not to be angry "—that she " didn't mean to
speak against Airlie—only against the sportsman class
generally ! " But I can give you no idea of her indiscretion
nor of the charm of beauty and childlikeness that makes one
always pardon her. What we have to do with her here is as
the involuntary cause of all this pain in my face—and teeth. I
shivered all the way home and in the course of the night awoke
wild—and have been going on more or less wild ever since—
obliged to give up a great party at Bath House last night—but
that was the compensation rather than a sacrifice.

Indeed dear Helen I was heartily glad to see your clear
lady-like handwriting on the back of a letter to me again
and very grateful to you for writing at such length tho' you were
quite mistaken if you made a point of saying next to nothing
about your health from the idea that anything else could be
more interesting to me. Understand this another time—that
what you think and feel about *yourself*, if it do yourself no harm
to write it, is just what I should like best to read, and *sometime*
it does one good to speak one's inmost feelings—tho' oftenest
harm I believe.

The German scheme is lying quiet, only now and then
such phrases as " it will do till we go to Germany "—" When
we go to Germany we will etc." strike a sudden terror into
my mind. For a little while well and good—but for a whole
year to have nothing to fall back upon under his and my own
gloom ! Mercy that *will* be awful ! *

Geraldine desired me to tell you " how very sorry she was
to hear of your having been so ill again "—I hear from her but
seldom at present, she has been in one of her perverse phases
which however is passing. " The fact is I believe (as Darwin
said the other day when I complained of some man being grown
disagreeable) " The fact is I believe we are all getting rather
old ! " And the wind has also been very long in the east—
and that I observe makes everybody quarrelsome.

I have been in rather intimate relations with the Sketchleys

* In the end, Carlyle went alone to Scotland in the last week of July and
then to Germany for six weeks from August 29.

lately. Pen was very *officious* in seeking superfluous charwomen
for me *after* I had suited myself in Helps—and now Ann being
found equal to the work I have made over my little girl to them
—until they get a grown servant—they had been without a
servant or anything instead for ten days—had parted with the
large woman because " she lied " and " was curious " and
" read novels." Pen is painting she says to order at a great
rate—but the fact is dear Helen, these people live on their—
" difficulties "—their *difficulties* are all their " visible means."
Penny is *kissing*-kind with me just now and has asked as a
favour that I would *sit* to her ! She " wishes to give me my
own picture as a proof of her *gratitude*." I shall sit because if
the picture has a shadow of resemblance it will be a great
Heaven-sending * to the Countess von Reichenbach.

Ann is much more effective and obliging than for long before
she went away and will do quite well " until we go to Germany."
Especially as I know now of an adorable cook to assist whenever
I want her—the woman who was with me daily at dinner time
and whom I got quite fond of. As for Mr. Carlyle he will
lament her loss I think all the rest of his life.

Good bye now dearest Helen and don't forget *the position*
in which I have had to write this letter ; that you may excuse
the illegibility and stupidity. Write soon again like a Dear.

Your affectionate cousin,
JANE W. CARLYLE.

163.   *To Helen Welsh*

Helen writes good letters, if too seldom—Carlyle's " bilious misery "
and its only suitable end as in Cavaignac's story—Returns early
from the Grange to finish the house—Thieves again—Carlyle
cannot endure new arrangements—Alterations described—John
and his wife—Funeral of the Duke of Wellington (18th Nov.).

5, Cheyne Row.
Sunday (14*th Nov.*, 1852).

As I have told you before, I think dear Helen, you write
exceedingly good letters ; the more's the pity that you write
them so seldom.

* Himmelsendung, as p. 7.

But in protesting against the silence of others just now, I feel quite in a false position. " Pluck the beam out of etc., etc."

I won't however lose time in excuses.

You seem to be in Cimmerian darkness as to *the condition-of-5-Cheyne-Row question*—don't even know if Mr. C. be returned. We here have known of his return only too well I can tell you; for he came home * (a month ago) in such a state of what he calls " bilious misery," that I really saw no more suitable winding up of the whole thing, than that in Cavaignac's Tale of " *L'Homme de Bien—L'homme de Rien,*" viz. that he and I should step out into the garden, and joining hands, each holding a loaded pistol in the other, calmly, and resolutely—blow each, his own brains out ! I had such a capital pair of pistols too, all ready at half cock ! † We did nothing so sensible however but went instead to the Grange, the second day after his return ; and stayed there a fortnight, where the " bilious misery " was increased to a pitch ! rather than assuaged, by eight o'clock dinner and the excitements of high life. I too caught a cold there as usual, which kept me very dull—and I was glad enough at the end of the fortnight to come home to my new painted house, leaving Mr. C. behind for three days till I should get things in some better order for him than they were on his arrival from Germany—for then the painters and paper-hangers, *three* of the one and *five* of the other, were just making a great effort to finish the staircase *before* his coming. I found that Fanny [the maid] had had the *thieves* again. Did I tell you of their first invasion ? But the last time they did not effect an entrance. Mr. Piper slept in the house during my absence, and my pistols were here—but nobody but myself I fancy would have had the spirit to fire them. You can't imagine how utterly strange and unhomelike all these improvements have made the poor house, I perfectly hate it as yet. And Mr. C. who can't bear anything not exactly as he has been *used* to it ; you may fancy how he likes having all his books and clothes and everything in new places !

* From Germany :—"' half dead ' out of those horrors of indigestion, insomnia, and continual chaotic wretchedness." (T.C. in L.M. ii. 208.)

† " The identical pistols with which old Walter of the *Times* was to have fought his duel, which did not come off." (L.M. ii. 207.)

Thank God it has been all his own doing—I suppose however the house is much improved—for those who haven't to live in it.

The drawing-room is a fine *square* room with new modern window and modern chimney—will be comfortable *perhaps* when it is papered and painted which it cannot be till next year. Meanwhile it has got the old furniture in it and Mr. C. sits there with bare walls. My old bed-room in which I still sleep, is prettily painted and papered in *pink*, but for practical purposes quite spoiled—three feet taken off it and the *large* bookcase set *into* it make it too small for my breathing in. The spare bed (its own being too large for it) stands facing the fire place and I have not had *one* good night's sleep in it since I was put into these new conditions. My imagination is tormented with all that various literature in the wall, and with the feeling of being in *The Iron Shroud* (do you know that story ?) and with the change in my curtains etc.—alas! when one's sleep is so easily scared away !

The up-stairs room—*yours*, is enlarged by having the chimney and closets taken back two feet—and has the centre window broken out, and the red bed is to be put up there and I am to sleep there—hereafter when it is papered and painted— but that also could not be finished this year on account of the damp of the walls. Mr. C.'s bed-room is as it was in size—but beautifully painted—*faint pink*—and there are wainscot closets for his clothes running all along the recess at the fire-place and he has got my pretty green carpet, and Mrs. Carlyle's picture over the mantelpiece, and is very smart indeed ; the closet at the top is half filled with a great cistern and the kitchen and back kitchen are flagged and painted anew and the larder smoothed up with a window broken into it—the same at which the thieves came in and took six pounds worth of things. There is also a window broken out in the upper staircase—and that I think is all.

John and his wife passed thro' last week to the Isle of Wight. I did not see them but they return for a week on Tuesday. I took yesterday a beautiful lodging in Sloane Street for them— at this end of it—and I expect to like my new sister-in-law from all I hear.

This end of London is in a quite horrible confusion at present with that *Lying in State* of the dead Duke. Thousands and Thousands of people thronging to see him and trampling one another to death ! I went yesterday along Paradise Row, meaning to see the thing myself if it were practicable—but when I saw the sea of human beings swaying to and fro I made off fast enough. I don't know for certain how many people were killed yesterday—Mr. Piper *saw* two dead women carried away on stretchers—and a Policeman said *four* bodies were lying in the workhouse, nine were taken to the Hospital but it is impossible to ascertain all the accidents in such a horrid confusion.

We are to go to Bath House to see the Procession—which will cost me a new black bonnet, not having such a thing. Numbers of men have been working all day (Sunday) and all last night and are to work all to-night putting up barriers to prepare against the crowd to-morrow. Better a great deal to have buried the Duke and been done with it.

God bless you all.

> Your loving cousin,
> JANE CARLYLE.

164. *To Helen Welsh*

A perplexing address and gift—For the dog, the feet, the teapot or a baby ?—Wants a fireside talk—Summer plans—The Reichenbachs : real friends—London friendships based on locality—John Greig—Lady Ashburton wants her company—Uncle John and his son—Death of William Gibson.

Saturday (25th Dec., 1852).

Well, certainly ! dearest Helen, anything like my perplexity over that beautiful piece of work yesterday morning is not easy to conceive. *Was* it a delicate attention to my *dog*, carried out on the most foolishly extravagant principles, both as to materials and pains ? to increase my confusion of mind I could not determine whether the address on the packet was in *your* handwriting or Geraldine's. You write my name and address—tho' nothing else—so excessively like Geraldine.

Now Geraldine *couldn't* have done that work herself, but she was quite *up to* having *imposed it* on some female friend, with an eye to *Nero !* then if it was *not* a bag to put my blessed dog into ; surely it *must* be to put feet into—but again " what a waste ! " (as Dwerkanaught said to Lord Ashley of the eighteen young women burnt in a Suttee).   The feet that went into *that* must be Venus's feet to begin with and attired in cobweb stockings and white satin slippers ! At night came " the solution," if solution it could be called ! to put over a teapot ! ! ! Mercy of Heaven ! all that lovely braiding put over a teapot ! *that* seems the absurdest *waste* of all ! Indeed my dear, I shall do nothing of the sort—I will keep it till—I have a baby ! and as it is likely to be " *a very small one* " it shall be a little bed for *my* baby !

I am glad to see such signs both in your letter and in this *labour of love* that you are about and active—much should I like to descend on a " wishing carpet " now and then and have a fire-side talk.   I wonder if I shall be in Scotland this summer —*Chi sa ?*   I am trying to get off from my visit to the Grange at Easter.   I shall be better here *with the house all to myself*— besides the Reichenbachs are going to America soon, almost immediately *—and I have been very intimate with them for the last year—and am become so deeply attached to them all, man, woman and children ! Oh such people they are when one *knows* them ! and the idea of their going away—under all the circumstances—is heart-breaking to me !   I did not think I had so much *heart-breakableness* left—and I *cannot* and *will not* cut off ten days of *them*, out of the little spell left—not for all the Lords and Ladies in the Kingdom.   There will be time enough for the Grange and any good that is to be done there, when I am again *without real friends near me*—for what do I *really* care for all these London people or do *they* care for *me ?* London friendship !   Ah God !   Henry Taylor truly told me long ago " its ruling principle was *locality* " and its minor principles are ennui, vanity, convenience,—I have found out for myself.

But—but—quietness is best.   Do you know if John Greig

* They settled near Philadelphia.

be still at Canandaigua—I should have heard surely if he were dead. I don't suppose the Reichenbachs will be in his direction—but I should like to know if he be still there, in case of *any* possibility of an introduction to him—which were as great a kindness to *him* as to *them*.

Lady A. is in town and was to have gone back to the Grange to-day but she has now sent a man on horseback with one line—" ill—and can't stir "—which means I suppose " will you come and see me—so I must go and put my bonnet on."

How glad I am dear Uncle has got his *little Benjamin* * back !—it will do him more good than all the medical advice in the world.

Poor old Gibson ! † I was thinking about a month ago where was he ? I would ask *you* and write him a letter ; it would please him so much. Now one can do nothing to please him never more. Oh that sad word *nevermore !*

Your affectionate,

J. W. C.

165. *To Jeannie Chrystal*

Photograph of Jeannie's baby—Death of Elizabeth Pepoli and Lady Sandwich.

5, Cheyne Road, Chelsea.
Saturday (Jan., 1863).

MY DEAR JEANIE,
        That Photograph gives me the queerest unearthly feeling ! I seem to be pitched suddenly back into the year 1820, and seeing yourself—as you lived and looked, when— " what shall I say ? "—*coquetting* with Dr. Carson or some other of your early admirers. I never saw a more perfect likeness—of *you !* Thanks for sending it, and for sending it on new year's day ! Your packet and a letter from Maggie were the only " delicate attentions " paid me this new year's day. And my " first foot " was a woman who bores me to death, and who performed that *mission* quite unconsciously.

* His son John (born 1826, died 1860), who was now returning from abroad.
† See note in Letter 119.

Well! the new year's day before—I had a quite satisfactory *first foot*; and beautiful new year's gifts—and a great many charming letters,—and God knows the good luck spent itself *all* on the first day! Three of those who tried to make my year lucky to my imagination, and sent me gifts and letters, were *dead*, one after another, within two months after! Countess Pepoli, The Countess of Sandwich and Mrs. Twisleton—and except that I got to Scotland for a little change and rest sorely needed, it has been a luckless year, the last, all thro'! It is time to give up speaking about luck when one has got past sixty. Indeed I am somewhat of the Suffolk girl's opinion who justified herself for strangling her aunt and robbing her; on the ground that " such old creatures shouldn't be allowed to live " ! . . .

A kiss to the Princess Royal—and thanks for her bonny little portrait. Kind regards to your Husband and a good new year to you all.

Yours affcly.,
JANE CARLYLE.

This letter, with the picture of Jeannie's baby so strangely recalling Jeannie's own baby days, concludes the series now brought to light. Save one letter to Maggie Welsh of November in the same year (L.M. iii. 187), it is the last recorded to one of the beloved family of Welsh. Twelve years had passed since any intimate letter had gone to the more than sister of old days, estranged since her marriage, not by time and distance only, but by the fatal pressure of alien interests. This letter could not but be kind, but it is not one of the old Babbie letters. After so long a silence it is the more pathetic because, though friendship had become only a memory, the detachment of the present could not escape the echoes of a beloved and irrecoverable past.

INDEX